BLOOD AND FIRE

DISLOCATIONS

General Editors: August Carbonella, *Memorial University of Newfoundland*, Don Kalb, *University of Utrecht & Central European University*, Linda Green, *University of Arizona*

The immense dislocations and suffering caused by neo-liberal globalization, the retreat of the welfare state in the last decades of the twentieth century and the heightened military imperialism at the turn of the 21st century have raised urgent questions about the temporal and spatial dimensions of power. Through stimulating critical perspectives and new and cross-disciplinary frameworks, which reflect recent innovations in the social and human sciences, this series provides a forum for politically engaged, ethnographically informed, and theoretically incisive responses.

For full series listing, please see end matter.

BLOOD AND FIRE

Toward a Global Anthropology of Labor

Edited by
Sharryn Kasmir and August Carbonella

First published in 2018 by
Berghahn Books
www.berghahnbooks.com

© 2014, 2018 Sharryn Kasmir and August Carbonella
First paperback edition published in 2018

All rights reserved.
Except for the quotation of short passages
for the purposes of criticism and review, no part of this book
may be reproduced in any form or by any means, electronic or
mechanical, including photocopying, recording, or any information
storage and retrieval system now known or to be invented,
without written permission of the publisher.

Library of Congress Cataloging-in-Publication Data
Blood and fire : toward a global anthropology of labor / edited by Sharryn Kasmir and August Carbonella.
    pages cm. — (Dislocations ; volume 13)
Includes bibliographical references and index.
    ISBN 978-1-78238-363-5 (hardback : alk. paper) — ISBN 978-1-78533-748-2 (paperback) — ISBN 978-1-78238-364-2 (ebook)
 1. Labor movement—History. 2. Working class—History. I. Kasmir, Sharryn, author, editor of compilation. II. Carbonella, August, author, editor of compilation.
    HD4841.B56 2014
    331.09—dc23
    2013050761

British Library Cataloguing in Publication Data
A catalogue record for this book is available from the British Library

ISBN: 978-1-78238-363-5 hardback
ISBN: 978-1-78533-748-2 paperback
ISBN: 978-1-78238-364-2 ebook

CONTENTS

Acknowledgments   vii

Introduction   Toward a Global Anthropology of Labor   1
August Carbonella and Sharryn Kasmir

Chapter One   Fragmented Solidarity: Political Violence and Neoliberalism in Colombia   30
Lesley Gill

Chapter Two   Labor in Place/Capitalism in Space: The Making and Unmaking of a Local Working Class on Maine's "Paper Plantation"   77
August Carbonella

Chapter Three   Flexible Labor/Flexible Housing: The Rescaling of Mumbai into a Global Financial Center and the Fate of its Working Class   123
Judy Whitehead

Chapter Four   Structures without Soul and Immediate Struggles: Rethinking Militant Particularism in Contemporary Spain   167
Susana Narotzky

Chapter Five   The Saturn Automobile Plant and the Long Dispossession of US Autoworkers   203
Sharryn Kasmir

Chapter Six	"Worthless Poles" and Other Dispossessions: Toward an Anthropology of Labor in Post-Communist Central and Eastern Europe *Don Kalb*	250

Notes on Contributors   289
Index   291

ACKNOWLEDGMENTS

This book is the outcome of a long collaboration that had its beginnings in our involvement in the Working Class Anthropology Project at the City University of New York Graduate Center during the late 1980s. We have accumulated many intellectual debts over the years, starting with the other members of the project, Geraldine Casey, Geoff Bate, and Bill Askins, who shared our initial interest in bringing working class life, culture, and organization to the forefront of anthropological research and theorizing. Ed Hansen, Louise Lennihan, June Nash, Bill Roseberry, Jane Schneider, Gerald Sider, Sydel Silverman, Gavin Smith, and Eric Wolf were early mentors and champions. Our development of the conceptual frameworks that anchor *Blood and Fire* has been greatly facilitated by our ongoing collaboration with the contributors to this volume, Lesley Gill, Don Kalb, Susana Narotzky, and Judy Whitehead, as well as the critiques of versions of our introduction presented at the Culture, Power, and Boundaries Seminar at Columbia University and the 2011 American Anthropology Association Meetings. We are especially grateful to Jane Collins, Linda Green, Massimiliano Mollona, and Gavin Smith for their careful readings and insightful comments on the manuscript. Thanks also to Margaret Abraham, Rebecca Busansky, Rex Clark, Timothy Daniels, Phyllis Droessler, Karen Judd, Art Keene, Chris Matthews, Patricia Musante, Cheryl Mwaria, Joy Nolan, Don Nonini, David Nugent, Ida Susser, Daniel Varisco, Robin Whitaker, and Jonah Zuckerman for the ongoing, enriching conversations and support.

August Carbonella would like to acknowledge Patricia Musante, for her insightful comments, probing questions, editorial advice, and keen sense of humor throughout the gestation and writing of *Blood and Fire*.

For Patricia, Travis, and Claire, and in memory of my sister, Michele.

Sharryn Kasmir thanks Benjamin Dulchin for his support for this project and for being a kind and generous partner in intellectual pursuits, political struggles, and family life.

For Benjamin, Ellis, and Zack.

INTRODUCTION
Toward a Global Anthropology of Labor

August Carbonella and Sharryn Kasmir

[T]hese newly freed men became sellers of themselves only after they had been robbed of all their own means of production, and all the guarantees of existence . . . And the history of this, their expropriation, is written in the annals of mankind in letters of blood and fire.

—Karl Marx

Recent protests—from the Arab Spring, to the European revolts, to Occupy, to the mass demonstrations in Turkey and Brazil—galvanized worldwide attention, as people in many different places demanded rights to livelihood, a livable wage, education, state services, and democratic freedoms. After years of steady pronouncements in the mainstream media that free trade was the source of universal prosperity and liberty, the widespread evidence of social precariousness and political exclusion on display exposed the underbelly of neoliberal globalization usually hidden from view. As a result, the protests pushed the problem of social inequality and the idea of class from the margins to the center of debate around the world. The general tenor of this discussion raises for us two key questions: How did we get to a situation in which labor was everywhere diminished? And, why had it been decades since labor demands were tied so explicitly to ideas about the greater common good?

After more than forty years of neoliberal hegemony, with its strong emphases on individualism and capital-labor cooperation, the connection we draw between labor demands and social betterment may strike readers as anachronistic. Even in the aftermath of the 2007/2008 global financial collapse, and its origins in corporate malfeasance, the notion that "what's good for capital is good for all" remains a broadly accepted truism, even among some labor unionists. Yet the recent political protestors across the world explicitly claimed rights and freedoms on behalf of a common humanity. In doing so they resurrected what Buck-Morss (2009) called "universalism from below," a set of demands for emancipation, human rights, and social equality made by common people throughout the *longue durée* of capitalist and colonial expansion. The rights and freedoms that are everywhere under attack in the early twenty-first century were initially won by the combined challenges of laborers—across space and social categories—to the reigning forms of economic exploitation and political oppression they faced. Those gains were not, however, secured for all time, but were subject to continuing efforts to restrict democratic freedoms to the privileged few. We invoke this dialectic of force and counterforce to remind readers of the suppressed histories of universalism that are now being reclaimed by popular movements of the dispossessed and disenfranchised around the world, and to foreshadow a theme that weaves its way throughout this volume.

The question of how we got here immediately calls attention to the global multiplication and political stultification of labor that has fed neoliberal capitalism and governance for the last four decades. In our view, though, adequate answers to this important inquiry requires a comparative focus on the making and unmaking of particular working classes over a longer time frame. The processes of dispossession and displacement at the root of this tripling of the global proletariat were experienced and lived differently in specific localities, countries, and regions, largely due to the historically specific ways these places were originally incorporated into the world capitalist order. At the same time, the global experience of what David Harvey (2003) calls "accumulation by dispossession" exposes heretofore hidden histories of connection among places and people. This understanding provides the rationale for the expansive geographical and historical scope of this volume.

Each of the contributors addresses the above issues through historical ethnographies that range from Colombia, India, Poland, to Spain and the United States. The six studies show how dispossession was lived by different local working classes at the end of the twentieth century. In each case, the authors document how the social movements, vibrant public spheres, and attempts to build organizations through which laborers tried to secure some greater measure of political and economic democracy for themselves and their societies were met by repression and violence. The chapters are longer than would be found in a typical edited collection. Our purpose in structuring the volume in this way is to represent the complexity of the struggles, histories, and social relations in each setting and to enable a comparison among cases to further our understanding of global precariousness. Notwithstanding the particularities of each case, commonalities among them quickly become apparent.

We elaborate below several overlapping themes that span the contributions to this volume, yet one important commonality needs to be stated upfront. A strong emphasis on the shifting spatial/temporal matrices of working-class life, culture, and organization animates each study. This is evident at the ethnographic level in changes in class experience, memory, and spatial perspective over time. The focus here is not, however, on the kind of local/global opposition that has captured the anthropological imagination in the last twenty years. Rather, transformations in the "common sense" (Gramsci 1971) within particular working-class places are seen in relationship to wider national, regional, and global sources of power and influence, which mediate, shape, and react to these local conditions, the type of confluence that Don Kalb (2009) calls "critical junctions." Taken together, the case studies not only attest to the mutability of class belonging, identity, and politics over time and space, but also constitute a strong argument for the continuing salience of class as both social formation and analytical tool for critical scholarship. In fact, as we discuss below, a sense of the mutability of class is central to an adequate understanding of its continuing relevance.

Our guiding questions fly in the face of the reigning academic wisdom that class as a social formation has simply disappeared over the last thirty-odd years. It is certainly true that no small amount of theoretical cunning was marshaled against the very idea of class or its historical-geographical existence (see Palmer 1994). Yet the elision of class is as much a consequence of contemporary scholars' mistaking the transformation and decline of the Fordist working class, a specific historical/geographical formation, for the end of class itself. This seems to be a recurrent misstep in social and historical scholarship, not least, as Michael Denning (2004) suggests, because cultural images and understandings of class last longer than actual class formations within capitalism. Denning argues that:

> While a capitalist economy continually reshapes workplaces and working populations, destroying old industries and working forces while drawing

new workers from around the globe and moving industry to new regions, we remain caught in the class maps we inherited from family, school, and movies. (2004: 229–230)

A central feature of the class maps or memories we have inherited is the opposition between "the stable working class" and "the poor," which, in turn, evokes a whole chain of signifiers—the affluent worker, aristocracy of labor, labor elite, on the one side; dangerous classes, the great unwashed, lumpen-proletariat, surplus populations, on the other. Moreover, this opposition is frequently traced on to all-encompassing distinctions between skilled industrial workers in the global North and racially marked and super-exploited laborers of the South. These typologies, whatever the particularities of their enunciation, greatly reduce our ability to apprehend the fluidity of class relations and experience.

It should be easy to see why our inherited class maps have become obsolete in our era when all "fast frozen" relationships and oppositions are, if not exactly "melting into air," at least being upended and remade. At the same time, new, transnational class formations, to replace the national classes of the Keynesian/state capitalist era, are not yet wholly apparent. We are confronted instead by a world of labor, in various stages of the making, unmaking, and remaking of class. The current moment of capitalist restructuring is producing a range of new social relations. Informal, criminalized, military, child, and bonded labors are once again as common as industrial and service sector work in both the global North and South, just as structural adjustment programs, penalization, and military and paramilitary violence serve to differentiate and regulate labor across the world. It is precisely these new or remade relations that compel us to move beyond old antinomies in search of explanatory frameworks capable of making sense of the changing experiences of labor and all they mean for social and daily life.

We take our cue here from "the shouts in the streets" (Berman 1982). The 99 percent versus the 1 percent equation that emanated roundly from the Occupy encampments or the poignant demands for economic and social justice wafting across national borders during the 2012 European Day of Solidarity and Protest demonstrated the widespread impulse and urgency among protestors to redraw class maps in the face of the growing aristocratic privilege of globetrotting elites who have withdrawn from all social compacts. This reemergence of grassroots universalism echoes the late-eighteenth- and early-nineteenth-century popular movements and sentiments that facilitated the early coalescence of class formations within and beyond national and cultural boundaries.

E. P. Thompson's strictures on essentialism thus seem especially trenchant and timely some fifty years after they were first lodged. As Thompson famously remarked in the opening paragraph of *The Making of the English Working Class:* "The working class did not rise like the sun at an appointed time. It was present at its own making" (1963: 9). Thompson traces the experiences and historical relationships of working people as they begin to consider their shared conditions and develop (or not) a shared identity. His emphasis on the making rather than always already accomplished structure of class (whether "in-itself" or "for-itself") is once again worth heeding in this moment of transition, and it serves as a guiding thread of our analysis. As such, we do not attempt to elucidate the already accomplished formation of a global working class, or any other such designation, nor do we suggest that outcomes can be known in advance. Rather, we draw attention to a politics of labor in the past and present as pointers to a processual and relational approach to the global anthropology of labor.

Toward a Global Anthropology of Labor

Our point of entry is what Karl Marx called the "multiplication of the proletariat," the continual expansion of those who were forced onto the market to sell their labor power, which he saw as the mirror process of capital accumulation. This notion of labor accumulation signals, for us, a sustained focus on the continual making, unmaking, and remaking of labor forces and working classes—politically, culturally, and structurally—through the dual lens of dispossession and disorganization. Expanding on Rosa Luxemburg's indispensable insight that primitive accumulation is not a one-time event but a constant feature of capital expansion, David Harvey's "accumulation by dispossession" brings the idea fully into the twenty-first century (2003). In a departure from the "expanded reproduction" of post– World War II Keynesianism in the North, when mass consumption, a burgeoning welfare state, and increased government expenditures for infrastructure did much to absorb surplus value, capital's strategies of privatization, creative destruction of assets, speculation, geographic mobility, etc. characterize the neoliberal epoch (see also Perelman 2000). Harvey's consideration of the inside/outside dialectic and the way that capitalism always creates its own "other" directs attention to the contingencies of labor and its forms of social reproduction. We would add to this the importance of placing the politics of labor at the heart of analysis. This is an initial step for a global anthropology of labor that centers on the dialectic of dispossession and incorporation in people's daily lives, as well as the ways working people make new divisions and alliances in the context of global accumulation. And it calls upon us to closely study working classes in their making, remaking, and unmaking, as this played out in kin relations, belief, social organizations, work relationships, and the many other arenas of life that are anthropology's long-standing concerns.

To realize this project, however, a critique of the analytical frames that Harvey uses to elaborate the concept of accumulation by dispossession is in order. First, he features capital as the driving force of this global process and relegates labor struggles to the proverbial back seat. This is not to say that the "class struggle from above" that Harvey so well documents is not hugely important, only that it remains incomplete without a reciprocal focus on "class struggle from below." Second, Harvey dichotomizes labor struggles in the global South and North, which he designates as progressive and retrograde, respectively; this is a problematic move. As Harvey shows, dispossession takes various forms around the globe: In the North workers lost pensions, welfare, national health care, and jobs. In the South, peasant and indigenous communities lost communal lands; environmental and genetic materials were patented by private corporations; and water, communications, and other public utilities were privatized. These wide-ranging processes can be traced to the shift in dominance from productive to finance capital that accompanied the rise of neoliberalism. Although these multiple forms of dispossession may have their origins in the overriding interests of finance capital, Harvey attaches distinct logics to the struggles they engender; hence he reinscribes a typology of global labor—North/South, forward-looking struggles/ rearguard action—that his theory should, by rights, dismantle. Unfortunately, this frame inhibits the remapping of past and present geographies of labor accumulation and struggle that we urgently need (see critiques by Collins 2012, Kasmir and Carbonella 2008). The reason for this misstep may be that Harvey sometimes slips into a narrow association of accumulation by dispossession with the loss of property rights, whereas he tends to neglect other forms (see Collins

2012, Wood 2007.) We develop a more *holistic* notion of dispossession that expressly refers to the varied acts of disorganization, defeat, and enclosure that are at once economic, martial, social, and cultural and that create the conditions for a new set of social relations.

As we are using it, labor—rather than "livelihood" as a collection of strategies for social reproduction, or "work" as a social activity, both of which are close companion concepts—is a pointedly *political entity*, whose social protests and quietude, organizations, and cultures reflect its multiple engagements with capital and state, as well as relationships with other workers locally, regionally, and globally. To be explicit, the designation labor is meant to convey several related ideas: First, it encompasses myriad ways of working—the manifold labors of slaves, petty commodity producers, coerced laborers, plantation workers, and domestic labor, within temporal and spatial processes of capital accumulation, as Eric Wolf described things for the early colonial period in *Europe and the People Without History* (1982). Second, it refers to the power-laden processes of categorizing, differentiating, or unifying those laborers. As such, it does not presume that the end point is full-on proletarianization, nor, with E. P. Thompson in mind, class-in-itself or class-for-itself at a global scale. Finally, a focus on labor in this political sense allows us to explore how states and other powerful institutions (such as, the World Bank and International Monetary Fund) intervene in capitalist processes to facilitate or hinder connections among working people, and it leads us to closely examine the creation of organizational forms such as unions and political parties.

Our development of this definition is heavily indebted to W. E. B. Du Bois's *Darkwater: Voices from within the Veil* (1969 [1920]). Du Bois argued that "the shadow of hunger" (a phrase that poetically captures the lived experienced of dispossession) and the production of difference and inequality are conjoined, simultaneous processes, and he framed the struggles of differently classified laborers within this broader context. Du Bois's mapping of recurrent processes of class composition and decomposition not only brings labor's political agency to the fore, but it also suggests that the outcomes of working classes' attempts to make themselves are multiple and uneven, resulting in attempts at solidarity, but also in racial, ethnic, and gender hierarchy, exclusion, and violence.

To expand upon Du Bois's political view of labor, we return to Wolf's grand synthesis in *Europe and the People without History* (1982). Wolf's perspective provided a still too little realized opportunity to reconceptualize anthropological subjects engaged in manifold labors, within temporal and spatial processes of capital accumulation, a move that encouraged a general, radical reshaping of the discipline (Roseberry 1989; see also Mintz 1985). Wolf's radical impulse was prefigured by others in anthropology. Monica Hunter Wilson and Godfrey Wilson, Max Gluckman, and Georges Balandier, and Wolf's fellow researchers in Julian Steward's People of Puerto Rico Project, especially Sidney Mintz, to note just a few examples, all paid considerable attention to questions of labor and power in colonial situations and developed innovative conceptual and methodological approaches for understanding the connections among the many, various forms of labor they encountered in the field (see Nugent 2002). Although Wolf's proposal for a critically engaged, global anthropology was eclipsed by the postmodernist celebration of all things cultural, in our view it remains extremely timely for the twenty-first century.

To this point, we have sketched a beginning for an overarching framework for a global anthropology of labor. In what follows, we review studies from anthropology, history, political economy, and sociology that are lodestones for our examination of labor in explicitly political terms. We use these works to enrich our ability to theorize the lived experience of various laborers across time and space and to consider the multiplication of the proletariat from an ethnological perspective, and we draw on them to elaborate several overlapping themes that we consider to be anchors for our project: *dispossession and difference; the politics of dispossession; place, space, and power;* and *the myth of "disposable people."*

Dispossession and Difference

The concept of dispossession has a long history in political economic theory. Marx's justly famous sketch of primitive accumulation remains the paradigmatic formulation. The story Marx tells has to do with the primacy of force and enclosure in creating both the preconditions for capitalism and the reduction of human beings to commoditized laborers. This process of "conquest, enslavement, robbery, [and] murder," in Marx's succinct summary "is written in the annals of mankind in letters of blood and fire" (1977 [1867]: 874, 875). Fiery prose aside, in some of his writings, Marx appears to assume that the plunder and terror that marked the earliest phases of capitalist development would subside with the steady advancement of capitalist relations. The continuing exploitation of labor would thereafter, he suggested, be secured through the silent compulsion of economic relations and the inculcation of tradition and habit. Yet as Rosa Luxemburg (2003 [1913]) and Karl Polanyi (1944) pointed out long ago, primitive accumulation (Marx's "original sin" of capitalism) could not be so easily relegated to the past. The title of this volume, *Blood and Fire,* refers to Marx's evocative phrase, and we revisit it to bring "primitive" accumulation squarely into the present, and to underscore the centrality of the process of dispossession and its manifold effects for the anthropology of labor.

If the current Great Recession has shown us anything, it is that waves of dispossession do not wash evenly over whole communities (Perelman 2000). Rather they are important moments in the political process of creating difference and inequality. The many examples of racism, exclusion, and anti-immigrant and right-wing populism that are one form of reaction to the enclosure and privatization of the contemporary global era underscore this important fact (Mullings 2005).

To better understand the connection between dispossession and differentiation, we need to decenter the wage relationship in our understanding of labor. In his provocative essay "The Spectre of a Wageless Life" Michael Denning (2008) recalls that the founding moment of capitalism is not the wage contract, but the imperative to "earn a living." This entails the wholesale divestment of the property and rights by which people had previously secured their sustenance. How a person or group enters the wage relation, if at all, is the stuff of multiple identities and cleavages, but the moment of wagelessness is one of commonality. This point serves to remind us that solidarity, as much as difference, is always a possibility. It also reminds us that the many ways of being without a wage—for a short term, for a lifetime, for generations, for whole communities or regions—is one manner in which people experience capital accumulation. We take this moment of wagelessness, with all its possibilities for solidarity *and* for division, and in all of its varied historical manifestations, as a starting point for analysis.

Jane Collins's (2003) study of the intersecting and mutually determined lives of garment workers in the United States and Mexico is highly suggestive in this regard. Collins describes the experiences of southern US women who lost their jobs when their employer declared bankruptcy. Their counterparts in Aguascalientes, Mexico, where the employer relocated, gained employment but nonetheless faced the persistent threat of plant closure. We see here the simultaneous making of wage labor and wagelessness and the precariousness of workers throughout the world, as well as the fledgling cross-border organizing efforts that resulted (see also Lee 2007).

The recognition that we need to decenter the wage contract also serves as a rejoinder to the increasingly common assertions that present forms of neoliberal accumulation are creating "surplus populations" that now constitute a permanent "outside" of capitalism, a problem we will address shortly. At the same time, it should not be taken to suggest a simple linear progression from wagelessness to wages, the trajectory usually associated with the idea of primitive accumulation. Historically, these two distinct existential relationships to capitalism have been produced simultaneously.

Indeed, the history of dispossession can be told as the simultaneous production of both wage labor and wagelessness. Silvia Federici (2004) documents the emergence of the sexual division of labor and the patriarchy of the wage during the long transition to capitalism in Western Europe. With other feminist scholars who advanced the theory of social reproduction, she knows that women's unpaid work is fundamental to the production of surplus value (e.g. Collins and Gimenez 1990; Federici 2012; Vogel 1983; Young 1981). The historical separation of men's and women's labors may be the least told aspect of capitalism's originating moment. Yet Federici's starting point is not this production of gender difference and hierarchy but an earlier experience of commonality dating to the fourteenth and fifteenth centuries, when there was an emergent popular consciousness, political sympathies and actions crossed linguistic and cultural lines, and there was widespread popular resistance. Elites and authorities were terrified of these developments (see also Robinson 2001).

By the mid-sixteenth century, capital, church, and state coordinated a counter response. They disciplined labor via mass incarceration of the poor in work and correction houses and "transportation" to the colonies, and they enclosed social reproduction through attacks on collective sociality and sexuality. The witch-hunt in the sixteenth and seventeenth centuries was central to the counter response, for it consolidated a range of assaults on women's bodies that were compounded during the witch trials, as men turned violently on women, and the young on the old. Rendered in situ within Europe, these cleavages mirrored the violent hierarchies of race that were mapped onto the global relationship of unwaged, enslaved labor in the New World and debased waged labor in the Old. As Federici tells us, these divisions set the terms for the later accumulation of difference and became a cornerstone of power for emergent capitalist classes:

> Primitive accumulation . . . was not simply an accumulation of exploitable workers and capital. It was also an accumulation of differences and divisions within the working class, whereby hierarchies built upon gender, as well as "race" and age, became constituent of class rule and the formation of the modern proletariat. (63)

If we recall that so-called primitive accumulation is a recurrent process, then we understand that the making and remaking of such divisions is the lifeblood of labor accumulation. Each wave of dispossession makes or remakes particular working classes again; old divisions are deployed and new ones institutionalized.

This dynamic also characterized London's docks at the turn of the nineteenth century. Dockworkers at that time were only nominally compensated for their labor with wages. Instead of regular monetary wages, dockworkers received their chief remuneration in "chips," the scraps and waste left over from shipbuilding. More specifically, chips referred to the prescriptive right of workers to appropriate a certain amount of the wood as payment. Chips together with "takings" from other workplaces along the Thames River constituted the primary medium of exchange among a network of marine-store dealers, grocers, peddlers, sex workers, alehouse keepers, and pawnbrokers. Efforts in the 1790s to regularize the money wage followed a dual strategy of criminalizing the customary takings and eliminating the nonmonetary community. At the same time, the construction of hydraulic dams and a massive system of docks and canals physically destroyed the nonmonetary community. As the existing material and cultural forms of everyday life were dismantled, new forms of social reproduction centering on the money wage were forcefully regulated. The newly formed River Thames Police were charged primarily with determining who would receive wages and who would not. The literal policing of the division between waged laborers and the wageless poor effectively separated the struggles of workers within the wage labor process from those outside it, and social hierarchy developed among the river proletariat as a result. This reclassification simultaneously intensified existing gender, ethnic, and racial inequalities. This late-eighteenth-century policing of the boundary between wage and wageless laborers was not a novel historical development. It paralleled and was preceded by numerous attempts to separate the labors of men and women, slaves and proletarians, and black and white workers (Linebaugh 2003).

A more recent twentieth-century example of wage struggle as the making of difference and hierarchy, especially with regard to racial inequality and the construction of "whiteness" can be found in Du Bois's "On Work and Wealth" in *Darkwater* (1969). The essay deals with the 1917 race riots in East St. Louis, Illinois. Du Bois begins his mournful sketch of the city with the growth of industrial capital in the first years of the twentieth century, when large numbers of eastern and southern European immigrants came to find work. Upon arrival, they encountered established tradesmen of mostly northern European descent who held fast to both their American Federation of Labor (AFL) craft unions and to their relative privilege. Consequently, the new immigrants faced insecure employment, intermittent and less than livable wages, and social exclusion. Nevertheless, the government's new restrictions on immigration and its conscription of white citizen-workers during World War I allowed these new immigrants a greater measure of bargaining power and a rising standard of living. Industrialists confronted labor's newfound strength by looking south to "the greatest industrial miracles of modern days—slaves transforming themselves to freemen" (89).

Rather than depress wages, though, the influx of African Americans to the city sparked fledgling attempts at solidarity. In the months before the riots, black, recent European immigrant, and even white workers joined together to confront their employers. Influenced by radical labor movements throughout North America and Europe, and counter to the overt racism of the AFL, black workers began to join the laborers' unions. This emergent solidarity was in Du Bois's frame as he imagined the possible materialization of a socialism that aspired to equality for all. But the constant remaking of global divisions cast a very dark shadow over that possibility. Du Bois foresaw that the demand to increase wages would benefit only white men, whereas people of color, immigrants, and white women would continue to suffer caste-like exclusion. Thus, he rightly predicted the continuation of white male privilege in the workplace and in labor in unions in the United States (see Roediger 1991). At the same time, he understood the classification of whiteness itself to be a highly fraught political process, one that fatefully depended on the use of terror and force.

As Du Bois well knew, capital never acts alone, and the wartime US government soon initiated a nationwide reign of terror aimed at forestalling emergent forms of working-class solidarity. Du Bois left out the larger political context of this government suppression in his portrait of the riot, but despite neglecting the details of this campaign, he pointed to its terror as a spark that ignited the violence. The not-quite-white eastern and southern European laborers were faced with the prospect of increasing insecurity or of joining with white workers in their attempt to banish African American laborers to a state of wagelessness. Many ultimately took sides with white workers and engaged in racial violence. The immediate aftermath was brutal, both for those African Americans who remained in the city and those forcefully exiled to an uncertain future in the South.

Building upon these conceptual advances, Bernard Magubane examines the relationship of race and class in South Africa (1979, 1983). Magubane recounts the making of the black working class in its dialectical relationship to the white working class and in a colonial context. He notes an initial possibility of class solidarity among landless black and white peasants who flocked to the slums of Natal during the first decade of the twentieth century. But ruling class and government fears of interracial solidarity pushed the government to enact policies of territorial segregation. Blacks were allowed entry to the city only as migrant laborers, but were precluded from permanent residence. As a consequence, white laborers became fully proletarianized, whereas blacks did not. White workers then defended their privilege as they fought for and won the right to organize white labor unions and secured laws that reserved skilled jobs for themselves. Thereby, they developed an allegiance to the state, and they participated in suppressing the emergence of an African working class (1983: 29). As a result, blacks continued to rely on household production in rural areas to subsidize their wages and ensure social reproduction, and labor brokers exploited their liminal position by recruiting them directly from rural areas and setting wages that were far inferior to those offered to whites. Magubane demonstrates how the simultaneous making of wage, wage insecure, and wageless labor depended crucially upon the production and maintenance of racial inequality and spatial segregation.

These studies clearly indicate that the process of defining waged and unwaged labor is inherently political, with long-term implications for working class formation and politics. The systemic power of capitalism may well lie in its ability to continually bring myriad forms of waged and unwaged labor into relation with one another across spatial scales. But attempts by laborers to similarly join together in solidarity across nations and empires have been only intermittently successful (Featherstone 2012; Kelley 2002; Silver and Arrighi 2001; Waterman and Willis 2001). This is a reflection of the persistent difficulty in crossing the color, gender, and status lines that demarcate different forms of labor around the world. It also spotlights the exclusionary practices of labor organization themselves. "White laborism," for example, found wide support among Anglo-Saxon workers across the British Empire, from England, to South Africa and Australia during the pre–World War I era. Labor unions in many different nations have used race, gender, ethnicity, and skill to draw boundaries around who was "cut in" and who "cut out" of the protections and benefits they won for their members (Brodkin 1998a; 1998b; 2000; Bush 2009; Du Bois 1969; Hyslop 1999; Mullings 2005; Silver 2003).

Contributors to this volume develop an understanding of relationship between dispossession and difference in a number of ways. August Carbonella's chapter on unionized workers in the twin cities of Jay/Livermore Falls, Maine, in the northeast United States shows how waves of dispossession depended upon the making of ethnic and social difference and inequality among workers in the paper and forest industry. Two protracted labor strikes against International Paper, in 1921 and 1987, frame his analysis. During the first, the company installed stark lines of demarcation to divide skilled and unskilled workers and to reinscribe an ethnic division of labor in the factory and town, a social cleavage that workers had successfully struggled to overcome in the 1910s. This legacy of difference hindered efforts to recreate solidarity across the industry and greatly contributed to the union's defeat in the latter 1987 strike. Sharryn Kasmir highlights the long dispossession of US autoworkers from the 1980s to the present, focusing on the ways in which GM's Saturn project produced difference and ruptured solidarity within the United Automobile Workers, precisely at a time when national and international alliances were critically important for labor. By locating the plant in the anti-union, right-to-work southern United States, GM sought to leverage Saturn's model of labor-management cooperation to encourage competition and division among union locals and to engender an individualist, entrepreneurial ethos among workers. Neither Carbonella or Kasmir take the existence of difference for granted. Instead we closely chart how, on the one hand, difference is made and sustained over a long period of time, and how, on the other, it is turned into inequality and disempowerment. More than providing clear expositions of the relationship between dispossession and the production of difference, then, we point to a larger politics of dispossession.

The Politics of Dispossession

By the politics of dispossession, we refer to the multiple ways in which capital and the state episodically undermine the power of working classes. Jerry Lembcke's (1991–1992) framing of "disorganization" is particularly useful for developing this point. US capital's flight beginning in the 1960s can be seen, Lembcke argues, as an effort to disorganize and defeat a domestic working class that had won position and leverage. Indeed, the move to neoliberalism in the 1970s–1980s restored power to the capitalist class after two decades of working-class empowerment through labor and urban social movements. We see this in the 1973 coup in Chile or the New York City fiscal crisis of the 1970s, when, in a very short time, working-class New Yorkers and their institutions were side-lined from their prominent role in shaping the city's social, economic, and political future (Freeman 2000; Harvey 2005). This exercise of the combined power of capital and the state over organized working classes takes place as well on a global scale, as cycles of disinvestment follow the accumulated victories of regional or national working classes (Silver 2003).

The concept of disorganization is also key for Steve Striffler's (2002) account of banana workers in southern Ecuador, who were unorganized, underemployed, and super-exploited despite the area's rich tradition of worker and peasant activism. State and military repression and violence played a central role in bringing about this wholesale defeat. "Regulation by fear" was equally used to discipline labor and to dismantle leftist culture and institutions in post–civil war Spain (Narotzky and Smith 2006). The Franco Regime used repression, murder, and exile to wipe out the traces of left politics, beliefs, and rituals from the public sphere. The regime thereby instituted new oppressive forms of daily life, which counted upon poverty, hunger, and food rationing to control its citizens. In rural Alicante, these conditions meant that when the post-Franco, democratic Spanish state promoted flexible labor contracts in the 1980s–1990s, there was little resistance. Workers had learned not to see themselves as political, and a public culture that might have sustained a political response had been destroyed.

We come, then, to a holistic understanding of dispossession as simultaneously economic, martial, social, and cultural. Lesley Gill develops this perspective in her chapter on the Colombian oil city of Barrancabermeja. Popular solidarity was systematically destroyed in the 1980s–1990s via a broad-based attack on working class, peasant, and guerrilla movements undertaken by a coalition of US military advisors, the Colombian state and military, and Colombian paramilitary organizations. Assassinations, mass murders, disappearances, arrests, and daily repression spread fear and insecurity, and social networks were steadily fragmented and dissolved. The profound salience of violence that Gill so eloquently describes contrasts sharply with the antiseptic portrayal of contemporary capital accumulation. Indeed, Gill's informants use the phrase "blood and fire" to describe their experience of displacement and to underscore the prevalence of terror in their lives, and to refer to Marx's depiction of the brutality and violence of capital accumulation.

In her chapter on Janata Colony, a slum in Mumbai, India, Judy Whitehead likewise details how neoliberal policies worked to fracture the Fordist work relationship and encourage real estate speculation. This "double dispossession" marginalized workers both from stable employment and from the city center, and Janata's working-class institutions consequently lost their power to influence and improve daily life. Tellingly, new forms of community organization and welfare come largely from the right wing, Hindu fundamentalist Shiv Sena, which uses gang violence in the service of labor discipline. Don Kalb, also charts the connection between political defeat and the rise of right-wing ultranationalism in his chapter on the declining fortunes of factory workers in Wroclaw, Poland, during the postsocialist period. The 1981 victory of Solidarity propelled a movement for worker control and self-government at the factory level. A year later, Solidarity was banned and the worker's control movement was pushed underground. Economic reforms, enacted after 1989 as "shock therapy" (Klein 2008) for Poland's membership in the EU and entrance into the wider capitalist world, paved the way for the sale of state-owned factories. A new class of technocrats, who had once been part of a broad coalition with workers to create Solidarity, planned these policies. The reforms are seen from the outside as having produced a "successful democratic transition," but Kalb argues that the "hidden history" of working-class dispossession—the loss of their political aspirations and control of their factories, their betrayal by technocrats, and their widespread unemployment—is at the core of his informants' right-wing populism and anti-liberalism.

In her chapter, Susana Narotzky writes about workers in the shipbuilding town of Ferrol in Galicia, northwestern Spain. Ferrol's workers organized the underground communist union CCOO and participated in a broad, popular movement that helped bring down the Franco Regime and force a democratic transition in the 1970s. The workers' annual labor contract, secure work, stable wages, and experience of solidarity, once enabled a class-based "structure of feeling," but Spain's preparation for entry into the EU in 1986 and the requisite, state-imposed neoliberal reforms forced the downsizing of the shipyards and the steel sector, such that there is no longer stable or well-paying work in Ferrol. Galicia's shipbuilding sector now relies wholly on a network of subcontractors and casual labor. Many young people have left in search of opportunities elsewhere. Those who remain are unable to afford housing, therefore, they live with their parents and delay marriage and childbearing. Narotzky describes the individual strategizing and networking that residents engage in to find a job and achieve social mobility, much in contrast with the collective action of earlier decades that had been the main avenue of security and advancement. Narotzky's informants no longer look to the union or left political parties for meaning, and they feel largely hopeless in the absence of a politics of solidarity.

The concept of dispossession developed in this collection speaks to the ways in which the alienation of political position, organizational capacities, culture, and consciousness are intimately connected with economic setback. As we have seen, emergent forms of solidarity often give way to class fragmentation and exclusion, and the multiple ways that people are displaced from their social ties—the bonds of kin and community, however configured—leave many isolated, passive, or in despair. This is brought about in some cases with violent repression, leaving fear and distrust in its wake (Gill.) In others, it is effected by the seemingly mundane mechanisms of worker insecurity produced in unremitting defeats and concessions of labor unions (Carbonella, Kasmir); by displacement from neighborhoods by real estate speculation and gentrification (Whitehead); by the loss of spaces of commonality where worker victories were reproduced through transgenerational memories (Narotzky); or by recriminations resulting from the appropriation of worker self-management (Kalb) (Linda Green, personal communication). It is important to note, however, that disorganization is not a one-way process but reflects, instead, the dialectic of organization and disorganization that plays a critical role in defining the politics of labor.

Place, Space, and Power

A focus on disorganization therefore implies a necessary, reciprocal attention to the problem of organization. The struggle for organization, in our estimation, is paramount for class politics. However, the above examples point to organizations not as permanently structured institutions. We instead see an active process of shaping, maintaining, destabilizing, and unmaking that depends upon the creation and rupturing of connections, alliances, and identities within places and across space (Wolf 1990). The importance of organization is at the heart of Eric Hobsbawm's (1984) critique of E. P. Thompson's history of the making of the English working class. For Hobsbawm, the making of the working class required more than the mobilization of culture and tradition, the realms of social life that Thompson stressed. In his view, class is a more decidedly political formation that requires institutions, most especially labor unions and political parties that cross national and international space. Although Hobsbawm emphasizes the progressive nature of working class institutions, it is important to keep in mind that a broadly encompassing solidarity is only one of many possible outcomes of organizing.

June Nash's ethnography (1979) of tin miners in Oturo, Bolivia, nicely foregrounds the relationship of organization and place/space connections and the ways that solidarity is created across social divides. Nash conducted fieldwork in 1969–1970, during a brief democratic opening before the brutal coup that destroyed mining communities. She witnessed militant activism and the reorganization of a powerful labor movement. The miners were largely indigenous, and they maintained an adherence to Marxist-Leninism along with their traditional beliefs. In the mining camps, they felt a double exploitation, since company-owned stores and housing were as much a source of expropriation of their surplus value as was their work in the mines. For this reason, and despite a gender division of labor, women and men joined together in the struggle against the company, making family life another source of class solidarity. They had strong local commitments—what Nash termed "communitas" and Raymond Williams would consider "structures of feeling"—while at the same time they saw themselves as part of a global proletariat. The union similarly sustained a tension between local-level activism and a broader understanding of the world market, neocolonialism, and imperialism informed by the international Marxism of the day.

An international labor geography likewise emerges from Karen Brodkin's (2007) monograph on young activists in Los Angeles. Most of Brodkin's informants were immigrants or children of immigrants whose parents brought histories of union and social activism with them to the United States. Their own or their parents' experiences of border crossing and confronting racism in the United States were in the forefront of their political consciousness, and their paths to political involvement included associations with labor unions and left groups in California. But their political biographies equally manifest a close identification with their parents' memories of labor and social activism in their home countries.

Nash and Brodkin each draw connections among locally situated identities and activism and general struggles and ideologies. Raymond Williams (1989) repeatedly returns to this relationship between local and universal scales in his analysis of working-class politics, as Narotzky discusses in her chapter. For Williams, working-class power always involves the necessary dialectic between what he calls "militant particularism" and "abstract universalism." These refer, respectively, to the immediate struggles and feelings developed at the local level (a mine, factory, or town) and the territory-spanning associations, networks, and political organizations that author solidaristic forms of identity (i.e., working class), build formal institutions (political parties), and develop projects (socialism) (see Harvey 2001; 2009). Williams directs our attention, thus, to the political work that is necessary to derive the general interest from specific claims, an effort that we might conceptualize as "universalism from below."

We can see the dialectical process of the particular and the universal in the efforts of workers to organize across geographic space and social categories in Suzan Erem and Paul Durrenberger's *On the Global Waterfront: The Fight to Free the Charleston 5* (2008). This struggle began in 2000, when members of the predominantly African American Local 1422 of the International Longshoremen's Association (ILA) in Charleston, South Carolina, picketed a ship being unloaded by nonunion workers. Their protest was ended by a police riot, followed by the arrest of five workers on felony charges. After this repression, the ILA and the AFL-CIO actively marginalized the besieged union local. Local activists, meanwhile, worked diligently with 1422 leaders to build a movement of independent-minded union locals, civil-rights organizations, leftist groups, black churches, and progressive white churches. In this way, they ensured that that their union was not isolated but linked to an array of community groups, and that wage laborers were thereby politically tied to those who did not earn a wage.

The map we construct from this account of the struggle begins in Charleston, but that city and its workers are not depicted as a circumscribed place or population. Dockworkers across the globe pledged an industrial action to close dozens of ports on the first day of the trial of the five workers. To avert this massive threat to international trade, the judge permitted the accused to plead no contest to misdemeanor charges. International Dockworkers Council (IDC), a progressive international labor federation, was fortified during the struggle, and after the victory, Local 1422 hosted IDC's first general assembly. The events extend from Charleston to New York City, which is home to ILA international headquarters and its union bureaucrats. The story also takes place in San Francisco, where the militant West Coast International Longshore and Warehouse Union contacted European unions and sketched a plan for solidarity on the global waterfront that sidestepped the conservative International Transport Workers Federation and instead bolstered the IDC. Events unfolded also in Denmark at the corporate offices of Nordana shipping, where there is intense competition in the global shipping industry, a sector that for decades used containerization to pioneer a worldwide assault on labor; in Liverpool, where an unsuccessful effort in the 1990s to organize internationally to save port jobs urged the founding of IDC and offered lessons to this new campaign; and in Seoul, where Daewoo Motor Workers lent their support.

The radically different forms of territory-spanning political networks and imaginations we have recounted raise important questions for a global anthropology of labor. In many ways, they reinforce the attempts to conceptualize continuous, interconnected space found in certain strands of anthropological and geographical theory (see Gupta and Ferguson 1997; Massey 2005). They also point to the problem of how connections across space, social barriers, and categories are produced in the first place. If, as Henri Lefebvre (1976: 21) notably wrote, capitalism reproduces itself by "occupying space . . . producing a space," the same may be said to hold true for working classes. While capital mobilizes states, transnational agencies, and militaries to create empires, ensure commodity and money flows, and establish global markets, a working class relies solely on its organizations, institutions, and affiliations to command and produce space. Labor's institutional presence is thus not simply a conduit for wage negotiations and the like, as it increasingly was in the global North during the Fordist period, but vitally important for its ability to command space and place. Political thinking and action beyond local, national, and social boundaries requires coordination, whether through the maintenance of alliances and networks or through more formal structures (see Bourdieu 2003).

Recognizing the importance of organization for connecting working-class places raises questions about contemporary scholarly understandings of the "local" within the social sciences and humanities. The local has increasingly come to mean resistance to the global. Indeed, local-global has become a common oppositional pairing that directs us to a culture of opposition strongly identified with and rooted in a particular place (Escobar 2008; Tsing 2005). The pointed interest in the social ties of place, however, frequently derails an investigation of their shifting relationship to institutions and networks that link local struggles to wider movements. Fred Cooper (2000) critiques the predilection for localism in social history along these same lines. He reminds us that defining a working class in the early nineteenth century "was indeed a political process and it took place not just in relation to communities in England and France, but in relation to imperial structure and the interrelated economies of sugar, cotton, and shipping. Capitalism was as local as community and radical politics was as 'global' as capitalism" (64). The point is not to privilege global forms of solidarity, association, or projects over local or particular struggles, but to argue that local working classes necessarily exist in state of continuing collaboration and/or tension with wider class formations, social movements, political networks, and forms of institutional power.

Carbonella and Kasmir argue in their chapters that the local is not a natural political or cultural space in which daily life is lived. Instead it is produced, involving the often-violent breaking of political connections, alliances, and networks that developed over time and that afforded workers some measure of power. In many of the cases in this collection, the localization of struggle is shown to be central feature of dispossession. This is not to say that the local is not also a site of solidarity, shared suffering, and common struggle (as it is framed in Narotzky's study of Ferrol or in Kalb's description of workers councils during the Solidarity movement). But when these structures of feeling are forcibly circumscribed at the local level (as they became at the Saturn plant and in Jay/Livermore Falls) labor's leverage is stultified.

An anthropology of labor must not, then, mistake the existence of the local as a given, but rather pose it as a problem to be explored.

From this perspective, the production of space and place is a critical component of what Eric Wolf (2001) calls structural power. Offered as a rephrasing and expansion of the older idea of social relations of production, Wolf maintains that structural power establishes the global fields of force in which capital is accumulated and labor is allocated. As seen throughout this volume, this often involves setting in motion recurrent processes of dispossession, differentiation, and disorganization to realign existing social relationships, Localities, regions, and nations are thus merged or disaggregated in the process of producing new spaces of capital accumulation. Structural power shapes, informs, and influences local outcomes, and it makes some kinds of action within them possible, while it renders others less likely or even impossible. Most importantly, the potential for creating and aligning local working class publics, national labor movements, and scale-spanning solidarities are highly determined by the changing forms and uneven geographies of structural power relations.

Disposable People?

The uneven processes of capital and labor accumulation outlined so far should serve to upset any notions we may still harbor about a homogeneous, global proletariat. As feminist and African American scholars have long argued, the singularity that some have too often attributed to "the" proletariat, white, male, industrial workers and their political institutions comes at the expense of a wider, heterogeneous social formation. Thus the continuing project of reconceptualizing labor brings us back to the insistence on the necessity of the multiple labors of slaves, peasants, plantation workers, household work, and others for the production of surplus value in previous phases of capital accumulation. This keystone of Wolf's (1982) reconfiguration of anthropological subjects situates them within relations of connection and mutual constitution, bridging the cultural and political divides between labor made *visible* by the capital/wage labor relation and the *invisible* labors outside of that relationship (Robinson 2001). To the extent that these labors are separated in space, they are not always apparent at the local level. Nonetheless, this relationship shapes the lives we seek to understand. If we hope to explain class or the production of culture, anthropologists cannot afford to miss these unseen connections (Narotzky and Smith 2006). Whitehead's chapter goes a long way to making these unseen labors visible, especially in their connections to capital accumulation in the global financial center of Mumbai.

At this new moment of capitalist restructuring we need to explore how the current multiplication of the proletariat is producing a range of new labor relations. This is not a wholly novel phenomenon, but a specific instance of the "general tendency of [capitalism] to create a 'disposable mass' out of diverse populations, and then to throw that mass into the breach to meet the changing needs of capital" (Wolf 1982: 379–380). The global scale and accelerated timeframe of the processes of dispossession, though, may be unprecedented. Certainly, the recent relentless movement and financialization of capital is simultaneously producing new enclosures (of land, property, commons, rights) and rustbelts (Midnight Notes Collective 1990).

There is a growing scholarly consensus around the notion that these new enclosures are creating people and communities who are permanently constituted as the "outside" of capitalism. Notwithstanding important corrections by those who expose the way states actively incorporate unwaged or unfree forms of labor (e.g., Collins and Mayer 2010: 147–159) or who theorize the "precariat" in relationship to capital and the state (e.g., Standing 2011), a range of concepts attempts to capture this purported outside. "The bare life," "disposable people," "surplus populations," "states of exception," and "wasted lives" all refer to what Mbembe calls "the biopolitics of permanent joblessness" (quoted in Denning 2008: 3). These ideas effectively dispense with the study of labor in favor of citizenship and exclusion, which has been a central analytical move over the last decade. This perspective also unfortunately reinscribes dualistic and outdated class maps, rather than confronting the actual, complicated global "multiplication of the proletariat" taking place in the present moment.

Jan Breman (1999) underscores the inadequacy of these oppositional formulations in his comments on the Indian industrial workers of the so-called informal sector. This "precariat," as we might describe it, has been comprised by a steady stream of displaced rural dwellers to Mumbai and other cities over four decades. Their numbers and output far outweigh the workers employed and goods produced in the formal economy. This informal sector is characterized by heightened insecurity of employment, debt bondage, withheld wages, and dispersed production sites—from domestic homework, to makeshift workshops, to relatively stable workplaces. It does not, however, constitute the "outside" of capitalism, but, increasingly, its center, as Gill's and Whitehead's chapters vividly demonstrate. Yet it is precisely this slum-dwelling precariat that Chatterjee (2004) sees as the embodiment of "surplus populations," and among whom a new politics, outside of class, is developing (see *Identities: Global Studies in Culture and Power* 2011). Chatteejee's analysis of the surplus populations' struggles for representation on the fringes of civil society thus comes at the expense of any attempt to understand their labor in the unregulated industrial sector.

Accounts of disposable populations thus make the mistake of substituting static social categories for a clear examination of the profound disregard for laboring peoples' lives that is exhibited by states, transnational regulatory agencies, global capital, and its local middlemen. They also miss the various ways that the surplus value produced by the precariat and nonwaged labor makes its way into the global circuits of capital, and they overlook the relationship between capital's prosperity and labor's deepening poverty. These scholars vaporize the contributions of these many laborers into the mist of what Marx called commodity fetishism by concealing "the social character of private labor and the social relations between individual workers" (Marx quoted in Merrifield 2002: 159). This perspective leaves us with a vision of people who are seemingly never "thrown back into the breach," nor chart an alternative. The end result of this analysis, we fear, is to remove laboring people from history.

Arundhati Roy (2011: 21) points the way to recovering this historical dynamic in her essay on the armed Maoist rebellions in central India. She asks,

> When people are being brutalized, what "better" thing is there for them to do than to fight back? It's not as though anyone's offering them a choice, unless it's to commit suicide, like the 180,000 farmers caught in a spiral of debt have done. (Am I the only one who gets the distinct feeling that the Indian establishment and its representatives in the media are far more comfortable with the idea of poor people killing themselves in despair than with the idea of them fighting back?)

Here Roy captures the dialectic between disposability and historical agency. In the one instance, impoverished, indebted peasants and proletarians appear as surplus populations whose way out is to end their lives. In the next, they rise up against their misery and command the attention and resources of the state and capital that furiously try to put them down. And they make history.

Rather than simply assuming that real people actually constitute capital's outside, we need to pay more attention to what relations of production and class fragmentation now look like. Future research will have to crack open these relations to include the disciplinary arm of the state (police, immigration services, military, penal institutions, labor laws, etc.), debt purveyors (large and small), and government functionaries, among others. The fact that the US-led military-financial empire, with its permanent war philosophy, has redirected the global spaces of capital and labor strongly suggests that we need to capture the relationship between the organization of oppression and the organization of accumulation to grasp labor politics fully (Robinson 2001). This framework will enhance our ability to revise inherited narratives of class and social inequality. The combined political and structural violence that today constitutes the key avenue of dispossession and the production of precariousness has rendered these narratives obsolete and suggests the urgency of ethnographies and ethnology of actually existing forms of labor and class relationships.

Conclusion

We have shown in this introduction that the defeat and unmaking of particular working classes is both the consequence of and grounding for neoliberal capitalism, and the six case studies in this volume make this abundantly clear. In examining class formation across both time and space, these studies closely consider the themes of dispossession and difference; the politics of dispossession; place, space, and power; and the myth of "disposable people," and they facilitate a comparative perspective on the uneven consequences of and reactions to the worldwide project to remake capital and labor. This comparison is our starting point for a global anthropology of labor.

As we intend it, a key feature of this subfield is an emphasis on the formal and actual connections and interrelations of distinct laboring populations. This strongly suggests that local and global are not separate spheres of human activity, as they are often portrayed, but interrelated spaces created together by the fields of force in which capital and labor are accumulated. The "global" is evident in each of our "local" historical ethnographies, as we refer to the flows of power, commodities, and labor across place and space, and to the territory-spanning networks and organizations that anchor local struggles. We trace how the coordination of demands and actions enhanced working class power, as well as how the weakening of those connections facilitated labor's defeat in case after case.

Although the fragmentation of working classes has been the hallmark of the last forty years, we do not see this as the end point, but as the interregnum between the unmaking of national working classes and the as-yet-unfinished class formations of the future. As we write, some sense of the shape of that identification, alliance, and politics is emerging. It is partly exemplified by the Occupy chant: "We are the 99 percent" and rephrased in the "people's" demands arising from public squares in many corners of the world. Whether explicitly or implicitly, these claims echo Thomas Paine's equation of the 1 percent against the 99 percent at the turn of the nineteenth century. At that juncture, that political slogan became a common identification for disparate laboring populations as they began gradually to coalesce into working classes. New alliances and networks are just emerging from the ashes of the long, recent defeat, and we do not yet know what forms will develop, but to apprehend them and contribute to this moment of political possibility, we need to recognize the manifold forms of labor and the changing class maps before us. This is the immediate project of the global anthropology of labor that inspires this volume.

References

Berman, Marshall. 1982. *All That Is Solid Melts into Air: The Experience of Modernity.* Harmonsworth: England.
Bourdieu, Pierre. 2003. "Against the Policy of Depoliticization." In *Firing Back: Against the Tyranny of the Market 2*. London: Verso Books.
Breman, Jan. 1999. "The Study of Industrial Labour in Post-Colonial India: The Informal Sector: A Concluding Review." In *The Worlds of Industrial Labour*, ed. Jonathan Parry, Jan Breman, and Karin Kapadia. London: Sage Publications.
Brodkin, Karen. 1998a. "Race, Class and Gender: The Metaorganization of American Capitalism." *Transforming Anthropology* 7, no. 2: 46–57.
———. 1998b. *How Jews Became White Folks: And What That Says About Race in America*. New Brunswick, NJ: Rutgers University Press.
———. 2000. "Global Capitalism: What's Race Got to do with it?" *American Ethnologist* 27, no. 2: 237–256.
———. 2007. *Making Democracy Matter: Identity and Activism in Los Angeles*. New Brunswick, NJ: Rutgers University Press.
Buck-Morss, Susan. 2009. *Hegel, Haiti, and Universal History*. Pittsburgh: University of Pittsburgh Press.

Bush, Roderick. 2009. *The End of White World Supremacy: Black Internationalism and the Problem of the Color Line.* Philadelphia: Temple University Press.
Chatterjee, Partha. 2004. *The Politics of the Governed: Reflections on Popular Politics in Most of the World.* New York: Columbia University Press.
Collins, Jane L. 2003. *Threads: Gender, Labor and Power in the Global Apparel Industry.* Chicago, London: The University of Chicago Press.
———. 2012. "Theorizing Wisconsin's 2011 Protests: Community-Based Unionism Confronts Accumulation by Dispossession." *American Ethnologist* 39, no. 1: 6–20.
Collins, Jane L., and Victoria Mayer. 2010. *Both Hands Tied: Welfare Reform and the Race to the Bottom of the Low-Wage Labor Market.* Chicago, London: University of Chicago Press.
Collins, Jane L., and Martha Gimenez, eds. 1990. *Work Without Wages: Domestic Labor and Self-Employment within Capitalism.* Albany: State University of New York Press.
Cooper, Frederick. 2000. "Farewell to the Category-Producing Class?" *International Labor and Working Class History* no. 57 (Spring): 60–68
Denning, Michael. 2004. *Culture in the Age of Three Worlds.* New York: Verso Books.
———. 2008. "The Spectre of a Wageless Life." Working Group on Globalization and Culture. Initiative on Labor and Culture, Working Papers 2008: 3, Yale University.
Du Bois, W. E. B. 1969 [1920]. *Darkwater: Voices from Within the Veil.* New York: Schocken Books.
Erem, Suzan, and E. Paul Durrenberger. 2008. *On the Global Waterfront: The Fight to Free the Charleston Five.* New York: Monthly Review Press.
Escobar, Arturo. 2008. *Territories of Difference: Place, Movements, Life, Redes.* Duke University Press.
Featherstone, David. 2012. *Solidarity: Hidden Histories and Geographies of Internationalism.* London: Zed Books.
Federici, Silvia. 2004. *Caliban and the Witch: Women, the Body and Primitive Accumulation.* New York: Autonomedia.
———. 2012. *Revolution at Point Zero. Housework, Reproduction, and Feminist Struggle.* Oakland, CA: PM Press.
Freeman, Joshua B. 2000. *Working Class New York: Life and Labor Since World War II.* New York: The Free Press.
Gupta, Akil, and James Ferguson. 1997. "Beyond Culture: Space, Identity, and the Politics of Difference." In *Culture, Power, Place: Explorations in Critical Anthropology.* Durham: Duke University Press.
Gramsci, Antonio. 1971. *Selections from the Prison Notebooks.* New York: International Publishers.
Harvey, David. 2001. "Militant Particularism and Global Ambition: The Conceptual Politics of Place, Space, and Environment in the Work of Raymond Williams." In *Spaces of Capital. Towards a Critical Geography.* New York: Routledge.
———. 2003. *The New Imperialism.* Oxford, New York: Oxford University Press.
———. 2005. *A Brief History of Neo-liberalism.* Oxford, New York: Oxford University Press.
———. 2009. *Cosmopolitanism and the Geographies of Freedom.* New York: Columbia University Press.
Hobsbawm, Eric J. 1984. "The Making of the Working-Class, 1870–1914." In *Workers: Worlds of Labor.* New York: Pantheon Books.
Hyslop, Jonathon. 1999. "The Imperial Working Class Makes Itself White: White Labourism in Britain, Australia, and South Africa before the First World War." *Journal of Historical Sociology* 12, no. 4: 398–421.
Identities: Global Studies in Culture and Power. 2011. Special Issue on Surplus Populations 18, no. 1.

Kalb, Don. 2009. "Conversations with a Polish Populist: Tracing Hidden Histories of Globalization, Class and Dispossession in Postsocialism (and Beyond.)" *American Ethnologist* 36, no. 2: 207–223.
Kasmir, Sharryn, and August Carbonella. 2008. "Dispossession and the Anthropology of Labor." *Critique of Anthropology* 28, no. 1: 5–25.
Kelly, Robin. 2002. "The African Diaspora and the Remapping of US History." In *Rethinking American History in a Global Age*, ed. Thomas Bender. Berkeley: University of California Press.
Klein, Naomi. 2008. *The Shock Doctrine: The Rise of Disaster Capitalism*. New York: Henry Holt and Company.
Lee, Ching Kwan. 2007. *Against the Law: Labor Protests in China's Rustbelt and Sunbelt*. Berkeley: University of California Press.
Lefebvre, Henri. 1976. *The Survival of Capitalism: Reproduction of the Relations of Production*. London: Allison & Busby.
Lembcke, Jerry. 1991–1992. "Why 50 Years? Working-Class Formation and Long Economic Cycles." *Science & Society* 55, no. 4: 417–446.
Linebaugh, Peter. 2003 [1991]. *The London Hanged: Crime and Civil Society in the Eighteenth Century*. London: Verso Books.
Luxemburg, Rosa. 2003 [1913]. *The Accumulation of Capital*. London: Routledge.
Magubane, Bernard. 1979. *The Political Economy of Race and Class in South Africa*. New York: Monthly Review Press.
———. 1983. *Proletarianization and Class Struggle in Africa*. San Francisco: Synthesis Publications.
Marx, Karl. 1977. *Capital. A Critique of Political Economy*. Volume One. New York: Vintage Books.
Massey, Doreen. 2005. *For Space*. London: Sage Publications.
Merrifield, Andy. 2002. *Dialectical Urbanism*. New York: Monthly Review Press.
Midnight Notes Collective. 1990. *The New Enclosures*. Midnight Notes, 10.
Mintz, Sidney. 1985. *Sweetness and Power: The Place of Sugar in Modern History*. New York: Viking Penguin.
Mullings, Leith. 2005. "Interrogating Racism: Toward an Antiracist Anthropology." *Annual Reviews in Anthropology* 34: 667–693.
Narotzky, Susana, and Gavin Smith. 2006. *Immediate Struggles: People, Power and Place in Rural Spain*. Berkeley: University of California Press.
Nash, June. 1979. *We Eat the Mines and the Mines Eat Us: Dependency and Exploitation in Bolivian Tin Mines*. New York: Columbia University Press.
Nugent, David. 2002. "Introduction." In *Locating Capitalism in Time and Space: Global Restructuring, Politics, and Identity*, ed. David Nugent. Palo Alto: Stanford University Press.
Palmer, Bryan D. 1994. *E. P. Thompson: Objections and Oppositions*. London: Verso Books.
Perelman, Michael. 2000. *The Invention of Capitalism: Classical Political Economy and the Secret History of Primitive Accumulation*. Durham, NC: Duke University Press.
Polanyi, Karl. 1944. *The Great Transformation*. New York, Toronto: Rinehart & Co.
Robinson, Cedric J. 2001. *An Anthropology of Marxism*. Burlington, VT: Ashgate Publishing Ltd.
Roediger, David R. 1991. *The Wages of Whiteness: Race and the Making of the American Working Class*. New York: Verso Books.
Roseberry, William. 1989. *Anthropologies and Histories: Essays in Culture, History and Political Economy*. New Brunswick: Rutgers University Press.
Roy, Arundhati. 2011. *Walking with the Comrades*. London: Penguin Books.
Silver, Beverly. 2003. *Forces of Labor: Workers' Movements and Globlization since 1870*. Cambridge: Cambridge University Press.

Silver, Beverly, and Giovanni Arrighi. 2001. "Workers North and South." In *Working Classes, Global Realities. Socialist Register*, ed. Leo Panitch, and Colin Lays. London, New York: Monthly Review Press, Merlin Press.

Standing, Guy. 2011. *The Precariat: The New Dangerous Class*. London: Bloomsbury Academic.

Striffler, Steve. 2002. *In the Shadows of State and Capital. The United Fruit Company, Popular Struggle, and Agrarian Restructuring in Ecuador, 1900–1995*. Durham, NC: Duke University Press.

Thompson, E. P. 1963. *The Making of the English Working Class*. London: Vintage Books.

Tsing, Ana. 2005. *Friction: An Ethnography of Global Connection*. Princeton, NJ: Princeton University Press.

Waterman, Peter, and Jane Willis, eds. 2001. *Place, Space and the New Labor Internationalisms*. Oxford: Wiley-Blackwell.

Williams, Raymond. 1989. *Resources of Hope*. New York: Verso Books.

Vogel, Lise. 1983. *Marxism and the Oppression of Women: Toward a Unitary Theory*. New Brunswick, NJ: Rutgers University Press.

Wolf, Eric. 1982. *Europe and the People without History*. Berkeley: University of California Press.

———. 1990. "Facing Power: Old Insights, New Questions." *American Anthropologist* 92: 586–596.

———. 2001. *Pathways of Power: Building an Anthropology of the Modern World*. Berkeley: University of California Press.

Wood, Ellen Meiskins. 2007. "A Reply to Critics." *Historical Materialism* 15: 143–170.

Young, Iris. 1981. "Beyond the Unhappy Marriage: A Critique of the Dual Systems Theory." In *Women and Revolution: A Discussion of the Unhappy Marriage of Marxism and Feminism*, ed. Lydia Sargeant. Boston: South End Press.

– Chapter 1 –

FRAGMENTED SOLIDARITY
Political Violence and Neoliberalism in Colombia

Lesley Gill

As the flight from Bogotá to Barrancabermeja begins its descent into the steamy Middle Magdalena River valley, cattle ranches and African palm plantations emerge out of the haze, and herds of Zebu cattle appear as tiny white specks against the undulating green pastures below. Oil pipelines crisscross the valley's alluvial plain, and the muddy waters of the Magdalena, laden with silt and the toxic effluence of the oil industry, churn northward to the Atlantic port of Barranquilla. The dark outline of the San Lucas mountains hovers over the western horizon. A few moments later, the sprawling refinery, wedged between the river and the city, and its two-hundred-foot flames come into view. Most of Colombia's oil is refined in Barrancabermeja, which developed as a foreign-controlled, oil-producing enclave and a center of militant working-class activism in the early twentieth century. Nowadays, "Barranca," as Colombians call it, is much more than an oil enclave. Its location on the Magdalena River, its access to a major road network and Atlantic port, and the presence of gold and mineral reserves in the nearby San Lucas mountains makes the city a major commercial entrepôt and transit point for Colombia's cocaine industry.

When the flight attendant announces that the plane will soon land, the mostly male passengers begin logging off computers and fiddling with cell phones in anticipation. They are engineers and contractors with ECOPETROL, Colombia's national oil company, and there are more of them than in the recent past. Business is booming in Barranca. After decades of brutal counterinsurgent terror against trade unions, neighborhood associations, civic groups, and left-wing guerrilla militias, the oil refinery is slated for expansion, a major hydroelectric project is underway, a new shopping mall, two large grocery stores, and an upscale hotel have opened in the city center; and Avianca—the Colombian national airline—has replaced the small propeller planes that once ferried passengers on the Bogotá-Barrancabermeja route with larger jets.

Business prospers on the ruptured lives and unmarked graves of thousands of working-class citizens. Violence has torn apart social solidarities, exposed peasants and working people to extreme social and economic insecurities, commoditized their resources, and created new hierarchies among them, all of which created the political preconditions for the imposition of a harsh neoliberal economic model. Colombia's largest and once powerful oil workers union—the Unión Sindical Obrera (USO)—is a shadow of its former self after losing more than one hundred leaders to state and paramilitary terror over the last two and a half decades. The partial privatization of ECOPETROL and the rise of subcontracting have further intensified economic insecurity, undermined workplace solidarity, and eroded the political networks of cooperation that connected the USO to working-class neighborhoods. Dozens of other unions find themselves in a similar situation or have ceased to exist.

What follows is an effort to explain the violent making, unmaking, and remaking of Barrancabermeja's working class. Sometime in the 1990s, as Colombia's economy became one of the most liberalized in the Americas, the country obtained the dubious distinction of being the most dangerous place in the world to be a trade unionist. The punishment of neoliberal capital became intertwined with a gruesome form of capital punishment—officially unacknowledged "disappearances," extrajudicial executions, and wholesale massacres—as the government pursued a military solution to a decades-long civil war by outsourcing the disreputable acts of warfare to right-wing paramilitaries. The paramilitaries used terror to facilitate the accumulation of wealth and power for themselves and an emergent right-wing alliance of drug traffickers-turned landlords, politicians, retired and active duty military officials, and neoliberal entrepreneurs. They did so through the violent dispossession of working people and peasants and the suppression of dissent. Private political-economic power then blurred with the state itself and deepened neoliberalism through the spread of regional sovereignties or parastates that operated alongside or in place of the official state, fueling the continued accumulation of wealth under conditions of extreme fear and impunity (Gill 2009; Hylton 2006; López 2010).

Nowadays, Barranca's urban periphery is characterized less by peace than a durable disorder,[1] and violence lurks just below the surface of an apparent calm. Downsized workers, displaced peasants, and poor urbanites compete for jobs within authoritarian, clientelistic networks in an outsized informal economy, where they are forced to struggle with the silences, ruptures, understandings, and ways of living that terror created. Like the residents of urban peripheries in much of the global South, excluding east Asia, they are characterized as a surplus population (Breman 2003; Davis 2006), one that raises questions of order and control for a government that must manage the disorder that its counterinsurgency war and neoliberal policies have created. It is therefore not surprising that Pentagon planners worry about the military challenges posed by so-called "feral cities" (Graham 2007; Norton 2003) and that militaries and police forces remain key to upholding the very order that neoliberal capitalism undermines. Yet viewing Barrancabermeja's downtrodden residents as an uncontrollable, surplus population removes them from the city's long history of working-class formation in which differently categorized laborers—informal, industrial, peasant—have bridged the cultural divisions among them to voice collective demands and create their own urban "order."

This essay argues that the installation and consolidation of neoliberal capitalism was the result of the reactive violence unleashed by a right-wing alliance of entrepreneurs, narco-paramilitaries, state security forces, and traditional politicians against left-wing insurgencies, peasant organizations, trade unions, and working-class communities that represented a variety of opposing views of the world. Violence, that is, brute force that aims to crush, eliminate, or mentally destroy an individual or group, is a recurrent feature in the periodic dispossession of working people, the disorganization of working-class power, and the reconfiguration of class relationships, but the importance of violence often passes unobserved in economistic accounts of capital accumulation that unfold at a high level of abstraction. Although Barrancabermeja represents an extreme example, the dismantling and reorganization of its working class offer insights into how violence becomes enmeshed with the interrelated processes of capital formation and working-class disorganization and dispossession.[2]

Grandin notes that political violence as an analytic category has moved from explanation to interpretation in recent years, as scholars have substituted analytic categories, such as exploitation, for humanistic ones, such as suffering, and focused on how violence is experienced (Grandin 2010). A spate of social science theorizing has sought to extend the concept beyond instrumentalized force to better understand how it pervades the fabric of social life. Notions such as "structural violence" (Farmer 1997) and "continuum of violence" (Scheper-Hughes and Bourgois 2004) promise deeper insights into the social, cultural, and economic dimensions of violence. Yet despite the utility of these formulations in certain contexts, they risk diluting the concept of violence by finding it everywhere and reifying it. Similarly, much human rights reporting enumerates the details of massacres, disappearances, and extrajudicial executions and documents incidents of torture, but it fails to explore the motivations that drive different groups of people into conflict (e.g., Human Rights Watch 1996; 2001). This kind of reporting removes targeted individuals from the history of social, economic, and political struggle that generated violence in the first place and treats them as passive victims.

A more dynamic, relational approach is necessary to grasp how violence works at the intersection of working peoples' changing relationships to each other and more powerful groups on the one hand and their feelings about these transformations on the other hand. In Chile, for example, Pinochet's assault on labor unions and activists aimed to disarticulate resistance to the dictatorship and terrorize working people into passivity so that the regime could enact neoliberal labor policies that were detrimental to worker interests (Winn 2004). And in Guatemala, the clash between the efforts of Coca-Cola workers to form a union and improve their working conditions, and the insistence of management and the Guatemalan state on maintaining the status quo, generated brutal military repression (Levenson-Estrada 1994). Although violence is, indeed, an experiential reality that has important meaningful and symbolic consequences, it cannot be dissociated from broader analyses of power, such as "the relational formation of subjectivity, the transformation of economic relations and the state, and the evolution of competing ideologies vying for common-sense status" (Grandin 2010: 7). In the Marxist tradition, political violence is understood as a by-product of class relations; violence itself is not the object of analysis but the broader social field from which it arises.

If, as David Harvey suggests, neoliberalism is a restoration of class power (Harvey 2005), it has been a particularly bloody affair in Barranca. The social crisis that arose from the one-two punch of violence and neoliberalism facilitated the incorporation of some working people into new exploitative forms of labor discipline, rent extraction, and political subjugation that deepened insecurity, weakened any collective response, and facilitated new forms of capital accumulation for a rising new right-wing bloc. The case of Barrancabermeja illustrates why an anthropology of labor must pay careful attention to how violence arises from, and simultaneously shapes, processes of capital accumulation and class formation. It also highlights how reconfigured urban proletarians on the expanding peripheries of Latin American, African, and Asian cities are negotiating violence, fear, and disorder, as well as the silences and new understandings that are arising from them.[3]

The essay is organized as follows: First, it explores the making of Barrancabermeja's working class in the early twentieth century and the creation of a dense institutional infrastructure of unions, civic groups, and neighborhood organizations that constituted a vibrant oppositional political culture. It then examines how privatized terror dismantled this working class and created new divisions that broke down old forms of solidarity. And finally, it considers the reconfiguration of a new working class through more authoritarian forms of labor discipline, rent extraction, and political subjugation and the current difficulties working people face in explaining and understanding, in shared ways, what has happened and continues to happen to them.

The Birth of a Militant Working Class: Oil and the Politics of Solidarity

During the 2010 celebration of Colombia's bicentennial, as official ceremonies in Bogotá extolled the heroes of the nation's nineteenth-century independence wars, surviving labor, peasant, and community leaders in Barancabermeja paid homage to different historical figures, including the labor organizers Raúl Eduardo Mahécha and María Cano, the assassinated oil worker and union leader Manuel Chacón, and the revolutionary priest Camilo Torres. These historical referents represented a long, independent tradition of nationalist, working-class radicalism that defined the Middle Magdalena region. The Barranca activists organized public fora, film screenings, and a march through the center of town, asserting that Colombians were still not independent. They also rededicated Camilo Torres

Park, unofficially known for years as the "Park of the Headless One" (Parque del Descabezado), after the repeated decapitation of a statue commemorating the fallen guerrilla cleric. Their courageous public actions symbolized the deep roots of Barrancabermeja's working-class political culture, which decades of savage violence had not completely obliterated.

Barrancabermeja emerged as a foreign-controlled, oil-export enclave in the 1920s, when the Rockefeller-owned Tropical Oil Company (TROCO)—a subsidiary of the Standard Oil Company of New Jersey—acquired the subsoil rights to a vast extension of tropical forest in the Middle Magdalena region. It grew up at the juncture of violent struggles over the organization of labor and the command of space, which brought together the managers and technicians of a global corporation, state officials, and diverse working people in far-flung relationships of domination and exploitation that were undergirded by the threat of US intervention. The enclave became what historian Paul Kramer calls a "strategic hamlet" of empire, one that concentrated extraordinary corporate power on the apparently seamless terrain of the sovereign nation-state (Kramer 2011: 1356). The TROCO extracted oil and accumulated capital through the careful crafting of sovereignty, that is, the ability to dictate the terms of life, by enclosing and isolating working people and severing territory from local jurisdiction. Yet because it controlled capital more easily than workers, it had to contend with the needs and demands of a heterogeneous group of immigrant workers, who created a radical political culture that challenged the oil company's right to command place and space and control labor.

Working-class radicalism defined the city's popular majority until the late twentieth century. It established deeper roots in Barrancabermeja than in other working-class centers, such as Cali, Medellín, and Barranquilla, because the city's birth as a foreign-controlled oil enclave undermined the emergence of a domestic bourgeoisie and the ties of deference, paternalism, and authoritarianism that entwined regional bourgeoisies and working classes elsewhere.[4] Together with the Atlantic Coast banana zone transformed by the United Fruit Company and immortalized in Gabriel García Márquez's *One Hundred Years of Solitude*, Barrancabermeja became one of the most important foreign-controlled enclaves to emerge in Colombia. But it was not unique. The labor struggles that shaped Barrancabermeja resembled those taking place between expanding oil corporations and nascent working classes in the Mexican Huasteca and Venezuela's Maracaibo basin (Santiago 2006; Tinker Salas 2009), as well as in emergent banana enclaves of Ecuador and the circum-Caribbean (Striffler 2002; Striffler and Moberg 2003).

Anti-imperialist labor organization was an important feature of early-twentieth-century, foreign-controlled, export enclaves in Latin America, and worker struggles in these zones—sometimes "industrial" and "urban," sometimes "agricultural" and "rural"—shaped the direction of national labor movements until well into the middle of the century (Bergquist 1986: 8). The opportunity to secure work in the nascent oil industry prompted peasants from the impoverished mountains of central Colombia and the northern coast to migrate to the Middle Magdalena region, where many settled small plots of frontier land and found jobs cutting roads through the jungle, clearing land, constructing buildings, and laying oil pipelines for the TROCO. Many others resided in Barrancabermeja, which rapidly acquired the largest concentration of urban proletarians in the country. From only nine hundred inhabitants in 1914, Barrancabermeja's population surged to over twelve thousand in 1927 (Vega Cantor 2002: 140). The initial migrants consisted mostly of young men, who, according to the 1938 census, constituted 61 percent of the population (Vega Cantor 2002: 203). The high concentration of single men supported the growth of a dynamic sex trade that played an important, albeit contradictory, role in the local economy. In 1926, for example, revenues generated directly or indirectly from prostitution in the proliferating number of hotels, bars, and bordellos accounted for fully half of the municipal income garnered from the oil industry. Yet even though prostitution underwrote a significant portion of the municipal budget, Colombian elites and foreign oil company mangers associated it with the moral degeneracy and undisciplined behavior that distinguished the emergent working class for them. They viewed Barrancabermeja as unruly and ungovernable and disparaged it as little more than "a bordello with a mayor and a priest" (Vega Cantor 2002: 206). The city became famous for "putas, plata, y petróleo" (whores, money, and oil).

Unlike the industrializing highland city of Medellín, which *Life* magazine called a "capitalist paradise" in 1947 (Farnsworth-Alvear 2000: 39), class conflict in Barranca was pervasive, raw, and violent. The small, transient group of US oil company managers, technicians, and their families were largely unfamiliar with the cultural practices and social mores of the mostly mestizo and Afro-Colombian workers, and they had difficulty developing cross-class relationships of respect and authority with them. The unmediated class divisions between the emergent working class and the foreign managers and technicians of "La TROCO" were most visible in a pattern of segregated residential housing. US and Canadian managers and technicians lived in the "barrio staff," which contained shaded, North American–style houses surrounded by spacious, well-tended lawns. Foreign residents enjoyed an array of services, including a hospital, a golf course, and a variety of sports facilities for their exclusive use. A fence separated this gilded ghetto from the impoverished working-class neighborhoods and encampments, where housing was rudimentary, basic services were nonexistent, and diseases, such as malaria, yellow fever, and intestinal disorders, were pervasive.[5] Patrolled by company guards from within the TROCO compound and monitored by the national police from without, the fence symbolized the hardening class and national boundaries that were dividing Barrancabermeja. Over the course of the 1920s, the installation of an army base and local, departmental, and national police forces reinforced these divisions and laid the basis for the intensified militarization of the city over the course of the twentieth century (Vega Cantor 2002: 208).

Not surprisingly, working-class political culture in Barrancabermeja became strongly nationalist and anti-imperialist, and it stood in stark contrast to the Catholic moralism that intertwined domestic textile mill owners and a largely female labor force in Medellín (Farnsworth-Alvear 2000). Anti-imperialist nationalism was not only the result of the inequalities and daily humiliations experienced by workers. It arose, too, from the 1903 loss of Panama to the United States, which prompted fears that the company would steal Barrancabermeja and claim it as a US possession, and from the twenty-one-year US occupation of Nicaragua (1912–1933). Moreover, a 1928 banana strike and subsequent massacre of thousands of workers in the United Fruit Company–dominated enclave on the Atlantic Coast further stoked oil workers' anti-imperialist sympathies, as the banana zone suffered from many of the same social and economic problems as Barrancabermeja. Although anti-imperialist nationalism expressed a strong antipathy to the abusive behavior of foreign corporations, it also gave rise to a budding international solidarity with oppressed peoples elsewhere. In 1928, for example, a workers' committee organized to support the struggles of Augusto César Sandino in Nicaragua, and it encouraged "our compatriots to march determinedly to Nicaragua to fight alongside General Sandino for the liberty of the continent" (Díaz Callejas 1988: 61).

From its beginnings, the labor movement in Barrancabermeja linked the struggles of Colombian oil workers to those of oppressed peoples elsewhere, and it built bonds of solidarity to urban merchants in the port city and to peasants in the surrounding Middle Magdalena region. Several prominent labor leaders, including the socialists María Cano and Raúl Eduardo Mahécha, drew on nationalist, anti-imperialist, and broad currents of Marxist thought to organize the immigrant working class in Barrancabermeja and other ports along the Magdalena River. Mahécha founded the Sociedad Unión Sindical, which represented oil workers and became, in 1937, the contemporary Unión Sindical Obrera (USO). He also led two major strikes against the TROCO in 1924 and 1927. These strikes underscored the accumulating strength, militancy, and organizational capacity of the oil workers, and they brought to light the emergent bonds of solidarity between different kinds of workers, urban merchants, and peasants that would shape the history of urban class struggles in Barrancabermeja for the next five decades (Vega Cantor et al. 2009). The growing organizational strength of working people enabled them to push against the grain of corporate efforts to localize popular struggles and partly reconfigure the TROCO's strategic hamlet into a nexus of broader relationships and connections among diverse urban working people and between them and rural peasants.

The labor strikes of the 1920s confronted the TROCO with a series of demands that underscored the miserable working conditions in the oil fields. These demands included wage increases, improvements in food and hygiene, an eight-hour workday, and Sunday as a day of rest. In addition, workers sought to ease the intense control that the TROCO exercised over their lives by asserting the right to read the national press in the work camps and insisting on the distribution of meals in company facilities "without the presence of the national police, as is the practice, which humiliates Colombian workers and places them in the position of convicts in the work camps" (Vega Cantor 2002: 255). Yet the strikers did not focus only on improving their wages and working conditions. They also took aim at the hardships that the foreign corporation imposed on other sectors of the population.

For example, the oil workers insisted on the right of Colombian merchants to operate on company territory and opposed the TROCO's attempt to monopolize local commerce by excluding merchants from its compound. Merchants, in turn, who depended on workers for business, gave money to support the labor strikes. The TROCO also ran roughshod over peasants, pushing them off recently settled lands in a bid to control access to the subsoil and to create a supply of laborers for its operations. Not surprisingly, land conflicts between peasants, who lacked legal titles to their plots, and the TROCO intensified during the 1920s, but because many oil workers were themselves semiproletarianized peasants, or recently dispossessed of their lands, supporting the land claims of rural cultivators blended easily with demands for better working conditions in the oil fields.[6] Peasants, in turn, provided food—yuca, plantains, squash, and rice—to sustain protesting workers and helped operate soup kitchens in Barrancabermeja during the strike (Vega Cantor 2002).

Although the strikes were ultimately suppressed, and workers could not force the TROCO to negotiate with their union until well into the 1930s, the protests underscored the radical political culture that was developing in the city. Protests erupted again on April 9, 1948, following the assassination of Liberal Party member and populist leader Jorge Eliécer Gaitán in Bogotá. The death of Gaitán set off riots between members of the Liberal and Conservative parties in many parts of the country and sent shock waves through Barrancabermeja, where working people declared the central government illegitimate and set up a revolutionary junta composed of communists, liberals, and supporters of Gaitán. The junta named a new mayor—Rafael Rangel, who was a Liberal Party member influenced by communist ideas (Díaz Callejas 1988), and he in turn authorized armed workers' brigades to maintain order and prevent pillage, as groups of enraged *barranqueños* tried to kill conservatives and representatives of the oil company and burn the churches. The oil workers made common cause with the junta by imposing a ban on alcohol and seizing control of the telephone, telegraph, water supply, and the police. They also organized the defense of the city through the distribution of small arms manufactured in the workshops of the oil company, the digging of trenches along the Magdalena River, and the mining of the port. The so-called Barranca Commune, combined with uprisings up and down the length of the Magdalena River, demonstrated the political power and the insurrectional leanings of a broad sector of the population inspired by Gaitán.

Yet the Barranca revolt represented the apex of working-class power in the twentieth century. Despite the challenges posed by the Barranca Commune and the uprisings in other parts of the country, radical popular movements never became strong enough to transcend regional strongholds, make common cause with oppositional movements elsewhere, and create a social movement capable of championing the cause of radical nationalism and working-class politics on a national scale (Hylton 2012). In the wake of Gaitán's assassination, the explosion of "La Violencia"—a "frustrated revolution" that generated extreme terror (Sanchez 2008: 47), especially against the left-wing political movement inspired by Gaitán—led to the death and displacement of hundreds of thousands of Colombians and destroyed worker and peasant organizations around the country. The Barranca Commune collapsed after the provincial government unleashed the army on the insurrectionaries and backed a wave of repression that pushed the mayor and others to join forces with Liberal guerrilla insurgencies that were forming in the region.[7] The sixteen-year period of national bloodletting that defined the Violencia (1948–1964) returned class and ethnic conflict to the clientelistic structures that had long defined Colombia's traditional political parties (Hylton 2006: 39; Roldán 2002). The end of Barranca's brief experiment with worker self-organization and direct democracy underscored the difficulty of scaling up the place-based forms of worker solidarity that Raymond Williams calls "militant particularism" (Williams 1989) to a more universal vision of social transformation with broad political purchase.

The uprising in Barrancabermeja, however, came at a moment when foreign-owned export enclaves were in decline almost everywhere,[8] including Barrancabermeja, where growing nationalism, worker pressure, and a government search for more export revenue gradually persuaded the TROCO to relinquish its oil concession to the Colombian state. Popular struggles had challenged the TROCO's right to exploit labor, control national resources, and claim a series of rights and privileges that were not available to Colombian workers. Moreover, when the Mexican government expropriated foreign corporations in 1938 and Third World nationalist movements began to rattle the chains of empire around the world, the global oil giants understood that the tide was turning. Oil executives became obsessed with preventing "another Mexico" (Santiago 2006: 8), and Colombian industrialists began to rethink how they wanted oil produced in their country, how they would deal with oil workers, and how they would safeguard private property. The reversion of the TROCO concession to the Colombian state and the creation, in 1951, of the state-operated Empresa Colombiana de Petróleos (ECOPETROL) soothed elite anxieties by avoiding the disruptions of expropriation and sidestepping worker participation in the new company, as had happened in

Mexico (Buceli 2006). The establishment of ECOPETROL also addressed the oft-stated desire of workers that oil production in Colombia take place under national control, but new tensions quickly emerged between an exclusionary state and Barrancabermeja's militant working class.

Popular Struggles and the State

By the middle of the twentieth century, popular struggles in Barrancabermeja turned less on strictly labor demands than on the widely experienced need for public services. "Civic strikes" became the primary tactic to express working-class anger, which had few legal channels of political expression in the aftermath of the bipartisan political agreements to end the Violencia and create the National Front government. The National Front (1958–1974) excluded any expression of radical or reformist politics and apportioned all government positions to members of the Liberal and Conservative parties, who alternated control of the presidency. This meant that in Barrancabermeja, the mayor was appointed by the provincial governor, who was himself a political appointee. The civic strikes expressed the friction between a municipality unresponsive to the growing needs of the population amid rising cold war tensions, a profitable oil company now in the hands of the state, and an assertive popular movement.

By the 1960s, oil workers constituted the core of the city's militant labor movement. They had achieved strong workplace bargaining power rooted in their location in a strategic industry vulnerable to strikes and disruptions in the flow of oil, and an increase in the number of public sector employees (teachers, civil servants, healthcare workers) had expanded the ranks of the urban labor movement as well. These workers were joined by legions of ruined peasants, pushed out of the countryside by landlord pressure and drawn to the city by dreams of well-paid jobs in the oil industry and the encouragement of relatives who had "made it." Migrants comprised 70 percent of the urban population in 1970 (Contreras 1970: 39), and they transformed the city from an oil enclave to an urban center in which the majority of the population was no longer connected to the petroleum industry. Even though ECOPETROL recruited more workers and engineers in the 1970s, when it expanded and diversified the refinery, the oil company only provided employment for about a third of the city's residents. Fewer and fewer new arrivals found permanent jobs with ECOPETROL and had to content themselves with temporary or part-time assignments (Toro Puerta 2004), while petty merchants and artisans comprised 53 percent of the economically active population (Contreras 1970: 45).

Divisions between the relatively well-paid oil workers of ECOPETROL and impoverished immigrants grew more acute. Two new neighborhoods—Galán and El Parnaso—with neat, two-story row houses near the city center displayed the relative prosperity of the oil workers, who, along with ECOPETROL engineers, pushed up the price of urban land and placed pressure on strained city services. Migrants populated the urban periphery, where they created new neighborhoods through land "invasions" opposite a rail line that separated them from the city center and symbolized the division between the city's "haves" and the "have-nots." Declared illegal by the state, migrant settlements lacked all manner of social services. Dusty, unpaved roads turned to quagmires in the rain and were dark at night; streams of black sewage flowed through open ditches; and mosquito-infested marshes were the only source of drinking water. Yet despite the emergent social and economic divisions between "modern," "industrial" workers who belonged to unions and the un- and underemployed "backward" migrants of the urban fringe, the USO did not limit itself to the defense of the wages and benefits of its membership and adopted a political practice that sought to unify working people across emergent differences.

The USO declared itself an alternative political project, one sustained by revolutionary nationalism and the defense of national resources for the entire population. This position enabled the USO to forge alliances with peasants, students, teachers, and informal workers and mobilize them (Vega Cantor et al. 2009). Former oil worker and USO leader Ramón Rangel, who was a high school student in the early 1970s, described his participation in an oil strike that lasted for six weeks. "I had a little chore. Every eight days, I took a bag of food to the houses of striking workers in the Northeast. They [the USO] assigned me at least six workers. Everyone had something to do. Here in Barranca, everyone participated in the USO's strikes, and [the participation] demonstrates the level of organization that the compañeros achieved."[9]

Despite periodic setbacks, defeated labor strikes, and the persecution of leaders, the oil workers' union played a leading role in a number of civic strikes, most prominently in 1975 and 1977 that took aim at Barranca's woeful public services. Of the numerous deficiencies suffered by urban residents, the absence of water in a city where the average temperature hovered in the upper nineties was felt most acutely. Although Barrancabermeja was surrounded by rivers, lakes, and marshes, it had no system to deliver water to immigrant neighborhoods; moreover, the oil company had for years poisoned local water sources with toxic waste.

The USO was not the only organization involved in the fight for public services. It formed part of a coalition of unions, political parties, churches, and community groups that gave birth to the Coordinadora Popular de Barrancabermeja in 1983. Although the organizers were the same as those who had led the earlier struggles, they conceived the Coordinadora as a more permanent link between Barrancabermeja's expanding poor neighborhoods and the local popular movement, a relationship that went beyond the episodic coordination of strikes. The Coordinadora included the defining presence of the USO, as well as left-wing political parties, members of the Catholic Church, and representatives from women's, peasant, and student organizations. "The idea," said a former member, "was that the urban social organizations would sustain it [the Coordinadora]. The Coordinadora was completely grassroots [netamente popular]."[10] Indeed, major decisions were made in popular assemblies and neighborhood-based *guardias cívicas* negotiated with the police and military during strikes (van Isschot 2010: 186–187).

Barranca was a hotbed of political ideas and projects of the left during the 1970s and 1980s, and as Vega Cantor et al. note, the political work of numerous unions and civic organizations generated a strong sense of "solidarity, altruism, commitment, and capacity to struggle" of the people affiliated with them (2009: 309). Activists who came of age in the late 1960s and 1970s used the word *mística* (mystique) to describe the intense emotional connections that they felt to each other and their commitment to the broader struggle for social transformation. Progressive Catholic clerics influenced by liberation theology nurtured these political sensibilities. Priests, nuns, and even a bishop spurred the formation of Christian base communities in poor neighborhoods, where the political thinking and practice of a generation of activists was forged. Trade union leader William Mendoza, for example, was introduced to political activism through the priests who ran his high school. "I lived in a very poor neighborhood," he explained, "and I got very involved with political activism through a priest, who was the principal of my high school. He believed in liberation theology, and we [students] used to go with him and other priests to their little farm, where they taught us about the ideas in Karl Marx's 'Capital' and about liberation theology."[11] Other prominent social leaders emerged from the same high school. Reflecting on the 1975 civic strike for potable water, Ramón Rangel recalled the widely cited statement of the bishop, who publicly affirmed the goals of the strikers when he declared that "the water in the city was too polluted to be any good for blessings."[12]

Nascent left-wing guerrilla insurgencies also began to forge ties with urban residents and establish a presence in Barrancabermeja during the 1970s. Two primary organizations started to develop that would establish a long-term presence in Barrancabermeja and the Middle Magdalena region: the Revolutionary Armed Forces of Colombia (FARC)—a peasant-based insurgency that organized in southern Colombia during the Violencia—and the National Liberation Army (ELN). Inspired by the Cuban revolution, the ELN had organized in the dense jungles of the Middle Magdalena region in the 1960s and would become the most prominent guerrilla organization in the city. Its founders chose the region for its history of resistance and popular struggle, especially the close ties between the peasantry and oil workers in the area around Barrancabermeja (Medina Gallego 2001: 78–79), and it built much of its strength in former strongholds of the 1950s-era Liberal guerrillas.[13] The ELN attracted radical clerics, students, oil workers, and peasants into its ranks, and it emphasized the defense of natural resources, especially oil. It also developed an urban network that supported the rural insurgency. A former ELN guerrilla, who joined the insurgency in the late 1960s, described the various ways that trade unionists supported the insurgency: "In addition to raising issues about imperialism and workers' rights in their union struggles, they sent supplies to us and helped to organize actions, such as the theft of weapons, in the city. In a couple of cases, the entire union directorates supported us."[14] Yet the ELN made little effort to develop a mass political base and largely ignored the strategic political importance of Barrancabermeja and its militant civic organizations and trade unions, especially the USO. Because of rigid adherence to the notion of an armed vanguard, or foco, it believed that support for radical social transformation would spring spontaneously from a peasantry inspired by the example and sacrifice of the guerrilla vanguard.

Consequently, the insurgency remained largely isolated in the countryside, where it was consumed by deep internal divisions and was nearly annihilated by the army in 1973 (Broderick 2000), but it eventually resolved its internal problems and embarked on a period of expansion following the 1979 Sandinista victory in Nicaragua. Aided by funds obtained through the extortion of oil companies, such as Occidental Petroleum, the reconfigured ELN emphasized political work and organization among peasants, students, and workers much more than in the past (Medina Gallego 1996: 150–155). The guerrillas established themselves in the northeastern and southeastern sectors of Barrancabermeja through the formation of militias,[15] and the ELN's identification with urban residents became so complete that guerrillas did not always adhere to the compartmentalized organizational structure that protected the identities of local cadres. A former resident of the northeast sector explained, "There was a time when you could walk into some of the neighborhoods in the northeast and stand in the middle of the street and shout out 'Who is the commander of the ELN in this neighborhood?' and people would tell you. Everyone knew the guerrillas, and people trusted them and each other."[16] Indeed, for urban residents accustomed to repressive police and military tactics during the labor and civic strikes that shook Barrancabermeja, the guerrillas offered them a form of protection. Evangelina Marín, a leading member of the Coordinadora, explained that "[m]any people considered the time of the popular miltias to be one of military accompaniment for them ... The fact that the militias were able to maintain a military presence for almost thirteen years in such a small city is because people accepted them and supported them" (Marín 2006: 356).

Indeed, the ELN—and to a lesser degree the FARC and other guerrillas groups, such as the Ejército Popular de Liberación (EPL) and the M-19—became part of the social fabric of working-class Barrancabermeja. The guerrillas' daily presence in the neighborhoods differed from other Colombian cities, where insurgents moved in and out of working-class areas but never established a permanent relationship with the residents. The current president of a contemporary neighborhood committee, who grew up in the northeast, remembered that even if people were not involved with the guerrillas, the insurgents were the sons, daughters, husbands, friends, lovers, and acquaintances of local people and were tolerated, if not actively supported, for these reasons. Echoing these observations, a social movement leader explained that "the culture of the guerrilla was part of the life of civil society. That doesn't mean that all civilians were guerrillas, but the guerrillas were part of our lives, part of our culture. Everyone struggled and lived together in one way or another."[17] Another resident recalled how the guerrillas backed urban squatters:

> What happens here in Barranca is that the army and the police have always been very violent. Whenever squatters invaded private land—because everything here was private property—the police or the army would always arrive to kick them out with a lot of blood and gunfire. They knocked down their homes, mistreated the people, shot tear gas at them, and then took them away. The guerrillas confronted the police and the army and tried to protect the people so that they could stay. The other thing that the guerrillas did was to help people build their homes. They helped people bring wood from the countryside.[18]

According to a long-time political activist, "whether you were actually a [guerrilla] miliciano, a collaborator, or simply a social movement member with no direct connection to the guerrillas, people more or less wanted the same things. This is not to say that everyone always agreed with the guerrillas; they [the guerrillas] sometimes made decisions that hurt the popular movement. But people in the Northeast, for example, were proud to have a guerrilla commander spend the night in their home, and they saw the guerrillas as a [political] alternative."[19]

Relationships with the insurgents were not seamless. Many workers did not support guerrilla attacks on the city's productive infrastructure, especially ECOPETROL, because they believed that such assaults posed a threat to their jobs. In addition, ties between popular organizations and the insurgencies raised a series of problems. Relationships with the guerrillas were dangerous for unarmed civilians amid the white-hot tensions of the cold war and exposed noncombatants to state repression. Moreover, the integration of local leaders into guerrilla structures, which varied from close working relationships to occasional discussions, raised prickly questions about autonomy that could cause friction. Finally, the capacity of the insurgencies to control criminality and thuggish behavior within their own ranks was a source of tension with residents. Given the explosion of the cocaine industry and the growth of organized crime that accompanied it, the guerrilla "popular militias" could easily devolve into predatory gangs, as both groups demanded payment from local residents for protection (cf. Ceballos Melguizo 2001), and the guerrilla "justice" meted out to presumed army collaborators or those accused of crimes by other residents was not always perceived as legitimate or distinguishable from criminal behavior.

The intricate and complex infrastructure of solidarity forged in Barranca would not survive the twentieth century. Although the Coordinadora continued to lead civic strikes into the 1990s, the 1987 murder of USO leader Manuel Chacón by a navy-controlled death squad infused these protests with a more defensive quality, as a new wave of political violence began to crash over the Middle Magdalena region. Escalating violence and the takeover of the city by right-wing paramilitaries backed by the state in the early years of the twenty-first century ruptured the interactions, routines, and social relationships that gave meaning to people's lives in the working-class neighborhoods of Barrancabermeja. Widespread terror, or "blood and fire" in the words of my informants, forced long-established residents to flee their homes for the relative safety of other cities; it was simultaneously an engine of urban growth, as it drove peasants from the countryside to Barrancabermeja.

Dirty War: Persecution, Rupture, and Fragmentation

Barrancabermeja and the surrounding Middle Magdalena River valley descended into a "dirty war" in the 1980s, one in which the state and allied paramilitary groups—organized first as clandestine death squads and then as nationally federated, standing armies—sought to roll back the power of the city's working-class organizations and the rising threat posed by guerrilla insurgencies. Privatized terror tore apart Barranca's institutional infrastructure of working-class solidarity, as well as the individual and social lives of many urban residents. It also laid the basis for remaking the working class and the creation of a reconfigured capitalist order in which barranqueños would participate on terms not of their choosing. Civic strikes became less demands for public services than protests against the assassination of union and community leaders, and the grassroots dynamics of the Coordinadora lost steam, as the leadership receded into the hands of a few political parties and grew more clientelistic. Social practices that once formed the integument of social life, such as talking to neighbors in the relative cool of the evening, chatting with coworkers during lunch, participating in church groups, unions, students organizations, and neighborhood associations, and involvement in the ceremonies that marked important life passages were suppressed or took place under the watchful eyes of the paramilitaries. They no longer provided working-class residents with a sense of coherence and connection to others that enabled them to grasp what was happening to people like themselves. This sense of coherence—or relative coherence—and the connections forged among ordinary people and the USO, the Coordinadora, the insurgencies, and other union and civic organizations in the city had helped shape a vision of possible futures, but this vision, as well as feelings of attachment and continuity, were shattered.

The dirty war became intertwined with the booming illegal drug traffic. Beginning in the late 1970s and 1980s, an emergent agrarian narco-bourgeoisie based in the cities of Medellín and Cali started to use the profits accrued from the illegal cocaine industry to buy their way into the landed gentry by purchasing some of the best, most fertile rural properties in the Middle Magdalena region. The massive infusion of drug money ignited a speculative market in land that led to the unprecedented accumulation of rural holdings at the expense of poor peasant cultivators, whose land claims were based less on property titles than settlement and use. This process represented an intensification of ongoing land struggles between peasants and landlords, in which the latter organized private armies to dispossess peasants and then used these same armies to "defend" their newly acquired properties in the absence of the state (Richani 2002: 118). Widespread dispossession constituted a veritable "counter agrarian reform." The consolidation of land holdings and the conflicts sparked by it aggravated a long-term agrarian crisis and quickened the decline of subsistence agriculture. Not surprisingly, many small cultivators formed alliances with guerrilla insurgencies to protect their interests (Richani 2002).

During the 1980s and 1990s, the FARC—Colombia's oldest guerrilla movement—expanded into over half of Colombia's 1,050 municipalities (Livingstone 2004: 64) and became the largest insurgency in the country. As the guerrilla established a stronger presence in the Middle Magdalena, it then extorted, kidnaped, and harassed landowners, some of whom were prominent members of the infamous Medellín drug cartel. The guerrilla harassment and persistent peasant demands for land placed the regional bourgeoisie on edge, and their disquiet only intensified with the advent of a series of national and regional political transformations. In 1982, President Belesario Bentancur opened peace talks with the FARC, and in 1985, the FARC launched a political party—the Patriotic Union (UP)—to act as a vehicle for the guerrillas to enter the political mainstream. While the government and the FARC talked peace, the 1988 decentralization of political power permitted the direct election of mayors for the first time in the twentieth century, heightening the political expectations of marginalized groups and unleashing a wave of intense electoral competition in the context of a growing armed insurgency. These changes alarmed regional power holders, who anxiously watched as the Patriotic Union attracted electoral support. They feared that the political opening would tip the balance of power in favor of the guerrillas and their supporters (Romero 2003).

The political decentralization also prompted closer collaboration between the armed forces, which had long opposed peace talks with the FARC, and the regional bourgeoisie, who claimed a right to "self-defense" in a region where property holders had long organized private armies to protect land acquisitions and where paramilitarism had deep roots. They complained that the state was not doing enough to protect it or to eliminate the guerrillas, and in response to their pressure, the state began to collaborate more closely with them to defeat the guerrillas in the Middle Magdalena region. With the technical support of the military and the financial muscle of major drug traffickers, the military promoted the growth of covert paramilitary groups to fight an expanding counterinsurgency war that increasingly targeted civilians.

The Middle Magdalena river town of Puerto Boyacá became the epicenter of paramilitarism in Colombia, when, in 1982, the town's mayor, the Texas Petroleum Company, cattle ranchers, drug traffickers, foreign mercenaries, and members of the armed forces financed and supported the creation of a paramilitary group to join the military's fight against the guerrillas (Medina Gallego 1990: 173). Puerto Boyacá was, at the time, a stronghold of the Colombian Communist Party (CP), and the newly formed paramilitary group and the army concentrated their efforts on disrupting the political organization of the CP and disarticulating the ties between the Party and the FARC (Medina Gallego 1990). They also launched a campaign of extermination against the Patriotic Union Party that led to the deaths of some three thousand party members. The dirty war did less damage to the guerrillas than to unarmed members of the CP, the Patriotic Union, and labor and peasant leaders, who were easier targets.

Despite the initial "success" of the Puerto Boyacá paramilitaries, they were little more than hit-and-run death squads that never expanded beyond the Middle Magdalena region. They did, however, serve as a source of experience and training for other paramilitary groups that emerged in northern Colombia and elsewhere (Madariaga 2006). Regional-based paramilitary entities subsequently morphed from roving death squads into standing armies with the enormous profits from the cocaine traffic, and, in the 1990s, their commanders began to dispute territorial control with the guerrillas (Duncan 2006). Regional armies obtained increasing autonomy from the state and federated, in 1997, under a national umbrella organization called the Autodefensas Unidas de Colombia (AUC) that centralized under its command eighteen different groups, or approximately 75 percent of Colombia's paramilitaries (Bejarano and Pizarro 2004: 110).

The AUC then grew more lethal with the passage in 2000 of Plan Colombia, a $1.3 billion, mostly military, US aid program that strengthened the police and the military, the AUC's closest allies. Not surprisingly, the paramilitary blocs consolidated their political power and territorial control in many areas once ruled by the guerrillas (Hylton 2006; 2010), and civilian displacement became less a consequence than a strategy of an intensifying dirty war. Refugees flooded from areas of the countryside once under guerrilla control to Barrancabermeja in the 1980s. Many could still believe that they would return to their homes after the soldiers and paramilitaries left. These hopes gradually evaporated as paramilitary control solidified and lands usurped from the peasantry passed into the hands of the paramilitaries and the drug traffickers, landlords, politicians, and entrepreneurs whose interests they served. Refugees from particular rural areas tended to cluster in certain urban neighborhoods, and it should come as no surprise that the guerrillas followed their support base into the city and established a strong presence among them.[20]

By the end of the twentieth century, Barrancabermeja was the only regional urban center not under paramilitary control, and many people believed that the paramilitaries could never gain a foothold in the city. Yet Barrancabermeja was not immune to the escalating violence, as state security forces within the city collaborated with increasingly powerful paramilitaries. A navy-controlled death squad, for example, helped pave the way for the AUC takeover by assassinating at least sixty-eight trade unionists, journalists, and human rights defenders in the late 1980s and 1990s (Loingsigh 2002; CINEP/CREDHOS 2004). The USO paid a particularly heavy price, losing thirty-three members in Barranca between 1988 and 1993 (Vega Cantor et al. 2009: 459–460). The oil port offered the AUC the possibility of capturing profits from the illicit sale of gasoline produced by ECOPETROL, of strengthening its grip on the cocaine traffic through control of commerce on the Magdalena River and the coca fields in adjacent Bolívar province, and of limiting the provision of supplies to guerrillas in the countryside. Moreover, the presence of various guerrilla groups in a city known for its militant social organizations made capturing Barrancabermeja an important political victory.

The Bloque Central Bolívar (BCB)—one of the most powerful blocs in the AUC—executed the takeover of the city. The late AUC leader Carlos Castaño had established the BCB in the northern province of Cordoba, and throughout the 1990s, the BCB extended its operations to some eleven Colombian provinces that spanned the length and breadth of the country, amassing a fighting force of seven thousand to eight thousand mercenaries. The BCB conquered and held territory by forcing guerrillas and other paramilitary competitors either to join forces with it, abandon areas that it claimed, or face destruction, and by expelling or massacring civilians who opposed it. Castaño and his brother, Vicente Castaño, also expanded the BCB's influence by "franchising" its activities to drug traffickers, such as Carlos Mario Jiménez, alias "Macaco," who had amassed a fortune and a private army through his affiliation with the North Valle drug cartel.[21]

In Barrancabermeja, the BCB's first objective was to eliminate the leadership and destroy the support base of any organization that represented an alternative to paramilitarism. This not only included the guerrillas but also trade unions, human rights organizations, student groups, and neighborhood councils, which, it claimed, were guerrilla fronts. To accomplish this objective, the BCB unleashed a wave of terror that killed or forcibly displaced thousands of people from the impoverished northeast and southeast sectors. Eighteen thousand people fled the city between 1998 and 2001. Yet the uncertain life of a refugee was better than the fate of others who remained behind. Between 1998 and 2001, eight hundred people died in the city, mostly at the hands of the paramilitaries (Romero 2003: 107), and Barrancabermeja had a per capita death rate in 2000 that was three times higher than the rest of the country (Madero 2001).

May 16, 1998, came to symbolize a major rupture in the life of the city for urban residents, one that divided urban history into two periods: "before" and "after." On that date, the individual assassination of social movement leaders, which had characterized the repression in Barrancabermeja, gave way to a full-scale paramilitary incursion, with backing from the state security forces, and the massacre of thirty-two people in ELN-controlled districts of the city. Three truckloads of heavily armed men dressed in civilian clothing entered the southeast sector shortly after soldiers had dismantled a checkpoint on a road leading into the city and inexplicably returned to their barracks. The mercenaries abducted three people on the way to a soccer field, where the lights and music of a bazaar had attracted hundreds of people. As the trucks roared to a stop before the crowd, hooded men jumped out and forced everyone to the ground, kicking and beating people with rifle butts and shouting insults. They then dragged several terrified people onto their trucks before continuing the rampage in the northeast. When they had finished, seven people were dead, and twenty-five others were "disappeared." Several days later, AUC leader Carlos Castaño announced that the Autodefensas de Santander y Sur de Cesar (AUSAC), an affiliate of the AUC, had carried out the massacre.

The massacre spread terror among the civilian population and announced the AUC's intention to take control of Barrancabermeja. It demonstrated the power of the paramilitaries and the impunity with which they could operate in the city. It also sent a powerful message to ELN supporters that the guerrillas could no longer defend their support base. One of the first human rights workers to talk to neighborhood survivors in the aftermath of the massacre reported that people were asking why the guerrillas had done nothing to protect them. "The people no longer had any faith [in the guerrillas]. They were tired, and they felt discarded. Nobody had given them any help," she explained.[22] Disillusionment with the guerrillas and a deepening dirty war corroded the infrastructure of solidarity that had developed in Barrancabermeja. "[May 16th] is where the whole debacle began," she insisted. "The social base weakened; people no longer showed up for events or protests."[23] In this way, paramilitary terror, death, physical displacement, and the chaos that violence created in peoples' lives fueled the unmaking of the working class. The mayhem set the stage for the accumulation of wealth and power by a rising group of far-right narco-paramilitary entrepreneurs and for the remaking of class relations on terms that favored the interests of Barranca's new over lords.

The paramilitary takeover of Barrancabermeja fed on the fears and vulnerabilities of the local population. It had less to do with the absence of the state than with its presence and active collaboration with the BCB. Barrancabermeja was one of Colombia's most militarized cities: two military bases, several fortified police stations, and the bunker-like headquarters of the Department of Administrative Security (DAS)—Colombia's maximum law enforcement agency—were among the state security forces that had a presence. They allowed BCB fighters to move freely about the city; they refused to respond to civilian pleas for help; and they looked the other way as the BCB committed gruesome atrocities.

The behavior of the guerrillas also eroded the legitimacy of the insurgents and created a climate conducive to the entry of the paramilitaries. Guerrilla attacks on police and military installations in densely populated urban areas had demonstrated a disregard for civilian life that alienated many residents. As the Colombian conflict became increasingly militarized in the 1990s, the guerrillas—especially the FARC—showed less interest in the political education of residents and local militias than in extracting more onerous "war taxes" from city merchants to finance military operations and in using the city as a source of recruits. Not surprisingly, despite the long history of merchant support for popular struggles in Barrancabermeja, storeowners increasingly saw the paramilitaries as a solution to the relentless guerrilla extortion and welcomed their arrival. Moreover, many of Barrancabermeja's flashiest commercial venues were controlled by drug traffickers-cum-paramilitaries who used them to launder profits from the cocaine traffic.

Growing military pressure on the guerrillas also gave rise to more severe "justice" in which suspected informants were executed without any serious investigation of the allegations against them. A resident of the northeast, for example, explained how the FARC murdered her husband and her fourteen- and fifteen-year-old stepsons who belonged to the FARC's urban militia. "Boys of this age," she said, "were used mostly to do errands. They hung out on the street corners to see if the police or the army was coming. But my husband eventually took them out [of the FARC], because he didn't want anything to happen to them ... But what happened? If you joined the guerrillas, you couldn't leave. You had to stay. The guerrillas killed the boys so that they wouldn't become informants [sapos] for the army ... Two years after they killed the last boy, they killed my husband."[24]

Finally, the terror and chaos of the paramilitary takeover arose not only from what happened to people but from what they did—or were forced to do—to each other. Poorly trained guerrilla milicianos with little understanding of the broader objectives of the insurgent struggle, or who simply sought to save their lives amid the rapidly shifting balance of power, intensified the mayhem when they switched sides and exposed their support networks. Residents no longer knew whom to trust, and merely leaving home for work became an act fraught with fear, as firefights erupted without warning, dead bodies with signs of gruesome torture littered the streets, and uniformed paramilitaries patrolled openly in some neighborhoods. The betrayals left people feeling deceived and broken. They provoked cynicism about the future and moved people to turn inward and seek individual solutions to their problems. Not surprisingly, residents became alienated from the insurgents, and relations with them soured, furthering the breakdown of social bonds.

As the paramilitaries expelled the guerrillas from the city and targeted the civilian population, the death and displacement of so many people ruptured community networks and severed the ties that bound Barrancabermeja's unions and social organizations to a support base in the city's northeast sector. The paramilitaries frequently seized the homes of the people they displaced and handed them over to supporters, who filtered into Barrancabermeja from other regions already under the control of the AUC. All of this undermined the neighborhood solidarities that had formed the bedrock of urban militancy in the northeast sector and furthered the disorganization of working-class power in the city. The disarticulation of Barranca's infrastructure of solidarity elucidates how violence plays a key role in the unmaking of working classes located within broader fields of power.

Once the initial wave of paramilitary terror had passed, wholesale massacres of suspected guerrilla sympathizers were no longer necessary, as the guerrilla militias had retreated from the city, but the paramilitaries used death threats and the selective assassination of social movement leaders and their family members to keep the opposition frightened. These tactics aimed to throw activists off balance by heightening feelings of vulnerability to a lethal, invisible enemy. They prompted suspicions about workmates, friends, and associates and incited rumors and speculation about imminent paramilitary "cleansing" operations. Daily activities that formed part of a predictable routine could, if widely known, jeopardize the security of a trade union leader or a human rights defender. The threats also destabilized the boundaries between zones of relative safety and threat, making activists feel insecure everywhere, and they aggravated cleavages between activists and their constituencies, who worried that associating too closely with targeted leaders could place their own lives in danger.

By 2003, the paramilitaries no longer operated as a mercenary army that waged a dirty war under the protective wing of the state. They had in effect become the state itself. The paramilitaries penetrated the official state apparatus and erected a mafia-like surrogate state in which organized crime fused with the politics of counterinsurgency. They manipulated elections by openly or tacitly supporting certain candidates, while intimidating others and dictating to people how to vote, and because of their enormous power, aspiring candidates for political office sought their support, albeit surreptitiously. Through the control of government office, the paramilitaries could thus tap into municipal treasuries, dictate who received government contracts, and demand kickbacks. They also monopolized the illegal cocaine traffic and the theft and sale of gasoline from ECOPETROL, and they operated a variety of legal businesses, such as the lottery, transportation enterprises, private security firms, and subcontracting agencies. In addition, they reterritorialized class power in the city. The boundary between the guerrilla-controlled neighborhoods of the northeast and the city center lost all significance, as the BCB laid claim to the entire city and displaced hundreds of presumed guerrilla supporters from their homes.

All of this made it extremely difficult for working people to explain and understand, in shared ways, what was happening to them and to chart a path for the future, and the total impunity with which the paramilitaries operated left residents feeling completely unprotected. Impunity highlighted the shifting dynamic of class struggle in Barrancabermeja. It enabled paramilitaries and their supporters to continue harming people without suffering any consequences, while simultaneously restricting the ability of working people to stem the physical violence and subsequent neoliberal policies targeted against them. And it drew strength from the contempt and indifference of broad sectors of Colombia's middling and dominant groups, who consumed television images of "dangerous classes" on the urban periphery tied to violent guerrilla militias.

Only by proclaiming one's "innocence," which meant renouncing political connections, could one hope for deliverance. Yet while affirming innocence contradicted the criminalizing rhetoric that made the brutal repression of so-called subversives more acceptable, it also implied that torture and extrajudicial execution would be acceptable if the person were less pure.[25] An imposed silence complicated the construction of a public narrative about what had happened and continued to happen. Working people had to contend with what had happened to them and their understanding of these experiences, on the one hand, and what they could debate, discuss, negotiate, and change, on the other hand.[26] The history of the political genocide of the left was reduced to the individual experiences of victims who were involved in particular events, and the institutional spaces that made working-class memories and experiences publically and politically available to others became severely constrained. Fragmented memories and the silences that sustained them opened the door for the elaboration of an understanding of the past that served the interests of those in power.

Trust vaporized. Social life grew more privatized and isolated as the public sphere shrank and a welter of authoritarian, personal relationships replaced the horizontal bonds that had connected people in the unions and popular organizations. People turned to evangelical churches, and away from politics, to find solutions to their problems. Surviving labor and social movement leaders lived under a shadow of death, surrounded by bodyguards and cloistered within their homes and offices. Weakened unions and social organizations found themselves poorly equipped to challenge new "flexible" work arrangements, and ruined peasants, downsized urban workers, and shell-shocked residents of the northeastern and southeastern neighborhoods had little choice but to rely on fragile personal networks for their daily survival. Yet they discovered that friends and relatives were not able to provide them with all that was necessary, and many people found themselves forced to turn to the paramilitaries for the support that they once provided each other.

The political transformations created new vulnerabilities and intensified old ones by disorganizing social life, eliminating or weakening the organizational forms through which working people had once channeled their demands, and exposing people to the intensifying discipline of the market at a time when employment opportunities were contracting in the city. One consequence was the growth of the informal economy in which the absence of rights, regulations, and bargaining power was a defining feature. As people toiled alone as itinerant vendors, part-time construction workers, motorcycle taxi drivers and so forth, they became vulnerable to violent forms of labor discipline, credit-debt relationships, and political subjugation.

Remaking Class: Labor Discipline, Debt, and Political Subjugation

The paramilitary takeover of Barrancabermeja presented company managers with a violent form of labor discipline that helped create the political conditions for the advancement of neoliberal policies. In response to working-class opposition to neoliberalism, which intensified in the wake of the Colombian government's embrace of free-market policies in the early 1990s, paramilitaries targeted labor leaders for assassination, torture, and constant harassment, especially during periods of labor unrest. Unlike the guerrillas, who opposed opening Colombia to greater foreign investment, the paramilitaries had no position against multinational involvement in the economy. According to Richani, "This allows for an affinity between the AUC and the foreign companies, particularly those invested in the conflict areas" (Richani 2005: 113). In contrast to the guerrillas, who had been the "uncomfortable allies" of Barranca's trade unions and civic organizations (Delgado 2006: 139), the AUC represented a far-right alliance of regionally based power holders. It was less concerned with overthrowing the state than with shoring up and participating in the status quo and serving as the violent enforcers of its most reactionary elements.

During the early months of the BCB occupation of Barrancabermeja, paramilitary commanders summoned labor leaders to meetings in which they laid out the new rules of social engagement—that is, no protests, no strikes, no public statements against employers—and they advised people to keep a low profile. One union leader who was an outspoken human rights advocate refused to attend these meetings. He explained: "[After the takeover], the paramilitaries began to send emissaries to tell me that I should meet with them. They did this to all the trade union leaders in the city, but we were one of the only unions that always refused to meet with the paras. We have a policy to never talk to any of the armed actors. So they started to squeeze me and to threaten me more." The pressure culminated with the attempted kidnaping of his four-year-old daughter when she was with her mother in a public park. When the mother's screams attracted attention, the kidnappers fled. The labor leader explained that two days later "a paramilitary boss reached me on my cell phone and called me a guerrilla son-of-a-bitch. He said that I was very lucky; they had planned to kill my daughter because I refused to meet with them."[27]

Trade union leaders who responded to paramilitary pressure for meetings were often fortunate to leave alive. A union leader and former worker for TELECOM—the state telecommunications company—was summoned to meetings during the months preceding the privatization of the company. Paramilitaries accused him and other workers of plotting to sabotage the company, of having ties to the insurgency, and of belonging to a "bad union for the company," one that publically protested the impending privatization of TELECOM. Yet because the trade union leader "had nothing to hide from them," and perhaps, more importantly, because he feared the consequences of defying the paramilitaries, he agreed to accompany emissaries to an occupied neighborhood of the northeast sector, where a commander wanted to question him. It quickly became apparent that the paramilitaries intended to murder him, and he credited his survival to a woman, known to his captors, who vouched for him and insisted that he had no ties to the insurgency.[28]

A similar terror-filled drama played out in other parts of Barrancabermeja. In the city's Coca-Cola plant, trade unionists observed plant managers talking with known paramilitaries whom, they asserted, extorted protection payments from the company.[29] Although it was well-known among workers that the corporation had once paid "war taxes" to the guerrillas, the extortion payments (*vacunas*) made to the paramilitaries guaranteed protection from the demands of labor. Paramilitary threats, harassment, and assassination attempts pushed workers to renounce their union membership and accept coercive buyout deals when the production line closed in 2003. Union membership plummeted, and the number of Coca-Cola workers with stable contracts and relatively good wages declined, as the plant was downgraded to a storage and distribution center. The company increasingly ignored collective bargaining agreements negotiated with the union, and a new generation of nonunionized, subcontracted laborers who earned lower wages entered the workforce. As the ties of familiarity that once bound workers to each other eroded, fears that paramilitaries operated in the plant limited workers ability to make effective demands on the company (Gill 2007).

By weakening or decimating the organized opposition to neoliberalism, paramilitaries hastened the elimination of full-time, unionized employment, the privatization of public entities, and the rise of subcontracting. By so doing, they aggravated long-standing problems of un- and underemployment, limited poor urban residents' access to basic services and forced them to pay higher fees. For example, a reduction of services at the only public hospital in Barranca not only eliminated jobs. It intensified a health-care crisis by forcing people to travel to the provincial capital and pay more for certain treatments that were no longer available in the city. Telephone service and electricity became more expensive in the wake of privatization, which cost additional jobs, and water rates shot through the roof, spiking 60 percent in 2007. Yet when hundreds of residents protested usurious electricity rates after newly installed meters malfunctioned in their homes, paramilitaries threatened them and the president of a consumer protection group that oversaw the cost of public services.[30]

The paramilitary presence empowered company managers and governmental officials to take advantage of weakened unions, the social disarray engendered by widespread terror, and the expulsion of the guerrillas to push more vigorously for the reorganization of labor relations. ECOPETROL's outsourcing of jobs to nonunion workers had already weakened the USO on the eve of the paramilitary takeover, and the strike had become an ineffective weapon of resistance, but the paramilitary reign of terror consolidated this process. It did so by displacing or assassinating the most dynamic union leaders and weakening the USO's ties to community organizations and the broader labor movement, which were already under siege. All of this debilitated the union's ability to challenge job loss and the reconfiguration of the oil industry; a 1999 civic strike, for example, was the last time that the USO led a major protest that shut down the city. The USO's storied solidarity with the urban working class became limited to the defense of its members benefits and privileges that had been won in the past.[31]

The USO's rearguard efforts to safeguard established privileges reflected the extent to which paramilitary terror had disorganized working-class power through the weakening of the city's most prominent trade union. The USO's anti-imperialist nationalism, once sustained by Barranca's vibrant political culture, was replaced by a more limited concern for human rights that highlighted a new defensiveness in working-class districts. Demands for the respect for human rights sought to address the immediate threat of overwhelming state and paramilitary terror, but human rights offered less a vision of a better world than a critique of what was wrong with the present. Rights discourse had little to say about what a collective political project might look like, having emerged at the historical moment when working-class solidarity and dreams of collective transformation were being snuffed out.[32]

In the context of rising terror and attacks on trade unionists, the restructuring of ECOPETROL, which began in 1991, led to the subcontracting of a greater share of work. The process advanced in 2003, when the government split ECOPETROL into two companies and opened the door for greater multinational involvement in oil production. It culminated in 2004, when a strike failed to win major concessions for workers. With the rise of subcontracting in the oil industry and elsewhere, the growing vulnerability and marginalization of barranqueños made clientelism more important to the well-being of ordinary people. Personal networks had long been necessary to secure a job, a house, and other opportunities in a city with persistently high levels of un- and underemployment, but as these networks fell under paramilitary control, they grew more authoritarian. The mercenaries used them not only to extort money from both workers and employers; they also dictated who worked and who remained unemployed. After murdering twenty members of the taxi drivers' union (UNIMOTOR) in 2000, for example, they transformed the organization into a source of rewards for supporters, who received jobs in exchange for using the taxicabs to carry out intelligence work (Loingsigh 2002). Workers with a trade union background or residence in a neighborhood stigmatized for its left-wing sympathies were either excluded or forced to remain silent and risk physical harm if their personal histories were revealed.

In the late 1990s, for example, ECOPETROL workers had organized the Sindicato de Trabajadores Disponibles y Temporales (SINTRADIT) to pressure the oil company to provide temporary jobs to members and thus to avoid the discounts and commissions charged by subcontractors and a plethora of newly constituted employment agencies. SINTRADIT organized at a time when un- and underemployment was deepening, as displaced peasants flooded into the city to escape rural violence and new neoliberal labor laws were undermining job security for those fortunate to have work. At its peak, the union organized two thousand people, but it did not survive the paramilitary takeover. The paramilitaries demanded that one of SINTRADIT's leaders pay a large sum of money as a condition for its continued work with the oil company. When he refused to pay, hitmen tried to murder him, and they ultimately forced him to leave the city. Yet the intimidation did not end with his departure from Barrancabermeja. According to the individual, a well-known paramilitary commander visited the home of a family member and explained that "he had given the order to capture me alive. He needed me alive so that he could tie me to a post with barbed wire and destroy me piece-by-piece so that the community would understand how guerrilla leaders died."[33] Such vicious repression shattered SINTRADIT, and workers' private experiences of terror were difficult to express publicly.

An unemployed worker described his fear of seeking employment through the so-called worker cooperatives and subcontracting agencies that the paramilitaries controlled. "The victimization of many people [by the paramilitaries]," he said, "has been because of the information that [they] have obtained about people through rumors and innuendo, even the unguarded comments of someone who says unknowingly in the presence of a paramilitary informant that 'ah, that guy was a guerrilla, or a guerrilla supporter.' So you see, there is this kind of fingering, even though indirect, and the information gets back to them."[34] The threat posed by rumor and gossip aggravated fear and, when combined with the imperative to find work, focused people on the immediacy of survival.[35] The ability of paramilitaries to control the labor market in contemporary Barrancabermeja highlighted the contingency and fragility of past labor victories in which workers largely succeeded in improving wages, winning benefits, and controlling the hiring process through their unions. As workers were either forced to maintain a low profile or were displaced from the city, they grew more divided from each other. Mistrust and uncertainty eroded social solidarity in an ever more fragmented working class, while access to jobs and benefits became gifts or favors from powerful, authoritarian patrons instead of social rights.

The brutal labor discipline and the erosion of economic well-being pushed some people into coercive debt relationships with the paramilitaries after a health crisis or a financial emergency overwhelmed their ability to cope. Many residents told how fliers offering generous credit started to appear in their neighborhoods after the paramilitary takeover. To access this money, one had only to call a cell phone number and a young man would appear on a motorcycle to negotiate the deal and provide the funds, which usually required repayment at 20 percent interest. The arrangement built on an older form of quasi-legal credit known as "*gota a gota*" (drip by drip), but it required no guarantors, collateral, or signed documents, and it turned on fear.

One woman explained that after surviving a traffic accident with a bus, she faced the task of paying for expensive repairs to the vehicle because the owner—a paramilitary—insisted that she bore responsibility for the accident. Yet neither she nor her husband were in a position to assume the cost of the repairs. The husband had lost his job with the state oil company, and the family of five depended on her wages as a nurse for basic necessities. Fearing what might happen if they neglected the damaged bus, husband and wife borrowed money from a local lender whom they suspected of paramilitary ties and then began to repay the funds immediately. When they fell into arrears, two paramilitaries came to their home and threatened them with harm if the payments did not continue on schedule. As the woman later explained, "I didn't know what to do. I could borrow from another paramilitary to pay off the first one, or I could plead with my relatives to lend me the money, which they don't have."[36] The paramilitaries wove exploitative relationships of credit and debt out of the vulnerabilities of local residents—vulnerabilities that, to a considerable degree, they themselves had created—and these relationships in turn allowed them to launder drug profits and siphon additional wealth out of the local economy. Debtors faced the impossible situation of living with the imminent threat of violence or squeezing their social networks to the breaking point and deepening their economic insecurity.

The paramilitaries enforced their rule through vicious political subjugation that was undergirded by impunity. In addition to the outright murder and intimidation of dissidents, the subjugation took various forms. In many neighborhoods, for example, the mercenaries set up protection racquets in which they extorted payments from residents in exchange for "security." One resident described how, in the aftermath of the takeover, a local commander called residents of the neighborhood to a meeting in a public school, where he explained that the paramilitaries had entered the city at the request of local citizens to deal with the "security problem" caused by the guerrillas. He then offered the services of his men to the community. Shortly thereafter, young enforcers began to visit individual households on Saturday afternoons, requesting weekly payments of two thousand pesos for neighborhood protection.[37] Most residents understood that their "contributions" to these individuals were little more than an exemption—sometimes only temporary—from the violence of the paramilitaries themselves.

The "security" that they provided included monitoring the comings and goings of residents and the enforcement of social norms, including evening curfews, the repression of prostitution and homosexuality, the prohibition of marijuana, and a ban on the wearing of earrings and long hair by men. Manuals that appeared in the city around 2003 spelled out the paramilitary moral code for poor urban neighborhoods, a code that sought to reestablish rigid gender, generational, and sexual hierarchies disrupted by years of violence and economic restructuring. People caught violating this moral code were subject to public humiliation and obliged to carry out "community service," such as sweeping the streets or cleaning parks, while wearing signs that announced their transgressions. Paramilitaries singled out certain young people, who, they asserted, engaged in delinquent behavior because of the failure of their parents to inculcate a proper moral education. A young man from the northeast sector noted the moral irony of paramilitaries, who monopolized the illegal drug traffic, enforcing a ban on marijuana consumption, and he lamented that some residents did not object to what is widely referred to as "social cleansing," because "seeing young men on the corner [smoking marijuana] makes them uncomfortable."[38]

Yet imposing a refashioned patriarchal order was not easy because of the mayhem that the paramilitaries themselves had created. The violent takeover of Barrancabermeja had primarily targeted men, who were believed to be the key actors and protagonists in the insurgency, and it produced hundreds of widows and fatherless children. Because residents were obliged to turn to the paramilitaries to resolve problems, they inadvertently legitimized the violent social order that the latter sought to create.

Nevertheless, the brute violence did less to create a legitimate social order than to generate widespread social malaise and establish the conditions for the continuing accrual of power and resources. As left social networks and political projects were destroyed, working people became incorporated into authoritarian, clientelistic relationships of power controlled by the paramilitaries and those they served. These opaque, often clandestine relationships created an ever present sense of menace for those dependent on them for their livelihoods, and they became a key mechanism for the transfer of wealth to more powerful social groups.

Legitimizing the Illegitimate: Low-intensity Peace, Daily Life, and the Informal Urban Proletariat

Nowadays, a deceptive calm hangs over Barranca. Civilian massacres no longer take place, and firefights between paramilitaries and guerrillas do not erupt on the streets of the northeast. People crowd the sunbaked streets of the city center; small boats, called *chalupas*, ferry passengers up and down the Magdalena River; and motorcycles clog the bridge that connects the impoverished northeast to the city center.

Unlike in the recent past, residents of the northeast can now escape in the evenings from the heat of their homes to the cool of the streets without violating a paramilitary curfew, and on Saturday nights, an eclectic mix of salsa, vallenato, and reggaetón music blares from the interiors of bars, restaurants, and living rooms, filling the streets with a festive air. Yet beneath the tranquil veneer, there is much discontentment even though the city is undergoing an oil boom. Neither the state nor the paramilitaries have incorporated poor urban residents into the neoliberal order in ways that insures their social reproduction.

Following the 2003 takeover of the city and the paramilitary expansion into former leftist strongholds in other parts of Colombia, mercenary organizations entered into "peace" talks with the government of present Álvaro Uribe Vélez, even though they had never been at war with the government. For a brief period, paramilitarism was officially acknowledged. The result was a government-brokered amnesty program, condemned by human rights groups for institutionalizing impunity, that sought to incorporate the mercenaries into civil society and dismantle their armies. Although some paramilitaries did demobilize, and several high-ranking commanders were extradited to the United States on drug-trafficking charges, the paramilitaries regrouped under new names and continued to target trade unions, peasant organizations, and human rights NGOs, while the government claimed that ongoing violence was the work of "emergent bands of delinquents" whose activities were not politically motivated.[39] By linking the ongoing violence to crime and locating paramilitarism in the past, the government attempted to sever the continuing connection between itself and the narco-bourgeoisie and neoliberal entrepreneurs who used violence for capital accumulation, as well as to obscure the reconsolidation of paramilitary groups in the present (Hristov 2010).

Moreover, in the aftermath of the peace accords, powerful paramilitaries sought ways to legitimate their power and consolidate their control through the publication of books and the creation of foundations and nongovernmental organizations. Ex-BCB leader Carlos Mario Jiménez, alias "Macaco," contributed to the Fundación de Ciencia y Tecnología para el Desarrollo Integral de las Comunidades del Magdalena Medio, based in Bucaramanga, the provincial capital. This foundation supported "development projects" on lands that were probably stolen from displaced peasants and thus strengthened the control of the new "owners" of these lands. In February

2007, the foundation also contracted three buses to take residents of Bucaramanga and Barrancabermeja to show support for Macaco, when he gave his public testimony in Medellín under the terms of the Justice and Peace law. On the eve of his testimony, Macaco contracted another NGO—la Fundación Villa de la Esperanza—to create a favorable history of him and then publish it in *El Espectador*, one of Colombia's most important newspapers. The "infomercial" was called "Entrepreneur of Peace" and appeared as a legitimate piece of journalism, presenting Macaco's humane qualities in interview format and describing him as a humble merchant who was driven to armed struggle by the exigencies of the war. The account, however, never mentioned the thousands of people that were assassinated and disappeared by the BCB.[40]

Semillas de Paz is another paramilitary-affiliated NGO that illustrates the depths of impunity in Barrancabermeja. Tied to the paramilitaries and comprised of demobilized members of the Bloque Central Bolívar, Semillas de Paz maintains an office in Barrancabermeja and presumes to counsel victims of political violence and document cases of abuse. In March 2007, it convened a meeting for the family members of victims of the armed conflict to promote its activities and gather documentation about the dead and disappeared from relatives. Meeting participants, however, realized only afterward that Semillas de Paz represented the victimizers of their loved ones and not fellow victims. The widow of a man murdered in a BCB massacre also recalled how members of Semillas de Paz visited her home and expressed a desire to "reconcile." She found their unannounced arrival extremely intimidating, and when they were unwilling to give information about the fate of her husband, she told them not to return.[41]

Such efforts at legitimation were repeatedly disrupted by shocking public scandals about the paramilitary-state relationship, including the so-called *parapolítica* scandal that led to the incarceration or investigation of over sixty members of congress for ties to the paramilitaries. Yet these scandals were always located in the past, while the consolidation of a far-right ruling bloc of entrepreneurial elites, narcotraffickers, politicians, and paramilitary leaders continued apace (Hristov 2010), deepening neoliberalism in Colombia. Labor leaders and human rights defenders in the Middle Magdalena region experienced little respite from the threats and harassment that they had endured for several years. In early 2007, for example, national and departmental leaders of the National Food and Beverage Workers

Union (SINALTRAINAL) who worked for the Coca-Cola Company received a written death threat from a new paramilitary group that called itself the Black Eagles. The threat listed four people by name, including their nicknames, and ordered them to "stop the noise against the Coca-Cola Company. The damage that you have caused is enough . . . we declare you military targets of the Black Eagles. How do you prefer to die—torture, dismemberment, or a shot in the head Middle Magdalena style?" It made clear the continuing ties between pre- and postdemobilization paramilitaries by linking the Black Eagles to the former AUC and warning the trade unionists that former AUC leader Salvatore Mancuso "doesn't like noise."[42]

The social decomposition generated by years of impunity-fueled violence and economic restructuring have eroded the economic security of many people, and part-time and temporary work are not always available to residents. The un- and underemployed complain bitterly about ECOPETROL contractors who bring workers from other parts of the country instead of hiring them for temporary jobs with the oil company, and small, local contractors, who once serviced the oil company now assert that larger, national and international firms have replaced them. Subcontracted workers may put in eighteen-hour days for thirty-five to forty continuous days without any time off. Carola Rojas, for example, has ridden a feast-or-famine wave of temporary jobs in the oil refinery and unemployment since 2002. When she is employed, she and her companion make ends meet on a monthly income of approximately one thousand dollars in a city where the oil industry has pushed the cost of living to higher levels than in other metropolitan centers. When the money runs out, Carola either sells hot dogs to prostitutes and their customers in the city's red light district or works illegally as a motorcycle taxi driver for which she has received repeated fines. As the numbers of un- and underemployed workers grows, competition for the available crumbs intensifies among ever more desperate people.

Indicative of the social unease are the tensions that have shaped relations between unlicensed, motorcycle taxi drivers and the licensed drivers of taxicabs. The ranks of both groups swelled with the downsizing, labor-outsourcing, and trade union decline that accompanied the violent imposition of neoliberalism in the city and the massive displacement of peasants from the countryside. In 2000, some 1,123,764 motorcycles circulated in Colombia, but by 2004, this figure had increased to 1,787,947, and sales of motorcycles experienced an increase of 65 percent between 2003 and 2004 (Hurtado Isaza 2007).

Discontentment among Barrancabermeja's urban transporters then deepened in the wake of the partial paramilitary demobilization, after hundreds of rank-and-file mercenaries found themselves in need of employment and took to the city streets on motorcycles to offer their services as unofficial drivers. Unlike the city buses, which were desperately slow and made numerous stops, the mototaxistas took people directly to their destinations for approximately the same fare as a city bus, one that undercut by 50 percent the rate licensed cabbies charged. To further complicate matters, these unlicensed drivers were not all independent operators. Some were controlled by paramilitaries who had not demobilized and who obliged them to hand over a percentage of their income for the right to operate. Paramilitary patrons further demanded that the mototaxistas use their position to collect intelligence on the ebb and flow of social life in the city. Such behavior threatened the security of urban residents and made it relatively easy to stigmatize all mototaxistas. As one licensed cabbie complained, "[T]hey are criminals who steal money from people and abuse women."[43] The conflict reflects a familiar pattern of creating new differences among working people that are difficult to overcome

Not surprisingly, the licensed cabbies demanded that the municipal government do more to control the proliferation of the mototaxistas, and they staged a series of protests that resulted in clashes with security forces. Following one of these skirmishes, in August 2007, the mayor's office emitted a decree that excluded the mototaxistas from the crowded center of town, where prospective passengers were abundant, but did nothing to address the economic issues at the root of the problem. This, in turn, sparked counter protests by the mototaxistas, many of whom argued that the public space could not be restricted in this way. Municipal officials then resorted to force to control the disorder created to a considerable degree by their own policies.

Nowadays, even though the extreme violence of the past has subsided, neoparamilitary groups that reconstituted in the wake of the demobilization continue to manipulate clientelistic networks in a context of widespread impunity. Challenging the impunity is difficult because of the absence of clear-cut distinctions between organized crime, politically inspired neoparamilitary violence, and state institutions, and because of the generalized social and economic insecurity that infuses every corner of daily life. Residents of the northeast describe in hushed voices how hooded men patrol their neighborhoods at night, and, unlike the recent past, they are uncertain of the provenance and identity of these nighttime marauders. The uncertainty heightens a sense of dread, undergirds the privatization of experience, and deepens the recourse to personal strategies to negotiate the hazards of life. All of this is reproduced and maintained by official denials about what is happening. Despite the murder of two union leaders and a rising number of homicides in the first half of 2009, a representative of the mayor's office could still assert that trade unionists and human rights defenders were not at risk in the city. He insisted that ordinary criminals posed the biggest threat to public safety. The city's rising death rate, he said, was the result of the settling of scores among criminals or people caught up in the competition among them for control over a wide range of profitable activities.[44]

The impunity, social fractures, and precarious economic situation have generated different personal experiences and understandings about the violent past and the still violent, disordered present. Despite the overwhelming military force that accompanied the paramilitary takeover of the northeast, and despite the reports of numerous national and international human rights organizations that attribute the vast majority of human rights violations to the paramilitaries, there are many residents of the northeast who blame the intense violence of the late twentieth and early twenty-first centuries on the guerrillas. Residents describe how their children were trapped in school or between school and home when firefights erupted out of nowhere; they explain their dilemmas when they woke up in the morning to find wounded guerrillas lying in the interior patios of their homes; and they recount the harsh guerrilla treatment of individuals suspected of collaborating with the security forces. Yet these stories and assertions are interwoven with deafening silences.

A resident, for example, says that she welcomed the paramilitary arrival, because it put an end to the violence in her neighborhood, which the guerrillas had controlled for at least a decade. The violence that she describes—a stray bullet hitting her husband in the leg, persecuted guerrillas seeking refuge in her daughter's school, and episodic firefights that erupted on the streets—is, she says, entirely the fault of the guerrillas, even though it took place between 2000 and 2002, when the paramilitaries abetted by the police and the military were pushing the guerrillas out and not during the previous decade in which the guerrillas had controlled her neighborhood with a considerable degree of popular acceptance. Significantly, too, in her recounting, she mentions nothing about a paramilitary massacre of several alleged guerrillas that took place in a house directly across the street from her home. The extent to which residents of Barrancabermeja can create—and even imagine—relationships that offer them an alternative to the authoritarian relationships, intimidation, and fractured memories that define the present remains an open question.

Conclusion

As this essay has shown, the systemic use of violence by the state, allied paramilitary organizations, dominant classes, and foreign corporations forms part of a long historical process in which the urban working class was made, unmade, and remade amid changing forms of capital accumulation. Although Colombia is an extreme example of the violence intrinsic to capitalism, it is indicative of a pattern that we must understand to grasp how dispossession and disorganization periodically unravel the institutions, relationships, understandings and ways of life that undergird working-class power. State and paramilitary terror have dismantled the dense social relationships and institutional structures of solidarity, including neighborhood organizations, unions, and Catholic base communities and reduced people to individual survival strategies. By so doing, the paramilitaries have divided working people from each other, abetted the reorganization of labor relations through subcontracting, debt, and political subjugation, and spurred the growth of the informal urban proletariat, which is more exposed to the discipline of the market and less protected than in the past. They have also usurped many functions of the official state, secured the rights of private property for a new right-wing power bloc through the violent displacement of thousands of peasants, and deepened neoliberalism through the proliferation of regional sovereignties. A far-right alliance of paramilitaries, neoliberal elites, politicians, and drug traffickers is now better positioned than in the past to siphon profits out of the regional economy, where the distinction between legal and illegal spheres has less meaning, and the targeted and strategic use of terror remains crucial to the accumulation of wealth through "flexible" labor relations, the appropriation of land, drug trafficking, and extortion.

Far from being meaningless or incomprehensible, political violence is deeply embedded in the unequal power relationships that shape the production and accumulation of wealth. The mid-twentieth-century expansion of worker rights and the decline of labor radicalism in the United States went hand-in-hand with the creation of foreign-controlled export enclaves in Latin America, where the use of violence to control labor was accentuated. Throughout the twentieth century, corporations and states continued to confront labor militancy in Latin America, despite, or perhaps because of, the extreme measures that dominant classes took to maintain the status quo (Bergquist 1986; Chomsky 2008) As Charles Bergquist notes, incorporating Latin American social movements into an expanding capitalist order has proven much more difficult for the United States and its regional allies than containing their counterparts in the United States. The violence and belligerence directed at them over the twentieth century reflects to a considerable degree the anxiety that they produced within government, corporate and elite circles, and it is not surprising that Latin American social movements have often acquired an insurgent, nationalist edge, even at times challenging the very foundations of capitalism itself (Bergquist 1996).

Nowadays, the proliferation of media and governmental narratives that equate the repression and criminality of left-wing guerrillas and right-wing paramilitaries have less to do with the past than with struggles over memory and power in the present.[45] They obscure a time when many working-class Colombians, especially in Barrancabermeja, embraced left-wing politics and often supported guerrilla insurgencies, even though these insurgencies never developed the broad political bases that characterized the FMLN (Farabundo Martí National Liberation Front) in El Salvador and the FSLN (Sandinista National Liberation Front) in Nicaragua. They also discount statistics: the security forces and paramilitaries have committed the vast majority of rights violations (e.g., Human Rights Watch 1996; 2001), and over the last thirty years, paramilitaries and those they serve have amassed legal businesses and thousands of hectares of rural land, while left-wing insurgencies have been weakened and pushed out of traditional strongholds (e.g., Hristov 2010; Richani 2002).

Obscuring the past opens the door for the establishment and legitimation of social truths that bolster the interests of the powerful and shape how working people understand the past and tell their stories about a time of devastating brutality. Violence has deprived men and women of the coherence necessary to grasp the connections between the past and present in ways that are broadly shared and that enable them to make a collective claim on the future. Consequently, barranqueños must simultaneously struggle against the order and coherence that dominant historical narratives impose on the one hand, and the chaos and fragmented memories that violence generated on the other hand. What sets the story of Barrancabermeja apart from the experiences of other towns in the Middle Magdalena is that surviving trade union leaders and human rights defenders have not stopped speaking out, and they provide alternative explanations for what has happened in the city. Many ordinary people also quietly refuse to give in to paramilitary extortion demands and threats. In these and other ways, they constantly push against the status quo, evaluate its strengths, and take advantage of its weaknesses. By so doing, they take stock of what they can do by themselves and with each other and make important strides toward revitalizing Barrancabermeja's radical popular tradition and refashioning a new form of solidarity that can strengthen challenges to impunity and capitalist privilege.

Yet despite the resilience and tenacity of these barranqueños, their story of social rupture and political disorganization is not uncommon in the early twenty-first century. Although it is particularly brutal, the tale has been rehearsed in less extreme forms elsewhere, as the case studies in this volume demonstrate, setting the stage for the incorporation of vulnerable people into new class relationships in which old solidarities and forms of struggle no longer held. An anthropology of labor that ignores the central role of violence in the making and unmaking of working classes does so at great peril.

Acknowledgments

I would like to thank August Carbonella and Sharryn Kasmir for several rounds of comments that greatly improved the final version of this article. Don Kalb and Judy Whitehead also offered helpful suggestions on an earlier version.

Notes

1. I borrow the term "durable disorder" from Romero (2007).

2. This process bears resemblance to the experiences of working classes elsewhere, for example, Winn (2004), Levenson-Estrada (1994), Linebaugh (1992), and Chomsky (2008).
3. See, for example, essays by Fontenot and Maiwandi, Bond, Rodgers, and Hylton in Davis and Monk (2007).
4. Compare, for example, Ann Farnsworth-Alvear's discussion of the intense paternalism that shaped early-twentieth-century labor relations between Medellín textile mill owners and female workers (Farnsworth-Alvear 2000) with the descriptions of worker radicalism in Barrancabermeja's foreign-dominated enclave in Vega Cantor et al. (2009).
5. The class and cultural divisions that shaped the early development of the oil enclave in Barrancabermeja resembled those that emerged in Venezuelan oil enclaves as described by Miguel Tinker Salas (2009).
6. For an insightful discussion of the land conflicts that shaped late-nineteenth- and early-twentieth-century Colombia, see LeGrand (1986).
7. Unlike the guerrilla insurgencies that would organize in the 1960s, the Liberal guerrilla groups did not seek the transformation of the social order. Their objective was to remove the Conservative party from power.
8. See Striffler (2002) and Striffler and Moberg (2003) for more discussion of the transformation of early-twentieth-century enclaves.
9. Interview with Ramón Rangel, Barrancabermeja, July 2009.
10. Interview with a former member of the Coordinadora, Bucaramanga, 2009.
11. Interview with William Mendoza, July 19, 2006, Barrancabermeja.
12. Interview with former USO leader Ramón Rangel, July 2009, Barrancabermeja.
13. Indeed, many peasants saw the arrival of the ELN as a continuation of the struggle waged by the Liberal guerrillas of Rafael Rangel. Yet, according to a former ELN guerrilla, the Cuban-inspired guerrilla tactics that ELN insurgents brought with them from training camps in Cuba were initially incomprehensible to peasants who had participated in the Liberal guerrilla struggles and wanted to engage in more frequent attacks on military compounds.
14. Interview with former ELN guerrilla, March 7, 2009, Bogotá.
15. The guerrilla militias were composed of urban supporters of the insurgencies who organized residents and channeled arms and aid to the rural forces.
16. Interview with trade union leader, Barrancabermeja, July 2009.
17. Interview with human rights worker, Barrancabermeja, July 2009.
18. Interview with urban resident, July 19, 2006, Barrancabermeja.
19. Interview with former Coordinadora member, July 2009.
20. Interview with Barrancabermeja human rights worker, Bogotá, April 2007.
21. "El intocable?" *Semana* (2007), http://www.semana.com.
22. Interview with human rights worker, Bucaramanga, 2009.
23. Ibid.
24. Interview with Barrancabermeja human rights worker, Bogotá, April 2007.
25. See Stern (2004: 39–87) for an interesting discussion about how claims to goodness shaped the formation of memory in Chile.
26. See Sider (1997) and Green (2012) for more discussion of the how silences shape historical processes of extreme inequality.
27. Interview with Barrancabermeja trade union leader, July 2006.
28. Interview with former TELECOM worker, Barrancabermeja, March 2007.
29. Interview with Coca-Cola worker, Barrancabermeja, 2004.
30. Interview with Jorge Elías Ramírez, Barrancabermeja, March 2007.
31. See Delgado (2006) for more discussion of the labor movement in the Middle Magdalena region and the role of the USO.

32. See Markarian (2005) for an interesting discussion of the politics of human rights among Uruguayan leftist who fled the country in the 1970s and 1980s. Markarian argues that activists only adopted the human rights frame after political repression in Uruguay made it impossible to make social and economic claims.
33. Interview with former SINTRADIT leader, Barrancabermeja 2009.
34. Interview, Barrancabermeja, 2007.
35. See Narotzky and Smith (2006: 56–74) for an interesting discussion of how fear and uncertainty regulated social life during the Franco era in Spain.
36. Interview with resident of Barrancabermeja, March 2007.
37. At the time, this amount was slightly less than one US dollar.
38. Interview with resident of Barrancabermeja, July 31, 2007. See also Taussig (2003) for more on paramilitaries and the "social cleansing" of so-called undesirables.
39. For more discussion of post-peace accord paramilitarism, in which criminality remains tethered to a defense of the status quo and the suppression of dissent, see Romero and Arias (2010) and Restrepo (2010).
40. "Un empresario de la paz." *El Espectator* (2007), http://www.elespactor.com; "El Espectator ofrece excusas por publicreportaje con 'Macaco'." *Semana* (2007b), http://www.semana.com.
41. Interview with massacre survivor, Barrancabermeja, February 2007.
42. Death threat faxed to the Bucaramanga office of SINALTRAINAL signed "Frente Aguilas Negras Lebrija," February 10, 2007.
43. Interview, Barrancabermeja, July 2007.
44. See the Colombian journal *Arcanos* (no. 15, 2010) for a series of articles that describe how a new wave of paramilitary violence and criminality has affected Colombian cities in the aftermath of the demobilizations.
45. This portrayal of the insurgencies resembles the "two demons" analysis of the Guatemalan counterinsurgency war in which scholars such as David Stoll asserted that peasants and indigenous peoples found themselves caught between two equally unacceptable armed groups (Stoll 1993). Subsequent scholarship, however, has debunked the methodologically flawed and presentist focus of this analysis (see, for example, McAllister 2010).

References

Bejarano, Ana Maria, and Eduardo Pizzarro. 2004. "Colombia: The Partial Collapse of the State and the Emergence of Aspiring State-Makers." In *States-Within-States: Incipient Entities in the Post-Cold War Era*, ed. Paul Kingston and Ian S. Spears. New York: Palgrave Macmillan.

Bergquist, Charles. 1986. *Labor in Latin America: Comparative Essays on Chile, Argentina, Venezuela, and Colombia.* Palo Alto, CA : Stanford University Press.

———. 1996. *Labor in the Course of American Democracy: U.S. History in Latin American Perspective.* London: Verso Books.

Breman, Jan. 2003. *The Labouring Poor of India: Patterns of Exploitation, Subordination, and Exclusion.* New York: Oxford University Press.

Broderick, Walter J. 2000. *El guerrillero invisible.* Bogotá: Intermedio.

Buceli, Marcelo. 2006. "Multinational Oil Companies in Colombia and Mexico: Corporate Strategy, Nationalism, and Local Politics, 1900–1995." Paper presented at the International Economic History Conference, Helsinki, Finland.

Ceballos Melguizo, Ramiro. 2001. "The Evolution of the Armed Conflict in Medellín." *Latin American Perspectives* 116, no. 28: 110–131.
CINEP (Centro de Investigación y Educación Popular)/CREDHOS (Corporación Regional para la Defensa de los Derechos Humanos). 2004. *Barrancabermeja, la otra versión: paramilitarismo, control social, y desaparición forzada 2000–2003*. Bogotá: CINEP/CREDHOS.
Chomsky, Aviva. 2008. *Linked Labor Histories: New England, Colombia, and the Making of a Global Working Class*. Durham, NC: Duke University Press.
Contreras, Victor. 1970. *Barrancabermeja: estudio socioeconómico y administrativo del municipio*. Bogotá: Centro de Estudios sobre Desarrollo Económico de la Universidad de Los Andes.
Davis, Mike. 2006. *Planet of Slums*. London: Verso Books.
Davis, Mike and Daniel Bertrand Monk, eds. 2007. *Evil Paradises of Neoliberalism*. New York: New Press.
Delgado, Alvaro. 2006. "El conflicto laboral en el Magdalena Medio." In *Conflictos, poderes, e identidades en el Magdalena Medio*, ed. Archila N. Mauricio et al. Bogotá: Colciencias/CINEP.
Díaz Callejas, Apolinar. 1988. *Diez días de poder popular: el 9 de abril en Barrancabermeja*. Bogotá: FESCOL/ El Labrador.
Duncan, Gustavo. 2006. *Los señores de la guerra: de paramilitares, mafiosos y autodefensas en colombia*. Bogotá: Planeta.
El Espectador. 2007. "Un empresario de la paz." http://www.elespectador.com. Accessed June 10, 2007.
Farmer, Paul. 1997. "On Suffering and Structural Violence: A View from Below." In *Social Suffering*, ed. Arthur Kleinman, Veena Das, and Margaret Lock. Berkeley: University of California Press.
Farnsworth-Alvear, Ann. 2000. *Dulcinea in the Factory: Myths, Morals, Men and Women in Colombia's Industrial Experiment, 1905–1960*. Durham, NC: Duke University Press.
Gill, Lesley. 2007. "'Right There With You:' Coca-Cola, Labor Restructuring and Political Violence in Colombia." *Critique of Anthropology* 27, no. 3: 235–260.
———. 2009. "The Parastate in Colombia: Political Violence and the Restructuring of Barrancabermeja." *Anthropologica* 51: 313–325.
Graham, Steven. 2007. "War and the City." *New Left Review* 44 (March/April): 121–133.
Grandin, Greg. 2010. "Living in Revolutionary Times: Coming to Terms with the Violence of Latin America's Long Cold War." In *A Century of Revolution: Insurgent and Counterinsurgent Violence during Latin America's Long Cold War*, ed. Greg Grandin and Gilbert M. Joseph. Durham, NC: Duke University Press.
Green, Linda. 2012. "To Die in the Silence of History: Tuberculosis Epidemics and Yu'pik Peoples of Southwestern Alaska." In *Confronting Capital: Critique and Engagement in Anthropology*, ed. Pauline Gardner Berber, Belinda Leach, and Winne Lem. New York: Routledge.
Harvey, David. 2005. *A Brief History of Neoliberalism*. New York: Oxford University Press.
Hristov, Jasmin. 2010. "Self-Defense Forces, Warlords, or Criminal Gangs? Toward a New Conceptualization of Paramilitarism in Colombia." *Labour, Capital and Society* 43, no. 2: 14–56.
Human Rights Watch. 1996. *Colombia's Killer Networks: The Military-Paramilitary Partnership and the United States*. New York: Human Rights Watch.
———. 2001. *The Sixth Division: Military-Paramilitary Ties and U.S. Policy in Colombia*. New York: Human Rights Watch.
Hurtado Isaza, Julia C. 2007. "'Llevaremos la situación hasta las últimas consecuencias': motopiratas." *Vanguardia Liberal*, July 9.
Hylton, Forrest. 2006. *Evil Hour in Colombia*. London: Verso Books.

———. 2010. "Plan Colombia: The Measure of Success." Paper presented at the Latin American Studies Association Meetings, Toronto, Canada.
———. 2012. *The Limits of Voluntarism: The Colombian Left and the Cold War that Never Ends.* Manuscript.
Kramer, Paul. 2011. "Power and Connection: Imperial Histories of the United States in the World. *American Historical Review* 116, vol. 5: 1348–1391.
LeGrand, Catherine.1986. *Frontier Expansion and Peasant Protest in Colombia, 1830–1936.* Albuquerque: University of New Mexico Press.
Levenson-Estrada, Deborah. 1994. *Trade Unionists Against Terror: Guatemala City, 1954–1985.* Chapel Hill: University of North Carolina Press.
Linebaugh, Peter. 1992. *The London Hanged: Crime and Civil Society in the Eighteenth Century.* Cambridge: Cambridge University Press.
Livingstone, Grace. 2004. *Inside Colombia: Drugs, Democracy, and War.* New Brunswick, NJ: Rutgers University Press.
Loingsigh, Gearóid. 2002. "The Integral Strategy of the Paramilitaries in Colombia's Magdalena Medio." Bogotá, unpublished manuscript.
López, Claudia. 2010. *Y refundaron la patria. . . .* Bogotá: Random House Mandadori.
Madariaga, Patricia. 2006. "Región, actores, y conflicto: los episodios." In *Conflictos, poderes e identidades en el magdalena medio, 1990–2001,* ed. Mauricio N. Archila, et al. Bogotá, Colombia: Colciencias/Cinep.
Madero, Régulo. 2001. "Human Rights Violations: Manifestations of a Perverse Model of Governance." http://www.colhrnet.igc.org/newsletter/y2001/spring01art/regulo101.htm. Accessed May 30, 2007.
Markarian, Vania. 2005. *Left in Transformation: Uruguayan Exiles and the Latin American Human Rights Networks, 1967–1984.* New York: Routledge.
Marín, Evangelina. 2006. "Eramos unos soñadores." In *Colombia: Terrorismo de estado-testimonio de la guerra sucia contra los movimientos populares,* ed. Vladimir Carrillo and Tom Kucharz. Barcelona: Icaria.
McAllister, Carlota. 2010. "A Headlong Rush into the Future: Violence and Revolution in a Guatemalan Indigenous Village." In *A Century of Revolution: Insurgent and Counterinsurgent Violence during Latin America's Long Cold War,* ed. Greg Grandin and Gilbert M. Joseph. Durham, NC: Duke University Press.
Medina Gallego, Carlos.1990. *Autodefensas, paramilitares, y narcotráfico en Colombia: orígen, desarrollo, consolidación.* Bogotá: Editorial Documentos Periódicos.
———. 1996. *ELN: Una historia contada en dos voces.* Bogotá: Rodrigúez Quito Editores.
———. 2001. *Elementos para una historia política del Ejército Nacional de Liberación.* Bogotá: Rodrigúez Quito Editores.
Narotzky, Susana, and Gavin Smith. 2006. *Immediate Struggles: People, Power, and Place in Rural Spain.* Berkeley: University of California Press.
Norton, Richard J. 2003. "Feral Cities." *Naval College War Review.* http://findarticles.com/p/articles/mi_m0JIW/is_4_56/ai_110458726. Accessed October 27, 2007.
Restrepo, Juan Diego. 2010. "Estructuras paramilitares desmobilizados en Medellín: de la unificación de la criminialidad a la fragmentación violenta." *Arcanos* 15: 64–77.
Richani, Nazih. 2002. *Systems of Violence: The Political Economy of War and Peace in Colombia.* Albany, NY: SUNY Press.
———. 2005. "Multinational Corporations, Rentier Capitalism, and the War System in Colombia." *Latin American Politics and Society* 47, no. 3: 113–144.
Roldán, Mary. 2002. *Blood and Fire: La Violencia in Antioquia, Colombia, 1946–1953.* Ithaca, NY: Cornell University Press.
Romero, Mauricio. 2003. *Paramilitares y autodefensas, 1982–2003.* Bogotá, Colombia: IEPRI.

Romero, Mauricio, and Angélica Arias. 2010. "Sobre paramilitares, neoparamilitares y afines: crecen sus acciones, que dice el gobierno." *Arcanos* 15: 34–45.

Sánchez, Gonzalo. 2008. *Guerra y Política en La Sociedad Colombiana*. Bogota: El Ancora Editores.

Santiago, Myrna I. 2006. *The Ecology of Oil: Environment, Labor, and the Mexican Revolution:* New York: Cambridge University Press.

Scheper-Hughes, N., and P. Bourgois. 2004. "Introduction: Making Sense of Violence." In *Violence in War and Peace: An Anthology*, ed. Nancy Scheper-Hughes and Philippe Bourgois. Malden, MA: Blackwell Publishing.

Semana. 2007a. "El Intocable?" http://www.semana.com. Accessed June 10, 2007.

———. 2007b. "El Espectador ofrece excusas por publirreportaje con 'Macaco.'" Accessed June 10, 2007.

———. 2008. "Ex-paramilitar aseguró que financió campaña de senador Gaviria." http://www.semana.com. Accessed July 19, 2009.

Sider, Gerland. 1997. "Against Experience: The Struggles for History, Tradition, and Hope among a Native American People." In *Between History and Histories: The Making of Silences and Commemorations*, ed. Gerald Sider and Gavin Smith. Toronto: University of Toronto Press.

Stern, Steve. 2004. *Remembering Pinchet's Chile: On the Eve of London 1998*. Vol. 1 Durham, NC: Duke University Press.

Stoll, David. 1993. *Between Two Armies in the Ixil Towns of Guatemala*. New York: Columbia University Press.

Striffler, Steve. 2002. *In the Shadows of State and Capital: The United Fruit Company, Popular Struggle, and Agrarian Restructuring in Ecuador, 1900–1995*. Durham, NC: Duke University Press.

Striffler, Steve and Mark Moberg, eds. 2003. *Banana Wars: Power, Production, and History in the Americas*. Durham, NC: Duke University Press.

Taussig, Michael. 2003. *Law in a Lawless Land: Diary of a Limpieza in Colombia*. New York: New Press.

Tinker Salas, Miguel. 2009. *The Enduring Legacy: Oil, Culture and Society in Venezuela*. Durham, NC: Duke University Press.

Toro Puerta, Mario Rafael. 2004. *Pendientes de un hilo: el proceso de desafiliación en un sector de Barrancabermeja*. Bogotá: Editorial Buenaventura.

van Isschot, Luis. 2010. "The Social Origins of Human Rights: Popular Responses to Political Violence in a Colombian Oil Refinery Town, 1919–1993." Ph.D. dissertation, Department of History, McGill University, Montreal, Canada.

Vega Cantor, Renán. 2002. *Gente muy rebelde: enclave, transportes y protestas obreras*. Bogotá: Ediciones Pensamiento Crítico.

Vega Cantor, Renán, Luz Ángela Núñez Espinel, and Alexander Pereira Fernández. 2009. *Petroléo y protesta obrera: La USO y los trabajadores petroleros en Colombia*. Volume 2. *En tiempos de Ecopetrol*. Bogotá: Corporación Aury Sará.

Williams, Raymond. 1989. *Resources of Hope:* New York: Verso Books.

Winn, Peter, ed. 2004. *Victims of the Chilean Miracle: Workers and Neoliberalism in the Pinochet Era, 1973–2002*. Durham, NC: Duke University Press.

– Chapter 2 –

Labor in Place/Capitalism in Space
The Making and Unmaking of a Local Working Class on Maine's "Paper Plantation"

August Carbonella

In March 2011, Paul LePage, Maine's newly elected Republican governor, ordered state workers to remove a recently installed mural honoring the history of the state's working class from the lobby of the Department of Labor building. One of the mural's panels portrayed the resolute solidarity that marked the 1987–1988 Paperworkers' Strike at the International Paper Company's (IP) Androscoggin Mill in Jay. It is likely that Governor LePage found this panel, representing as it did a bitterly protracted labor struggle that still stirred the passions of Maine's citizens, to be among the most offensive images confronting "business leaders entering the building" (the official reason cited for the mural's removal). Nonetheless, all representations of labor history in the mural were seemingly egregious affronts to elite sensibilities. In the midst of global protests against neoliberal austerity politics, the governor may well have feared the power of artistic images of labor's past struggles to fuel resistance to his own budget slashing and draconian anti–public sector union proposals. Ironically, his attempt to erase the past from the politics of the present ignited an internet-based "free the mural campaign," which now serves as the hub for communications and mobilizations by social justice, workers' rights, and "Occupy" activists in Maine.

The governor's mural makeover caps a long history of efforts by Maine's corporate and political elites to suppress any form of labor movement connectivity across space and time (i.e., traditions of solidarity) that facilitated democratic demands for better working and living conditions, the expansion of the social wage, and a more equitable distribution of social wealth. As we will see, the imposition of autocratic rule in the paper mill towns during the 1920s and 1930s played a key part in undermining democracy in the state for over sixty years, creating what Osborn (1974) later called the paper plantation. Big-stick tactics, alone, were never sufficient to accomplish corporate goals. Force went hand-in-hand with hegemonic projects initiated by this elite to reshape extant forms of common sense in ways that facilitated, and even naturalized, cooperation between labor and capital in each town.

In this chapter, I focus on the making and unmaking of a local Fordist working class in the neighboring towns of Jay and Livermore Falls, Maine, over the long arch of the twentieth century. My reference to a local working class, however, should not be construed as shorthand for a social formation with an almost organic relationship to place and tradition. As the brief discussion of the mural controversy already suggests, the making and unmaking of class at any spatial scale necessarily involves fierce struggles over geography, history, and class composition itself. These struggles may be separated for analytical purposes, but rarely in practice. Particularities matter immensely, though. In every case, it is how this tripartite struggle is articulated (in both senses of the word), and by whom it is fought, that powerfully shapes the place/space nexus and past/present relationship of a specific class formation.

Over the course of the twentieth century, the working-class community straddling the borders of Jay/Livermore Falls participated in two such tripartite struggles—the paper workers' strikes of 1921–1926 and 1987–1988; the sixty-year period between these strikes was one of relative working-class quietude. In what follows, I explore the making and unmaking of this local working class via the lens provided by these explosive strikes, as well as the forms of historical and geographical common sense that took hold during the interregnum, to chart the powerful, shaping influence of historical and spatial relationships on class composition and experience (Thompson 1966; Mitchell 2005).

Big Paper, Industrial Unionism, and the Making of a Regional Working-Class Public Sphere

The corporate push to solidify autocratic rule began in earnest in 1921, when a newly formed consortium of paper manufacturers, led by International Paper Company (IP), provoked a strike throughout the region. As we will see, this strike was the opening gambit in the consortium's battle to impose new labor relations, destroy unions, and undermine the vibrancy of a regional working-class public, linked and consolidated by a network of central labor councils in several localities. In spite of these widespread efforts to consolidate the power of capital, working-class solidarity in the region proved too powerful for the majority of monopoly paper corporations to surmount. Only IP—the region's largest paper corporation that was rapidly expanding its operations throughout Eastern Canada and the US South— was able to prevail. It used its power to import scores of replacement workers, hire a small army of armed guards, and clog the courts with requests for injunctions leading to mass arrests of union officials and labor organizers.

IP's assault on labor did not occur in a vacuum. The immediate post–World War I period witnessed a double effort by powerful ruling classes, driven largely by US interests, to create, on the one hand, a hospitable global environment to reinvest stores of over accumulated capital and, on the other, to shore up their power in the face of the growing militancy of national working classes and the successes of the Russian and Mexican revolutions (Silver 2003; Smith 2003; Wolf 1999). Prefiguring the combination of neoliberal exuberance and neoconservative nativism characteristic of George W. Bush's presidency, national borders were increasingly tightened to stem mass labor immigration, while they became ever more permeable for the flow of commodities, money, and investment. These efforts by ruling economic and political classes to free markets and immobilize labor simultaneously were consolidated in the imposition of what Silver (2003: 143) argues were the equivalent of today's structural adjustment policies by the International Gold Standard Committee (a precursor to the International Monetary Fund) that served to redistribute social wealth upward and create massive social dislocation and precariousness among the working classes.

In the United States, government and corporate campaigns were initiated that focused on producing or widening differences among laboring populations. Toward this end, the first targets were the associations, clubs, and unions with large immigrant memberships, in an attempt to destroy the forms of cross-ethnic and cross-skill cooperation fostered by the burgeoning industrial labor movement of the 1910s. These attempts to disorganize the industrial union movement crystallized in a series of repressive government actions that came to be known as the Red Scare of 1919–1920. Secretary of War Newton Baker sent federal troops into the steel strike of 1919 to route out the "Bolsheviki and radicals counseling violence and . . . social revolution" (Dawley 1991: 248). Attorney General A. Mitchell Palmer orchestrated a succession of "red raids" on a range of immigrant organizations between 1919 and 1920 that culminated in the arrests of somewhere between five and ten thousand immigrants and the mass deportation of over 250 others (see Levine 1988; Nelson 1989). And in 1920, the well-publicized arrests of Italian working-class activists Nicola Sacco and Bartolomeo Vanzetti on what many considered to be false charges sent numerous other immigrant radicals into hiding.[1] The most insidious action during the Red Scare, however, may well have been the military intelligence's classification of *all* southern and eastern Europeans, Jews, and African Americans as enemies of the state, justifying the mass criminalization and surveillance of whole communities, populations, and organizations (Dawley 1991: 249). Above all, the criminalization of whole populations effectively undercut the influence of radical workers and peasants from other lands in the burgeoning US labor movement and thus dampened organized opposition to the flattening of the wages and intensification of work for all laborers.

IP clearly drew inspiration from these national and international political projects to remake class relations in its localities and persevered in its efforts to implement the American Plan long after the other regional paper corporations had settled the strike. The American Plan was a well-coordinated campaign promoted by the National Association of Manufacturers during the late 1910s and 1920s to create nonunion, or open, shops (see Levine 1988; Montgomery 1987). Its central tenet that workers should not be required to join unions was later enshrined in the "right to work" laws of individual states made possible by the passage of the 1949 Taft Hartley Amendment. IP's intention to operate its mills with nonunion labor was forcefully reiterated by its president, P. T. Dodge, in a statement printed in the *Livermore Falls Advertiser* (April 19, 1922) shortly before the strike's one-year anniversary:

> As long as I am president, no outside union leader will cross the threshold of any of my mills. I am unilaterally opposed to any third party trying to run our business. The strike we had over a year ago [sic] was directed especially against my company and was most unfair. We are now organizing and running our business on The American Plan.

Yet IP did not limit its efforts to a one-dimensional drive to install an open shop, as the American Plan is usually understood. Instead, it deployed a double movement of force and cultural regulation in its determined effort to reshape the work, family, and community relations of its employees. Toward this end, IP marshaled its considerable power and influence to accomplish two primary goals: to disorganize the regional labor movement that linked many of the industry's localities and nurtured labor's collectivized moral order; and, in turn, to localize class relations within each of its mill locations. The company deployed its tactical forces to cultivate both ethnic and geographic difference by provoking "the greatest strike that ever took place within the paper industry" (Gross 1964: 192).

Sizing up equally, perhaps, the looming global and regional threats to unfettered capital accumulation posed, first, by the successful Russian and Mexican revolutions and, secondly, by the growing militancy of the regional labor movement,[2] IP's concern to reestablish control over its workforce clearly outweighed considerations of the financial costs to the company such a strike would unleash. The company had good reason to be worried. Radical and socialist union organizers had become increasingly influential during the 1910s. Despite significant differences of style and perspective, Industrial Workers of the World (IWW, or Wobbly) and Socialist Labor Party leaders, such as Big Bill Haywood and Morris Hillquit, were among the many advocates of radical industrial unionism that struck a chord with a growing population of immigrant mill workers throughout the state during the first two decades of the twentieth century (see Buhle 1995). A huge crowd of mostly Lithuanian and French Canadian immigrants, for example, gathered to hear Elizabeth Gurley Flynn, the young organizer of the 1912 "Bread and Roses" strike in Lawrence, Massachusetts, speak at the IWW Paper Workers Union Local in the IP town of Rumford. When events in Lawrence detained her, Wobbly spokesperson Benjamin Legere quickly stepped in to take her place. Eugene Debs, the Socialist Party leader, similarly drew large audiences during his speaking tours of the state (Scontras 1985). These labor leaders were among a strong cadre of travelling lecturers on Maine's central labor council circuit, who managed to foster a lasting commitment to industrial unionism and working-class solidarity that far outlasted their rather short-lived organizational achievements in the state (Scontras 1985).

Without diminishing the critical importance of the travelling lecturers, it was the more routine organizational, cultural, and political initiatives of the central labor councils themselves that fostered the culture of militant unionism, often incorporating socialist, Wobbly, and AFL affiliates, across the region. This was especially true of the emergent industrial union movement within the paper industry. The industry's two major unions, the International Brotherhood of Papermakers (IBPM, or Paper Makers) and the International Brotherhood of Pulp, Sulfite, and Paper Mill Workers Union (IBPSPMW, or Pulp Sulfite) overcame their fractional differences in 1910 to create an effective alliance, enabling them to organize workers across skill and ethnic lines. They adopted the "one big union" idea, though not the organizational form, of the IWW. In essence, the two unions agreed to compromise on jurisdictional matters and, more significantly, to negotiate and strike together, if necessary. Although the dual union form was a major political weakness that IP would, in fact, later exploit during the 1921 strike, this alliance exemplified the cooperative spirit of the new unionism.

In many respects, interest in both formal and informal cooperation between so-called skilled and unskilled workers grew out of an intensifying technological assault and a series of managerial rationalizations since the turn of the twentieth century.[3] Consequently, workers across all skill levels found employment in IP's mills increasingly dangerous, alienating, and precarious (Gross 1964). Technological assault was central to IP's competitive strategy and centered on the continual reinvestment in faster, wider machines. This strategy was not without significant drawbacks, however. The constantly increasing capital/labor ratio resulted not only in a declining profit margin, but recurrent overproduction. Mills were periodically shut down and large quantities of paper sat in storage. IP frequently used the stores of surplus paper as a weapon to instigate strikes. Forced work stoppages were simultaneously a way to reduce surpluses and an opportunity to increase what Marx called absolute surplus value by pushing workers to accept an extended workday and reduced wages as the terms of a settlement.[4] At the same time, a vigorous standardization program and the subdivision and fragmentation of jobs undermined craft control over various production processes (Smith 1970: 189–218). Between 1900 and 1910 the mills of IP's Otis Division in Jay/Livermore Falls nearly doubled their production capacity while reducing the workforce by almost 40 percent.[5] Meanwhile, wages for skilled papermakers entered a significant downward spiral over the same period of time.[6]

Yet despite these steadily worsening conditions of employment, solidarity between so-called skilled and unskilled workers was stalled for more than a decade by a rigid system of ethnic segregation operating within the mills, residential areas, and the unions themselves. IP's triply enforced segregationist policies temporally forestalled what Mike Davis (1986: 42) elsewhere called "an explosive homogenization of status."[7] IP initiated this coordinated strategy of labor regulation in the 1890s, when it and other monopoly paper companies began their colonization of Maine's economy. A cohort of skilled paper workers, primarily of Irish ancestry, together with others who traced their lineage to elsewhere in the British Isles, were lured from the older paper-making areas of Massachusetts, primarily, with the promise of relatively high wages, profit-sharing plans, and decent housing. At the same time, a much larger group of French Canadian immigrants from Quebec, the Atlantic Provinces, and Maine logging camps, together with smaller but still significant numbers of Italian and Polish immigrants from Massachusetts, were recruited with a promise of steady, albeit low-waged, work in the mills.

With this diverse workforce in place, labor discipline at IP's Otis Division in Jay/Livermore Falls revolved around a system of overlapping ethnic and skill hierarchies.[8] While the machine-driven pace of production and a new managerial mode of coordination[9] made the directive role of skilled machine tenders and pulp engineers increasingly vestigial, IP took great pains to maintain the status differentials that these and other skilled workers had enjoyed in the pre-monopoly paper industry (Smith 1970: 189–218). Skilled papermakers and beater engineers, who had learned their craft in Massachusetts, thus retained the power to hire and fire crews and were noted for their verbal and even physical abuse of subordinates.[10] Meanwhile, French Canadian, Italian, and Polish immigrants were blocked from advancing beyond the status of semiskilled labor.

As noted above, these ethnic and status differences were inscribed in the built environment as well. The tightly packed tenements inhabited by the growing immigrant population in the Chisholm section of Jay stood in stark contrast to the more charming single-family cottages of the adjacent neighborhood of Livermore Falls Village, home to skilled workers and mill supervisors alike. This residential segregation only served to inflame ethnic prejudices of the working-class elite, as the concentrated poverty of the Chisholm neighborhood was attributed to personal failures of the French, Italian, and Polish immigrants who lived there. The renowned poet Louise Bogan's memories of her early years in Livermore Falls, where her father was briefly a mill superintendent, revolved around the brutality that was enacted upon Chisholm residents who dared to cross the town boundaries (see Frank 1986).

These ethnic and status differences ultimately sparked protracted struggles over appropriate forms of union organization and leadership, sustaining a bitter rivalry throughout the first decade of the twentieth century (Graham 1970; Gross 1964; Zieger 1983). The local union hall of the IBPM was the center of social life for skilled workers in Livermore Falls. The IBPM originated as a craftsmen's fraternal order in Holyoke, Massachusetts, in the 1890s, just as monopoly firms were transforming social relations in the paper industry. Eagle Lodge, the name of this first local, emphasized craft solidarity, mutual aid, and male camaraderie. Secret initiation rites and rituals of sociability formed the raw materials for an ideology of craft privilege (Graham 1970; Zieger 1983). The fraternal order, then, provided a social context for the reinvention and recreation of craft traditions and ideals that were increasingly marginalized at the point of production. Skilled papermakers in Livermore Falls maintained this fraternal tradition throughout the first decade of the twentieth century. Frequent meetings, parades, "smokers," and dinners as well as the use of a ritualized discourse of worker respectability, dignity, and fraternity integrated and sustained the craftsmen community (see Clawson 1989).[11]

As may be imagined, the fraternal solidarity of craftsmen did not extend to the newer immigrant groups. In fact, the Paper Makers adopted a protectionist and nativist posture toward the new immigrants, refusing them membership. When they began to form independent local unions, as they did in Jay as early as 1902, the "Brotherhood" pressured the AFL to deny charters to these upstart organizations. The Paper Makers then assumed jurisdiction for all workers in the industry, but tellingly restricted leadership to a close circle of skilled workers. Much like the anti-immigrant hysteria in the United States today, the skilled paper workers blamed their heightening job insecurity and declining fortunes on the rising population of immigrant workers, who were charged with undermining their craft traditions and power (Gross 1964; Graham 1970).[12]

Faced with the Paper Maker Union leadership's intransigence, French Canadian, Italian, and Polish immigrants joined the open rebellion erupting within the IBPM in 1906, which shortly led to the formation of a rival union organized on an industrial rather than a craft basis. Founders of the new International Brotherhood of Pulp, Sulfite, and Paper Mill Workers Union (IBPSPMW, or Pulp Sulfite Union) were clearly influenced by the industrial union model of the one-year-old IWW, an organization that James Fitzgerald, Pulp Sulfite president, expected would soon rival the conservative AFL for power and influence.[13] Like other emergent industrial unions of the period, the Pulp Sulfite Union attempted to unify and represent a sharply divided industrial labor force as part of a larger political project to widen the scope of workers' power on and off the job (Gross 1964). The radical upstart union rapidly developed a strong social base despite the AFL's refusal to grant it a charter. Immigrant workers in Jay/Livermore Falls organized one of its first locals.[14]

Skilled workers who emphasized craft identity above class cooperation were not likely to align themselves with this union movement attempting to transcend their privilege. And the members of the Paper Makers did not disappoint. A bitter rivalry ensued, reaching a critical point when Pulp Sulfite members broke a strike called by the Paper Makers against IP in 1908. The ability of the former to staff and run the paper mills during the strike underscored the actual leveling of skills that had occurred in the paper industry, despite the existence of the industrial caste system and the concurrent discourse of craft. Consequently, the Paper Makers Union was weakened considerably and forced to negotiate jurisdiction with the upstart organization. The two unions reached an accord in 1909, which conceded the majority of paper workers to the Pulp Sulfite Union, with the important exception of the machine tenders, beater engineers and their immediate crews.[15]

Nonetheless, full-blown cooperation across skill and ethnic lines did not emerge until another major strike called by the IBPM in 1910 to protest the punitive conditions that existed at IP since the 1908 strike. Briefly, returning strikers were required to sign a nonunion pledge as a condition of employment. Additionally, they were compelled to work overtime at straight pay, while nonstrikers received the standard overtime rate of time-and-a-half. Most irksome, though, was the installation of a "spy system." Company spies were placed in every department of the mill in an elaborate attempt to root out union activity. Surveillance was maintained outside the mill as well, as spies attended union meetings and informal gatherings. The scope of this company intelligence unit was revealed when a small cohort of workers who attended a secret union meeting found "blue cards" in place of time cards the following morning.[16] The one hundred members of the Paper Makers Union in Livermore Falls walked out in protest. But, more general conditions—tours of eleven and thirteen hours, seven days a week, for barely subsistence wages—brought out the four hundred members of the Pulp Sulfite Union in sympathy.[17]

Even before the 1910 strike, however, a mood of conciliation between the two unions was apparent. The previously conservative *Paper Makers Journal* began carrying political cartoons from the socialist *New York Call*, a paper that regularly called for the reorientation of the Socialist Party toward the mass of immigrant proletarians (Buhle 1995: 68). One suggestive political cartoon portrayed a brutish personification of the "paper trust" beating back the proletarian "slaves" with the twin clubs of "oppression" and "wage cuts."[18] The incipient cooperation symbolized by the cartoon materialized in a stunning victory for members of both unions in the 1910 strike. The two unions negotiated with IP as one entity for a contract that instituted the eight-hour day, a 5 percent immediate wage increase—leading to 20 percent over five years—and the establishment of grievance committees for all workers.[19]

The collaboration of the two unions within the mills created significant momentum for a broader-based collaboration within the public sphere as well. As we will see, the creation or expansion of existing institutions, constituting a regional working-class public, dramatically altered the political and cultural landscape within and among the paper mill towns in Maine and New Hampshire and served to anchor regional working-class solidarity. The regional network of Central Labor Unions (CLU) became the primary institutional anchor of this emergent working-class public among spatially distant communities. Although formally associated with the Maine and New Hampshire Federations of Labor, the CLU's, as mentioned above, were becoming a bastion of socialist influence in the region. One result of this rising socialist influence was their coordination of a dynamic regional program of working-class political and cultural activity across industry, skill, and ethnic lines (Scontras 1985: 120). A growing sense of solidarity was apparent in Jay/Livermore Falls shortly after the 1910 strike. Theatrical performances (featuring performances by members of both paper unions), benefit dances for striking workers in other areas, and visits by travelling union and socialist lecturers were among the kinds of weekly events hosted by the CLU.[20]

The local CLU, in effect, constituted a sphere of cooperation and continuing self-formation for the steadily expanding labor movement. By 1920, ten unions regularly held biweekly or monthly meetings in the CLU, representing, among others, retail clerks, glove factory seamstresses, carpenters, woods workers, musicians, along with the paper workers.[21] And the types of activity offered by or in conjunction with the CLU were considerably expanded to reflect the increasingly diverse membership. Weekly dances, a consumer cooperative, and baseball leagues, supplemented the lectures, political forums, and union meetings.[22] Sports competitions, for one, served as an important means to ritualize and, ultimately, negotiate tensions between ethnic groups. Heavily attended parties and dances frequently followed the games. An indication of the extent to which a vibrant working-class public lessened ethnic hostilities is indicated in local workers' memories of the growing proclivity for interethnic marriage during the 1910s.[23] Other forms of cultural production were equally important for instilling a sense of common identity and solidarity among this diverse population, including union journals that published worker poetry and fiction (reflecting the pervasive influence of the IWW, perhaps), as well as news of labor conditions throughout the paper industry, the region, and the country. The constitution of this local working-class public sphere through the CLU's participation in a regional network of labor councils allowed geographically separated, and ethnically divided, working populations to create a language of labor; this language helped them make sense of their shared conditions and, ultimately, forge a common class identity.

Moreover, it was the union's control over hiring within the area's paper industry that significantly enhanced this common class identity. This tactical power facilitated the circulation of workers in and around the region and gave them a measure of informal control over their working lives. They could take short "vacations" or "French leave" from the increasingly dangerous working conditions of the mill to work on family farms in Quebec during planting or harvest seasons, find temporary work in area sawmills or logging camps, or even test out the working conditions in another paper company. This element of tactical power seems to have been specific to the region as it is not mentioned in the historiography of the national unions.[24] It does, however, turn up in the oral histories and reflections of local and regional paper workers, who recall that initial hiring and continued employment was contingent upon union approval.[25] IP's official history of the Otis Mill in Jay/Livermore Falls also refers to a continual rehiring of workers who "went off on a lark," as well as the high rates of quits and truancies during the 1910s.[26] This migratory practice significantly built up a network of intimate relations throughout the region and even beyond. Workers in other towns and mills were no longer an abstraction, but former work mates, drinking buddies, and confidantes.[27] This expanded spatial perspective created an intimate sense of class belonging and solidarity, a perspective both sustained by and sustaining of the regional working-class public sphere.[28]

The production of this working-class commons[29]—via the production, practice, and valuation of collectivity—went way beyond what would become the rather ordinary union focus on the wage bargain. Instead, an emphasis on the common good was fostered within this regional space. It was not only within this space, however. Wider organizational, political, and ideational networks linked regional struggles to national and international movements. The traveling lecturers, the socialist organizers, and the union publications, carrying news and ideals from elsewhere, were the embodiments of these networks that enabled Maine's working class to withstand attacks on their rights to organize and a livable wage for over a decade, while creating a powerful counterargument to outsized corporate greed and the social inequality that always follows in its wake. But as we previously saw, powerful corporate and government forces were already planning their war of maneuver and creating the social hysteria necessary to whip up support. The consequent political disorganization of the working-class commons should not, however, be seen as a single act of enclosure. It is better understood as the inaugural moment of a slow process of dispossession that would end in 1987, with the erection of a chain-link fence around IP's flagship mill in Jay that served to keep replacement workers in and Jay workers out.

Americanism and Fordism: The Remaking of a Local Working Class

We are now in a better position to understand both IP's unyielding stance during the 1921 strike: in particular why its drive to create localist affinities and identities were critically important to its strategies of labor regulation and the advancement of Fordist moralities. Over the course of the 1920s and 1930s, IP's mill towns were reimagined and remapped during a massive campaign to rearticulate workers' patterns of loyalty and allegiance to a new political/cultural configuration dominated by capital. Toward these ends, IP employed a broad repertoire of powers to reassert its control of labor and the entirety of social life outside the mills, an affirmation of Mario Tronti's notion of the social factory avant la lettre. Over time, and under pressure of IP's regulatory regime, localism would violently replace solidarity as the key word of working-class life and experience.

IP's provocation of the 1921 Paperworkers' Strike was not in any way an isolated event, however. It was, as we have seen, part of a wider campaign by US industrialists to install the American Plan or, to use Antonio Gramsci's (1971) more apt formulation, Americanism and Fordism.[30] Corporate/industrial elites' ability to marshal a powerful configuration of forces—state, police/military, and paramilitary—that were gathering strength in the late 1910s around the "Americanist" project, buoyed their belief that the moment was right to mount a frontal assault on labor and, more importantly, to win. The consolidation of this repressive power bloc began with the Wilson administration's successful pressuring of Congress to pass the Sedition Act of 1918, which legalized the repression and deportation of immigrants associated with radical causes (especially anarchists, socialists, and Wobblies). The Palmer Raids, or Red Scare (1919–1921), spanning both the Wilson and Harding administrations, took full advantage of the Sedition Act to terrorize and deport immigrant labor and political activists. At the same time, the Ku Klux Klan (KKK) experienced a rebirth in the North as an anti-immigrant paramilitary organization and the American Federation of Labor (AFL) deployed an increasingly nativist stance on immigration. Both of these developments were nurtured within the Red Scare's vortex of racial hatred and anti-immigrant hysteria, providing radically different poles of support for the attacks on the rights and power of organized labor.

If nothing else, the constellation of powers marshaled against the industrial labor movement indicates the strength that the latter had achieved during the 1910s. When IP's workers went out on strike, then, they acted from this position of strength. And they did not act alone. They were part of a large industrial force across the country that struck en masse to protest both the well-coordinated assault on their right to organize and the increasing corporate regulation of their work, family, and social lives (Levine 1988; Montgomery 1987). The standoff of these two powerful blocs of capital and labor, while never equal, suggests why all elements of the American Plan could not be introduced simultaneously or as a package in all places.

In Jay/Livermore Falls (and I imagine elsewhere) celebrations designed to encourage forms of interclass conviviality and patriotic citizenship, for example, were only gradually incorporated into local commemorative festivities. Tensions ran quite high for years. Yet, once a significant number of workers had returned to the mill, others permanently left the area, or found work elsewhere, William Murray, IP's local mill manager, made a number of paternalist gestures and initiated a hegemonic project to reorient working-class political affinities and identities to the locality and a carefully constructed cultural localism. The critical focus of IP's corporate hegemony was more than simply cultural; it involved the restructuring of "community as a relation of production," to draw upon Daniel Nugent's (1993: 150) useful formulation.

The creation of IP's localism necessarily involved, of course, the destruction not only of unions, but the regional labor movement, its culture of solidarity, and its socialist-inspired emphasis on the greater common good. Given IP's manifold mandate to transform labor organization, culture, and politics, it may be easy to see why members of its corporate hierarchy did not hesitate at times to deploy all available means—from court injunctions and police or militia violence, to mass firings and mill closures—to achieve their goals; nor why at other times they turned to paternalism. A single-minded emphasis on increasing corporate profits appeared to justify all means to that end.

As the most powerful monopoly corporation in the paper industry, IP's hard-line position may well be attributed to the fact that it, alone, was well poised to take immediate advantage of the expanding geography of paper production. Recent political and technological developments facilitated the expansion of the paper industry, both beyond national borders and to new areas of production. Protective tariffs were removed in 1913, erasing the constraints of shipping newsprint across the US/Canadian border. At the outset of the 1921 strike, IP already was shifting newsprint production to Canada. By 1923, the *Weekly Financial Review* designated IP's paper mill in Three Rivers, Quebec, as "the most modern and efficient in the world."[31] More, the 1921 invention of a new pulping process made soft pine a viable substitute for spruce and fir in paper production. Soft pine was abundantly available in the southeastern United States, an area long known for its harsh, anti-union laws and policies. IP's corporate heads had to know that they would shortly be able to expand into the South and take advantage of its relatively cheap labor supply. Indeed, by the end of the strike, IP had opened a half dozen mills in the South.[32]

These political and technological advantages offered IP secure ground to demand a restructuring of its "relations-in-production" (Burawoy 1985). By the end of the strike's first month, company officials made it known that there would be no return to the status quo. While its mills were still closed, IP presented a number of ultimatums to union representatives, stating that, henceforth, employees across the board would receive wage reductions of 15 to 30 percent (depending on skill level); the working day would be lengthened from eight to twelve hours (eliminating one shift and therefore involving a massive reduction in the labor force); most jobs would be reclassified as unskilled; and a whole category of workers, to be designated as "common labor," would be removed from the union's bargaining unit by corporate fiat and paid "locality" wages. At the same time, IP declared its intention to continue bargaining with "representatives of skilled employees." As we will see below, this rather obvious attempt to drive a wedge between the Paper Makers and Pulp Sulfite Unions coincided with both explicit and more subterranean efforts to rejuvenate earlier forms of ethnic antagonism. Further, the corporation used the local press and strategically placed fliers to reaffirm its position that "all contract proposals were nonnegotiable" and that it would not hesitate to open its mills if necessary with "competent new employees."[33]

IP made good on its threats during the summer of 1921. The paper giant reopened its mills with strikebreakers, all of whom were transported by train to each locality; broke off relations with its unions; placed heavily armed private guards around its mills; and evicted strikers from company-owned housing. In response to IP's provocations, violence erupted in all IP locations in the northeast, but nowhere as intensely as along the sixty-mile stretch of the Androscoggin River, from Berlin, New Hampshire to Jay/Livermore Falls, Maine—the epicenter of IP's corporate empire. In each Androscoggin locality, strikers protested, picketed, rioted, and stormed trains filled with their incoming replacements to defend their rights to livelihood, decent wages, security, and union representation.[34]

Nonetheless, IP remained resolute in the face of the strikers' sustained resistance and used its vast power to solidify its autocratic power in each locality. IP's oppressive reign began with its successful petitions to the courts for injunctions, which treated the fact of a strike as sufficient evidence of a crime. Over fifty years later, a local paper worker vividly recalled the intensity of the resulting prosecutory climate:

> Well the thing to watch during that time was, ah, about every week there was a list of injunctions served by the court. You couldn't even walk the streets, you

see. It was a violation of court order, and all you had to do was have somebody accuse you of violating the order and bang, you were in for thirty days.[35]

Armed with these injunctions, sheriffs randomly stopped motorists and pedestrians, intimidated and arrested pickets, and attempted to stop nonresident union organizers and officials from entering town.[36] The correspondence of a Pulp Sulfite regional labor organizer, who was arrested three separate times for violating court orders in Berlin, Rumford, and Jay/Livermore Falls, hints at the damage caused by the consequent legal costs and time lost to the union's effectiveness: "[I]t seems so as if we all [are] going to be arrested, at least a large number so we will not be able to secure bonds."[37]

The legalized repression of union organizers and the state-sanctioned intimidation of strikers and their supporters in the company towns heightened the political discourse surrounding the strike, if not always the strategic analysis. During a mid-August rally in Chisholm, Paper Makers Union President James Carey charged that IP's relentless pursuit of power and profit had turned workers into industrial slaves.[38] Notwithstanding its fiery political rhetoric, what was not said in Carey's speech that day provides a hint that IP's multifaceted attack was already taking its toll on the solidarity of the two dominant paper industry unions. It is not surprising that such sustained structural and physical violence would cause a rift, especially given that the Paper Makers Union had always been the weak link in the regional labor movement and that its membership stood to gain substantially from crossing the picket lines. Hence Carey's silence that day carried much significance. Carey made no mention at all of the divisive potentialities embedded within IP's reclassification of labor. Nor did he proffer any strategies for defeating the company's politics of ethnic differentiation, providing an early hint of the Paper Makers' eventual retreat into "bread and butter" or business unionism.

Carey's silence on the matter would be easy enough to chalk up to the exigencies of rallying support for the unions if the Paper Maker–dominated local publicity committee had not similarly remained mute on the issue, as it elaborated on Carey's pronouncements on "industrial slavery" some months later with a call for the emancipation of workers. In both cases, the evocations of "slavery" and "emancipation" were deployed to call for the restorations of workers' rights to a livelihood, union protections, and a livable wage, not to advance a vision of a new social order based on principles of economic and social justice. In the context of unchecked repression and unrestrained capital accumulation, Carey's and the committee's statements certainly served as critically important public interventions. Yet their combined thematic emphasis on jobs, wages, and trade unionism suggests the extent to which socialism was already becoming an absent signifier in local and regional political discourse.

It is not possible to know if any effort to "speak for hope" (Williams 1989: 322) at that moment of danger would have served to bolster strikers' resolve or even stem the ever growing trickle of skilled workers (IBPM members) back to the mills in the days and weeks between Carey's speech and the committee's publication. In any event, what emerged as the Paper Makers' "hands-off" approach to IP's coded ethnic segmentation of labor, an issue already of growing concern to the leadership and the largely immigrant membership of the Pulp Sulfite Union, signaled the growing divergence of foci and concerns that would shortly lead to a deep rupture in the forms of cooperation and solidarity that had united the two paper industry unions and their members throughout the previous decade.

Despite Carey's hesitation publically to acknowledge the revival of the industrial caste system, now officially classified as an ethnic segmentation of labor, during the strike's first months, he could not have been unaware of the growing tensions between members of the Paper Makers and the Pulp Sulfite unions. At the time of his fiery speech in Chisholm, IP was already two months into its concerted campaign to lure Irish and Anglo machine tenders, beater engineers, and other skilled laborers back to the mill with promises of permanent jobs, increased authority, and even supervisory positions.[39] At first, the campaign was only moderately successful. But by the late fall, a significant cohort of skilled Irish and Anglo laborers had broken the picket lines to return to work. Their defection created an immediate domino effect. The correspondence of Pulp Sulfite labor organizers chronicled this privileged cohort's accelerating rush to reclaim jobs in all IP mills along the Androscoggin River. They also contained frequent entries about the ongoing efforts of "scabs" to convince more adamant strikers to follow suit.[40] Although a small number of French Canadian, Italian, and Polish skilled workers also returned to work, they were nonetheless reassigned to less responsible positions than were their Irish and Anglo peers. Despite these desertions, the majority of immigrant workers, classified en masse as "common labor" in absentia, remained determined, as one local labor organizer noted, "to see the strike through to the end," an end, as it turned out, that would not be officially declared for another five years.[41] But a sizable contingent of immigrant workers stayed out as long as they could, some to the very end of the strike, as they returned to farms or millwork in Quebec and Acadia, sought factory work in Massachusetts and beyond, or found work in Maine's textile factories, lumber camps, sawmills, or other paper mills. Unionist activists, placed on IP's blacklist, experienced this precariousness for many years.[42] For all intents and purposes, however, the skilled workers' return to work throughout the fall of 1921 and winter of 1922 marked the unofficial end of the strike.

IP's reintroduction of a stark ethnic segmentation of labor had the desired effect. It severed the fraternal ties between the two unions and their members and therefore crumbled the very foundation of the regional working-class public. A deep bitterness remained in its wake. Despite the fact that a small number of French Canadian skilled workers, for example, also broke ranks and returned to work, it was the perceived eagerness of Irish and Anglo workers (increasingly identified jointly as Yankees) to profit from IP's favoritism that provoked the greatest ire. After this, ethnic affiliation rather than class solidarity rapidly became the key axis of social life, albeit with an interesting twist. During my conversations with elderly French Canadian residents, I noticed a frequent slippage in ethnic categories. When talking specifically about their childhoods or early adulthoods, they frequently referred to the close relations among French Canadians, Italians, and Poles in Chisholm. However, when talking about the tense relations of all three groups with their Irish and Anglo adversaries, only two ethnic categories seemed relevant: French and Yankees. This condensed classificatory scheme seems to have been based, in part, on the small numbers of Italians and Poles left in Chisholm after the strike, as well as the perceived ascendancy of Irish Americans to "Yankee respectability" at the same time. More importantly and accurately, it captures both the broad classifications used for IP's ethnic segmentation of labor, as well as the deep social divisions between the "French" and the "Irish" that followed in the wake of the "strike of '21." Further, these "everyday" classifications suggest that the 1920s, and the vortex of racial panics and state violence that characterized the "age of anxiety," was the moment when the Irish began fully to enjoy the "wages of whiteness" (Roediger 1999).

Evidence of the lasting ethnic enmity can be seen in the way that mental maps were subsequently redrawn. This is strikingly illustrated in the contrasting descriptions of local social relations offered by two retired French Canadian workers from Chisholm, who differed in age by fifteen years. The older worker came of age in the 1910s and served as recording secretary of the Pulp Sulfite Union during the late 1910s and early 1920s. His map thus included both Chisholm and Livermore Falls:

> Oh, this was a strong union town. The union hall was like a club. We used to go down there [the Central Labor Union in Livermore Falls] for entertainment; we had weekly dances there, parties, card games. There wasn't much else to do around here, so we all got together there.

The younger worker, who came of age in the 1930s, drew much starker boundaries:

> There were no businesses in Jay or Chisholm. We had to shop in Livermore Falls. At one point, we even intermarried with the Irish [before 1921]. We all worked for the IP. But, the people who lived in Livermore Falls were considered lousy Yankees. Even now [1991] the people of Jay and Livermore Falls are enemies, especially in sports. After World War II, when all the returning GIs started having kids all at once, it was suggested that one big school be built for both communities to save money. Do you think us Frenchmen are going to do anything with those goddamn Yankees? Never!

Although little more than a decade separates the youths described by these recollections, the younger worker's heavy emphasis on boundary maintenance and ethnic hostility clearly differentiates his community from the more inclusive one described by his elder. The reimagined ethnic community he describes accurately captured the growing insularity of social life in Chisholm, which came increasingly to center on St. Rose of Lima Catholic Church and *la survivance*, a resurgent nationalism that historically articulated resistance to British colonialism in New France (Quebec). In Maine, from the 1920s on, la survivance facilitated the revitalization of "French" identity and culture. Although Italians and the remaining Poles also attended mass at St. Rose's, the clergy's primary concern was the conservation of French Canadian faith, language, and culture (see Gerstle 1989), preaching from the pulpit the importance of family obligation, group loyalty, and communal reciprocity and supervising "French only" social functions in the parish hall.

The revival of French identity was not an isolated phenomenon. Italian social life and identity increasingly centered on the local chapter of the Sons of Italy, though without the almost millenarian intensity evident among the French. The Knights of Columbus Hall became one bastion of Irish sociability, IP's Murray Hall, named after the local mill manager and built in 1926 to replace the CLU as the center of local social life, became another locus of Irish male camaraderie, shared with their Anglo counterparts. Although officially a community center, the Irish and Anglos were disproportionally represented on Murray Hall's governing board and greatly influenced its social and cultural activities. Most tellingly, Murray Hall became a key site for the revitalization of craft and fraternal rituals from the early era of the Paper Makers' craft unionism. The monthly boxing matches, for one, preceded by a "smoker" (with free cigars supplied by the company) restored the forms of male camaraderie and fraternity that earlier sustained the "craftsmen community."

The feverish production of difference—centered on family, church, lodges, and exclusivity—created a local public sphere that, if not exactly bourgeois, largely existed "behind closed doors" (Habermas 1991: 35). Doors, however, never seemed to be closed to IP's powerful mill managers, who increasingly assumed the roles of local patrons. William Murray, superintendent of mills in the 1910s and 20s, was ever present at the Murray Hall smokers and the Knights of Columbus dinners. He headed the local "citizens' committee" that yearly evaluated the cleanliness and neatness of workers' homes during "citizenship competitions," which he also organized. Murray also established a health department, whose function was not to provide medical care, but to send nurses to workers' private homes to instruct families about diet, abstinence from alcohol, and sanitary practices. Murray's replacement, T. G. Magnan, held a permanent perch in the back pew of St. Rose's to ensure that all workers attended the 8:00 a.m. mass at St. Rose's on Sunday, their only day off. Local lore during my initial fieldwork in 1990–1991 even had it that Magnan had direct access to the confessional via his regular meetings with priests, where workers' most private fears and frustrations were discussed.

In the face of such heavy-handed paternalism, there was literally no place left for an autonomous working-class culture or practice of solidarity. Members of the different ethnic groups increasingly came together only as part of the "IP family." And Murray Hall steadily replaced the CLU as the center of social life. Within that corporate space "citizen education weeks," not socialist forums, held sway. "IP family" picnics pushed aside the Labor Day Parades and festivities that so recently had held preeminence on the social calendars of workers and their families. And ethnic difference trumped class solidarity.

To return to the enclosed mental map of the younger French informant, we can now see why, over time, the increasing insularity of ethnic culture and identity wound up providing an unintended support for dominant social divisions and hierarchies. Specifically, especially among the French, memories of the strike were increasingly framed by ethnic hostilities, while IP's role in the perceived ethnic betrayal was registered only by its gaping absence. But material, political, and social circumstances in the decades following the strike also facilitated the production of this selective memory. Of these, the classification of most immigrant workers as "common labor," and the increasing precariousness that followed in its wake, was the most significant.

In any event, IP's massive reclassification of labor was registered more as a result of political betrayals and collaboration with the enemy than with IP's original act of structural violence. The older resident of Chisholm, mentioned above, recalled bitterly that the AFL did not support the strike in any way, but he found the AFL's nativism during the early 1920s to be far more of a betrayal. Well into his nineties when we spoke, he offered few details beyond saying, jaw clenched, that the national AFL leadership worked against the French. We can imagine, however, that as recording secretary of the union he participated in many discussions with the socialist leadership of the Pulp Sulfite Union about the AFL's campaign to restrict immigration from Canada, which only fanned the flames of a more generalized panic about the porosity of the Canadian/US border. He was just as likely to have had read the article by James Davis, US Secretary of Labor, in *The American Federationist (AFL Journal)* alluding to French Canadians as illegal aliens or perhaps to have directly experienced the Ku Klux Klan's violent assaults on French Canadians in Maine's logging camps during the early 1920s (see Ramirez 2001; Scontras 2002). What he did talk openly about, however, was his twenty-plus years of insecurity as a result of being blacklisted and only being able to find work in the woods or shoveling coal for the railroad, often making less than ten dollars a week.

Common laborers in the paper mills did not fare much better. During the 1930s, IP paid common labor less than twelve dollars a week, a figure well below half of what the US Bureau of Labor Statistics considered the minimum necessary for a family of four.[43] This made subsistence on one wage packet virtually impossible for French Canadian families, to take the most numerous immigrant group, who usually had six, and sometimes as many as ten, children. In addition, their insecure employment derived from the petty despotic power of mostly Irish and Anglo foremen and department supervisors, who hired, fired, and assigned work on the basis of ethnicity and favoritism. As one French Canadian recalled about his work experience at IP in the 1930s: "Irishmen made all the hiring decisions. Of course, their friends and family got jobs on the paper machines first. We Frenchmen might wind up in the wood yard."[44] Once hired, the possibilities for promotion were extremely limited, if not nonexistent. The classification of almost 70 percent of job categories as common labor left little room to move up.

The control of promotions and everyday job assignments by foremen, boss machine tenders, beater engineers, and department supervisors, in fact, solidified a system of clientage, centered on the performance of "favors." To take a commonly mentioned example, foremen could, and regularly did, demand that workers provide a steady supply of liquor during a vacation week at their hunting cabins, on their birthdays, for holidays, or just on a whim. Workers who did not comply with these demands were often reassigned to the most odious and backbreaking jobs. Or a worker might simply be summoned out of bed to work an extra shift, since being on call twenty-four hours a day was a condition of employment.[45] Moreover, personalistic hiring practices often served as an informal reinforcement of IP's blacklist. The new bosses, who benefited substantially by crossing the picket lines, were not likely to hire the union activists who angrily confronted them as they entered the mill.[46] Local workers recalled that these discriminatory hiring practices frequently included members of labor activists' extended families.

More, during slack times, only married men were kept on the payroll; single men were laid off. Given the paper industry's general propensity toward overproduction, frequent shutdowns or slowdowns were common. These selective layoffs intensified during the depression; unmarried men had to shape up for work at the beginning of each shift. The foreman of each department would pick from the assembled group of workers according to need and favoritism. The instability inherent in this system meant that single men could not save enough to get married and start a household; all the wages they were able to earn went to the reproduction of the parental household. The expanded nuclear family thus became an important social form that enabled a reserve labor force to wait out periods of underemployment or joblessness. At the same time, the relative surplus labor of unmarried men served both to suppress wages for all workers and ensure an adequate labor supply during peak periods.

Mapping the Kingdom of Freedom: Localism in Jay/Livermore Falls

A society can proclaim the Kingdom of Freedom is at hand when compulsion passes for spontaneity and adaptation no longer exists either in word or concept.
— Henri Lefebvre, *Everyday Life in the Modern World*

When I first began my field research in Jay/Livermore Falls, I asked local workers how or why they decided to work for IP. Most simply scowled at my ignorance. Those who took pity on me answered in one of two ways. The first focused on geography: "If you're going to live around here, you work for the IP." The second focused on family and history: "It's what my father did, my grandfather too; basically, that's all there's ever been around here." Over the course of my fieldwork, I came to understand the scowls. My question was naively posed with an assumption of (free) choice. In contrast, workers' responses to my questions revealed a tightly constructed sphere of circulation, articulating and defining a terrain of work, family, and community. Workers identities, aspirations, and values were shaped and defined on this terrain; their movements constrained within it as well.

Their responses also revealed a silent, if unwitting, testimony to the success of a hegemonic project begun by IP in the 1920s. Since that time, a constructed localism and an enforced isolation were the twin axes around which IP's claims to community, history, and morality were advanced and sustained. The genealogies and mental maps of local workers expressed the taken-for-granted nature of this produced social geography and history. But other understandings of territory and tradition were potentially available. During the 1910s, as we have seen, the regional labor movement fostered and sustained very different spatial perspectives and traditions. Yet some seventy years later, the class-based historical and geographical common sense produced within the regional working-class public sphere had long been displaced by the transformations of tradition and territory that literally took *place* in the interregnum. The story of how local workers learned to forget the previous geography and history of class identity and solidarity is embedded within IP's profound reorganization of work and daily life since the 1930s. And it is to that story that I now turn.

IP's strategies of labor control were necessarily modified following the passage of Wagner Act of 1935. This centerpiece of New Deal legislation provided a charter for union organization and established the National Labor Relations Board (NLRB) to regulate the capital/labor relationship. The return of unions to IP mills, and with it the systemization of grievance procedures, significantly reduced the arbitrary and personalistic power of the foremen, for one. But as one may suspect, given IP's unyielding anti-union stance,[47] the paper giant found ways to use components of the Wagner Act to consolidate its 1920s initiatives to localize class relations and center the regulation of labor on "rationalized" family life. Here I refer specifically to two constituent elements of the new legislation: first, its linkage of collective bargaining to local level negotiations and elections, making the creation of a system of decentralized labor relations a real possibility; second, the tying of wage gains to increases in productivity, bringing the "family wage" within reach of a growing segment of the labor force.

The devil is, of course, always in the details. The meaning of any law is not determined by its codification, but rather unfolds over time via the struggles that ensue over its perceived implications, subtexts, and underlying principles. That certainly held true for the Wagner Act. It was put into practice in a rather piecemeal manner, as unions and corporations squared off against each other to expand or limit, respectively, the geographical span of union organization, the wage bargain, grievance procedures, and workers' rights to strike, for starters. History and geography figured prominently in workers' struggles, particularly, as existing loyalties, organizational forms, spatial networks, and command of space served either to bolster or weaken their ability to shape the evolving labor/capital compact.

The Wagner Act codification of labor's right to organize, together with mandated collective bargaining, inaugurated an explosion of union organizing drives and the emergence of the CIO on the national stage (see Davis 1986; Negri 1994). The reverberations emanating from both New Deal labor legislation and the revival of militant unionism were immediately felt throughout northern New England. The United Mine Workers' District 50 waged successful organizing drives in Maine and New Hampshire during 1937 (Graham 1970: 19–23). District 50's resounding organizing victories in Rumford, Maine, and Berlin, New Hampshire, two of the critically important nodes of the 1910s regional labor movement, clearly signaled that labor activists had not completely disappeared from the region after the defeats of 1921. Rather, it seems, they were laying low waiting for a political opening in which to reclaim some strategic advantage (Zieger 1984: 184).[48]

Yet, as we will see, the unions' defeat in the strike of 1921 ultimately set the terms of organized labor's return to IP's mills. Union organizing drives taking place on the West Coast greatly influenced this outcome, if in a rather unexpected way. Two progressive CIO affiliated unions—the International Woodworkers of America (IWA) and the International Longshoremen and Warehousemen Union (ILWU)— were threatening to organize paper workers in the Pacific Northwest (Lembcke and Tattam 1984). Paper companies throughout the region immediately attempted to reestablish relations with the Paper Makers and Pulp Sulfite unions (Graham 1970). The AFL unions' complicity in this corporate "war of maneuver" quickly reversed their sagging fortunes, as one after another West Coast paper corporation rushed to sign labor contracts in an attempt to forestall the return of militant unionism (Graham 1970). Both unions had been all but moribund since the 1921 strike. More, John Burke, president of the Pulp Sulfite Union and former socialist, had been humbled by defeat. The rest of the socialist leadership was long gone, and with it went the union's emphasis on mobilization and solidarity. Now representatives of each of the AFL paper unions approached the major paper companies with metaphorical hats in hand.

IP management similarly jumped at the chance to sign with its erstwhile foes. In 1937, as the organizing drives were heating up along the East Coast, IP held secret negotiations with the two AFL unions, securing from each an assurance of future labor peace. The AFL unions thus signed a labor agreement in October 1937 that (re)unionized IP's mills without conducting any organizing drives or, most tellingly, making any contact with workers.[49] In fact, local workers in Jay/Livermore Falls first heard about the agreement from their foremen, who simply told them that they had to get a union card before they reported for work the next morning. There were many cynical reactions to this news. Retired workers frequently told me that the company simply wanted to stick union labels on the paper rolls. In the aftermath of the Wagner Act, unionized printers were said to be rejecting paper made in nonunionized plants. One former union official told me that the mill superintendent kept the "union labels in the safe. He watched them like they were dollars." But apathy was the most common response. Many veterans of the 1921 strike joined only under protest. Others simply adopted a wait-and-see attitude toward the unions.

Meanwhile District 50 continued to exert significant pressure on its AFL rivals. Its negotiating strategy suggests the radical union's growing appeal among "common laborers." By insisting on across-the-board flat wage increases for all workers, District 50 achieved a significant reduction of wage differentials between common laborers and their skilled counterparts. As may be expected, this move alone created a groundswell of support for District 50 among labor's lower ranks.[50] The Pulp/Sulfite Union only adopted this strategy in 1941 in an effort to stave off defections to District 50 and the CIO. And it was done over IP's vociferous objections and the extreme hesitations of the Paper Makers' leadership.[51]

The other significant gain associated with unionism was the institution of the seniority system beginning in the 1940s. This again was a reaction to District 50's successful undermining of the personalistic and/or arbitrary power of foremen by instituting an internal job ladder in the mills within its jurisdiction; a procedure that significantly extended the Wagner Act's original linkage of wage gains to increases in productivity, but that was instituted only as a result of a shrewd negotiating strategy by District 50. The job ladder rationalized job placement and promotion by defining a regular procedure based on seniority. An expansion of job classifications accompanied the seniority system, resulting in a steady decline in both the length of time workers were employed as common laborers and the unskilled/skilled worker ratio.[52] The expansion of semiskilled jobs and the seniority system was considered a significant victory for workers and helped bolster support for the unions.

The two AFL unions could not ignore the success of District 50 and the CIO unions in establishing the seniority system, nor could IP, since the threat of radicals displacing the AFL unions was ever present. In the neighboring town of Rumford, for example, District 50 and the now chastened Pulp Sulfite Union constantly engaged in open warfare and raids on each other's membership.[53] Once instituted, the seniority system allowed workers greater control over their work lives. Now, job promotions were fundamentally based on skill level and seniority. When skill levels were relatively equal, seniority determined promotions. It also regularized layoffs; no longer were marital status or family connections the deciding factors.

We can already begin to see how ethnicity steadily lost its power as a social and labor classificatory scheme under the double impact of the Wagner Act and radical unionism. Steadily rising incomes and advancements had a profound social and cultural impact within the community. Ethnic hostilities were significantly reduced in the postwar period. In fact, ethnicity itself played a far smaller part in social organization. And the expanded nuclear family form faded, as young workers were increasingly able to start their own households in their early twenties and even in their late teens.

Militant Particularism in Boom Times: IP's Postwar Consolidation of Power

By the onset of the postwar era, collective bargaining procedures had rationalized production within the paper industry, as elsewhere, and were radically transforming its social relations of production. IP workers, like their counterparts in other heavy industries, gained a substantial degree of control over their work, family, and social lives. For IP, however, any amount of worker autonomy, no matter how slight, seemed to reignite the question of labor control. Notwithstanding its initial hostile reception to the Wagner Act, IP began to exploit collective bargaining procedures to secure two outcomes: forestall the possibility of its workers' uniting in coordinated action across space and intensify work within each place.

Throughout the postwar period, militant particularism and familial authority defined working-class life in Jay/Livermore Falls. IP's heightened search for new mechanism of labor regulation during this period demonstrates this process well. Within the framework of collective bargaining procedures, IP successfully relocalized the capital/labor relationship and reinvented patriarchy as a significant form of labor regulation. Yet localism was now maintained more through economic incentive and compulsion than through cultural intervention. And patriarchal authority now served to maintain a strict sexual division of labor within nuclear families, rather than guarantee a flexibly deployable labor force.

We may begin by looking at the process through which IP relocalized the capital/labor relation. In a skillful manipulation of collective bargaining procedures, IP played one locality off against another in a process unionists call whipsawing (see Kasmir, this volume).[54] Whipsawing exploits the system of decentralized labor relations by putting one location in competition with another for jobs, raises, and security. IP entered into a series of localized negotiations that simultaneously expanded the opportunities for capital accumulation and limited the ability of the unions to bargain effectively over local issues, much less to mobilize united actions across space. A longtime union organizer and negotiator captured this dynamic well in our conversation. Discussing the events leading up to the two union locals' decision to withdraw from the regional bargaining unit,[55] he noted (and it is worth quoting him at some length):

> We were in the northern division, which bargained together for certain issues like wage rate raises. But the company would bleed that, saying things like: "If you want a raise then we'll have to shut this or that mill down. We won't be able to keep them going." Now all the mills in the northern division were marginal mills until they built the Androscoggin Mill in Jay [1964]. That mill was going to town, new machines, new everything. All the other mills could do was hold us back. I was around when other mills got held back because they wanted to help out their brothers in another mill. The

members said, "Let's not take the raise now because if we do they'll close the other mill down." Well, guess what, they closed it down anyway. That's when I started pushing to opt out of the northern division. I didn't want the Jay mill to be stuck in that trap, so I stood up to it. IP wanted us to join the northern division. Then they could start shutting mills down. They shut a lot of them down anyway. Corinth was taken out of the northern division. The company was always playing one local against another. Locals often fought more amongst themselves than with the company. Everybody's out for blood for their local. Local 14 of the IBPSPW was the biggest local, and they backed me in pulling out of the northern division. Then Luccarelli [local president of the IBPM] got his guys behind the idea. After that I got four 10 percent and two 10.5 percent raises.

No one ever talked about going into the northern division again. Then the company started shutting down mills. Everyone said "Whew," this is the way it works. No matter what they said, they'd shut down the mills anyway. You can't trust them. But they used the older mills for leverage. See, they wouldn't shut them down right away. They learned the game. They'd start pounding on you way ahead of time, saying something like they were going to run a mill five more years. We'd better start using this plug now. They'd say, "Hey, if you want that mill to keep running or run better, give us some leeway. We need some money to put into the mill to keep it running. So if you demand the raise, well okay, we'll give it to you, but we're going to have to shut that mill down." Then everybody says, "Let's help our brothers out; let's not take the raise." But the company did long-range planning. They would run a mill for five more years while they built another and got it going. Then they'd say we [the unions] fought them every inch of the way, and that's why they closed the mill down. But they planned to shut it down right from the get-go. Once the divisions were broken up, all the locals were given different expiration dates for their contracts. It's hard to back up another local on strike if your contract still has another year-and-a-half to go.[56]

The increasing geographical isolation evident in this passage dramatically affected the politics of unionism. Paper workers in Jay/Livermore Falls increasingly became indifferent to the plight of their peers in other localities, especially after the new Androscoggin Mill was built in the 1960s. The limited spatial perspectives of workers in Jay/Livermore Falls during this period is illustrated by common expressions of confusion after they were displaced during the 1987 strike: "I always thought we *were* the IP"; "I barely knew that IP existed *anyplace but here*." The homogenizing tendencies inherent in the Wagner Acts' socialization of the wage contract thus had the ironic effect of increasing territorial divisions and antagonisms within the paper industry and most others as well.[57] National labor laws, both the Wagner Act and the 1947 Taft-Hartley Amendment, which made unified labor action exceedingly difficult, bolstered corporate spatial strategies, such as IP's. Nonetheless it took the cooperation of the unions to make it work. The Pulp Sulfite and Papermakers unions, now raised from the ashes of 1921, were only too willing to cooperate.

The political actions of local workers in the postwar period, in those rare moments when they happened at all, were extreme expressions of what Raymond Williams (1989) called "militant particularism," or placing a heavy emphasis on protecting existing wage bargains to the almost total exclusion of all other political considerations. In 1972, for example, IP organized a protest against Maine's new Land Use Regulation Commission. Buses of paper workers from Jay/Livermore Falls traveled to LURC hearings to protest its attempt to regulate timber harvesting.[58] A few years later, local unionists started a letter writing campaign to protest a settlement by the Indian Lands Claim Commission in Washington that restored three hundred thousand acres of paper industry–controlled land to the Penobscot Indians, a settlement that the paper industry's public relations campaign painted as a threat to the livelihood of paper and timber workers. No mention was made, however, of the fact that the paper industry controlled over seven million acres of land in Maine.[59] Nor, for that matter, was there mention of the ecological devastation that paper industry toxins caused to rivers, forests, and reservoirs.

As the labor negotiator's discussion of whipsawing indicates, the postwar era witnessed IP's unrestrained expansion. Workers agreed to higher levels of technology, faster, wider paper machines, and extensions of the working week in exchange for higher wages and job mobility. Intensified capital investment dramatically increased the capital/labor ratio in the Androscoggin Mill. The ever-expanding scale of the operation surprised even longtime paper workers. Paper machines, which even in the late nineteenth century symbolized the automatic production process,[60] were now massive monuments to alienated labor. The length of two football fields and two to three stories high, the paper machines established a grueling pace of production that completely consumed workers' physical and mental energies. An anecdotal story may serve to illustrate this point. During fieldwork, I set up a series of interviews with a displaced paper worker. A physically vibrant man in his early forties, "Joe" answered my questions with a great deal of wit and insight. One day he announced that he had been "called back" to the mill as temporary summer help, so the next time we met would have to be after his shift. When he arrived for our next meeting, I barely recognized him. Within a week, he seemed to have aged ten years. Physically and mentally exhausted, he could barely speak and our conversation ended quickly.

There are two intimately related points to be made here about the high rates of capital investment. First, the monumentally asymmetrical capital/labor ratio dramatically reduced IP's profit margin. The machines had to be run constantly for profit to accrue. Second, workers had to be available to staff the machines at all times. IP addressed this dual necessity by reinventing patriarchal authority within nuclear families.

As mentioned earlier, the family structure changed significantly in the postwar era. As a regularized system of promotions and steady wage increases eliminated the necessity for a multiple-wage strategy, the nuclear family became increasingly important. The postwar boom in housing construction also provided significant support and encouragement for smaller families. Houses built in Jay/Livermore Falls after the war were largely single-family homes, with two or three bedrooms. Family networks retained their social importance, however. They provided the primary social group for all leisure and mutual aid activities. For example, kitchen doors were never locked so that family members and friends of the family could simply "pop over" for a visit, for dinner, or for a favor. This "pop over" tradition is well captured in a local saying: "If you have to knock, you're not welcome."

The nuclear family may also be profitably seen from the perspective of the tactical uses it served in the transformation of the social relations of production (see Bloch 1971). We can start by exploring how patriarchal authority was significantly reinvented to make it more functional for IP's regime of intense capital accumulation. The implementation of the "Southern Swing," a revolving tour system, in the early 1950s was the primary catalyst for the reinvention of patriarchy. The Southern Swing, named for its origins in the historically anti-union US South, required employees to work one week on the day shift, the next on the overnight shift, and the next on the afternoon shift. Another significant feature of the Southern Swing is that it required workers to remain on the job until their replacements arrived. Thus, workers were often required to work double, even triple shifts. This tour system virtually eliminated machine "downtime," therefore accomplishing one of IP's central goals. But it was not simply a function of having adequate staffing arrangements. It served to enforce a strict sexual division of labor within the family. Wives' abilities to work outside the home were severely curtailed by the demands placed on them by the Southern Swing. Without fixed schedules or any predictability to the working week, wives found it difficult to keep jobs. Having to leave work to pick up a sick child from school, or to miss a night shift, or a few shifts because one's husband could not leave the mill, provide a sense of how precarious women's employment outside the home had become. More, no family emergency or special event was considered reason enough to refuse a shift. IP employees say they often missed crucial events like a child's high school graduation because of work demands. Moreover, the whole life of the family revolved around the husband/worker. They slept odd hours, sometimes for whole days to recuperate. They ate meals at odd times, and always shifting times, requiring the preparation of multiple meals for different members of the family. Family life was defined by production schedules and the needs of exhausted mill workers. The comments made by wives of workers displaced during the 1987–1988 strike give a sense of the impact of the Southern Shift on an entire family. One commented:

> Before the strike, [he] would come home and just sit on the couch. He seemed depressed all the time. I actually thought it was caused by his experience in Vietnam. We never really knew what they went through in the mill. The guys never talked about it. Once the strike began, there was a guy I had never seen before living in our house. He was smart, funny, and seemed to have enormous energy.

The second wife's comment indicates how this exhaustion impacted the family:

> I never knew my husband had a sense of humor. He was grumpy all the time. We literally walked on eggshells when he was home. He was always yelling at the kids to be quiet so he could sleep. I only got to see his lighter side after he left the mill and began working for the union.

Steadily, workers' lives had become routinized into a seemingly endless round of working, eating, and sleeping. The Southern Swing ensured that this "simple reproduction of labor power" was not interrupted by other demands on workers' time. A working wife, for example, would have created multiple conflicts of interest. Meals would have to be prepared; children shuttled back and forth to school or childcare; and attention paid to the multiple details that are necessary to maintain a household.

Increased mobility within the company and steadily rising wages can only partially explain why workers and their families put up with long days, multiple shifts, and the exhausting pace of work. A fuller explanation is given by IP's and other paper companies' control over external labor markets. The large paper companies controlled most of the state's major timber resource and sold access to it in ways that systematically discouraged the development of potential competitors for labor, especially after 1945. Sawmill and lumber industries in Maine were given only short-term permits to harvest timber, if they could secure them at all, while Canadian firms were given more favorable considerations. The unreliability of the wood supply has continually discouraged the financing of large sawmills within the state. The ones that did exist were low-profit, labor-intensive ventures, whose pay and benefit scales, if any, were well below those found in the paper industry. For a sense of contrast, we need only look to the northwest coast, where huge lumber mills set wage and benefit standards for the entire timber industry, including the paper industry.[61]

IP's social landscape of power, constructed over the span of sixty years, had an enormous impact on the way workers' life histories were eventually constructed and understood. Adult life histories were seen as a series of movements from insecure jobs in area sawmills to a more secure position in the paper mill. Or, alternately, as a movement from one position to the next within the paper mill itself: from woodpile worker, to pulp room operative, to machine tender, or, perhaps, foreman. Family chronicles were articulated in similar fashion as a movement from poverty and precariousness to relative security. One paper worker recounted how his father, who worked in area lumber mills and shoe shops all his life, never had much money. He, on the other hand, could regularly afford to buy "meat and good stuff, not just baked beans or macaroni and cheese." As the angry stares of workers subjected to my naive questions about their career choices suggested, these genealogies and mental maps represented the taken-for-granted nature of IP's transformations of tradition and territory since the 1920s. And, they underscore the company's success in creating a tightly circumscribed sphere of circulation that shaped and informed workers' identities, aspirations, and values. But they would soon find that nothing at all could be taken for granted. The 1987–1988 Paper Workers' strike in Jay, to which we now turn, marked the violent end to the labor accommodations characteristic of the Fordist era in that locality and, ultimately the demise of this local working class.

The 1987 Jay Strike and the Unmaking of a Local Working Class

The top-down unionism that displaced the more horizontal organizational forms exemplified in the regional labor councils provided the institutional backbone for the development of militant particularism, or struggles over the local wage bargain and the protection of jobs to the exclusion of all other political considerations. This bifurcation of work from politics was instrumental to the vitality and longevity of the corporate rule that characterized the region for seventy years.

It was interrupted in 1987 by a strike in Jay, which started out as a form of militant particularism—a protest against the imposition of flexible labor practices, as well as massive salary and workforce reductions, understood as direct threats to job security and the existing wage bargain.[62] This concern was not based on idle speculation. During the early 1980s, IP signaled its intention to dismantle its social compact with labor by publicly mocking its founding tenet and basis: localism. The corporation radically reversed its policy of decentralized decision-making with the creation of a new human relations department in 1984 to push through sweeping changes in work rules. The HR department was charged with implementing programs and policies developed at corporate headquarters, a move that, among others, significantly reduced the decision-making responsibilities of the local superintendent of mills. From its very inception, then, the HR department held a malign significance. Casey Lavoie, a former "local boy" who made his way into management via a stint as president of Local 14 of the United Paperworkers International Union (UPIU) in Jay, was transferred from Wisconsin to head this new department.[63] Lavoie's reputation as a "born-again" anti-unionist augured sweeping changes in corporate labor relations. But lest the point be lost, Lavoie announced his assigned mission to break the union within three years at a family gathering shortly after his return. If the full significance of the setting of this announcement was not immediately apparent, it became obvious during the paper workers' strike of 1987–1988. With Lavoie's appointment, IP was reorienting and restructuring the cultural/ideological terrain on which its corporate hegemony was built. At stake was IP's ability to remove itself from the notion of community it had so carefully constructed since the 1920s, and from the sense of mutual responsibility between capital and labor that this concept then evoked.

IP reinforced this point before the strike even began by installing a massive, barbed-wire security fence around the mill and setting up a trailer park within this new enclosure that would eventually house replacement workers imported from southern states by the infamous strikebreaking firm, B.E. & K. Much to the strikers' chagrin, they realized how dramatically the rules of the game had changed over the past decade; a local strike action—even when joined by locals from three other IP mills across the country in a loosely coordinated action—was not sufficient to halt a global corporation's aggressive assault on what they saw as their very "way of life." As labor strategist, Peter Kellman, put it to a community-wide assembly in Jay's newly anointed "Labor Temple" in the early fall of 1987: "The strike won't be won here. It can certainly be lost here. But it can be won only by expanding to the state and national levels." Over the next fourteen months, the strike morphed into a broad-based social movement for economic and social justice, mobilized around the idea of working-class solidarity.

While attempting to develop an adequately spatialized response to looming dispossession, the ambiguous memory of the five-year-long strike of 1921 repeatedly flashed up in conversations in the union hall, around dinner tables, and with elders. The question of what exactly had been lost during that earlier strike seemed particularly urgent in these discussions, as strikers, their families, and local supporters struggled to make sense of both the hushed tones and vague warnings of the few old-timers still around to remember. When I began my research on the 1987–1988 strike in the early 1990s, in fact, I was more than a little surprised to be continually directed back to the "strike of '21," especially since very few folks seemed to know much about it. In time, I came to understand that their evident interest in that vanquished history centered on the very radical question of whether or not another life had once been possible and could be again. In that moment of political and economic dispossession, the need of local workers to chart a new communal life course turned on efforts to restore the reciprocities of past, present, and future.

Yet the transformations of class composition, territory and traditions in the intervening years had, as mentioned, imbued the strike of '21 with incommunicable significance, to borrow E. P. Thompson's evocative phasing (1980: 132). The ensuing political consequences for strikers laid not so much in the loss of some liberationist potential of the past, à la the utopian interpretations often given to Walter Benjamin's (1969) more nuanced identification of the Janus-faced nature of history. Rather, the reigning historical amnesia precluded a politically enabling discussion of how the past defeat of the regional labor movement produced the present, and what that might mean for the creation of a viable response to the mounting neoliberal assault they faced in the 1980s. In the end, the strike of '21 lived on in the present as a variant of Marx's "dead weight," conjuring up more fear than hope.[64]

We can begin to see here the politics of space and its importance in facilitating or hindering the retrieval of historical legacies of class struggle. Yet IP's exercise of power over the preceding sixty-odd years did more than make some narratives possible while silencing others (Trouillot 1995). It also forestalled the consolidation of a political strategy to link strikers from different localities in united action across space (Harvey 1989). Not only had the historical legacies and spatial practices of the 1910s regional labor movement been rendered unavailable by IP's half-century-long production of its geography of power, but also the consolidation of regional solidarity in the present was similarly foreclosed. The marginalization of woods workers, both in the regional economy and in the consideration of paper mill workers, increased significantly in the post–World War II era. Their precarious employment, remote residences, and increasingly tension-fraught relations with mill workers seemingly made them unsuitable collaborators in what would become one of the most significant US struggles to rebuild working-class solidarity in the 1980s.

This long process of spatial enclosure and political isolation prompted Peter Kellman's enunciations during the tactical arguments of the 1987–1988 strike's initial stages. Within a very short time, striking members of Local 14 of the United Papermakers International Union in Jay had managed a remarkable feat; they revitalized a working-class public that centered on weekly mass meetings of over two thousand people in Jay's Community Center, now renamed the Labor Temple. These mass meetings evolved from their origin as forums for union business to central sites for strikers and their supporters to both imagine and enact an oppositional community to that put forward by local corporate functionaries and their political allies in the region. The mass meetings were the crux of Local 14's strategy to usurp local political power. And this strategy worked extremely well. Union members, for example, ultimately won all five seats on the town council.

Yet it remained a pyrrhic victory at the dawn of neoliberal globalization. When the paper workers protested IP's abrupt withdrawal from the labor/capital deal that had long defined their working lives by calling a strike in 1987, they were genuinely surprised to see how quickly they could be replaced. There was no shortage of woods workers, for example, willing to cross picket lines given their precarious existence, which they partly attributed to the paper workers' continuous refusal to support their demands for higher prices. Moreover, the strikers were astonished by IP's relentless pursuit of profit over loyalty to both place and employees long professed in its civic endeavors. Perhaps most perplexing, however, was their realization that their national union lacked both the mechanisms and the desire to empower them by connecting their labor struggle to those in other IP locations. As Local 14 activists began to travel throughout the United States to build support for the strike, for example, they were stunned to find that their strongest opposition came from the majority of regional representatives of the UPIU. Their own regional representative refused even to supply Local 14 activists with contact information for other IP union locals.

Institutional complacency within the national union was, in part, the product of the codification of locality bargaining procedures in both the Wagner Act and the anti-solidarity prohibitions of the Taft-Hartley Amendment. Yet the failure of regional UPIU officials to grasp the immediate threat to collective bargaining, and unionism itself, served as a wake-up call. Reading the signs, Kellman and Local 14 President Bill Merserve argued persuasively that business-as-usual bargaining procedures were wholly inadequate in the face of sustained and coordinated assaults on workers' rights. Indeed, the contours of the consolidating neoliberal attack on worker and citizen rights were already made clear in a global chain of antidemocratic political actions: the 1973 US-backed military coup in Chile that installed the brutal dictatorship of Augusto Pinochet, Ronald Reagan's mass firing of striking air traffic controllers in 1981, and Margaret Thatcher's brutal repression of the 1984–1985 UK miners' strike. Such repressive political regimes, and the manifold enclosures and expropriations that they enacted, ushered in a new era of enhanced global capital investment, production, and finance (Midnight Notes Collective 1990).

In this new global political and economic climate, Local 14 activists realized that solidarity would have to be built from the ground up and increasingly drew upon Kellman's long experience in the antiwar, civil rights, and labor movements in their effort to create new class-based alliances to bolster the declining power of unions. Local

14's emphasis on alliances and new political practices was evidenced by their innovative (yet ultimately unsuccessful) use of cross-country caravans to establish solidarity with other unionists, garner public support, and bring the geographically dispersed UPIU locals into a common bargaining and strike pool.

Clearly, this innovative action by Jay strikers' to build a workers' movement across space posed a direct challenge not only to the postwar geography of capital accumulation, but also to the geography of unionism that facilitated it. Yet here we can see the political consequences of the forestalled rapprochement of the socialist past and radicalizing present. The mentalities and strategies of 1980s strikers were clearly approaching those that flourished during the heyday of 1910s labor movement, especially within the regional working-class public sphere. Had the strikers of the 1980s actually been able to draw on the lessons of the past, however, they may have placed a greater emphasis on building a working-class movement that addressed the neoliberal project to restore capitalist power in a more holistic manner. Their effort to increase negotiating power through the creation of a common bargaining and strike pool was certainly a step in the right direction. But their failure to attempt the mobilization of all workers in the forest industry—from the precarious woods workers, to the independent wood haulers, up to the highest-paid machine tenders—registered the lingering influence of the US labor movement's political insularity. Ultimately, the historical legacy of restrictive labor laws, corporate localism, and labor differentiation within Maine's "paper plantation," together with the mounting neoliberal assault on workers' rights proved too much of an obstacle to surmount.

In the end, all twelve-hundred-plus workers lost their jobs, and only a small percentage of them were ever called back to work. As it turned out, IP's provocation of the strike was merely the first step in a long relocation strategy to move jobs and investments to areas with even less stringent labor, environmental, and wage regulations. A simple list of some key transactions will suffice here. In 1998, the paper giant began buying up paper mills in Russia and has steadily increased its investments in the former Soviet Union ever since. In 2004, IP sold off all of its forestlands in Maine and New Hampshire, some 1.1 million acres. And the next year, the company sold its Androscoggin Mill in Jay to Verso Paper Company, which now operates the plant as an open shop.

From this perspective, it is clear that the unmaking of this local working class did not happen from a single act of enclosure alone, dramatically announced with the erection of the barbed-wire security fence around the mill. Instead of a one-time event, it is better understood as a long process that began with the previous enclosure of the working-class public in the 1920s, along with the systematic dismantling of its linkages to wider organizational, political, and ideational networks. This disorganization of working-class power was subsequently consolidated by the localism and militant particularism that increasingly defined workers' political perspectives between 1921 and 1987. Consequently, while Jay workers' worldview hardly extended beyond the tightly circumscribed borders of IP's company town, the corporation itself increasingly secured its profits within the interconnected spaces of its continually expanding global empire. As in 1921, IP used its enormous spatial advantage to defeat the strike and destroy the union. While the strike was still on, for example, IP began what Funding Universe[65] called a decade-plus buying spree, acquiring corporations in the United States, France, Germany, New Zealand, and Poland, among others.

Conclusion

Jay's paper workers' enormous difficulty in establishing the political connections among IP company towns, their UPIU affiliates, and the full range of forest industry workers necessary for victory was the result of protracted twentieth-century labor battles, hegemonic campaigns, and political/legal resolutions that increasingly tied working-class resistance to particular places while, at the same time, allowing capital to transcend spatial scales in pursuit of lower labor costs and higher profits. This produced what I call the historical geography of US Fordism, characterized by cultural localism, political isolation, and geographic unevenness. Corporations and their supporters in public office ably exploited these spatial features during the transition to neoliberalism to permanently disorganize the Fordist working class and, ultimately, secure new labor relations centered on what we now understand as a generalized global precariousness.

It thus becomes clear in hindsight that Local 14's scale-jumping initiatives did not, literally, go far enough. Although certainly innovative and far-reaching for the time (and threatening to the status quo within the national union's hierarchy), they remained caught within the outdated local/national nexus mapped during the 1920s and 1930s at an important transitional moment when IP and US capital, more generally, were globalizing their operations at warp speed. Encumbered within this spatial nexus, they were forced to direct their petitions for redress to the very same Reagan-appointed National Labor Review Board charged with ringing the death knell for unionism and collective bargaining. Despite their innovative and far-reaching efforts to revitalize radical unionism in the face of the neoliberal attack on their rights, then, Local 14's most progressive activists could not ultimately overcome the political and organizational hurdles imposed over the previous fifty years of corporate rule and increasingly restrictive labor legislation, even within their own local. There was a sizable cohort, led by Local 14 Vice President Felix Jacques, who strongly objected to what they called Kellman's "outside" interference in local affairs and who worked with UPIU's regional representative to limit union activity to proscribed collective bargaining procedures. For this latter group, at least, the long slippage into forgetfulness hindered their ability to confront the past in the present and fully envision another historical geography of organization and activism.

Almost a quarter of a century after the unionized paper workers' defeat, it is worth pointing out that the provocative actions by the current republican governor of Maine, Paul LePage, have had the ironic effect of ensuring that the lessons of the 1987 strike are not lost on the current generation of Maine activists. This historical memory is shaping their evolving public conversations about how unions were destroyed, the connections between the assault on collective bargaining and the flattening of the social wage, and how the 1 percent plundered the global social wealth. In short, the governor's attempt to foreclose a discussion of working-class history has served, not to erase "class," but to push it dramatically to the center of public attention and discussion. Now, however, class is increasingly understood as a global relationship. The connection between IP's displacement of Jay workers and its global investment and production strategies is certainly not hard to see. And most importantly, questions are erupting on how best to think through the remaking of the neoliberal global order. With access to this historical knowledge, their spatial imaginations are becoming grounded in both place and space, paralleling the flows of capital and labor: locally, regionally, *across* borders, continents, and oceans.

Acknowledgments

My research was funded by grants from the Robert F. Wagner Sr. Institute for Urban Public Policy at the City University of New York Graduate Center and Wenner Gren Foundation for Anthropological Research. I thank Gavin Smith and Jane Collins for their careful reading and editorial suggestions; Michael Blim, for his discerning comments on a much earlier draft that remained helpful; Lesley Gill, Don Kalb, and Rex Clark for the enriching conversations; Sharryn Kasmir for the many insights shared during the long development of this project; Peter Kellman, for sharing his vast knowledge of Maine's labor history, pointing me to crucial archival documents, and facilitating my fieldwork in countless ways; and Patricia Musante, my first editor, for the thought provoking conversations, close reading, and theoretical acumen that kept me from getting mired in the details, and most of all for making the process of writing fun. Special thanks are due to all the people of Jay/Livermore Falls who invited me into their homes to share their experiences and stories.

Notes

1. The Saco and Vanzetti arrests and subsequent death sentences were a flashpoint of radical sympathies and anger in the 1920s. Their case was the inspiration of numerous books, poems, and stories, most notably John Dos Passos's *U.S.A.* trilogy, which was started just one day after he was arrested at a Massachusetts protest for clemency (see Barbara Foley 1993: 434–435; Cary Nelson 1989: 148).
2. See Charles A. Scontras's (1983; 1985; 2002) studies of Maine's labor history.
3. David C. Smith (1970: 189–218, 593–661); 20th Annual Report of the Maine Bureau of Industrial and Labor Statistics.
4. Maine Bureau of Industrial and Labor Statistics, 1908.
5. Maine Bureau of Industrial and Labor Statistics, 1899 and 1910.
6. Reports of the Department of Labor and Industry, 1902, 1903, 1906; Maine Bureau of Industrial and Labor Statistics, 1908, 1910.
7. Edwin Riley, the first general manager of IP in Jay/Livermore Falls, organized skilled workers of Irish and English descent in patriotic associations that facilitated their socialization and identification with the town's petty-bourgeoisie. *Livermore Falls Advertiser* (April 20, 1908).
8. International Paper Company (1948a).
9. "Taylorism," named after Frederick Taylor, the well-known inventor of scientific management. Taylor, in fact began his career in Maine's paper and pulp mills.
10. International Paper Company (1948).
11. The IBPM's local activities were regularly reported in the *Livermore Falls Advertiser* between 1900 and 1910, much like any other fraternal organization in the town.

12. International Paper Company (1948); Maine Bureau of Industrial and Labor Statistics, 1910 report.
13. James Fitzgerald correspondence to IBPSPMW Executive Board; cited in Keith Emery Voelker (1969: 44).
14. Maine Bureau of Industrial and Labor Statistics, 1906 report; for a wider perspective on the IBPSPMW's social base, see Robert Zieger (1983).
15. Maine Bureau of Industrial and Labor Statistics, 1910 report; Robert Zieger (1983: 25); Harry Edward Graham (1970: 4–5).
16. Maine Bureau of Industrial and Labor Statistics, 1910 report.
17. Maine Bureau of Industrial and Labor Statistics, 1910 report.
18. *Paper Makers Journal*, June, 1908.
19. Maine Bureau of Industrial and Labor Statistics, 1910 report.
20. *Paper Makers Journal*, February, 1911.
21. Reports of Maine's Department of Labor and Industry (1913; 1920).
22. Wilfred Gonya, 1971 interview. Tape 600, Maine State Federation of Labor Collection, Northeast Archives of Folklore and Oral History, University of Maine, Orono; Dossithee Gossilin, 1991 interview.
23. Reported numerous times by elderly informants.
24. See, particularly, Robert Zieger (1983); Harry Edward Graham (1970); James Gross (1964).
25. Dossithee Gossilin, former recording secretary of Local 8, Pulp/Sulphite Union in 1919–1925, interview 1991; Joseph White, tape 672, Maine State Federation of Labor Oral History Collection.
26. International Paper Company (1948).
27. An exchange of marriage partners within the paper mill towns of Jay/Livermore Falls, Rumford, and Berlin, New Hampsire, appeared to be a fairly regular occurrence, as indicated by the recollections of elderly informants and by the weekly listings in the *Livermore Falls Advertiser* during the 1920s of local residents en route to or returning from visiting kin in the wider region.
28. Eric Hobsbawm (1964) discusses the importance of the "tramping artisan" for the development of a nineteenth-century English labor culture.
29. I draw here on such diverse scholars as De Angelis (2007), Linebaugh (2009), and Harvey (2010), who equate commons with the production, practice, and valuation of collectivity.
30. The Fordist marriage of Taylorism and the assembly line or drive had already become an established fact of industrial work life by 1921. In the paper industry, however, it was the combination of Taylorism and the continuous process paper machines that set the pace of work and determined the organization of labor.
31. *Livermore Falls Advertiser*, January 31, 1923.
32. International Paper Company (1948), *International Paper After Fifty Years*.
33. *Livermore Falls Advertiser*, July 27, 1921.
34. Stories of strike violence, not just in the Androscoggin River region but throughout the IP system, were carried almost daily or weekly in Maine newspapers, especially the *Lewiston Evening Journal* and the *Livermore Falls Advertiser*, during the summer of 1921.
35. W. E. Gonya (ibid.).
36. *Livermore Falls Advertiser*, October 5, 1921.
37. Correspondence of PSPMW organizer Jacob Stephans to John Burke, dated November 8, 1921, International Brotherhood of Pulp, Sulphite, and Paper Mill Workers Union Records, 1906–1957, Cornell University Library, Collection No. 5432mf.
38. *Livermore Falls Advertiser*, August 15, 1921.
39. This was a growing concern all through the strike. John Burke, president/secretary of the IBPSPMW, appeared worried about the company's practice of getting "as many

men on salary ... and out of the union" as possible in a letter to a local organizer. See John Burke correspondence to Jacob Stephan (July 21, 1921).
40. Correspondences of Jacob Stephan and George Brooks (IBPSPMW organizers in Maine and New Hampshire) to John Burke: Fall, 1921.
41. Correspondence of Jacob Stephan. Papers of the IBPSPMW.
42. Dossithee Gossilin, former recording secretary of Local 8, Pulp/Sulphite Union in 1919–1925, interview 1991; Joseph White, tape 672, Maine State Federation of Labor Oral History Collection.
43. This figure is derived from interviews with elderly French Canadian residents, but finds support in Robert Zieger (1983: 70).
44. Interview, October 30, 1991. In this case, the interviewee requested anonymity, a common request during the time of my initial fieldwork in the early 1990s, which itself spoke volumes about the repressive atmosphere in this mill town. People were afraid not necessarily for themselves, but the repercussions for their families if it became known that they had cast IP in an unfavorable light.
45. Workers frequently referred to Doc Allen, whose only job it seemed was to roust paper workers from their sleep and bring them back to work.
46. *Livermore Falls Advertiser*, September 27, 1922.
47. In their important study of the contemporary global forest industry, *Pulping the South*, Carrere and Lohann (1996: 107) still found it necessary to characterize the now global paper giant in terms of its "aggressive anti-union stance."
48. IP closed its mills in Rumford and Berlin after the 1921 strike. IP was never able to break the strike in Berlin and arranged to sell its mill in Rumford while workers there remained on strike. The very different political trajectories of Berlin and Rumford, on one side, and Jay, on the other, was very likely the result of the fact that other large paper companies existed in the former cities, and other employment was available. Berlin, especially, still exhibited a vital working-class public into the 1930s. Indeed, it was one of the few cities in the United States where the Labor Party was victorious during the depression (see Davin and Lynd 1979: 118–169).
49. Harry Edward Graham (1970: 31–33). Graham argues that the 1934 Longshore strike had much to do with the paper companies decision to sign with the AFL unions, who now presented themselves as moderate alternatives to the CIO unions. See also Robert Zieger (1983: 135–142).
50. Robert MacDonald (1956: 108–128).
51. Robert MacDonald (1956: 108–128); Robert Zieger (1983: 195–201).
52. George Lambertson, 1991 interview. Lambertson was a longtime organizer for District 50 in the western Maine and New Hampshire region. He later became a regional representative for the IBPSPMW. See also Robert MacDonald (1956: 124).
53. Lambertson interview (ibid.).
54. The politics of "whipsawing" is well documented in Eric Mann's (1987) piercing monograph of a local UAW campaign in Los Angeles.
55. Representing workers now at IP's flagship Androscoggin Mill in Jay, which opened in 1964.
56. George Lambertson, 1991 interview.
57. See Sharryn Kasmir (this volume), Gordon Clark (1989), and Andrew Herod (1998).
58. Details of that meeting are found in William C. Osborn (1974: 240–247).
59. Fact sheets and form letters for the mail campaign were given to me by members of Local 14 in 1990 to show how, as they put it, politically naive they were in their unquestioning support of IP. See William C. Osborn (1974) for an expanded discussion of the paper industry's elaborate public relations apparatus in Maine.
60. See Karl Marx's (1976: 503) discussion of the paper industry.

61. See William C. Osborn (1974: 129–136) and David C. Smith (1971: 419–430). For the northwest, see Harry Edward Graham (1970), Jerry Lembcke and William Tattam (1984), and Patricia Marchak (1983).
62. See Julius G. Gettman (1999), Peter Kellman (2004), and David Richer (1990) for deeply insightful discussions of the political implications of the 1987–1988 Strike in Jay, Maine, and Minchin's (2006) important expanded focus on the three other UPIU locals participating in the strike.
63. Holding local union office became the surest path to a management position from the 1960s on with the opening of the Androscoggin Mill.
64. Expressed, especially, in the dire warnings from older residents that IP would marshal unimaginable force to break a strike.
65. http://www.fundinguniverse.com/company-histories/international-paper-company-history/. Accessed October 23, 2012.

References

Primary Published Sources

American Federation of Labor: *American Federationist* (1912–1923)
International Brotherhood of Paper Makers: *Paper Makers Journal* (1901–1920)
International Paper Company: *Otis News* (1959–1965)
International Paper Company: *The Scroll* (1966–1970)
Lewiston Daily Sun (1986–1990)
Lewiston Evening Journal (1903–1921)
Livermore Falls Advertiser (1908–1990)
Maine Bureau of Industrial and Labor Statistics, Annual Reports (1899–1910)
Paper Trade Journal (1910–1915)
United Paperworkers International Union: *Local 14 News* (1986–1987)
US Census Reports, Characteristics of the Population, Maine (1950–1980)

Primary Unpublished Sources

Maine State Federation of Labor Oral History Collection (taped interviews), Northeast Archives of Folklore and Oral History, University of Maine, Orono
Peter Kellman Papers, Jay Strike Collection: Folger Library Special Collections, University of Maine, Orono
Wayne Glen, Letters, box 4
Bill Merserve, Letters, box 4
Strike Video Collection, box 9
Paper Makers Journal, Papers of the International Brotherhood of Pulp, Sulfite, and Paper Mill Workers: Labor-Management Documentation Center, Catherwood Library, NYS School of Industrial and Labor Relations, Cornell University
George C. Brooks Correspondence
S. Ed. Launer Correspondence
Jacob Sephan Correspondence

Secondary Sources

Benjamin, Walter. 1969. "Theses on the Philosophy of History." In *Illuminations: Essays and Reflections*. New York: Schocken.
Bloch, Maurice. 1971. "The Moral and Tactical Meaning of Kinship Terms." *Man* 6: 79–87.
Buhle, Paul. 1995. *A Dreamers' Paradise Lost: Louis Fraina/Lewis Corey (1892–1953) and the Decline of Radicalism in the US*. Atlantic Highlands: Humanities Press.
Burawoy, Michael. 1985. *The Politics of Production: Factory Regimes Under Capitalism and Socialism*. New York: Verso Books.
Carriere, Ricardo and Larry Lohman. 1996. *Pulping the South: Industrial Tree Plantations and the World Paper Economy*. London: Zed Books.
Cernek, Stephen Rea. 1978. "Beyond the Return to Normalcy: The Decline of Organized Paper Workers, 1921–1926." Ph.D. dissertation, Ball State University.
Clark, Gordon. 1989. *Unions and Communities under Siege: American Communities and the Crisis of Organized Labor*. Cambridge: Cambridge University Press.
Clawson, Mary Ann. 1989. *Constructing Brotherhood: Class, Gender, and Fraternalism*. Princeton: Princeton University Press.
Davin, Eric L., and Staughton Lynd. 1979. "Picket Line and Ballot Box: The Forgotten Legacy of the Local Labor Party Movement." *Radical History Review* 22: 43–63.
Davis, Mike. 1986. *Prisoners of the American Dream: Politics and Economy in the History of the U.S. Working Class*. London: Verso Books.
Dawley, Alan. 1991. *Struggles for Justice: Social Responsibility and the Liberal State*. Cambridge: Harvard University Press.
De Angelis, Massimo. 2007. *The Beginning of History: Value Struggles and Global Capitalism*. London: Pluto Press.
Foley, Barbara. 1993. *Radical Representations: Politics and Form in U.S. Proletarian Fiction*. Durham, NC: Duke University Press.
Frank, Elizabeth. 1986. *Louise Bogan*. New York: Columbia University Press.
Gerstle, Gary. 1989. *Working Class Americanism: The Politics of Labor in a Textile City, 1914–1960*. Princeton: Princeton University Press.
Gettman, Julius G. 1999. *The Betrayal of Local 14: Paperworkers, Politics, and Permanent Replacements*. Ithaca, NY: ILR Press.
Graham, Harry E. 1970. *The Paper Rebellion: Development and Upheaval in Pulp and Paper Unionism*. Iowa City: University of Iowa Press.
Gramsci, Antonio. 1971. *Selections from the Prison Notebooks*. New York: International Publishers.
Gross, James A. 1964. "The Making and Shaping of Unionism in the Pulp and Paper Industry." *Labor History* 5, no. 2: 183–208.
Habermas, Jurgen. 1991. *The Structural Transformation of the Public Sphere: An Inquiry into a Category of Bourgeois Society*. Cambridge: MIT Press.
Harvey, David. 2010. "The Future of the Commons." *Radical History Review* 109: 101–107.
———. 1989. *The Condition of Postmodernity: An Inquiry into the Origins of Cultural Change*. Oxford: Blackwell Publishing.
Herod, Andrew. 1998. "The Spatiality of Labor Unions: a Review Essay." In *Organizing the Landscape, Geographical Perspectives on Labor Unionism*, ed. Andrew Herod. Minneapolis: University of Minnesota Press.
Hobsbawm, Eric. 1964. *Labouring Men*. London: Wiedenfield and Nicolson.
Kellman, Peter. 2004. *Divided We Fall: The Story of the Paperworkers' Union and the Future of Labor*. New York: Apex Press.
Lembcke, Jerry, and William Tattam. 1984. *One Union in Wood: A Political History of the International Woodworkers of America*. New York: International Publishers.

Levine, Rhonda. 1988. *Class Struggle and the New Deal: Industrial Labor, Industrial Capital, and the State*. Lawrence: University Press of Kansas.

Linebaugh, Peter. 2009. *The Magna Carta Manifesto: Liberties and Commons for All*. Berkeley: University of California Press.

MacDonald, Robert. 1956. "Pulp and Paper." In *The Evolution of the Wage Structure*, ed. Lloyd G. Reynolds and Cynthia Taft. New York: Yale University Press.

Mann, Eric. 1987. *Taking on General Motors: A Case Study of the UAW Campaign to Keep GM Van Nuys Open*. Los Angeles: Institute for Industrial Relations, University of California Press.

Marchak, Patricia. 1985. *Green Gold: The Forestry Industry in British Columbia*. Vancouver: University of British Columbia Press.

Marx, Karl. 1976. *Capital: A Critique of Political Economy. Volume One*. New York: Vintage Books.

Midight Notes Collective. 1990. *The New Enclosures*. Midnight Notes 10. http://www.midnightnotes.org/newenclos.html. Accessed March 20, 2011.

Minchin, Timothy J. 2006. "Labor's Empty Gun: Permanent Replacements and the International Paper Company Strike of 1987–1988." *Labor History* 47, no. 1: 21–42.

Mitchell, Don 2005. "Working Class Geographies: Capital, Space, and Place." In *New Working Class Studies*, ed. John Russo and Sherry Linkon. Ithaca: Cornell University Press.

Montgomery, David. 1987. *The Fall of the House of Labor*. New York: Cambridge University Press.

Negri, Antonio. 1994. "Keynes and the Capitalist Theory of the State." In *The Labor of Dionysus: A Critique of the State-Form*, ed. Michael Hardt and Antonio Negri. Minneapolis: University of Minnesota Press.

Nelson, Cary. 1989. *Repression and Recovery: Modern American Poetry and the Politics of Cultural Memory*. Madison: University of Wisconsin Press.

Nugent, Daniel. 1993. *Spent Cartridges of Revolution: An Anthropological History of Namiquipa, Chihuahua*. Chicago: University of Chicago Press.

Osborn, William C. 1974. *The Paper Plantation*. New York: Grossman Publishers.

Ramirez, Bruno. 2001. *Crossing the 49th Parallel: Migration from Canada to the United States, 1900–1930*. Ithaca: Cornell University.

Richer, David. 1990. "The Struggle Against Enclosure in Jay, Maine: An Account of the 1987–88 Strike Against International Paper Company." *Midnight Notes* 10. http://www.midnightnotes.org/newenclos.html. Accessed March 20, 2011.

Roediger, David R. 1999. *The Wages of Whiteness: Race and the Making of the American Working Class*. New York: Verso Books.

Scontras, Charles A. 2002. *Organized Labor in Maine: War, Reaction, Depression, and the Riseof the CIO, 1914–1943*. Orono: Bureau of Labor Education, University of Maine Press

———. 1985. *The Socialist Alternative: Utopian Experiments and the Socialist Party of Maine, 1895–1914*. Orono: Bureau of Labor Education, University of Maine Press

———. 1983. *Organized Labor in Maine: Twentieth Century Origins*. Orono: Bureau of Labor Education, University of Maine Press.

Silver, Beverly. 2003. *Forces of Labor: Workers' Movements and Globalization since 1870*. Cambridge: Cambridge University Press.

Smith, David C. 1970. *A History of Papermaking in the United States, 1691–1969*. New York: Lockwood Publishing.

Smith, Gavin. 2011. "Selective Hegemony and Beyond: Populations with No Productive Function: A Framework for Analysis." *Identities: Global Studies in Culture and Power*, 18, no. 1: 2–38.

Thompson, E. P. 1980. *Writing by Candlelight*. London: Merlin Press LTD.

———. 1966. *The Making of the English Working Class*. New York: Vintage Books.
Trouillot, Michel-Rolph. 1995. *Silencing the Past: Power and the Production of History*. Boston: Beacon Press.
Voelker, Keith Emory. 1969. *The History of the International Brotherhood of Pulp, Sulphite, and Paper Mill Workers from 1906 to 1922*. Ph.D. Dissertation. University of Wisconsin.
Williams, Raymond. 1989. *Resources of Hope*. London: Verso Books.
Wolf, Eric 1999. *Peasant Wars of the Twentieth Century*. Norman: University of Oklahoma Press.
Zieger, Robert H. 1984. *Rebuilding the Pulp and Paper Workers' Union, 1933–1941*. Knoxville: The University of Tennessee Press.

– Chapter 3 –

FLEXIBLE LABOR/FLEXIBLE HOUSING
The Rescaling of Mumbai into a Global Financial Center and the Fate of its Working Class

Judy Whitehead

Mumbai's redeveloped skyline over the past decade has led conservative commentators, such as Boris Johnston, the mayor of London, to herald Mumbai as an emerging Singapore, modern, spacious, and uncluttered. Yet the spatial reshaping of south and central Mumbai into a center of business and residential "excellence" hides a dramatic dispossession of the city's industrial workers. This process involved double waves of dispossession over the past quarter century: the first involved the loss of stable industrial jobs, while the second comprises the "clearance" of former workers' habitation. Mumbai led the way in India's transition from Fordism to finance in India. It was the first city to experience wide-scale deindustrialization of large-scale enterprises, and then later to reshape its built environment and economy into an important node in global financial networks, specializing in financial and producer services, back-end office operations, real estate, insurance, and entertainment industries (Sassen 2001). Simultaneously, former industrial processes were outsourced to small-scale units on Mumbai's hinterlands in edge cities that are now major locales of India's large and growing "informal sector." The spatial and historical aspects of changing class relations, and class dispossession, are thus etched into central and south Mumbai's built environment. The presence of gleaming office towers, apartments, wide thoroughfares, and, especially noted by Boris Johnston, the decline in "slums," pavement dwellers, and beggars in south and central Mumbai was and is being accomplished through what Marx termed the "bloody discipline of primitive accumulation" (Marx 1976: 716).[1]

This chapter will map the changing landscapes of labor, capital, and space in central Mumbai, focusing especially on the past three decades, as the city's business and government elites have responded to economic liberalization by reshaping the central and southern parts of the megacity to their new requirements. It will utilize historical materials to chart the changing class, colonial, and ethnic divides in the city, showing how these changing configurations have impacted the built environment of the city. It thus covers the labor history of the early colonial period (1850–1920), the later colonial period that was marked by the rise of a mass independence movement and the "national question" (1920–1947), the Nehruvian period in which import substitution policies encouraged the growth of large-scale domestic industries (1947–1985), and the period since 1984–1985, when economic liberalization has been the predominant economic policy at both state and national levels. It places special emphasis on the social transitions from Nehruvian policies for import-substitution industrialization to neoliberal capitalism of the past twenty-five years. Finally, it will utilize ethnographic material from fieldwork carried out in a large "slum" colony that still remains in central Mumbai, Janata Colony in Worli neighborhood, to show how the change from Fordist industry to financial services and real estate speculation has dramatically shrunk both the livelihood options and living spaces of former industrial workers and their families.

To be sure, the process of spatial restructuring is still ongoing, and during the periods of fieldwork, in the summers of 2004–2005 and the spring of 2010, it was far from complete. Mumbai, a megacity with more than fifteen million inhabitants, with over half being "slum-dwellers," presents special challenges to rapid drives of gentrification and redevelopment. Yet the lineages of change are clear, even if the process is incomplete. Mumbai's future reliance on the FIRE sector (finance, insurance, real estate, and entertainment) was explicitly spelled out in a McKinsey & Company report, Vision Mumbai (2003), that was adopted almost wholesale by the Brihamumbai Municipal Corporation (BMC) (i.e., the municipal government) in 2005. At the time of fieldwork, between 2004 and 2010, however, central Mumbai was in the process of massive flux. Forms of informal habitation, commonly referred to as slums in municipal documents, that had previously housed industrial workers, existed cheek by jowl with gleaming office towers and high-rise apartments. But while over 50 percent of the city's inhabitants still lived in informal habitation,[2] there was a noticeable decrease, recorded in BMC statistics, of such dwellings in south and central Mumbai between 2001 and 2011 and a corresponding increase of new "slums" in northeastern Mumbai. Not coincidently, the municipal and state governments are pursuing increasingly revanchist policies toward former industrial workers still living in south and central Mumbai "slums." These policies included a massive eviction drive in 2004–2005 that destroyed the houses of about three hundred thousand "slum-dwellers" in central and south Mumbai (Whitehead and More 2007). Many of these people are now being resettled in officially sanctioned areas in less desirable parts of the city. One of these areas, Rafiq Nagar, is in the midst of the municipal dump in the eastern Mumbai suburb of Mankhurd (Doshi 2012).

The double waves of dispossession in central Mumbai, first of stable jobs and secondly of housing, were unleashed through India's policy of economic liberalization, beginning in the mid-1980s (Corbridge and Harris 2000). These neoliberal economic reforms accelerated after a balance of payments crisis in 1991. The opening of India's industries to international competition through the withdrawal of tariffs and quotas led to a virtual collapse of Fordist production in Mumbai. In its place poorly paid, flexible work, often carried out in home-based industries, in small-scale units located on the outskirts of the city, or in poorly paid jobs in the lower rungs of the service sector became the dominant form of employment. Nowhere is this change more obvious than in central Mumbai. An important center of textile, pharmaceutical, and electronics production until the mid-1980s, it experienced steep deindustrialization in the late 1980s and early 1990s that resulted in the loss of about one million jobs. These changes have resulted in an altered political, economic, and cultural landscape for labor in India that has greatly enhanced the power of employers and virtually flattened the bargaining power of workers.

The shifting contours of labor, capital, and the built environment in central Mumbai is indicative of wider trends throughout the country. Most of the contemporary employment generated in India's growing economy has occurred through flexible contract work, often referred to as "the informal sector." Defined as unregulated employment that requires little capital input, self-employment in the service industry, petty commodity production, work in small industries employing fewer than fifty people, contractually based or temporary work in large enterprises, and self-employment in agriculture, the informal sector now constitutes about 92 percent of India's jobs. While this definition of the informal sector conflates middle-class, contractual employment in large enterprises with the work of the precariat, and thus obscures contemporary trends, a 2007 central government report noted that 77 percent of those employed in the informal sector earned less than $0.50 US per day (Sengupta 2007). This is 50 percent less than the World Bank's figure denoting absolute poverty. Moreover, since economic liberalization began in earnest in 1991, formal sector employment has remained virtually stagnant at about 7–8 percent of total employment.

The change in Mumbai from Fordism to flexible, contract-based work has been marked by massive changes both in the organization of labor and in the spatial organization of central and south Mumbai as a global city characterized by new forms of social-spatial exclusion. These simultaneous movements of capital involved both the destruction of Fordist production and the creation of a financialized real estate boom in south and central Mumbai, alongside the outsourcing of industrial processes to small-scale, informal enterprises on the city's outskirts. The concept of accumulation by dispossession enables us to understand both the changing livelihoods and forms of habitation of central Mumbai's working classes in the past thirty years. It foregrounds the mutability of class relations in this transition, enabling us to understand how new divisions between the privileged urban middle class and the increasingly "undeserving" poor in Mumbai are being forged in the context of India's recent GDP growth of between 5 and 10 percent per annum.

Spatial and Economic History of Mumbai

Mumbai (known before 1995 as Bombay) emerged as the major commercial center in western India in the mid to late nineteenth century, functioning both as a major port and commercial entrepôt. During this period, India was perhaps the most important single economic prop for the British Empire, supplying cheap raw materials for Britain's textile industries, a transfer of wealth through land revenue, and the largest protected market for its finished goods: the Indian market absorbed two-thirds of all British cotton textiles, which themselves accounted for 75 percent of England's exports. Bombay became a major commercial center because of its port facilities and later saw the growth of large-scale indigenous industry. This industrial base, most significantly textiles, started operation about 1850, in opposition to colonial government policies that discouraged Indian industrialization. Hence, Bombay's textile and industrial magnates became important supporters of the nationalist movement and of the Congress Party in the twentieth century. The Congress Party, which officially formed in 1875, claimed to unite all classes, religions, and regions in the fight for political independence. Mumbai's working classes, which became the most militant section of Indian labor in the early twentieth century, were thus defined both by colonial/racial and class contradictions (Fanon 1967). As the nationalist movement gained momentum in the early twentieth century, these dual loyalties came to the forefront, with nationalist goals sometimes overshadowing class politics. Indeed, even during the Nehruvian and neoliberal phases, national goals of economic development have continued to compete with the economic interests of India's workers, while being continually redefined to meet different policy agendas.

Once independence was achieved in 1947, the drive to catch up with the West led to the diversification and expansion of Mumbai's industrial base. Under India's import substitution policies, the newly independent government encouraged domestic capital in both producer and consumer goods sectors. Between 1950 and 1985, pharmaceuticals, chemical production, and engineering products emerged as important industrial sectors in central Mumbai alongside the textile industry. Nehru's Five-Year Plans, which privileged industrial development over agriculture and provided policy support to new industries, were important in stimulating the growth of these sectors in newly independent Bombay.

However, Bombay's textile industry remained the major manufacturing sector in Mumbai between 1950 and 1985 in terms of both output and labor force, employing about 250,000 workers and including nearly sixty mills until the mid-1980s. Most of the mills were privately owned, although thirteen became state-owned after experiencing declining profitability in the 1960s. Along with other "sick" mills in Kanpur and Ahmedabad, these mills became absorbed into the National Textile Corporation, a public sector enterprise.

Most of the mills were built in the late nineteenth or early twentieth century in what was then the northern border of the city. As housing and commercial development expanded into the northern suburbs after independence, the mill areas came to occupy the central zone between the southern business and financial districts and the northern residential suburbs. These neighborhoods, including

Worli, Parel, Dadar, Lalbaug, Prabhadevi, Byculla, and Saat Rasta, were the centers of a distinctive working-class culture that supported the first trade union in India, the Girni Kamgar Union (Textile Workers' Union), and the first major industrial strikes in the 1920s (Chandarvarkar 1994). Indeed, between 1919 and 1940, there were eight general strikes in the Bombay textile industry and numerous work stoppages.

Girangaon (The Mill Districts): Working-Class Neighborhoods

The organization of the textile workers in early-twentieth-century Bombay was shaped not only by the division of labor and capital/labor relations, but also by the neighborhoods in which they lived. Due to labor recruitment patterns that produced a convergence between residential neighborhoods and sites of employment, a remarkable synergy emerged between working-class neighborhoods and trade union organizing. Due to the high demand for mill jobs, employers were often able to defeat early workers' unions that had formed in the workplace by firing militant workers (Chandavarkar 1998: 117). Consequently, unions changed their strategy and began organizing in the neighborhood and the street. By the mid-1920s, 90 percent of workers lived within fifteen minutes walking distance from their workplace, a pattern that continued into the post-independence period. The housing stock consisted of *chawls*—apartment buildings of one-room dwellings and shared bathrooms, built by the colonial government following scandals about high rates of child mortality among workers' families—informal habitation built on open land called "slums," and private rental accommodation. The neighborhoods were spatially characterized by clusters of cross-cutting social solidarities defined by caste, region of origin, and religion. These neighborhood clusters, however, did not so much reflect the persistence of primordial (caste) loyalties in an urban setting, but rather the particularistic networks formed in the process of labor recruitment from surrounding regions. Personal networks became the major form of labor recruitment. Labor contractors, or jobbers, became crucial middlemen who recruited from their own outlying regions and often from their own caste. Upon arrival in Bombay, jobbers also provided temporary housing and sometimes informal credit facilities for newly hired workers. They were also important middlemen between workers and employers. More established workers also attempted to find jobs for relatives and friends from within their region, thus reestablishing rural connections and solidarities within an urban setting (Chadavarkar 1984; 1998). These residential clusters that were loosely defined by region and caste also facilitated arranged marriages, since region, caste, and personal connections mattered in marriage choices. This pattern increased the density of kinship ties, adding to class solidarities within neighborhoods. As Gupta (1984) has pointed out, caste and regional identities did not prevent horizontal class solidarities from forming during important social movements, such as during the Bombay trade union movement. The Girni Kamgar Union provided the major organizational linkages across factories and neighborhoods. Its activists were able to strike strong roots in the mill districts because they situated their politics within local cultures and neighborhoods.

Street life imparted its momentum to politics, as well. Trade unionists organized on the streets, and labor organizers often used local street theater, called *tamashas*, to promote recruitment drives. During strikes, relatives and neighbors, along with grain dealers, merchants, and moneylenders from the neighborhood, provided informal credit to striking workers, enabling them to maintain their resistance for long periods of time. These cross-class alliances indicate that the trade union movement possessed widespread support in Girangaon. Other neighborhood associations that contributed to solidarity were the *akhadas*, or gyms, that trained young men in physical fitness and fighting, and were sometimes pulled into industrial action. Tea shops that were frequented almost daily by neighborhood workers were also centers of union recruitment, as well as of sociality. The physical and social control of neighborhoods by textile unions was doubly important during strikes, as the neighborhoods constituted a site where strikebreakers could and would be shamed into compliance with work stoppages. The overlapping ties of work, neighborhood, and region of origin produced a social and moral cohesion that undoubtedly contributed to Bombay's reputation as an "insurrectionary city" between 1920 and 1950. Union organization also spanned across the various neighborhoods of the mill districts, with the Communist Party of India, formed in 1925, and its union, the Girni Kamgar Union, providing the major connecting link.

Bombay's reputation as the leading center of trade unionism in colonial India attracted numerous artists and writers to the mill districts, collectively known as Girangaon. The *tamashas*, or street plays, became institutionalized in theaters by the 1940s. Playwrights associated with the Indian Progressive Theatre Association made Girangaon their home, and the Communist Party of India also chose Girangaon for its central office location in 1927. Many of Bombay's most important visual artists of this period also drew their inspiration from the popular struggles in Girangaon (Chandavarkar 2004: 26, 27).

The Girni Kamgar Union (Textile Workers' Union, or GKU) led important and long-lasting strikes in 1927–1928 and 1936–1937 and was dominated in this period by the CPI, the undivided Communist Party of India. It eclipsed previous workers' combinations that had been led by prominent social reformers of Mumbai who lacked the organizational dedication and radicalism of the Communist Party. The Communist Party of India, almost from its inception in 1925, became part of the Communist International, sending delegates to the Third International and receiving literature, advice, and funding from the Soviet Union. The CPI underwent a number of policy changes from 1925 to 1945 that reflected international communist theory, dominated by the Communist Party of the Soviet Union, on building a workers' and peasants' revolutionary force in a colonized country. The major policy shifts centered on the relation of the communist movement to what was viewed as the "bourgeois nationalism" of the Indian Congress Party. At some points, the Communist International held that a bourgeois democratic revolution necessarily preceded communism, and hence the Congress Party should be supported. At other points, it held that the class character of the Congress Party should be critiqued and exposed. In hindsight, however, it seems that the various shifts in relation to the nationalist movement mirrored the Comintern's overriding goal of saving socialism in one country, that is, the Soviet Union. These policy shifts had a major negative effect on the Girni Kamgar Union and the CPI in the 1940s . Between 1925 and 1929, the Comintern placed emphasis on building trade union militancy and on exposing the class character of the Indian Nationalist Congress, led by M. K. Gandhi. When this policy largely failed, the policy of a united front with socialist elements inside the Indian National Congress was pursued, as an anti-colonial bourgeois-democratic revolution was then seen as a necessary precursor to an eventual proletarian revolution. This policy was predominant between 1936 and 1939, when a socialist group, the Congress Socialist Party, was formed inside the Congress and led by Nehru. However, the most extreme policy change, and one that nearly erased the Communist influence within the Mumbai labor movement, was the switch from a political line viewing the outbreak of World War II as war between imperialist powers during the Hitler-Stalin pact of 1939–1941, to declaring it a People's War once the Soviet Union joined the allied side in 1942. Hence Britain, on its last legs as the colonial power in India, now became defined as the "people's friend" by the CPI. This policy change occurred simultaneously with the Congress Party launching the Quit India movement in 1942. During this movement most of the nationalist leadership was jailed, but gained prestige through their incarceration. The Quit India movement erupted as a more or less spontaneous mass movement involving hundreds of thousands of demonstrators demanding immediate independence for India, with the British government capitulating, and promising independence once World War II ended.

Since Indian independence was a mass popular demand by the 1940s, the fact that the CPI aligned itself with the colonial government led to a dramatic drop in its popularity. In the 1947 elections after independence, the CPI was not able to win a single constituency, while the Congress Party swept the elections, both in Maharashtra and federally. This had repercussions for the trade unions affiliated with the Congress and Communist Party in the Bombay mills. In the late 1940s and early 1950s, the Girni Kamgar Union, the union linked to the Communist Party of India, was eclipsed by the Rashtraya Mill Mazdoor Sangh, a union affiliated with the nationalist Congress Party. The immense popularity, indeed hegemony, of the Congress Party immediately following independence derived from the fact that it was perceived as the main organization that led India to independence from Britain.

Once in power, however, the Congress Party followed a policy of "responsible trade-unionism" that demanded significant concessions from workers. It also relied upon landed elites to deliver votes in rural areas and hence reached compromises with landlords and rich farmers on agrarian issues, such as land reform. The militancy that had been unfurled by the socialist section of the Congress Party and the Communists in the 1930s had now to be blunted by the exigencies of rule. The developmental state created by the Congress Party involved a policy of what Gramsci has termed "a passive revolution," that is, a process that attempts to absorb and simultaneously neutralize radical elements, while protecting corporate and landed interests behind a rhetoric of socialism. The Indian state that emerged following independence was dominated by both industrial and landed elites, with neither being able singly to exert control over it. Nor was industrial capital, hampered by its history of colonial restrictions, able to drive a capitalist revolution in the countryside. In this balance, or stalemate, of political forces, the educated middle class and intelligentsia, employed largely in the public sector, came to assume a dirigiste role in governance and looked to the state to drive India's development process (Chatterjee 1997; Kaviraj 1988).

Due to the overriding interests of both industrial capital and landed elites, compromises from both workers' and peasants' organizations were required by the newly independent state. Often this was framed as promoting rapid industrialization and national development. All political parties possessed trade union fronts, whose policies followed the electoral platforms of their respective parties. In 1946, a year before formal independence, the ruling Congress Party in Maharashtra passed the Bombay Industrial Relations Act, whose aim was to ensure that "efficient production was not hampered by thoughtless and needless work stoppages" (Chandavarkar 2004: 45). In keeping with this policy to secure labor peace, the RMMS, the congress-affiliated trade union, was declared the only official union in the textile mills, with exclusive powers to represent textile workers. The Bombay Industrial Relations Act also set out the criteria for approved union policies, which involved renouncing strikes until all other means of resolving differences had been attempted (2004: 47). The pro-management stance of the RMMS led to a gradual accumulation of grievances among workers in the decades following independence, as many of the workers' demands were sacrificed to the overriding goal of industrial development.

Due to the compromises that the RMMS struck with management from 1950 to 1970, other unions were trying to gain or regain supporters within the textile industry after 1970. These included unions affiliated with the Shiv Sena and the CPI. The RMMS was increasingly viewed by workers as a management union. Simultaneously, a major political movement was growing in Bombay that also impacted the trade union movement. This was the Samyukta Maharasthra, a political movement to separate Maharashtra, the state in which Bombay is located, from neighboring Gujarat on linguistic lines. Since most of the mill workers were from rural Maharashtra and were Marathi speakers, while many of the mill owners were either Gujarati or English speakers, the demand for a separate Marathi-based linguistic state was a popular demand among them. Due to the convergence of class and ethnicity in the Samyukta Maharashtra movement, all non-Congress parties supported it. This included the Communist Party of India, who wished to regain its historical prominence in the mill districts. However, the support for Maharashtra statehood also provided an opening for purely ethnically based political organizations to gain adherents among the mill workers. Most prominently, this included the Shiv Sena, a Marathi-based regional party that was strongly anti-Communist, which became active in the mill areas during the Samyukhta Maharashtra movement and later took Marathi nationalism in a right-wing direction.

The Shiv Sena, which means "Shiv's Army," was founded in 1966 by political cartoonist Bal Thackeray. It was named after the Marathi warrior king Shivaji Bhonsale, who successfully fought the Mughals in the late 1600s, establishing the Mahratta empire in the process. The Mahratta state, ruled from Pune in Maharashtra, was the most successful anti-British force in India until it was finally defeated in 1818. In addition to strongly promoting Marathi linguistic identity, the Shiv Sena campaigned for job reservations for Marathi speakers, targeting both South Indian migrants and Mumbai Communists as responsible for job losses and unemployment in Mumbai. Its early adherents belonged mainly to white-collar, lower-middle-class employees and shopkeepers for whom in-migration to Mumbai was perceived as diluting Marathi predominance. The Shiv Sena did not gain electoral success in the mill districts until the 1990s. However, it did manage to establish trade unions in nine mills during its early phase from 1966 to 1980 (Bhowmik 1999: 40).

The Communist-affiliated trade unions had also gained or regained considerable influence among those textile workers in central Mumbai, particularly among those who desired greater industrial militancy in the 1960s, but who rejected the Shiv Sena's racist stance toward outsiders. Hence, the overall situation of union organization in the Bombay textile mills of the late 1970s was that the RMMS constituted the officially sanctioned but increasingly unpopular trade union, while the other unions affiliated with either the Communist Party or the Shiv Sena were jostling for influence among disaffected textile workers. None was able to gain overall leadership over the trade union movement in Mumbai in the 1970s. Hence, this decade was marked by escalating street conflicts between supporters of the Shiv Sena and the Communists. Violent incidents involved the Shiv Sena setting fire to the CPI offices in Parel and culminated in 1970 with the murder of a prominent CPI leader, Krishna Desai. Many observers date the most recent decline of the CPI and its affiliated union

GKU in Girangaon to Krishna Desai's murder and the subsequent fear that Shiv Sena street fighters instilled in the mill areas.

Deindustrialization: The Textile Strike and the Fate of the Mills

The Bombay mills were already under pressure by the late 1970s, suffering from lack of reinvestment. There was also increasing competition from the new, small-scale power-looms in edge cities on Mumbai's eastern and northern outskirts, such as Thane, Bhiwandi, and Ichalkaranji. Indeed, the textile industry overall was beginning to undergo major changes, the most important of which was outsourcing weaving processes to these small-scale factories on Mumbai's outskirts. Several observers at the time noted that, faced with rising import costs of machinery from Germany and Japan, mill owners followed a strategy of substituting labor for capital, becoming increasingly reliant on low wages to maintain profitability. Hence, labor productivity had been declining in the textiles mills for at least a decade, and the mills were increasingly uncompetitive with the power-loom sector by the beginning of the 1980s. This was shown by the nationalization of thirteen textile mills in central Mumbai in the 1960s. Because of the labor substitution strategy by management, workers' wages in the textile industry had been declining relative to other industries in Bombay. In addition, the real wages of most textile workers had also declined during the 1970s due to strong inflationary pressures. Most workers, however, were largely unaware of the threat that power-loom subcontracting posed to the very existence of the mills.

Given the long-standing grievances over pay, working conditions, and the increasing hiring of temporary workers, called *badli*, major industrial action was to be expected at some point and finally erupted in early 1982. The Bombay Textile Strike lasted for one and a half years, from 1982 to 1984, and is considered a major watershed in Indian labor history. It was renowned for its militancy, for its size—with about 250,000 workers involved—and for its ultimate and dramatic collapse. The initial spark of the 1982 strike, raised at first by Shiv Sena unions, was an issue of bonuses being cut in nine textile mills, leading to work stoppages in those mills. However, once it became obvious about a month later that workers from the nine mills demanded a general strike throughout the mills, the Shiv Sena rescinded its support, because its leaders viewed a general strike as an "extreme" tactic and class conflict was anathema to their nativist stance. They argued instead that an agreement should be sought between the nine mills and their unions, with the state's chief minister acting as mediator. In frustration, a group of workers' representatives from the nine mills approached Dr. Datta Samant, a charismatic labor leader independent of any political party who had won significant pay rises for workers in the chemical, electronics, and pharmaceutical industries in Bombay. They convinced him to lead their strike and urged a general strike in all sixty mills, arguing that the support of all textile workers was necessary for success. Although pay and cuts in bonuses were the initial issue in the original nine mills, there were long-standing grievances in the other mills. These included the increasing use of temporary work contracts for certain processes inside the mills and the general docility of the RMMS in relation to management (Lakha 1989). Accumulated grievances compelled workers in other factories to join those in the nine mills striking over bonuses and also imparted an extra militancy to striking workers. Datta Samant was initially reluctant to call an indefinite general strike in Mumbai's entire textile industry, due to his (and other union leaders') perception that the outsourcing of weaving to the small-scale power-loom sector weakened the textile workers' bargaining position. However, he was compelled to do so by workers' representatives, who staged a protracted sit-in at his home, prior to a major rally on January 17, 1982. This rally marked the official commencement of the general strike (van Wersch 1992).

The workers were adamant that they needed a union that was independent from all political parties. They believed that the connection between political parties and trade unions, so prevalent in India's industrial landscape, meant that unions had a divided allegiance. Often party platforms and electoral tactics could override workers' democratic interests. For instance, the Communist-affiliated unions believed that the textile workers' position was weak and that their demands were hence impractical. In addition, they judged that supporting a major strike would make the Communist Party unpopular with a middle-class electorate. They also feared that independent trade unionism, exemplified in the leadership of Data Samant, represented reformism that would wean workers away from Communist ideology. For the most part, they advised the unions they controlled to refrain from the participating in the general strike. However, they were overruled by their membership, most of which voted with their feet and joined the new union. The new union was called the Mumbai Girni Kamgar Union (MGKU) to both connect it to and differentiate it from the GKU that had led workers' strikes in the 1920s and 1930s. Once the strike started, the Communist Party extended support to striking workers through the TUJAC, the trades' union council that was formed during the strike to coordinate efforts among all the non-Congress unions active in the textile industry. They provided little logistical or manpower support, but did organize food donations for the striking workers. Due to their lukewarm support for the general strike, their membership declined steeply during this period, from about twenty thousand to one thousand members (van Wersch 1992).

From the beginning of the strike, the mill owners ensured that they were in a strong position. By outsourcing their production to the power-loom sector, hiring new, nonunion scabs on a temporary basis, and stockpiling finished goods, they were able to maintain operations throughout the strike. There appears to have been no decline in the supply of textiles in Bombay over the eighteen-month duration of the strike (van Wersch 1992). In addition, since the central government had nationalized numerous textile mills in Ahmedabad and Kanpur, as well as Bombay, it worried that rising wages and bonuses in Bombay would spill over into wage demands in other state-owned enterprises. Hence, the Congress Party had an added reason to support the mill owners in Bombay. In addition, Indira Gandhi, then prime minister, personally wished to prevent Datta Samant from emerging as a national trade union leader. Not only would a victory for Samant undercut the role of Congress-led trade unions, it could also end the period of "responsible" trade unionism. Hence, the central government was keen on opposing Datta Samant from the beginning of the textile strike. With the central government on its side, the mill owners were able to wear down the striking workers over an eighteen-month period and conceded, finally, to none of their demands.

There appeared to have been numerous attempts by the state government of Maharashtra to produce a compromise solution throughout the eighteen-month strike, including the establishment of a High Powered Committee that recommended substantial wage increases. However, these compromises were always jettisoned by either the mill owners or the central government mediators that represented the National Textile Corporation, owners of the state-managed mills (van Wersch 1992).

Although the strike was never officially called off by either Datta Samant or the Mumbai Girni Kamgar Union, its final date is given as August 8, 1983, after a decision was taken by the union to allow workers to return to the mills. The strike was characterized not only by its length and size, but also by ongoing violence among the police, striking workers, and hired strikebreakers, including, in some cases, gangsters. Although violence was perpetrated by both sides during the strike, the mill owners held the overwhelming balance of force, being supported by the police, the RMMS, and notable gangsters. This violence was the leading edge of worker dispossession, as the following interviews show.

Personal experiences of violence was a common motif of the interviews I conducted with former textile workers in Worli in central Mumbai, in the spring of 2010, about the history of the strike. One man in Worli, Ravindra Patel, suffered from long-term depression, alcoholism, and an unstable work history following the strike. He had moved to Mumbai and Worli from the neighboring district of Raigar, acquiring a job first as an apprentice and then as a winder in Century Mills, in Worli in 1978. He was hired on a temporary basis, and hence the demand to make temporary workers permanent employees was very important to him. He had been a strong supporter of Datta Samant, as was everyone I met in Worli. He felt that the RMMS, the Congress trade union, ignored the problems of temporary workers, while the Communist unions paid lip service to the issue, but did little about it. The strike became violent, according to Ravindra, because the mill owners hired goondas (thugs), to disrupt union meetings and to protect strikebreakers who wanted to work. One night, when the MGKU had organized picket lines at Century Mills in Worli to dissuade new temporary workers from entering the mill, a fight broke out with armed thugs. Two of Ravindra's friends who were stabbed died that night. In all, five of Ravindra's friends died during the strike.

Another worker from Century Mills, who was also an activist with the MGKU, had both his hands broken during a scuffle with RMMS thugs outside the local bus station. "What happened was I'd told some bhaiyyas[3] who were working that the strike was for everyone's benefit, so you shouldn't go to work. They complained to the RMMS, and the next day four RMMS workers attacked me with *lathis* [long wooden sticks often used by the police to control crowds]. When they aimed the *lathis* at my head, I lifted my hands and they were broken. Then they kicked me in the stomach and hit me with the *lathis*. They left me for dead; but I only had a broken rib and fractured hands." He stated that "the RMMS tried to break the strike by bussing in workers from other places. They also broke up the union meetings outside the gates." He didn't see anyone get killed, but knew there were scores who died in the violence.

Violence was also experienced through police repression of striking workers. One ex–textile worker, who had been a well-known activist of the MGKU, recounted how the secretary of the union at Century Mills in Worli, one of the forty-seven private companies, was arrested after workers at this mill stoned a bus full of strikebreakers, although he had not been present at the incident itself. After receiving bail, he was re-arrested on charges of robbery and was beaten for three days continuously, only receiving bail after three weeks. By isolating and targeting neighborhood leaders of the strike committees, the police and state government aimed to terrorize and demoralize the striking workers.

As a result of the violence, some of the more visible and prominent activists of the Mumbai Girini Kamgar Union went underground for long periods during the strike, while their relatives and families were harassed by the police. Many of the striking workers tried to return to their villages in rural Maharashtra or moved to seek work in the power-loom sector in Bhiwandi.

The end of the strike was marked by widespread retrenchment and the gradual closing of the forty-seven private and thirteen government-owned mills (Bhowmik and More 2001). In the first two years following the strike, about 120,000 retrenchments occurred, with dismissals targeting those who had been active in the Mumbai Girni Kamgar Union (van Wersch 1992). For example, neither Ravindra nor fellow striker Ramesh were retained after the strike. They also did not receive Voluntary Retirement Scheme (VRS) payments to which they were entitled and which other workers received once the mills closed. Ramesh believes he was blacklisted due to his visible activism during the strike. In addition, new migrants who had no union experience and were easier to control, were increasingly hired by mill owners on a temporary basis for any positions that remained open. Within ten years after the strike ended, the number of workers in the industry had shrunk to one-fifth their number in the early 1980s (van Wersch 1992). Today, the mills are almost all completely closed. Large-scale pharmaceutical, electrical, and chemical industries, located in central eastern Mumbai, followed the example of the textile industries in outsourcing production to small-scale, informalized units in Mumbai's hinterlands, where they could escape government regulation, health and safety provisions, and minimum wage regulations. This shift in spatial class relations would have major implications for future forms of employment and for real estate speculation and finance capital that would further reorganize the landscapes of class in Mumbai.

The MGKU, although demoralized by the failure of the 1982–1984 strike, continued to be active in helping workers return to their jobs and in pressing for Voluntary Retirement Scheme benefits to be paid out once employment had been terminated. However, they ceased to wield much local influence, at least in Janata Colony, where there was no office and there were no active union members in 2005. In 1997, Datta Samant was himself murdered, apparently by members of the Chota Rajan gang, who were reputedly hired by the owner of Khatau Mills, which was involved in an ongoing dispute with retrenched workers over their VRS payments (D'Monte 2002). However, the attackers have never been arrested or charged.

Post-Fordist Livelihoods in Central Mumbai

Through the deindustrialization of textile and other industries in central Mumbai throughout the late 1980s and 1990s, about one million people lost their jobs. The more fortunate were sometimes able to access Voluntary Retirement Scheme payments, although they often waited several years, or even a decade, after their loss of employment before receiving compensation. Those who were visibly active in the strike, however, were often denied their VRS benefits, and many just left Bombay. A 2002 study of the lives of ex–textile workers in central Mumbai indicates that many had moved, mainly to the edge cities of Bhiwandi and Thane, where the textile industry had reorganized itself in small-scale units. There, they were hired on a contractual, piece-rate basis, earning between one-fourth and one-third of the wages they had formerly received in the mills (Bhowmik and More 2001). They often had to work ten- to twelve-hour days, six days a week, to acquire the equivalent of a minimum wage. Most of the power-loom operations were extremely small-scale, utilizing unpaid family labor to raise profitability. Here, extremely low wages offset low capital intensity, and the power-loom sector emerged as leading textile producers in India, selling to both domestic and international markets. Its competitiveness was aided by liberalizing reforms that eliminated tariffs on imported machinery and allowed labor market "flexibility" in the late 1980s and early 1990s. These small-scale units were also supported by government financial incentives available through the Export Development Corporation, set up to facilitate export-led growth. The fate of those who stayed in central Mumbai is more varied, due to stress in finding new types of informal work in the late 1980s and early 1990s. I conducted research in one slum neighborhood in central Mumbai, Janata Colony in Worli, in the summers of 2004–2005 and again between February and March 2010. The experiences of Janata Colony residents since the end of the strike reflect their increasing marginalization to the new spatial economy of central Mumbai and the difficulties they have experienced in simply making ends meet.

Janata Colony, Worli Neighborhood, Central Mumbai

The majority of inhabitants in Janata Colony had migrated to Mumbai from rural districts along the Konkan coast and also from some of the more drought-prone districts in southeastern Maharasthra such as Satara, Sangli, and Kolhapur. They came seeking work in the mills, starting in the 1950s and continuing until two decades ago. The caste composition in Janata Colony is mainly *agris, bhandaris,* and *kunbi Marathas. Agris* and *kunbi Marathas* are middle-caste groups historically connected to farming and often considered dominant castes in the rural areas from which they migrated. *Bhandaris* are considered a Scheduled Caste (i.e., a caste group defined as ex-untouchables by government census). There was also a sizeable population of Goan Christians, with a similar history connected to farming, but from a formerly Portuguese colony, that had become largely Catholic during Portuguese rule, which ended in 1971. According to the local municipal councilor, a Communist Party member who started a school in Worli, prior to independence in 1947, Worli village was solely a fisherman's colony inhabited largely by Kolis. The Kolis are a Scheduled Tribe, defined by the Indian Constitution as a group deemed to exhibit "primitive traits," i.e., to live by fishing, hunting, or subsistence agriculture. They have retained this designation, despite the fact that the Kolis are located in the center of a megacity and are mostly now commercial fishermen. The Kolis are considered the original inhabitants of the Mumbai island, and, as Scheduled Tribes, receive some government benefits, including reserved places in education and in public sector jobs.[4] The migrants to Janata Colony now far outnumber the original fishing families, with the Koli families residing in the original fishing village from which Worli neighborhood acquired its name, and consisting of 25,000 people. The 150,000 migrants reside on what was formerly public land behind Worli village, built up through the "illegal" construction of informal housing over a forty-year period. This "slum" area became known as Janata Colony, or People's Colony. There are also a few more recent migrants from Uttar Pradesh. Houses in both Janata Colony and Worli village are generally two-story structures that have been added onto and renovated extensively over the past three decades. Some people said that they had invested about one lakh[5] rupees in house construction and renovation in the past thirty years and would have done more if the Bombay Municipal Corporation allowed higher structures. While earlier migrants had constructed their dwellings on squatted, free land, more recent migrants purchased land from local informal contractors who utilized "muscle power" and bribery to gain control over most remaining public space in and near Janata Colony and who reputedly had connections either to the local Shiv Sena ward office or to local, independent gangs. There is now no noncommodified space left in Janata Colony.

My interviews with women from eighty households in Janata Colony in Worli in the summers of 2004 and 2005 show that the late 1980s and 1990s, the decade following the strike, was a time of great hardship. To survive, children were often removed from school to contribute income to the household. With the loss of male employment in the mills, most of the women began working as domestic servants in the high-rise apartments mushrooming on the Worli sea face, or as cleaners in nearby office towers, both of which grew up as Mumbai developed into a financial center. Indeed, seventy-three of eighty women interviewed in 2004 were still working as domestic servants. A high percentage of women who were engaged in domestic service acquired their employment through friends in Janata Colony. Rates of pay, working hours, holidays, and working conditions varied considerably from one family to the next. Most worked for two to three households and for between three and six hours per day, and most reported rather mixed feelings toward domestic service. On the one hand, they welcomed the opportunity to work outside the home; on the other hand, they were often disgruntled about the conditions of their work, especially its low pay and lack of holidays. Like many women in central Mumbai, following the relocation of textile to Mumbai's hinterlands, their work constituted the "feminization of survival" during the early years of industrial restructuring (Sassen 2003). As in many other parts of the world, early neoliberal restructuring involved the loss of secure, male employment, meaning that women have often been forced into low-wage employment to maintain the viability of their households.

Although a National Union of Domestic Workers was established in Mumbai in 2001, and has had some legal success in having a minimum wage, pensions, and job security laws formally applied to this sector, none of the women in Janata Colony had joined it. This was because, as several noted, "competition for this work is very high." They felt that joining the NUDW might result in their loss of employment, since few household employers were willing to pay minimum wages or provide job security to domestic workers. Since domestic service is "hidden in the household," women were isolated from each other and felt unable to assert demands for higher wages or holidays from their employers.

In addition to domestic service and household work, a number of women engaged in petty commodity production or service work at a very small scale: two women made south Indian rice pancakes, called *iddlis*, every morning for a south Indian restaurant in Worli, four worked as vegetable vendors in a nearby market, one woman made incense sticks that she sold to nearby apartment dwellers, two did tailoring from their homes, while one woman sold fish at the Koli fishmarket in Worli village. In addition, two women who had formerly been domestic servants now worked as child-care workers in a crèche run by Pragati Kendra (Progress Center), an NGO associated with the Catholic Church, while another worked in the same NGO as a social worker.

Significantly, most women worked within the circumscribed space of Worli, with only a few engaging in domestic service in nearby Parel and Lalbaug neighborhoods that were about ten kilometers away. Not only did this keep their transportation costs low, but it also constituted a moral boundary of respectability that bus travel could transgress. As one respondent cautioned, "[E]ven though nice women work outside the home nowadays, it's not good to travel long distances on the train or bus because we have to look after the home also." In other words, while work outside the home was accepted by their community, long commuting distances to work, especially in the evenings, could be associated with the taint of prostitution.

Male Livelihoods

While women's work exhibited a readily discernible pattern based on domestic labor, both paid and unpaid, the work of men was more varied and fragmented. With one exception, all the men had insecure, contractually based jobs, and all but one experienced a drop in income—between one-fourth to half of their previous wages. Seventy-eight of eighty had previously worked in the textile industry, and two were still employed in nearby Century Mills in 2005, but as watchmen. Several men expressed reluctance to discuss their current work; first, they felt that their current insecure, contractual work was not a real job and were embarrassed to discuss it. Secondly, a number of younger men were active members of the Shiv Sena and distrusted research work carried out by non-Marathi speakers. The nativist stance of the Shiv Sena meant that Shiv Sena members were both distrustful of and hostile to non-Marathis working in Mumbai and particularly in research on potentially sensitive topics. In addition, one woman told us that her husband felt shame at being a retrenched mill worker. Hence, some of the data on their employment and conditions of work was acquired through interviews with their wives or daughters.

Twenty-six men were employed in the construction industry in 2005, helping to build the apartment buildings and office towers that were mushrooming in central Mumbai due to the growth of financial capital. These constructions were crowding out the squatter colonies that had previously provided housing for industrial workers. This work was based either on temporary contracts of several months duration or was daily wage work. Hence, working days and income varied considerably in the construction trades, from a minimum of four days per month to a maximum of twenty-three. Daily wages also varied between employers, between 100 and 180 Rs, per day, depending on the company. All the men who agreed to be interviewed complained about the contract system and the irregularity of their employment. They also had lost many of the benefits (e.g., pensions, sick leave, and holidays) that had accompanied their work in the textile mills.

Many worked at other part-time jobs to make ends meet. Five men worked as security guards either at industrial estates, office towers, for construction sites, or for the nearby Nehru Science Center. Eleven men, who were not employed in construction, plied auto-rickshaws in the northern suburbs, while thirteen had been able to plough their Voluntary Retirement Scheme payments[6] (VRS) from the textile mills into purchasing taxis. Two were street hawkers, selling tea from roadside stalls, called *dhabas*,[7] while one rather fortunate man was able to use his VRS payment, plus a loan from his sister, to retrain as a mechanic. He found a stable job with a garage in north Mumbai and by 2010 had moved to the northern suburbs with his wife. He had the most secure and well-paid work of all the people interviewed. Finally, one man worked for a nearby printing press, although his work was contractual and intermittent, and he was financially supported by his wife who worked in day care. Three men were currently unemployed—two due to alcoholism and the other due to a chronic illness.

All the men I interviewed believed that they had experienced a decline in their living standards, ability to take care of their families, long-term security, and also in social status following retrenchment from the mills and subsequent work in the "informal sector." A number believed that they were still unemployed, since they did not see temporary work in the informal sector as a real job. There were several, newer migrants to Janata Colony from Allahabad who were hired on temporary contracts after the strike ended. While they did not suffer the same degree of violent dispossession that striking workers experienced, they also viewed their present employment outside the mills as less secure, lower paid, and with fewer benefits than millwork. Deepak Verma, for example, migrated from Allahabad sixteen years ago and found a job as a winder in Century Mills in Worli in 1992 through an uncle. He was hired on a temporary basis; all workers after the strike, he asserted, were hired only on temporary contracts. By the time the mill closed permanently in 2003, he was making 5,000 Rs. per month. He also received a VRS payment of 75,000 Rs. in 2006. With this, and a 145,000 Rs. bank loan, he was able to purchase a taxi and has been a cab-driver ever since, from which he makes about 4,000 Rs. per month net profit. He has increased his working time in the past two years: he now works between eight and twelve hours per day and twenty-eight to twenty-nine days per month. However, he estimates that basic living expenses for himself, his wife, and one child are 7,000 Rs. per month. His wife has joined one of the microcredit circles recently to pay his daughter's school fees, which have doubled in the past two years. He remembers his work as a winder, with its regular hours and pay, the promise of a pension and other benefits, with nostalgia (interview March 26, 2010).

With varying degrees of intensity, all the male interviewees recounted a personal history of dispossession after the strike: first of stable jobs, second of the pensions and benefits that accompanied industrial work in Mumbai, and thirdly of their social status. Although work in the textile mills was not the highest-paid industrial work in Mumbai, its stability and benefits ensured that mill workers had a high status within Mumbai's working class and sons of mill workers were sought-after husbands. In the past two decades, marriages of sons and daughters have sometimes had to be delayed as parents struggle to find money for weddings and younger, underemployed men became less desirable husbands. I met several young men between the ages of twenty-five and thirty who were still living with their parents for financial reasons. Although people in Janata Colony do not pay dowry, due to the influence of social reform organizations in Worli, they often have to take out loans to pay for wedding expenses.[8] Some households accessed wedding loans through local microcredit organizations that began operating in Worli in the early 1990s. One man explained that the "respect" (*izzat*) of Marathi men was based on economically supporting their wives, children, and community, and this was lost after the strike. Prominent women from Janata Colony often referred to their husbands as useless loafers. They were particularly disparaging about a local community men's organization, the Mitra Mandal, referring to it as merely a place where idle men played cards, drank, and passed the time. The dispossession of stable jobs involved a loss also of social and cultural capital, witnessed in the difficulties that some families experienced in securing the marriages of their children.

Unemployment and underemployment of the children of ex–textile workers was a major anxiety in the community. While a few of the younger people had managed to attend college, and some had secured white-collar work, most were unable to attend college, mainly for financial reasons. In one case, a college principal had demanded bribes to admit a young man into an accountancy program for which he had already been accepted, which the family was unable to pay. As I was leaving Worli in 2010, the family was considering applying for a loan to pay the bribe, since an accountancy career for the son would immediately upgrade its status. In addition, most of the children of ex–textile workers were educated in Marathi-medium state schools and lacked the English language and westernized habitus that is now required for service work in the shopping malls and office towers that are overtaking central Mumbai. Hence, they are virtually excluded from the cosmopolitan imaginary that now shapes middle-class Mumbai's cultural ideals in an emerging global city.

The Decline of the MGKU and Rise of the Shiv Sena in Central Mumbai

The massive retrenchments that followed the failed textile strike led to increasing impoverishment and insecurity for ex–textile workers and their families and demoralization for the MGKU, the union that led the strike. The decade after the strike also witnessed a steep decline of support for the Communist Party in central Mumbai. This decline was mainly due to the fact that the Communist unions only gave lukewarm support to the striking workers (van Wersch 1992). In addition, many of the older Communist functionaries believed that the industrial proletariat in large scale factories was the vanguard class and that informal sector workers did not possess a revolutionary consciousness. Communist Party of India members I spoke to in Worli believed this was true even of men who had lost their previous jobs in the textile industry. They have largely remained aloof from the quotidian travails afflicting ex–textile workers in central Mumbai and even expelled some members who began organizing soup kitchens and microcredit organizations during and after the strike, believing these to be reformist deviations from class struggle (interviews 2004–2005).

One of the major political consequences of the failed strike was a political vacuum in central Mumbai at a time of large-scale retrenchment. This vacuum began to be filled by the militant Marathi-nationalist party, the Shiv Sena. The Shiv Sena gained its first electoral success municipally in middle-class neighborhoods by promoting Marathi linguistic identity during the Samyukta Maharashtra movement and later campaigning for job reservations for Marathi speakers. In its early phase, between 1970 and 1980, the predominantly working-class areas of central Mumbai were largely immune from the appeal of the Shiv Sena (Bhowmik 1999: 40). While the Shiv Sena gained a foothold in some mills prior to the strike, its early withdrawal of support for the textile strike led to its declining popularity among ex–industrial workers throughout the 1980s. In addition, Datta Samant's view that the Shiv Sena was a fascist organization discouraged many former mill workers from lending it their support. The major base of support for the Shiv Sena during this decade came from Marathi-speaking white-collar workers.

Yet by the early 1990s, the Shiv Sena had broadened its electoral appeal and organizational clout, reaching out especially to unemployed youth, many of them the children of ex-textile workers. It created employment centers and took over many of the akhadas (gyms) in central Mumbai, places where unemployed male youth often congregated. In the late 1980s, the Shiv Sena linked itself with the pan-India Hindu nationalism of the Bharatiya Janata Pary, in which Muslims became the feared and hated "other," targeted for their supposedly seditious, anti-national tendencies (Hansen 2001). The Shiv Sena also projected a militantly masculine image, idealized in the symbol of the warrior king Shivaji Bhonsale who founded the Maratha empire. In the 1990s, the Shiv Sena organized informal health centers and ambulances, as well as providing latrines in slums. It also created local- or ward-level recruiting and training centers in Mumbai, known as *shakas*. By 1990, there were about 220 *shakas* established throughout Mumbai (Katzenstein et al. 1997: 383). One was located in Janata Colony, the site of my fieldwork. These centers trained young men in physical fitness and in *dada-giri* (i.e., the use of force, extortion, and paternalism to gain political and economic ends, such as providing services in "slums").

The Shiv Sena has projected a plebeian and sometimes violent masculinity as an ideal subjectivity, standing partly outside the legal structures of the state. Yet they also claim to represent the moral order of the common Marathi citizen, of Marathi manus, policing the cultural boundaries of Marathi family values through rejecting both Western "liberal" culture and Muslim influences. Bal Thackeray has constantly berated his followers to be active and independent, to start some business or open a shop if there are no jobs. The Shiv Sena combines acquiescence to neoliberal policies of dispossession with psychological appeals to traditional forms of masculinity, now equated with individual entrepreneurship and responsibility. Hence, the Shiv Sena, and Thackeray in particular, projected an idealized image of what Marathi masculinity could and should be: individualistic, physically active and assertive, and competitively successful, rather than a reflection of the present state of underemployment and "degeneracy." For Thackeray, this present state of underemployment and poverty derived both from others taking jobs away from the Marathis and from the effeminacy and weakness of Marathi men. The Shiv Sena "offered young, powerless, insecure men the opportunity to view themselves as strong enterprising men, accepting of their male desires, able to control women and to command respect by their association with Shiva Sena" (Hansen 2001: 92–94).

The finances of the Shiv Sena are reputed to include donations from larger industrial houses and to be raised through *khandan*, or "gifts," a language of reciprocity that dates from the patronage of the Mahratta empire. Yet these "gifts" were often extorted from local shopkeepers and small businesses to "prevent" violence in their neighborhoods or to protect neighborhoods from violence in areas in which violence—often instigated by the Shiv Sena itself—might occur (Katzenstein et al. 1997: 370; Lele 1995). A number of government inquiries have implicated leaders and militias of the Shiv Sena in inciting and carrying out massacres of Muslims during the communal riots of 1992–1993 in which about a thousand people—mostly Muslim—lost their lives.

Its efforts at organizing recruitment, employment, and training centers, as well as providing for social services in central Mumbai resulted in Shiv Sena winning municipal elections after 1985, the year following the failed textile strike. The Shiv Sena enlarged its financial clout through its involvement in real estate transactions, increasingly becoming a major real estate player in Mumbai's transformation into a global financial center. Connections between the Shiv Sena, the real estate market, and large, organized criminal gangs also became prevalent in the late 1980s, as the latter provided the muscle and financial power for slum conversions, encroachments, and territorial control. In the late 1980s, several well-established gangsters, slumlords, and local thugs ran on a Shiv Sena ticket (Hansen 2001: 99; Weinstein 2008), as organized crime moved from "black market" activities in the 1970s to real estate development from the late 1980s onward (Weinstein 2008, Whitehead and More 2007). The Shiv Sena continued to dominate municipal elections throughout the 1990s, occasionally losing control over Mumbai's administration to the Congress Party, as in 2004. More recently, the Shiv Sena split into a faction led by Bal Thackeray's son, Uddhay, and another led by his nephew, Raj Thackeray, renamed the Maharastra Navriman Sena (MNS). Policies and practices of an exclusive Marathi nationalism continue to dominate MNS strategy.

Despite the recent division in the Shiv Sena, it is safe to say that militant Marathi nationalism continues to exert a hold over significant sections of the younger people living in Mumbai slums in central Mumbai. The psychological and discursive appeal of the Shiv Sena and the MNS cannot be attributed solely to economic factors. However, the psychological insecurities generated by mass unemployment and deindustrialization throughout the late 1980s and early 1990s undoubtedly played their part in making the totalizing organizational culture and hypermasculine discourse of the Shiv Sena appealing for the children of ex–textile workers. In addition, "the mutual supportive activities of the Shiv Sena in the slums gave the Shiv Sena workers a sense of direction and control in an otherwise chaotic existence" (Lele 1995). Neither the MGKU, the union leading the strike, nor left political parties could transcend a "rational" analysis of unemployment to match the organizational, cultural, and psychological support offered by the Shiv Sena. Indeed, the Shiv Sena came to control neighborhood spaces in central Mumbai in similar ways that the early Communist Party dominated Girangaon neighborhoods in the late 1920s and 1930s.

The ascendance of the Shiv Sena in former working-class neighborhoods in central Mumbai is reflected in a generational gap between ex–textile workers and their children. As one young man explained to me, "The Communist Parties and Datta Samant blamed capitalism for the loss of jobs and told us to wait for socialism. The Shiv Sena gave us work when we had nothing and promised to save jobs for Maharashtrians." Bhowmik reports a similar generational difference emerging in ex–textile workers' families in the 1990s. A middle-aged retrenched worker and former activist in the MKGU, now working as a street hawker, complained about his sons making fun of his politics: "What have you got from your support of the communists? Unemployment and a useless ideology . . . at least the Shiv Sena gives us a steady income" (Bhowmik 1999: 44).

However, the support for the Shiv Sena and/or the MNS was both fragmentary and partial in Janata Colony. Some ex–textile workers, undoubtedly, joined the Shiv Sena in the late 1980s and early 1990s. Yet none of the ex–textile workers I spoke to were supporters of the Shiv Sena or the MNS. They claimed to have retained their allegiance to the MGKU leadership, still idolized Datta Samant, and agreed with his view of the Shiv Sena as a fascist organization. Some joked in 2010 that the Shiv Sena was now a paper tiger, because it had to pay people to attend its demonstrations, for example the boycotting of a Bollywood film, *My Name is Khan*, which presented Muslims in a sympathetic light. In addition, the major NGO in Janata Colony, Pragati Kendra (Progress Center), promoted liberal, secular ideals and community empowerment and was connected to the Catholic Church and to the ideals of liberation theology. The municipal corporator (or councilor) for the Worli neighborhood, an elected official, was a member of the Communist Party, who had successfully held off the advance of the Shiv Sena in Worli for twenty years. Indeed, it is the children of ex–textile workers, who face an extremely insecure future and have never experienced industrial solidarity, who have become vulnerable to the appeals of the Shiv Sena in Janata Colony.

Neoliberalization of Space in Central Mumbai

The failure of the textile strike of 1982–1984 and subsequent deindustrialization of central Mumbai occurred simultaneously with the reshaping of the southern and central neighborhoods of the city into India's major financial center. Indeed, following the strike, many MGKU and other activists turned their attention toward housing activism, as they believed that the gentrification and redevelopment of central Mumbai was already laid out in plans drawn up by the textile industry and the central government during the strike itself (D'Monte 2002: 4–5). Following the strike, many textile owners transformed themselves into real estate developers and shifted their investments to commercial and residential real estate (personal communication, P. Deshpandey). The MGKU housing activists formed a housing NGO known as the Bombay Environmental Action Group, which also included progressive architects and urban planners. It lobbied the state government to retain and upgrade the residential spaces of ex–textile workers, as well as providing for more green space in a city that had a minuscule amount—0.03 acres per one hundred inhabitants—of park and green space.

This double movement of capital in central Mumbai possessed two simultaneous movements, both of which produced dispossession: the first involved industrial destruction, and the second was directed toward financial and real estate speculation, with the major plan being to link the southern business districts in Fort and Nariman Point with the northern residential suburbs. Real estate speculation led to a spatial redevelopment of central Mumbai that reflects its new profile as an aspiring global city (Banerjee-Guha 2002; D'Monte 2002; Whitehead and More 2007). Areas of central Mumbai are giving way to office towers, shopping malls, upscale high-rise apartment buildings, and entertainment complexes. The redevelopment of central Mumbai has led to an influx of middle-class professionals and business elites there, often living side-by-side with remaining "slum-dwellers" and ex–textile workers.

The reshaping of both capital and place was driven by the underlying political economy of declining rates of profit in large-scale industries and rising potential ground rents in the central city. Specifically, rent gaps were emerging between existing rents in chawls and "slums," and the potential ground rent to be realized from redeveloping both the mill lands and the workers' residential spaces into upscale office towers and apartment complexes, and then leasing these spaces to the FIRE businesses and middle-class professionals. As Mumbai became repositioned as in the 1990s as India's major financial center, rents and land prices rose in tandem in both south and central Mumbai.

Neil Smith's (1996) notion of rent gaps has explained the process of deindustrialization followed by gentrification and redevelopment that accompanied the expansion of financial centers such as New York and London during the past thirty years. Yet the analysis of changing rent gaps also applies to Mumbai. Ground rent is a claim made by landowners on users of the land; it represents a reduction from total surplus value created above the cost price by producers. For Smith, actual, capitalized rent is the quantity of ground rent that is appropriated by the landowner, given existing land use. Potential rent is the amount that might be capitalized under the land's "highest and best possible use," or at least a "higher and better use" than the present one (Smith 1996: 68). The rent gap is simply the disparity between actual and potential ground rent.

Smith analyses the gaps between actual and potential rents in New York, London, and Amsterdam, focusing especially on neighborhoods sandwiched between the central financial districts and outer suburbs. Such neighborhoods are spatially and structurally similar to central Mumbai, sandwiched between the southern financial core and the northern suburbs housing the middle class. Smith notes that rent gaps can arise in these middling neighborhoods due to normal cycles of disinvestment and also following rapid inflation, or where older uses of the land have become unprofitable, or immediately after a period of economic liberalization (Smith 1996: 76). All such neighborhoods face strong gentrifying pressures once these cities become inserted into global capitalism as financial centers.

Since all these conditions operated either singly or in combination in Mumbai over the past few decades, it is not surprising that rents in the southern zone (i.e., the central financial district) rose in the 1990s to become the highest in the world, shortly after economic liberalization occurred. Financial liberalization after 1991 led to an influx of multinationals seeking commercial real estate and interested in real estate speculation (Nijman 2000). A stock market downturn in 1992, fuelled by a financial scam, also led to a flood of domestic equity into Mumbai real estate (Nijman 2000; Tiwari 2000). The speculative nature of the real estate market led to a collapse of 30 percent in the late 1990s, but prices quickly rebounded by the beginning of 2000. Prices in central Mumbai also rose substantially (i.e., by about 450 percent in the early 1990s) and with a few downturns (i.e., in late fall 2008–early 2009) they have continued their upward climb. In other words, rent gaps were rising very markedly in the former mill neighborhoods of central Mumbai. Between 2005 and 2010, south and central

Mumbai had among the top ten real estate prices in the world. In contrast, the average income in Mumbai was about US $4,500 in 2006, making Mumbai one of the most unaffordable world cities from the mid-1990s onward.

The mill owners' shift from manufacturing to gentrification of mill neighborhoods began in earnest after the collapse of the strike. They accelerated the process of declaring their mills "sick" by not modernizing their machinery and by closing them down piecemeal. Yet there were a number of legal hurdles to overcome in this transformation, since the mill lands had been originally leased to companies for industrial purposes only. They overcame this legal problem through subcontracting production elsewhere, so that the mills appeared to be losing money. Their unprofitability qualified them for loans from the Board for Industrial and Financial Reconstruction (BIFR), a central government agency that helped industries modernize their facilities. The applications for mill modernization included an appendage with residential, commercial, and leisure facilities added to the application. The second phase, however, involved using monies sanctioned by the BIFR to sell some of the land for commercial or residential uses. This process provided mill owners with even more reasons to lay off remaining workers.

The most infamous example of this process is the Phoenix Mills in Parel, now a posh shopping center and apartment complex (Krishnan 2000: 4–5). In 1978, a fire, which many workers believe was set by management, allowed for a car dealership to be built where the former mill canteen stood. In 1984, a new proposal to "revive" the mill allotted an additional twenty-three thousand square meters for commercial purposes to provide rent to offset the mill's losses. A further application in 1995 gave Phoenix Mills tax exemption on the basis of further reviving the mill.

In 1998, the management applied to BIFR for additions to the mill, including recreation facilities such as a club, indoor sports facilities such as billiards, and "a number of bowling alleys" as well as a health club, spa, and sauna for the staff of the mill (Krishnan 2000: 10). The recreation facilities, however, were not really meant for Phoenix Mills staff, but instead became the famous Bowling Alley restaurant, which opened to much fanfare in May 1999. Alongside it was a high-end discotheque, Fire and Ice, plus numerous restaurants and shops, including the ubiquitous McDonalds, Marks and Spencer, the Gap, and Rita Kumar, a Delhi-based fashion designer. The "integrity" of the mill structure was preserved through retaining one of the chimney stacks, painted over to resemble a bowling pin and through renovating some of the mill sheds into offices (Krishnan 2000: 6). Meanwhile, areas for two major apartment complexes, Phoenix Towers A and B, were constructed by Mittal Towers and were selling for approximately 14,000 Rs. per square foot in 2006 (interview, P. Deshpandey, 18 December 2006). Needless to say, no bowling alleys, billiard rooms, or other recreational facilities were built for the staff of the mill.

Retrenchments at Phoenix Mills accompanied the transformation of the mill structure. After the strike, the mill retained only twelve hundred of its seven thousand workforce, and all were temporary workers. In 1988, the Processing Department was closed and its tasks—winding, framing, blowing, etc.—were subcontracted to power-looms in Bhiwandi. This process caused the retrenchment of five hundred more employees (Krishnan 2000: 12). By 1999, there were only 150 contract workers remaining at Phoenix Mills, a year after it was claiming the need for recreational space for a thousand workers and staff. By 2000, all remaining 150 workers had been let go; and some are still waiting for their Voluntary Retirement Scheme payments (interview, December 18, 2006). While Phoenix Mills pioneered the way, other mills, including Matulya Mills, the Kalpataru Heights in Mahalaxmi, the Belvedere Court, and Century Mills in Worli, where I carried out fieldwork, soon followed suit, transforming the mills into shopping malls, office towers, and high-end apartment buildings.

Debate over, and Fate of, the Mill Lands

The land attached to the mills is considered a major source for housing and office redevelopment, consisting of over five hundred acres in central Mumbai. There has been a great deal of public debate over these lands (D'Monte 2002), as mill owners wish to receive the highest rent from their "best possible use," while housing activists want a substantial portion to be reserved for low-cost housing and public amenities. A major barrier to their transformation into high-end commercial and residential real estate was the Development Control Regulations. These were brought into force by the state government through legal cases filed by Bombay Environmental Action Group during the early 1990s, when the working class of Mumbai still had a fairly strong political presence. Rule 58 of the Development Control Regulations specified that one-third of mill lands should be reserved for low cost public housing since retrenched workers needed to be accommodated. One-third was to be reserved for public purposes, such as parks or other amenities, and only one-third was to be used for real estate development. The rationale of this formula was that most mill lands were not specifically owned by textile firms, but had been leased for extended periods provided they were used for industrial purposes. In addition, Bombay already had a very high built-up area in relation to green spaces; hence one-third of the mill lands should be devoted to public parks.

Nevertheless, the huge rent gaps that had emerged gave developers strong incentives to bypass the legal requirements for redevelopment and push for changes in the Development Control Regulations (DCR). C. Prabhu has shown that real estate companies could engender an 80 percent increase in profit rates through dismantling the regulations (C. Prabhu, quoted in D'Monte 2002: 192), hence the incentives for changing these rules were very great.

With a change in government to the Congress Party in the state elections of 2000, subtle changes in the wording of the DCR were instituted, so that the amount given over to the Brihamumbui Municipal Corporation (BMC) and Maharashtra Housing and Development Authority (MHADA) was only one-third of open land (i.e., that outside the perimeters of the mill buildings). This amounts only to about 10–12 percent of the land surface in mill areas. This change also held only if the mill owners demolished the buildings. For those mills in which renovation into shopping malls took place, however, no land had to be parted with, as with Phoenix Towers. This modification in the DCR led the Bombay Environmental Action Group to file a public interest lawsuit with the Mumbai High Court, charging that the change in phrasing subverted the purpose of Rule 58. While they won their case in the Mumbai High Court in October 2005, the National Textile Corporation, which owned thirteen of the sixty mill sites, filed a counter petition with the Supreme Court in October 2006. Their major argument was that the leases of many of these lands had already been sold to developers. In March 2006, the Supreme Court sided with the National Textile Corporation. Most of the lands are apparently slated for shopping malls. Indeed, the sale of the twenty-five National Textile Corporation mills between March and July 2005 covered an area of fifty acres at prices that surprised even those Mumbaikers jaded by stratospheric real estate market. In addition, although the mill owners possessed only lease rights, the lands were sold as if they were freehold properties.

Although protests against this ruling were organized by the MGKU and seventeen other groups, including the Trade Union Congress, the Center of Indian Trade Unions, the Documentation Research and Training Center, the Communist Party of India, Communist Party of India (Marxist), and others, there has not been widespread resistance to this conversion of mill lands into zones of "residential, commercial and recreational excellence" (P. Deshpandey, personal communication). While mass rallies during the textile strike attracted tens and even hundreds of thousands of demonstrators, the numbers protesting against gentrification have never been more than several thousand. This was true even for demonstrations against slum clearances in 2004–2005. The lack of major overt resistance may be partly due to the memories of the failed textile strike, and the sense of defeatism it engendered, and partly due to fear of the pervasive underworld involvement in the real estate market.

As Weinstein (2008) notes, the shift from import substitution to economic liberalization in India was also accompanied by a shift in Mumbai's underworld activities. Since import quotas were relaxed in 1991, the black market smuggling of contraband goods was no longer profitable, and organized crime diversified into real estate speculation and development. In addition, the land market in Mumbai is oligopsonistic: supply is constricted by geography and especially by historical factors. First, major public bodies own large tracts of land, including the Mumbai Port Trust (two thousand acres), the Airport Authority, and the National Textile Corporation (NTC) (four hundred acres) (Singh 2003: 10). Second, privately owned land is highly concentrated, due to land grants originating in the colonial period, in which large tracts were leased as a reward for political loyalty to the British. In this way, Parsi merchants and businesspeople, who had cooperated with the British conquest of the Mahrattas, acquired land trusts that covered most of Mumbai islands (*Times of India*, 31 July 2005, p. 4). Today, about nine developers and trusts control all available private land on Mumbai island (Singh 2003: 6). Given the rising real estate values throughout Mumbai, neither developers nor trusts are willing to sell much of the land they currently possess. Hence, forceful encroachments of private land and forceful conversions of both public and private land are common. Gangland involvement (both related and independent of the Shiv Sena) in real estate transactions has been a feature of Mumbai's real estate development for decades, but has increased markedly during the liberalization phase. The role of the underworld is crucial in lubricating the transition from manufacturing to an economy dominated by real estate and financial services, both in disciplining ex-workers' resistance to moving out from chawls and "slums," and in mediating conflicts between real estate developers. As one housing activist told me: "Developers need to get 70 percent of the population of a site to agree for redevelopment in order for it to take place. People in an area who refuse to agree to redevelopment are met with muscle-power and sometimes, bribes. Gangs in the city are regularly used for extortion and for persuading people to move. Also, the builders take money from financiers, with the return being based on 'respect'; however, very often 'respect' is not enough and gangs must be employed for repayment" (personal communication, P. Deshpandey). The increasing infiltration of Mumbai's land mafias into all major political parties, including both the Shiv Sena and the Congress Party, and their ability to combine bribes with extortion has enabled them to circumvent existing regulations and ensure a speedy completion of shopping malls, office-towers and entertainment complexes (ibid).

The "slum-dwellers" of central Mumbai, including those in Janata Colony who squatted on "free" if illegal land, now occupy land that is among the most expensive in the world. In Worli, real estate was priced at 9,000 Rs. per square foot in 2004, the price of the middle-class apartment buildings that have mushroomed along the adjacent Worli Sea Face. This price rose to 14,000 Rs. per square foot in 2005. By the spring of 2010, with the completion of the Bandra-Worli Sea Link in 2009, these prices again doubled. Hence, the real estate mafias have strongly pressured the state government to rid these neighborhoods of any informal habitation, including "slums" and chawls. Clearly, more revanchist municipal policies toward "slum-dwellers" in central Mumbai have been surfacing in the past decade.

The first opening to private sector slum development occurred through the Slum Rehabilitation Scheme, instituted by the Shiv Sena municipal government in 1995. Under this policy, private developers were encouraged to build apartment blocks on demolished "slum" land, which they received free of cost, as long as 25 percent of the housing stock was reserved for the former "slum-dwellers." The remaining 75 percent was to be sold to middle- and high-income earners or as commercial real estate. In addition, developers were given an increased FSI (floor-space index) for the private apartments as an added incentive to reserve 25 percent free housing for "slum-dwellers." In practice, this meant that apartments and commercial towers could be built 25 percent higher than in the past. Each apartment for a "slum-dweller" or chawl-dweller was to be 225 square feet, including a kitchen and bathroom area. In addition, the developer had to acquire 70 percent approval for the scheme from the local population. As the informant quoted above indicated, sometimes force, intimidation and bribes have been used to gain this legal approval.

As a result of the spiraling real estate gains in central Mumbai, developers have been keen to bypass the Slum Rehabilitation guidelines and redevelop all "slum" lands as upscale real estate. They have been aided by prominent NGOs, such as Bombay First and the McKinsey Foundation, who aim to recreate Mumbai as the next Shanghai by 2015. The housing policies of the municipal government have largely followed these recommendations and the plans of the gentrification mafia. As a result, "slum" evictions are now the norm. In December 2004–January 2005, the state government, elected on a platform of regularizing and redeveloping "slums" where inhabitants had been established after 2000, began instead a policy of widespread demolitions of "slums" in both south and central Mumbai that had been regularized after 1995. Those people who had settled in informal habitation prior to 1995 received a photopass, which gave them the right to vote and also protected them somewhat from future evictions. About three hundred thousand people who had settled in Mumbai after 2000, and who did not possess a photo-pass, had their houses and hutments demolished during this period, including about forty people in Janata Colony who had built their houses on the side of the road leading to the high-rises on the Worli sea face. In July 2005, there were further demolitions in Worli, and a further one hundred people lost their houses, without compensation.

These demolitions were certainly met with protest. A coalition of twenty organizations that were either active in the strike or were active in housing issues, including the MGKU, the Communist Party of India, the Communist Party of India (Marxist), the Trade Union Joint Action Committee, the Committee for the Right to Housing, the Indian Center for Human Rights and Law, Yuva Janata, and the National Alliance of People's Organizations, was formed to organize legal and political protests to the demolitions. Various street protests were organized, including one on January 13, 2005, in which about one hundred people stormed the provincial government legislature dressed as nineteenth-century Mahars, or "untouchables," with spittle boxes hanging from their necks (interviews 2005). This form of dress was meant as a dramatic symbol equating today's "slum-dwellers" with the former rural "untouchables," who were required in the nineteenth century to wear spittle boxes around their necks to stop their bodily pollution from defiling Brahmins. The demonstrators were arrested and held in jail for two days, with one young girl dying following a police charge with lathis. The injured were often refused entry into local hospitals, because the medical staff feared that documentation of these cases could lead to legal charges against the police and potential police harassment if this occurred. On February 13, 2005, five hundred people laid siege to the offices of the Congress Party, and following this, the ruling party ordered the demolition stopped.

However, smaller, piecemeal demolitions and evictions have been reported from various neighborhoods from 2005 to 2010. In Janata Colony, about 150 people were evicted in 2008 and 2010 from informal houses that had been erected near the bus stand and along Sasmira Marg, the main thoroughfare to the Worli sea face. The rationale was that such houses would be in danger from the increased traffic due to the opening of the Bandra-Worli Sea Link bridge in July 2009. Although the Bombay Municipal Corporation has promised to build a three-story apartment building for them, the former residents of Sasmira Marg are still unhoused at present.

Despite the legal protests by civil society organizations, the street protests in 2005 did not result in huge demonstrations of ex–textile workers and their families. The relative quiescence of a formerly activist working-class community can be explained by a congruence of factors. First, the major organizations of the Mumbai working class, especially the trade unions, had been decimated by the failure of the textile strike and Mumbai's ongoing deindustrialization. Second, with most "slum-dwellers" now working in the informal sector, few have the time or resources to forgo a day's work to participate in the demonstrations. Third, the Shiv Sena, then influential in many of Mumbai's "slums," supported the demolitions, arguing that it was mainly recent Bangladeshi Muslim migrants whose hutments were being demolished. Fourth, one cannot discount a general sense of defeat in the face of powerful neoliberal government and corporate interests in Mumbai that shapes the political horizon of many former textile workers and their families. The following extract from my field notes recounts what happened to two households whose hutments in Janata Colony were demolished in 2005. It shows how finding alternative, affordable accommodation in Janata Colony had become extremely difficult. It also illustrates the municipal government's view of the ex–textile workers and their families as basically expendable populations.

Vanita and Mina recounted the hardships they underwent for at least one year following the demolitions of their homes on Sasmira Marg in 2005. In both cases, they and their families had to live under tarpaulins for a year. Vanita is an activist who was hired as a social worker for a local NGO in 2003 and possesses a high degree of social capital in Janata Colony. Hence, after hearing of her plight, the lawyer for this organization finally rented her family a single room in her apartment on Worli Sea Face. However, the rent was 5,000 Rs per month, and tensions erupted when Vanita could not pay, since her salary as a social worker was insufficient and she is the sole breadwinner in her family. Fortunately, a friend of the family in Koliwada who had secured a permanent job at the Docks after the strike, came to their rescue by renting them a two-room apartment for Rs. 3000 in the fishing village, where they now reside. Her daughter and son-in-law live next door.

Mina had an even more difficult experience, because she did not have the same influence in the community that Vanita possessed. Mina protested to the BMC many times about the demolition. She had been living in Janata Colony for 30 years and possessed a photopass, i.e. a document that registers "slum-dwellers" on the basis of their long-standing residence on a squatted property. The photopass enables its owner to vote in elections, and also gives rights of compensation if displacement occurs. The BMC's response was to send goondas (thugs) to physically harass and threaten them, after which they gave up trying to reclaim their house space or to petition for a new space. Mina and her husband, who works at a printing press, were finally able to find a tiny, rented room in the Koli fishing village through acquiring a loan from a local microcredit NGO. She, her husband, and two sons live in a 20 foot by 35 foot room (field notes, March 2010).

Both Vanita and Mina and their families are fairly resigned to their situation and to the general process of gentrification currently engulfing central Mumbai and eroding the spaces in which they and other "slum-dwellers" live and work. This sense of resignation in the face of overwhelming odds seemed to characterize most of the people I spoke to in Janata Colony concerning their housing problems and possible evictions in the future. The former industrial workers and their families lack a strong, unified form of protest. Their labor market fragmentation in various "informal sector" jobs complicates organization at the point of production. Attempts to organize "slum-dwellers" against housing, eviction, and other issues have been mainly neighborhood based and divided by their limited geographical scope. In addition, local NGOs tend to be overstretched in terms of both resources and personnel. Under these conditions, it is easy to empathize with Vanita's current resignation and her dream to move to north Mumbai, where rents, food, and other living costs are more reasonable. Finding a job there for herself and her unemployed husband, however, remains a barrier to their move.

The changed policies of the state government, and the urban policies of both the state and central governments, promote the continued sale and redevelopment of mill lands and of "slum" areas in ex-working-class neighborhoods. Street hawkers were banished from south and central Mumbai in 2008, removing simultaneously both a source of employment for ex–textile workers and the informal markets that sold food and household articles cheaply. Scooter rickshaws, a relatively inexpensive mode of transport and means of informal employment, are also banned from south and central Mumbai because their slow speed and low-cost clients do not conform to the image of a global city, with its high-speed freeways transporting air-conditioned business people from the southern financial districts to the northern residential suburbs. The stores close to Janata Colony now consist of high-end designer outlets, coffee shops, and shopping malls, which are far too expensive for most Janata Colony residents to frequent. The only major food and clothing market left in central Mumbai is in Parel, several kilometers and a thirty-minute bus ride away from Janata Colony. As Sassen notes, the replacement of low-cost neighborhood shopping locales that cater to local needs by upscale boutiques and restaurants is a common feature of global city redevelopment, putting additional spatial demands upon the urban poor (Sassen 2006: 86).

In addition, two public parks near Janata Colony were sold to real estate trusts in 2010 and closed to the general public, although open to high-rise residents. Hence, ex–textile workers and their spouses and children have experienced dispossession both in the spheres of consumption and production, constituting a kind of pincer movement that makes daily living increasingly difficult. Residents of Janata Colony are increasingly hemmed in by the class and spatial politics of central Mumbai, being viewed by real estate companies, municipal government agencies, and the state development agencies as "matter out of place." The sentiments of the new middle class in Mumbai, constituted as global consumers in a rising Indian economy, increasingly hinge on a politics of erasure in relation to ex-workers and "slum- dwellers." Middle-class citizens groups frequently gain media exposure by objecting to the "encroachments" of small shops and street hawkers on public spaces and walkways and have spearheaded drives to have street-hawking, microenterprises, and microshops declared illegal. Such sentiments represent a change in middle-class attitudes toward the urban poor, from a formerly "chelta hai," or "anything goes," ideology that symbolized the sometimes anarchic, but still-functioning, character of Indian cities, toward much more exclusionary sentiments in which formerly mixed spaces are to be cleansed, redeveloped and reordered (Fernandes 2006).

Conclusion

The class and spatial politics in central Mumbai over the past thirty years have been closely intertwined, and their combined effect has been a shrinkage or outright dispossession of livelihood security, and spaces for work, housing, consumption and leisure. Ex–textile workers are trapped in the interstices of an urban geography produced and reproduced in such a way as to increasingly exclude them. The class cleansing that has accompanied Mumbai's transformation into a global financial center has produced increasingly polarized spaces of work, life, habitation and leisure: the image of "slum" dwellings still standing alongside gated high-rises, replete with swimming pools and tennis courts, has become a visual synecdoche of the city's increasing fragmentation and polarization in terms of class, consumption, and cultural capital.

The fragmentation of both work and domestic space economies in central Mumbai has been accompanied by increasing political fragmentation of working-class organizations. No single organization today possesses the reach that former trade unions and left political parties possessed during the Fordist era. Indeed, the remnants of the CPI in Worli tend to be dominated by a revisionist leadership that views informal sector workers as lacking "revolutionary potential," an attribute that only the industrial proletariat apparently possesses (Nitin More, personal communication). With most of India's working population now employed in the informal sector, it is safe to say that such *doxa* has inhibited Communist support in Janata Colony (and elsewhere). In addition, the fragmented space economies of central

Mumbai has rendered the MGKU relatively ineffective in Worli, due to the difficulties of organizing at the point of production. In addition, those organizations that oppose gentrification and argue for upgrading existing slums are small-scale NGOs, such as Pragati Kendra in Janata Colony or SOS (Save our Slums) in Parel, that are neighborhood-based, and lack the personnel to devote to citywide political coordination.

In addition, the Shiv Sena, and its offshoot, the MNS, has hitched a plebeian Marathi cultural identity to a triumphalist and exclusionary majority nationalism. This nationalism seeks to insert India into the global economy as a rising, economic superstar, based on the region's possession of a low-cost, skilled labor force. Hence, the fragmentation and informalization of work and its exploitation in small-scale factories or service industries, is seen as a necessary "social cost" of India's rapid development. Indeed, this attitude toward labor is true not only of the Shiv Sena's platform, but of all major political parties: it is India's "comparative advantage" at this particular stage of its insertion into global supply chains. Once again, India's workers are being forced to sacrifice their class interests to national goals, this time for the demands of national competitiveness at a global scale.

The nationalist character of the supposedly temporary sacrifice of workers' rights is a signal feature of contemporary competitive neoliberalism in India. It is reflected in the fact that not only central and state governments, but the major trade unions rejected the insertion of a social clause including environmental and labor standards, into World Trade Organization agreements in the late 1990s. They viewed the social clause as a means for workers in the developed world to retain their existing geospatial (and imperialist) privileges, since it imposed greater relative costs on "developing" regions, where cheap, skilled labor power was the main attraction for investment (Chan and Ross 2003). Hence, until trade unions in India forgo the "cheap labor" advantage of India's drive for export-led growth, it seems unlikely that much organizational militancy can be expected from that sector in the near future. Class contradictions have been largely subsumed under national imperatives in the global shift from western to eastern (and southern) production platforms, while neoliberal governmentality produces a global discipline of divide-and-rule that seems to emanate from rational considerations of specific comparative national advantages.

In the 1930s and 1940s, the Communist trade unions were able to forge a wide community of political sentiment in the central Mumbai mill districts based on innovative organizational strategies focused on the neighborhood as well as the workplace (Chandavarkar 2004). Today, the fragmentation of working-class livelihoods in small-scale informal enterprises and service sector jobs makes organizing at the point of production extremely difficult. A new national union, the National Trade Union Initiative, that is independent of all political parties and dedicated to organizing informal sector workers, emerged in 2006 through the amalgamation of three hundred independent, small trade unions. It launched a relatively successful nationwide general strike in February 2013. However, it is not yet active in Janata Colony or in Worli itself. If it is possible to imagine and create or recreate innovative organizational forms that can encompass the fragmented work and living spaces across the geography of central Mumbai, it is from groups such as the ex–textile workers of Mumbai, with their militant labor history, that a revindicative class politics might arise in the near future.

Acknowledgments

I would like to thank the Shastri Indo-Canadian Institute and the University of Lethbridge for providing the funding that made this study possible. I would like to especially acknowledge the contributions of my research assistant for the earlier part of this study, Nitin More. Nitin and I discussed many of the political, historical, and cultural issues covered in this chapter, and his insights contributed a great deal to its themes. Nitin was working as an activist/scholar for LEARN (Labour Education and Action Research Network) in central Mumbai, organizing women workers in Dharavi's informal sector, when he met an untimely death through an "apparent" electrical accident in 2011. He was only 30 years old and had recently married and started a family. The son of a mill worker from Parel, Nitin understood firsthand the hardships faced by the families of retrenched mill workers that were kept going in the 1980s and 1980s by women's informal labor, both inside and outside the home. Indeed, he believed it was through his mother's sacrifices that he was able to attend college. He made it his life's work to help women informal workers organize themselves to attain basic social security such as fair wages, health-care, and access to food and cooking fuel, a life's work ended by his untimely death. I therefore dedicate this chapter with respect and admiration to his memory.

Notes

1. All informal forms of habitation in Mumbai are referred to as slums in official documents. Due to the perjorative connotations of the word slum, often connected to criminality and lack of hygiene, I have put the term in quotation marks. Indeed, many "slums" in Mumbai have been renovated over time, and they often house people with lower-middle-class or even middle-class occupations.
2. Falzon 2004 notes that seventeen wards of the northern suburbs witnessed a population growth of 50 percent between 1981 and 1991.
3. The term *bhaiyya* refers to Hindi-speaking migrants from Uttar Pradesh and Bihar.
4. Indeed, Worli was one of the seven original fishing villages of Mumbai.
5. One lakh is one hundred thousand in quantity.
6. VRS is short for Voluntary Retirement Scheme. It refers to the payments that ex–textile mill workers received after they lost their jobs in the late 1980s and early 1990s. Although these payments were substantial, often amounting to several lakhs, many interviewed stated that they had to wait between five and ten years to receive them.
7. Street hawking was banned in south and central Mumbai in 2008, thus removing another employment possibility for ex–textile workers.
8. Dowry was not an issue in Janata Colony for the people I interviewed. Several interviewees remarked that two local NGOs had been active in campaigning against dowry and would not allow them to access microcredit if they were known to pay dowry. However, marriage ceremonies in the kunbi Maratha and agri families are quite expensive and often require recourse to microcredit loans.

References

Banerjee-Guha, Swapna. 2002. "Shifting Cities: Urban Restructuring in Mumbai." *Economic and Political Weekly* 37, no. 2 (January): 121–128.

Bhowmik, Sharit. 1999. "Communalism and Labor: Political Process and Textile Labor in Mumbai." In University of Mumbai, Refresher Course.

Bhowmik, Sharit, and Nitin More. 2001. "Coping with Urban Poverty: Ex-Textile Workers of Mumbai." *Economic and Political Weekly* 36, no. 52 (December): 4822–4827.

Chan, Anita, and Robert J. S. Ross. 2003. "Race to the Bottom: International Trade Without a Social Clause." *Third World Quarterly* 24, no. 6 (June): 1011–1028.

Chandavarkar, Rajnarayan. 1984. *The Origins of Industrial Capitalism in India: Business Strategies and Working Classes in Bombay, 1900–1940*. Cambridge: Cambridge University Press.

———. 1998. *Imperial Power and Popular Politics: Class, Resistance and the State in India, 1850–1950*. Cambridge: Cambridge University Press.

———. 2004. "From Neighborhood to Nation: The Rise and Fall of the Left in Bombay's Girangaon in the Twentieth Century." In *One Hundred Years, One Hundred Voices: The Mill Workers of Girangaon, An Oral History*, ed. Meena Menon and Neera Adarkar. Delhi: Seagull Books.

Chatterjee, Partha. 1997. *State and Politics in India*. New Delhi: Oxford University Press.

Corbridge, Sturat, and John Harriss. 2000. *Reinventing India*. London: Routledge.

Doshi, Sapana. 2012. "The Politics of the Evicted: Redevelopment, Subjectivity, and Difference in Mumbai's Slum Frontier." *Antipode*, Early View (Online Version): 1–22.

D'Monte, Darryl. 2002. *Ripping the Fabric: The Decline of Mumbai and its Mills*. Delhi: Oxford University Press.

Fanon, Franz. 1967. *Black Skin, White Masks*. New York: Grove Press.

Falzon, Mark Anthony. 2004. "Paragons of Lifestyle: Gated Communities and the Politics of Space in Mumbai." *City and Society* 16, no. 2 (June): 145–167.

Fernandes, Leela. 2006. *India's New Middle Class: Democratic Politics in an Era of Economic Reform*. Minneapolis: University of Minnesota Press.

Gupta, Dipankar. 1984. "Continuous Hierarchies and Discrete Castes." *Economic and Political Weekly* 19, no. 46 (November): 1955–1958.

Hansen, Thomas Blom. 2001. *Wages of Violence: Naming and Identity in Postcolonial Bombay*. Princeton: Princeton University Press.

Kaviraj, Sudipta. 1988. "A Critique of the Passive Revolution." *Economic and Political Weekly*, Vol. 23, no. 45, pp. 2429–2442

Katzenstein, Mary Fainsod, Uday Singh Mehta, and Usha Thakkar. 1997. "The Rebirth of Shiv Sena: The Symbiosis of Discursive an Organizational Power." *Journal of Asian Studies* 56, no. 2 (May): 371–390.

Krishnan, Shekhar. 2000. "The Murder of the Mills: A Case Study of Phoenix Mills." Report Prepared for the Girangaon Bachao Andolan.

Lakha, Salim. 1989. "Organized Labor and Militant Unionism: The Bombay Textile Workers' Strike of 1982." *Bulletin of Concerned Asian Scholars* 20, no. 2: 42–54.

Lele, Jayant. 1995. "Saffronisation of Shiv Sena." In *Bombay: Metaphor for Modern India*, ed. Sujata Patel and Alice Thorner. New Delhi: Oxford University Press.

Marx, Karl 1976. *Capital*, Volume I. New York: Penguin.

Mckinsey & Company. 2003. *Vision Mumbai: Transforming Mumbai into a World Class City*. New Delhi: Cirrus Repro.

Nijman, Jan. 2000. "Mumbai's Real Estate Market in 1990s: De-regulation, Global Money and Casino Capitalism." *Economic and Political Weekly* 35, no. 7 (February): 575–582.

Sassen, Saskia. 2001. *The Global City: New York, Tokyo, London*. Princeton: Princeton University Press.

———. 2003. "The Feminization of Survival: Alternative Global Circuits." In *Crossing Borders and Shifting Boundaries: Gender on the Move*, ed. Mirjana Morokvasic, et al. Berlin: VS Verlag.

———. 2006. "Cities and Communities in the Global Economy." In *The Global Cities Reader*, ed. Neil Brenner and Roger Keil. London: Routledge.

Sengupta, Arjun. 2007. *Report on the Conditions of Work and the Promotion of Livelihoods of the Unorganized Sector*. New Delhi: National Commission for Enterprises in the Unorganized Sector. Delhi: Dolphin Pinto Graphics.

Smith, Neil. 1996. *The New Urban Frontier: Gentrification and the Revanchist City*. London: Routledge.

Singh, Gurbir. 2003. "Who Owns Mumbai? It's a 7,000 Acre Reality Check." *Economic Times* October 10.
Tiwari, Piyush. 2000. "House Price Dynamics in Mumbai, 1989–1995." *Review of Urban and Regional Development Studies* 12, no. 2 (December): 149–163.
van Wersch, Hubert V. M. 1992. *The Bombay Textile Strike: 1982–1983*. Delhi: Oxford University Press.
Weinstein, Liza. 2008. "Mumbai's Development Mafias: Globalization, Organized Crime and Land Development." *International Journal of Urban and Regional Research* 32, no. 1 (March): 22–39.
Whitehead, Judy, and Nitin More. 2007. "Revanchism in Mumbai? Political Economy of Rent Gaps and Urban Restructuring in a Global City." *Economic and Political Weekly* 42, no. 25 (June): 2428–2434.

– Chapter 4 –

STRUCTURES WITHOUT SOUL AND IMMEDIATE STRUGGLES
Rethinking Militant Particularism in Contemporary Spain

Susana Narotzky

This chapter examines the connection between the production in the present of memories of the past and the ability to frame present-day conflicts in relation to particular or universal claims and political projects. Through referring to past struggles and their outcomes, the process of framing will clarify what renders certain possibilities legitimate while excluding others. This connection between past and present realities, memories, and struggles will appear in the reading of past struggles in terms of heroism or defeat, and in the way of incorporating those memories into present-day struggles in positive or negative terms. These processes express interlinked and diverse forms of dispossession that were shaped by and, in turn, delimit the possible spaces and scales in which struggle can be meaningfully waged.

My aim is to analyze a particular case, in an industrial corner of Europe, in order to unveil the processes of defining and framing conflict, setting the contending field of force, and designing the battlefield where struggle will be waged. These processes are themselves part of the struggle, waged both in discursive terms and in material ones. On the one hand, tensions and contradictions in the way people access resources (economic, political, and symbolic) produce cleavages in terms of spaces and identities of contention, but they are also the grounds for producing instruments that can help unify pluralities of experience. On the other hand, the construction of a wider collectivity appears as an oriented process, that is, it has a purpose, one that addresses subjects in their projection into the future (their livelihoods, their careers, their family lives, their children, their retirement, their pensions). The time dimension is thus embedded in people's struggles to gain control over their lives at different levels of abstraction: the more proximate level traces connections between past and present generations of concrete people (parents and children, mentors and pupils); an intermediate level traces connections between institutions, between the past and the present of organized groups; finally, there is a more abstract plane that traces connections at the structural level, between past and present logics of systemic reproduction, between logics of historical development. These connections between past and present at different levels of abstraction, in turn, enable people to operate at distinct spatial scales and result in different types of impact. This is how memory is expressed in practice, and how it gets involved in a very real sense in the framing of present-day struggles, and the defining of projects for the future.

The chapter is based on fieldwork in the town of Ferrol (A Coruña), Galicia (northwestern Spain), which I began in 2003, and where I am still working at the time of writing. Ferrol has the doubtful honor of having been the birthplace of General Franco, who renamed it after his glorious crusade as Ferrol del Caudillo. However, very few people in Spain know that it was also the birthplace of Pablo Iglesias, the founder of the Spanish Socialist Party (founded in 1870). This is symbolic of a space of tensions, where the military (the navy) and the shipyard workers have simultaneously confronted and cooperated with each other, starting in the eighteenth century. What attracted me to Ferrol was precisely the tension that emerged so powerfully during the Franco regime (1939–1975): between on the one hand, the utmost expression of the regime's repressive might, the military;[1] and on the other, the utmost expression of working-class struggles, by the organized workers of the Empresa Nacional Bazán, the nationalized shipyards. By the early 1970s the public military shipyard (Bazán) and the initially private commercial shipyard (Astano) employed some twenty thousand workers and provided almost every household with a living wage. The definition of this industry as "strategic" and key to developing the strength of the nation resulted in stable, relatively well paid employment for the male population, which in turn produced a strong, well-organized working-class movement.

The experiences, practices, and narratives of different generations of workers in Ferrol shed light on a critical question, one which is particularly relevant today: what kinds of collectives need to be produced to achieve a radical transformation of capitalist relations of production and a substantively democratic political space? To answer this question, however, it is necessary to understand how common emancipatory projects and forms of solidarity might be discovered or created by ordinary people who are constantly faced with two kinds of work: the everyday work of earning a livelihood and imagining a future for their children; and the work of fighting to change a reality of hardship and uncertainty. This duality in turn relates to different ways to engage in struggle: through immediate mobilization for claims, linked to direct experience, on the one hand, or through long-term organizing toward structural transformation in the general interest, on the other. It therefore refers to the immanent tension between the particular experience of dispossession and the more abstract argument (or category) through which it is communicated and shared, and eventually the construction of a larger structure—a theory—where the particular position makes sense, and which should be transformed.

Experience, Abstraction, Struggles and Theories

This tension among different levels of abstraction was underlined by Raymond Williams in a series of political essays (1989) about what the struggle for socialism had to be in the present (late twentieth century). His analysis was based on Britain's experience in the 1980s (e.g., the Thatcher reforms, the miners' strike, the gradualism of the Labour Party and its abandonment of a real socialist transformation,) and it drew on his own experience as a border person, from having been raised in a small community in South Wales to go on to one of the centers of abstract thinking (Cambridge). It is from this border position that he explained two different kinds of feelings of responsibility, two different modes of "community": (a) one linked to a (rural) place and to immediate proximity, to the "recognition of certain kinds of mutual responsibility" and of "a level of social obligation which was conferred by the fact of seeming to live in the same place and in that sense to have a common identity"; and (b) another one (industrial) linked with more abstract forces which nevertheless had concrete and place-bound effects: "a community that had been hammered out in very fierce conflict, the kind of community that was the eventual positive creation of struggles within the industrialization of

South Wales" (1989 [1977]: 114). For Williams, however, present-day historical realities forced the need for abstraction and a politics of negation (of immediate experience) that came with it:

> Something had happened which put certain of the basic elements of our social life beyond the reach both of direct experience and of simple affirmation, affirmation followed by extension. In came, necessarily, the politics of negation, the politics of differentiation, the politics of abstract analysis. And these, whether we liked them or not, were now necessary even to understand what was happening.... New characteristic social relations which have, in a sense, to be discovered, not only by factual enquiry but by very complex interpretation, discovering all kinds of new systems and modes. And these things which are the determining tendencies in modern history can be put into conflict with those other affirmative notions which, whether they come from older kinds of rural communities or from militant working-class communities, are always more closely tied to experience. And around them still centres the notion of community, contrasted now to what? Often I found, as this argument continued, contrasted with "real politics" or "practical politics." (1989 [1977]: 116)

What appears then is that, often, these more abstract realities are pictured as "real politics" or "practical politics," that is, the politics of the organizations (mainly the party and unions) and *confronted* to the politics tied to "communities." It is this tension between the real weight of abstraction in our lives, and the immediacy of experience that Williams sought to capture in the dialectics of affirmation (experience, community, the extension of community) and negation (distance, abstraction, practical politics) inherent in the struggle for socialism. The process of "negation" (the method of abstraction) was in itself a part of the hegemony of capitalism, and had not yielded the expected results (through Labour Party politics), but the process of simple community "affirmation" (the method of experience and place proximity) was also inadequate for the struggle to be successful:

> We have learned all too harshly and bitterly the truth of these latest phases, the phase of negation, the phase of knowing that you have to go beyond the simple community, the phase of the quick identification of enemies, the phase also of very conscious and prolonged political abstraction. If we merely counterpose to that the forms of a simpler kind of politics, I very much doubt if we shall engage in the central struggle. On the other hand, if that negative politics is the only politics then it is the final victory of a mode of thought which seems to me the ultimate product of capitalist society. Whatever its political label it is a mode of thought which really has made relations between men into relations between things or relations between concepts. And yet to re-establish

the notion of politics as relationships between men, to re-establish the ideas of community politics, would mean superseding, going beyond, that kind of politics rather than merely in turn negating it. (1989 [1977]: 117–118)

In a very central way, overcoming this 'negative politics' became the key issue that had to be resolved for orienting and waging a successful struggle for a different—a socialist—society. This recognition led him to develop his concept of "militant particularism," one which tries to address the tension between the politics of "negation" and the politics of "affirmation," which is also the tension of defining a project that can be shared. That is, it points to the need to find the general interest in the particular interests of communities struggling for a better life. The question of survival of particular communities becomes not a special case but a general case, reviving the labor *movement* by driving at the general interest through the particular claims of, for example, the mining communities in the 1980s (1989 [1985]: 125–127). Instead of negating the particular through a superior set of abstract concepts defining the general interests of the "economy" or the "nation":

> The unique and extraordinary character of working-class self-organization has been that it has tried to connect particular struggles to a general struggle in one quite special way. It has set out, as a movement, to make real what is at first sight the extraordinary claim that the defence and advancement of certain particular interests, properly brought together, are in fact in the general interest. That, after all, is the moment of transition to an idea of socialism. (1989 [1981]: 249)

However, it is the struggle for that moment of transition to the *idea* of socialism that has been largely lost by working-class organizations today and that needs to be reconstructed through a "necessary and workable settlement between particular interests and the general interest" (1989 [1981]: 254). For Williams the problem with labor in its institutional forms (party, union) has been their transformation into "part of the mechanism of a modern capitalist society" (1989 [1981]: 250). Only the immediate experience of particular interests has preserved the truth of the socialist version of the general interest, "yet not consciously, not at the level of argument, only really at the level of feeling, of mood" (1989 [1981]: 254). It is, then, from this position that "the concept of a practical and possible general interest, which really does include all reasonable particular interests, has to be negotiated, found, agreed, constructed" (1989 [1981]: 255). In the end, in

Williams's view, both the "affirmative" aspect of experience in immediate struggles, and the abstract intellectual "negation" of distanced analysis were necessary to construct "in convincing detail ... the general shape of the new social order" (1989 [1981]: 255).

This debate, however, was a political one in which academics on the left were trying to make sense of the actual role of institutions that were meant to represent working-class interests (Labour Party, trade unions), the significance of new social movements appearing in the 1960s and 1970s (anti–Vietnam War, civil rights movement, feminist movement, environmental movement) and the substance of class as a category and a praxis defining a collective movement. The debate, of which Williams was part, expressed a dissatisfaction over the formal institutions of labor and a need to understand new forms of conflict within capitalist societies. In the wake of the systemic turn of the 1970s, after the collapse of the Bretton Woods financial system and the liberalization of exchange and financial markets that ensued, labor institutions became increasingly coopted in what was described as neocorporatist regimes, based on reaching agreement through institutional negotiation within the existing social framework, instead of seeking a total transformation of the system through sustained conflict and an idea of socialism. For those involved in the debates the questions were (1) was class an abstract category or was it a praxis?; (2) what was the articulation between experience (immediate struggles) and formal organizations (political struggles), between particular and general interests?; and (3) what was the link between concrete and abstract understandings of class position (structures of feeling, class consciousness)? The thread connecting these different questions was the tension that Williams identified between the concrete and the abstract in the lived experience of class, but also the need to incorporate this duality (concrete/abstract) in any organization that really expressed the interests of the dispossessed. E. P. Thompson criticized French Marxist structuralism for understanding class as an abstract structural category (in the *Poverty of Theory*, 1978) and proposed instead an understanding of class that was tied to concrete collective action and struggles that would eventually build up a culture of class, where social situations would acquire a shared meaning (Thompson 1966). Hobsbawm's (1984 [1971]) position was, on the contrary, that:

> Class has two levels of aspiration ... the immediate, day-by-day specific demands and the more general demands for the kind of society which suits it (1984 [1971]: 26).

Working-class consciousness at both levels implies formal organization; and organization which is itself the carrier of class ideology, which without it would be little more than a complex of informal habits and practices (1984 [1971]: 27).

"Socialist consciousness" through organization is thus an essential complement of working-class consciousness. But it is neither automatic nor inevitable (1984 [1971]: 28). The necessary mediation of organization implies a difference, . . . a divergence, between "class" and "organization," i.e. on the political level, "party." The further we move from the elementary social units and situations in which class and organization mutually control one another—e.g. in the classic case, thè socialist or communist union lodge in the mining village—and into the vast and complex area where major decisions about society are taken, the greater the potential divergence. (1984 [1971]: 28)

What Hobsbawm stresses also, through the historical example of "The Making of the Working Class 1870–1914" (1984 [1981]) in a direct critique of Thompson is that organizations (mass unions, Labour Party) are central to the development of class consciousness and of class as a collective force and as a movement with direction. Organizations are also key in training and framing the leaders that emerge in concrete mobilizations during immediate struggles, but they also produce particularly formalized kinds of leaders for institutional aims (1984 [1981]: 210). As different from spontaneous and reactive forms of protest by subaltern groups, class becomes a subject of history *only* when it is formalized. However, often organizations acquire dynamics of their own tied to long-term perspectives of their institutional social reproduction that might get in the way of effective mobilization in the interest of ordinary workers (1984 [1977]: 293). What the organizations of the left provide is their capacity to produce policies and bodies capable of implementing them from within the system (1984 [1977]: 295). It is both Thompson's and Hobsbawm's positions that Williams tried to supersede through retaining the contradiction between concrete and abstract, particular and general, immediate and organized struggle as central to the socialist *idea* and project.

These various strands of theory have in common their central preoccupation with the possible forms of struggle, with trying to understand what makes oppressed and exploited people come together, how they attempt to transform their situation in a durable way, and in what direction, following what design of a society. Struggle has often been defined as the necessary process by which spaces of possibility are opened for those who were excluded from them. It is the means toward greater inclusion in the polity and in civil society. Struggles attempt to force participation through confrontation and mobilization that may push toward the transformation of the rules that frame social interaction. Struggle is about conflict and about how conflict is defined. William Roseberry, in his essay "Hegemony and the Language of Contention" pointed to the fact that "unity is [for both the ruling and the subaltern classes] a political and cultural problem" (1994: 359). It is in the light of this central problem that hegemony appears as a process of construction of the languages, contours, and practices of struggle, in an always changing confrontation between dominant and subaltern subjects. However, as Roseberry reminds us, "The concept's value for Gramsci [when trying to understand the *failure* of the Piedmont bourgeoisie to lead and form a unified nation-state] lay in its illumination of lines of weakness and cleavage, of alliances unformed and class fractions unable to make their particular interests appear as the interests of a wider collectivity" (1994: 365). For anyone observing the situation of subaltern classes in Europe, the issue of cleavages emerging in opposition to unity is central. For anyone even remotely interested in changing the direction of the distributive structure, not to mention a more profound transformation, it becomes imperative to analyze what are the conditions of possibility of struggles being waged today in Europe. This chapter seeks to do that through an analysis of the connection between the historical production of shared identities and particular collectives of struggle—militant particularism—and the experienced structure of present-day capitalism in an industrial town in Southern Europe.

In Ferrol, as elsewhere in Europe, the task is to analyze the processes people engage in and the instruments that they develop in their struggle to try to control their lives. What we see from the ethnography, however, is that these processes are disharmonious and contradictory and do not produce unity or orientation in and of themselves. To address this problem, I will explore three axes of analysis that emerge from my fieldwork and explain the construction of structures of feeling: *history*, the understanding of a logical structure to the development of events in the past leading to the present; *experience*, as a psycho-physical fact and interpretation of the position of the self in the real world; and *collective identity*, as a construction by which to make sense of, and interact with, forces that appear too impersonal and abstract to be dealt with otherwise. In industrial Ferrol, these axes are locally depicted as "defeat," "suffering," and "struggle." Defeat describes an *understanding* of the Transition from Franco's dictatorship to parliamentary democracy (1975–1982) in terms of hopes and expectations of socialism that were disappointed. Suffering expresses the *experience* of workers' daily work, of mobilization and repression and of the recognition of defeat. Struggle tells about collective *action* aimed at transforming the existing situation into a better one; about hope and project for a better future in the general interest. Memory emerges as the bridge that enables people to link these different scales, define projects and stabilize boundaries for struggle.

Defeat, Suffering, and Struggle: History

The aftermath of the Spanish civil war (1936–1939) transformed the realities of making a living for everyone in the country. The industrial town of Ferrol had a history of socialist, communist, and anarchist working-class organizations before the war that resulted in a strong repression after Franco's victory. However, the importance attributed to the shipyards by the regime had the somewhat paradoxical effect of creating a strong and organized working-class movement.

The nationalist economic policies of the early Franco regime favored an import substitution program that aimed at strengthening the country's industrial base, resulting in a peculiar mix of repression and paternalism for the working classes (Babiano 1993). Repression was extreme in the areas under the control of the "National" Francoist army during the civil war and during the first ten years after it ended (1939–1949). It included summary executions, prison, concentration camps, and work camps together with systematic encouragement of denunciations of republicans or "reds" and continuous police surveillance of the conduct and political affinities of citizens. It also implied massive purges in private and public workplaces of workers who had mobilized for the Republic or the revolution and against the Francoist "National" rebels. In private industry, purges happened immediately and applied mostly to workers who were imprisoned or in exile as a result of the conflict. In the public sector, a law-decree (*decreto-ley*) of August 25, 1939, reserved 80 percent of employment in the civil service to "ex-combatants, disabled veterans, ex-prisoners of war, orphans and kinspersons of the 'fallen'" on the National side during the war (Riquer 2010: 153). At the same time, employers were legally forbidden to dismiss workers for economic or business reasons[2] without government permission and had to pay a strong penalty for doing so, while workforce minimums were statutory, established, and enforced for all firms by the government. Strikes were illegal and severely repressed, free unionization was forbidden, salaries were tightly controlled and their value deteriorated by inflation, and rationing provided scarcity at controlled prices while black market prices rocketed (Molinero and Ysàs 1990; 1993; Vilar 2004; Riquer 2010). Male employment stability became the programmatic hallmark of labor relations during the regime and produced a system of internal labor market where sons entered as apprentices in their fathers' firms, especially in the large strategic industries. This was coupled with a closing of the labor market to women, whose main calling was defined by the National Catholic regime as housework, especially after marriage.

The participation of the state in heavy industries grew steadily until the end of the regime in 1975 and continued growing through the restructuring of the early 1980s until the privatization of the 1990s.[3] In addition, two different periods of trade protectionism can be defined in the first twenty years after the civil war: (1) autarky (1939–1946), the *Falangista* model of self-sustaining economic autonomy; and (2) import substitution (1946–1959), aimed at developing domestic industry in order to reduce dependency and achieve competitiveness. These were followed by gradual liberalization after 1953 and the treaties concluded with the United States under the Madrid Pact.[4] A 1963 report on Spain by the International Bank for Reconstruction and Development (IBRD, later the World Bank) prescribed the adoption of monetary stabilization policies, liberalization of trade and foreign investment, deregulation of the labor market, while it opened up aid credit. It can be said that starting in 1959 the economic policies of the Spanish Francoist governments (referred to as "technocrats") follow the model of development that the United States had exported to the rest of Western Europe after World War II. However, this liberalization model was compatible with state intervention intended to regulate the excesses of the market but not to substitute for it. "Indicative planning" was a model of economic regulation initiated in France after World War II that was linked to postwar reconstruction, but that had intellectual antecedents both in right-wing corporatist ideas as well as in Soviet socialist central planning of the interwar period (Ramos-Gorostiza, José Luis, Pires Jiménez, and Luis Eduardo 2009). One of its major proponents was Jean Monnet, one of the founders of the European Economic Community (EEC). It was mostly meant as a technical device based on macroeconomic data (input-output tables, national accounting) that would enable economic actors to make rational decisions. The role of the state was to gather and make available this macroeconomic information and to coordinate the national economy and its different sectors in relation to long-term economic development targets. The state's intervention had to interfere minimally with market forces, but it had to make decisions as to which "sectors" of the economy should receive incentives because they were thought to represent the ground base of any further development. Spain followed the French model of "Development Plans," centered in strong key industries (steel, energy, shipbuilding) that would be given preference by the state. Indicative planning was a model widely discussed by European nations after World War II, and it had the endorsement of US reconstruction planners. In its 1963 report, the IBRD supported the adoption of "indicative planning" as a way to liberalization and economic development for Spain. The results of Spain's development plans during the 1960s have been strongly criticized by Spanish economists on various grounds, although most stressed their inefficiency and constraints to full liberalization (Ramos-Gorostiza, José Luis, Pires Jiménez, and Luis Eduardo 2009).

Indicative planning did have two fundamental consequences that are central for the discussion in this chapter. First, it introduced a particular *technical* language into economic practice, one that seemed to supersede the political language that had infused economic thinking and decisions up to that moment (*Falangista*, socialist, communist, anarchist). Macroeconomic data were to be the guides of economic policies, and they appeared as devoid of political intention, while the group of economists that came to power with that project were aptly called "the technocrats," foreshadowing the neoliberal arguments for a politics of austerity today.[5] Macroeconomic arguments would eventually become such a hegemonic force as to pervade the discourse of democratic trade unions, putting an end to the revolutionary aspect of unions that had reemerged during the Franco regime (Martínez-Alier and Roca Jusmet 1988). Second, indicative planning, through favoring the key sector industries that were also those that could benefit from economies of scale and Fordist modernization, gave workers in these industries jobs that were protected not only through labor laws but also through longer-term economic policies. Indeed, the articulation of production and consumption that is the hallmark of Fordist organization, trading stable employment and better wages for increased productivity, which creates a simultaneous rise in demand and supply and a dream of middle-class aspirations, was tied in Spain to the "strategic" industries and framed in a context of repression. Some of these industries had been nationalized (such as the military shipyards) but those that were private also benefited from special state support and protection. These policies thus strengthened workers' position within these sectors in the short term and eventually enabled the reconstruction of class-based trade unions.

These modernizing plans were undertaken by the victorious side of a civil war that had been mostly a class war, aimed at the suppression of alternative (socialist, anarchist) models of political-economic organization, and in an environment of absolute political repression. Liberalization of the economy was a first step and signaled the regime's intention of siding with the "free" world in the polarized environment of the Cold War. Nevertheless, if the goal of integration with Western international powers was to become a reality some political gestures toward democratization needed to be forthcoming.[6] During the "development decade" (1960s), government intervention was progressively reduced and committees representing workers within large firms (more than five hundred workers) became legal within the framework of the corporatist "vertical" national union. The turning point appeared with the *Ley de Convenios Colectivos* (Law of Collective Agreements) of April 1958 that established the legality of *economic*—as distinct from political—collective action as part of the process of negotiation of workers with their employers. In the following years, the institutional framework of labor committees enabled workers to legally organize and voice collective claims (Sánchez Recio 2002). These worker committees, democratically elected by workers, negotiated in-firm collective agreements with representatives of the enterprises and under state supervision. After 1965, "economic" strikes were decriminalized, although unions would remain illegal until Franco's death in 1975. During this period, the argument of "modernization" was central to the liberal political economists (many of them members of the Opus Dei Catholic congregation)[7] in Spanish governments from 1957 up to 1982 and the advent of the Socialist Party to power (Anderson 1970; González 1979; Graham 1999; Viñas 2003).

In the Ferrol shipyards, a sustained expansion of demand that existed until the early 1970s provided male jobs and decent wages from one generation to the next and reinforced the effects of state protection to "strategic" industries. Both state intervention and a favorable market conjuncture contributed to stabilizing workers' expectations. Stable employment lasted until the early 1980s and was crucial in the reemergence of a clandestine but very active class-based trade union (Comisiones Obreras, CCOO) in the early 1960s. Many today speak of the situation of shipyard workers in that period as one of privilege, but it was the result of a particular historical conjuncture and of struggle. It was the organization of the labor movement in class terms within the "vertical" corporatist union of the Francoist regime, by a coalition of social Catholic, communist, and anarchist groupings, that enabled workers in the "strategic" industries to better their salaries and work conditions. Annual collective bargaining became established in all sectors of heavy industry by the early 1960s. Often these were moments of strikes and violent confrontation that developed a particular male identity centered on values of justice, struggle, and solidarity among peers. Clandestine union leaders were in and out of prison continuously during the 1960s and early 1970s. In Ferrol, the negotiation of a collective agreement in early March 1972 resulted in numerous strikes and demonstrations that were severely repressed, leading to the death of two workers and sixteen wounded on March 10, while more than 100 strikers were put under arrest, 60 imprisoned, and 160 disciplinary redundancies occurred. Those involved in the organization of the movement were put on the blacklist. In commemoration of this, March 10 became instituted as the day of the Galician worker. The shipyard union became the model for the entire working class in Ferrol and was very active at organizing other local industrial struggles.

After the transition to democracy, the first socialist government of President Felipe González initiated a restructuring of all national state industries in order to prepare Spain for incorporation into the European Economic Community and the free market challenge of competitiveness. Complying with demands from Brussels, the shipyards were brutally downsized. From 1984 to 1987 thousands of jobs were lost; unemployment and early retirement became a generalized feature in the region. While the economic rationale for restructuring was generally accepted by unions as the "need" to transform what was admitted to be an inefficient industrial system resulting from the state intervention policies of the preceding regime, workers asked for better conditions of severance and unemployment coverage, as well as guarantees that new industries would be developed in the old industrial areas. Labor conflict increased during those restructuring years, and unions succeeded in obtaining better overall conditions for those made redundant, but this appeared to many as a tradeoff for becoming a new type of union, a "responsible" union in the context of Europe, but one that in fact explicitly abandoned the revolutionary path.

During the Transition period the unions had become progressively bureaucratized after the Moncloa agreement (Pacto(s) de la Moncloa, 1977) and generally compliant with the macroeconomic technical projections of the economists, their growth objective, competitive arguments, and interest in European integration. The Pacto de la Moncloa was a political agreement to stabilize the economy, signed by the major political parties (including the Communist Party and Catalan and Basque nationalist parties) in October 1977. It had the tacit support of the unions and rested on the shared objective of making the transition to democracy possible. The raison d'état of the political transition and the fear of involution appeared to all as a strong argument for the agreement. In a conjuncture of high inflation (27 percent) the Moncloa agreement was aimed at containing salaries and increasing productivity to enhance competitiveness and stimulate growth. The practice of "agreements" among employers, workers' unions, and the state has since become strongly instituted in Spanish economic policy.

The early Transition years (1975–1976) had seen the power of the unions increase[8] and openly express (through strikes and demonstrations) both political objectives (democracy, free unions, legalization of the Communist Party) and labor and social issues (salaries on a sliding scale, better working conditions, social benefits). This had resulted in a progressively better distribution of work rents to capital rents in the GDP up to 1977, with real salaries following the increases in productivity. From then on, work rents would decrease steadily as a result of salaries stagnating or even decreasing while productivity continued to increase (Gutiérrez 1990: 122–126; Martínez-Alier and Roca Jusmet 1988: 52; Zaragoza and Varela 1990: 61). The Pacto de la Moncloa, and all the subsequent agreements that were subscribed by unions[9] and employers under the supervision of the state, had as their main objective wage contention in order to control inflation and foster economic recuperation (Zaragoza 1990). The politics of "agreement" (*concertación*) between the different actors in the economy have been described as neocorporatist because they implied the loss of a revolutionary objective and the incorporation of trade unions into the neoliberal policies of democratic governments: "[N]eo-corporatist structures also assimilate politics to the economy in another sense, because macroeconomic orientations become the basis of social agreements" (Martínez-Alier and Roca Jusmet 1988: 59).[10] The process of cooptation of labor conflict by the technical guidelines of macroeconomic planning continued in the same way it had been initiated during the technocratic governments of the Franco regime. This situation produced a hegemony that would frame industrial workers' protests and struggles in a particular "language of contention" (Roseberry 1994) that was that of the dominant groups but appeared to be neutral, technical and universal:

> The macroeconomic reasoning and objectives, which appear a lot more neutral [than traditional corporative ideologies] might better serve the aim of getting trade union leaders to accept "social peace" and convince their followers, so long as they abandon the Marxist or anarcho-syndicalist language and start discussing about how much should the inflation rate be reduced or how much should the GDP increase. (Martínez-Alier and Roca Jusmet 1988: 56)

This trend of technical reasoning and justification has continued until the present, through various moments of restructuring and job loss in the 1990s and 2000s that have seen how workers' struggles were driven toward negotiation and agreement by the unions.

By 2009 the structure of the shipyard industry in Ferrol had become a flexible one relying on a network of subcontracting auxiliary firms. Parallel to this transformation, the region has experienced the increase of small- and medium-sized enterprises (SME), primarily in textile and garment manufacturing and in service sectors, in new industrial parks surrounding the town of Ferrol (such as Narón). These "new" jobs are intended for women and younger people and are highly volatile and unprotected. Little unionization or collective action mark this new area of employment where a stronger sense of individual strategizing and networking is the main instrument of social mobility. In economic terms there is a demise of the traditional "Fordist" shipyard industry and an emergence of a "flexible" regionally integrated structure of SME. For most people job precariousness and career instability render a vision for the future very difficult. Migration to the big cities of Madrid, Barcelona, or London has soared for young people in this region in the last ten years as they attempt to find better opportunities in urban centers. Today, Ferrol has the second largest emigration rate among Spanish towns, and over a third of its households live on state subsidies, often that of an older generation that accessed early retirement in the restructuring struggles of the 1980s, 1990s, and 2000s.

Defeat: Workers' Reading of History

The concept of defeat was associated during my fieldwork with the understanding of experiences related to the Transition and the restructuring years. It produced a particular framework for capturing the logic of the present in relation to the events of the past. This reasoning of historical experience was one of the aspects entangled in the local structures of feeling of the working class that enable or inhibit solidarity and mobilization.

Early in my fieldwork (2003), in a debate around memories of the past and political activism organized by a cultural association in Ferrol, Raúl,[11] one of the leaders of the working-class movement of the 1960s and 1970s, said:

> [In the 1960s] anarchists, communists and socialists had different experiences [of the Republic and civil war period] it was very difficult to make them agree . . . [We had to do] invisible underground work in order to produce the new working-class movement out of all these different opinions. Many have contributed to this final result: to bring the dictatorship to an end. (R., 2003)

This is a very succinct statement of what seems to have been one of the grounds for overcoming cleavages in the past: the fight for democracy. In the same meeting however, several people started voicing what would become a leitmotiv throughout these years: that the fight had, in the end, been lost.

There was a sense of defeat, their defeat as the working class and as the "left," but also a defeat of a particular idea of democracy, that of *popular sovereignty* going beyond institutional forms. Both these aspects were linked, because, as Raúl declared in 2010, "the war [civil war] was lost by the working class, not by the Republic." The aim in recuperating democracy was to widen the spaces of struggle for the working class, the spaces of solidarity, of respect, and of hope. The generation now in their seventies feels they were deceived by political leaders: "We became orphans of the left; we gave everything, we believed in people who today are not on our side" (L., 2003). Prominent leaders of the left during the transition came into power in 1982 only to conduct industrial restructuring and destroy thousands of jobs in Ferrol. The expectations of democracy were misleading, remarks María, an activist woman: "We thought that through voting for those parties we believed in, they would be doing the work [for us], but that did not happen. We made ourselves comfortable; we thought that we didn't have to keep fighting, because they were there to do the job" (M., 2005). Here, she expresses a perception that the fault lay also with the working class for abandoning their active participation and leaving things in the hands of formal institutions such as parties and unions. By legalizing unions and parties, channels for conflict expression were constitutionally regulated: "democracy" not only produced the demobilization of the working class, it also produced a profession out of political activism, and a "realist politics." Union and party representatives became "experts" in "politics," distancing themselves from ordinary people's experiences and preoccupations.

The older generation was able to produce a unity during the Franco years and against all odds, by agreeing that working-class struggle was foremost a fight for democracy and against the dictatorship. During the Transition, all over Spain, the left very soon discovered the fragmentation produced by a battle around new interests and resources that often pitted the old allies against each other. The popular saying *"Contra Franco vivíamos mejor"* [Against Franco we fared better], common by the early 1980s, expressed growing cleavages and the reconfiguration of the stakes at play. In Ferrol, the generation that reconstructed a unified class struggle during the 1960s is defined by the next generation (now in their forties) in ambiguous terms: they appear as an heroic group of people, a collection of significant personalities that were able to powerfully transmit their analysis of the situation and engage the solidarity of everyone in the region. They are also described as the "lost generation," the generation that lost the transition challenge, the generation of unionists who were trapped literally in the industrial restructuring that destroyed the shipyards. They lost their jobs while the increasingly fragmented structures of production impaired the capacity of unions to organize.

There is a general agreement in seeing the present as a loss in relation first, to the unfulfilled expectations of the Transition; second, to what did get accomplished in those years in respect to the rights of workers and civil liberties; third, to the promised stabilization of the economic situation after the tough years of restructuring; and fourth to the unity and solidarity of the workers' movement during the dictatorship. As a retired worker who had a son working in one of the subcontract auxiliary firms for the shipyard put it:

> In the last twenty years workers have lost 40 percent of their gains. People work without social security, without labor security. Young people have to accept precarious jobs, dangerous jobs in the shipyards. The unions cannot do much in the small auxiliary firms, workers don't find support when they have a problem, there is competition among workers and there is no solidarity. But these are all workers' problems. (M. B., 2003)

The precarity that the young generation endures appears here as the mirror of a double loss, that of the social and labor conquests that were obtained through hard struggles, and that of the capacity for engaging in that form of struggle in the present, for lack of solidarity. Indeed the youngest generation, in their twenties, is also defined as a "lost generation" in that their fragmentation is complete and their confidence gone. They are individualists; they go it alone. They do not trust the unions because they see them as corrupt. In the words of Juli, in his late twenties and a union member: "Mine is an unbelieving generation. Politics is of no use to solve problems. Everything remains the same whoever is in power (*gobierne quien gobierne*)" (J., 2007). This disbelief is an expression of the failure of the heroic generation that produced a strong working-class union during the dictatorship. It underscores their failure to produce a real democracy, where "politics"—institutional channels and representatives—would make a difference. It very explicitly refers to their defeat in material terms—what they did not, in the end, accomplish. But it also refers to their inability to transmit their values, their tools of analysis, their conscience, and their consciousness to the next generations. Above all, it points to their shortcomings to transmit the capacity for struggle. The clear sentiment that, as María said, "Perhaps we have been unable to transmit it" (M., 2005) gets repeated over and over by the elders as a *mea culpa*. These difficulties of transmission are in part related to the consequences of the restructuring period that dismantled the shipyard apprentice school and the mentorship process that had structured intergenerational knowledge transfers within the factory. Indeed, for the older generation, this mentorship system is described as crucial in their political initiation. Through it, they learned the trade together with particular ways of analyzing their position in the world.

The import substitution period of the dictatorship, and the particular structure of state industries that were considered "strategic" for the development and security of the nation (energy, steel, chemicals, coal, and military industries) created the perfect space for transmission. Because these industries required specialized workers, training was provided in "apprenticeship schools" (*escuelas de aprendices*) within the factory. Instruction seems to have been excellent in many accounts although infused with Falangist rituals and ideology. The last two years (out of four spent in apprenticeship) were spent learning the trade by teaming with senior mentors in the shipyard workshops. Workers speak of it as a "University" where, together with the practicalities of the trade, they learned about past history, politics, society, and culture. There was a clandestine library in the shipyard were they could read forbidden works (in their words: "From Marx to Lorca"). Here they found the transmission of memories of struggle, they learned about labor strikes during the Republic (1934), they learned about confrontations among the left during the revolution and the civil war (1938), learned about the repression that was particularly devastating in the area, but also about anti-colonial struggles abroad, about civil rights movements, etc.

All of it contributed to a widening of their understandings of conflict and to the capacity to address more abstract scales of struggle. Moreover, this was not only a theoretical transmission of knowledge but one that was put into practice constantly through the analysis of present-day situations and the design for action and solidarity with other mobilizations. Some of these mentors in the shipyard have become heroic symbols. (Julio Aneiros, for example, who was defined as a mentor by many, was a member of the clandestine Communist Party and a key player in the reorganization of a class-based union in the 1960s.) One can easily follow the lineages of mentorship up to the present because all politically active workers articulated them explicitly. The vocational school was transformed into a short-term training space in the 1980s, when workers were hired already holding degrees from technical schools, and was finally closed in the early 1990s, coinciding with the second restructuring period. The shipyard space (Bazán) remained for a while the working-class "University" through the union activism of the restructuring years, making transmission of "social conscience" still possible. However, after the second wave of restructuring was finished in the late 1990s, two generations of mentors had disappeared and the structure of the industry was fragmented in a multitude of small auxiliary firms that were positioned differently in the physical and social space of shipbuilding. According to Raúl, the early retirement aspect of restructuring was planned so as to separate the leaders that had been active during the Transition from the following generations of workers. It sought to disrupt transmission chains, and it succeeded.

In these circumstances, the workers' reading of history situates the generation who struggled during the dictatorship as losers, even when they thought they had accomplished their objective by attaining democracy and what came with it: free unions, the legalization of the Communist Party and civil rights.

Suffering: Workers' Experience of Defeat

The material aspects of this loss are the basis for what workers define as "suffering." This concept refers to the embodied realities of being part of the working class, and it reveals an important aspect of the structures of feeling that can be shared and mobilized to produce a collective identity. For industrial towns such as Ferrol, the restructuring periods of the 1980s and 1990s had a major impact on the livelihoods of most households, producing a pervasive sense of fear (*miedo*) and pain. In the context of recent political and economic transformations the meaning of fear has changed from a mostly political[12] to a mostly economic value form while retaining a logic of dismantling organized working-class struggle: from fear of repression during Franco to fear of economic destitution in the present. Those with permanent employment are afraid of losing their jobs. They are afraid the shipyard will not get any new orders, and the menace of total closure looms. Casual workers are afraid of not being rehired. Workers in the small auxiliary firms are afraid these will shut down, move elsewhere, or find a cheaper workforce. During the year 2012, more than a thousand direct jobs were lost, all of them in the auxiliary companies that are subcontracted to work in the shipyard. Precarity is becoming widespread and young people are increasingly dependent on subsidies or obliged to migrate.[13] Parents are afraid their children will not get proper jobs or any jobs at all and that they will have to leave, as many are doing. Many households live off the pensions of the workers who were forced into early retirement. In between precarious jobs people live on unemployment benefits. They are afraid the state will reduce social benefits, and this is indeed occurring with the cuts resulting from the structural adjustment program imposed by the European Commission since 2011. Young people cannot leave their parent's home; they cannot have children; they remain dependent. One of them explains:

> There are very few casual workers that are union members, because of fear. Nobody wants to go in the list [of the union] because you have to show your face and confront the company. We are moving back in time. They want to destroy the stability conquered by the labor movement. When you see that, you are afraid. You live to the limits. You live with fear. You don't even dream of having a child or of buying a car. (J. C., 2006)

For a town that had stable employment and accomplished gains in social benefits for almost half a century this has come as a shock. Indeed it has come as a counterintuitive reality: democracy has led to a disastrous situation in their material economic conditions, but also in that institutional channels allegedly opened to facilitate the struggle to gain control over their lives, have in fact become dead-ends. "People are afraid. Those that are meant to defend you are not going to defend you," says Xaime, a radical union leader (2006). He then describes how political parties are only interested in getting power, they have lost touch with ordinary people's problems, and they do not care. Unions are bureaucratized, and they lack an alternative project. They submit to the arguments of employers (labor market deregulation, increases in productivity, job flexibility) and to the state's macroeconomic analysis and neoliberal projects. They are seen as profiteering from the fragmented and precarious labor market structure, where they increasingly function as a "placing agency" using clientelist procedures, through their statutory participation in the Instituto Nacional de Empleo (INEM, or National Employment Institute), and make money through their control over occupational retraining courses tied to unemployment benefits. In fact, the participation of trade unions, together with the employers' associations, in the national employment and retraining programs was a result of the neocorporatist agreements they made during the early 1980s as a tradeoff for accepting restructuring policies.

The relative power of unions as an institution in the official employment organisms puts union bureaucrats in a patron-client relation with the mass of ordinary members, and it prevents the development of internal democracy and discourages dissent within unions, while another form of fear creeps in. Xaime, leader of a critical faction (Trotskyite) of the major union Comisiones Obreras (CCOO-Críticos), explains a recent conflict in an auxiliary company. Five groups of workers (totaling around sixty individuals) started legal action against the main shipbuilding company Navantia (the old Bazán, state owned) on the grounds of "labor lending" (*prestamismo laboral*), a form of illegal subcontracting where de facto employee-employer relations are with the main company and not with the subcontractor. With this legal action, workers had bypassed the unions, who did not like this. The nationalist union Confederación Intersindical Galega (CIG) tried to dissuade the workers and, confronted by their decisiveness, told them not to use the legal frame of "collective conflict" but to present demands individually, which they did, and lost their cases. In Xaime's opinion, the union committee assumes the production model based on subcontracting and supports the company's decisions while monopolizing collective action.

However, he understands the issue as a structural one reflecting the fact that unions have not been able to organize the auxiliary industry (whose individual firm size is too small) into a strong unified union movement that jointly addresses the problems of auxiliaries.

The unions in these private firms need to coordinate with those of the main shipyard, which is state owned (and colloquially called the *principal*), because they are an integral part of it irrespective of the legal fragmentation. Their problems are articulated and the struggle should be coordinated. In a pamphlet written in July 2006 at the height of the conflict with an auxiliary firm, Nervión, the critical Trotskyite magazine *El Militante*[14] stated:

> This strike reveals an important aspect: that the auxiliary companies are now part of the labor movement of this factory on equal footing with those of the *principal*. . . . It is imperative that . . . a *coordinating committee of auxiliary companies* is instituted that addresses their problems in a global manner and represents all the companies. This will also permit better coordination with the union committee in the *principal*, something necessary as this strike has shown us (stress in the original).

But this unity is yet to materialize. This real pain of fear and betrayal is compared with other forms of suffering in the past, primarily the suffering of the heroic generation fighting the Franco police: many were tortured and imprisoned; some died when demonstrations were repressed (1972). Women talk about the suffering of the wives of these fighters who lost their husbands and fathers to the demanding hours and dangers of political struggle. This created an intimate distress within the family resulting from the tension between what women perceived as the abstract collective fight of men versus their own personal immediate struggles to get by every day. Most shipyard workers' spouses were full-time housewives. Their view of the struggle differed markedly from that of working women in other local industries, such as canneries (see Narotzky 2010). The latter fought with their comrades in the battlefront while the former preserved the rearguard in an ambivalent space between the intimacies of family reproduction and the public militancy of support to the fighters (providing for them and the family while they were in prison, for example). The difference between past and present suffering seems to be one of purpose. *Then*, suffering was directed toward an identifiable goal, it was part of the struggle, it led toward a better future, and it was worth it. Suffering *now*, however, appears as a function of defeat, of passive acceptance of what is perceived as overwhelming forces: the market, the economy, the European Union.

Faced with the betrayal of institutions, workers try to explain what is amiss, when and why their elected representatives stopped caring for them, and how to redress the situation. The major point that is underlined over and over is that these elected representatives lost touch with the immediate reality of work and hardship. This is explained as a result of the union leaders being given time off and even total release from work when they became officially elected, a legally recognized right that is meant to compensate for the hours dedicated to union work. The argument is that they lost touch from ordinary hardship when they got paid for being union representatives, when they started thinking of themselves as "politicians" instead of workers. Social distancing mirrored spatial separation, office work instead of work in the slip or the workshops. And in the process they "lost their souls"; because they did not suffer what their fellow workers suffered, they became part of an institution instead of "real people." Now they are alienated from the rank and file.

But suffering also has a positive side. Those in the younger generation who try to organize some sense of collective purpose put suffering as the cornerstone of any possible unity. They say: "In order to struggle and make things better one must suffer them" (J. P., 2007) or "People believe in those that suffer with them" (M. C., 2010). So collective suffering, the shared embodiment of work and hardship, is seen as being the basis for any possible collective identity and action. And purposeful suffering, sacrifice, becomes a means to an end: "Without sacrifice there is no victory" (C. F., 2010).

Struggle: The Construction of Solidarity

The last aspect involved in creating the structures of feeling of workers in Ferrol is struggle itself, as it is part of the production of a collective identity that can be mobilized for transforming reality. Struggles waged in the present refer to past modes of collective identity formation both as models to follow and as a warning of pitfalls to avoid. Present struggles, however, have to confront new forms of cleavages that fragment the subaltern classes today. What sorts of instruments are now being used to produce coherence and unity?

This chapter has described how in Spain, as elsewhere, present-day fragmentation of the production structure together with the opening to a competitive market from the 1980s onward and the rise of unemployment, casual and precarious jobs has run parallel with the institutionalization of political and labor conflicts, the hegemony of macroeconomics and a culture of *"concertación"* (agreements). As a result, previous institutionalized forms of collective identity such as classical trade unionism have lost public confidence. On the other hand, there are increasing reasons to mobilize: *as workers* in the face of a consistent loss of rights and employment opportunities, *as citizens* in the face of life-threatening environmental assaults, and *as ordinary people* in the face of the difficulty to make a living. All of these issues could be analyzed and framed in seemingly simple political-economic terms producing a structure of common positionalities. However, people experience these commonalities in a particular and fragmented way, from within a structure of feeling embedded in place and personal hardship. Militant particularism is pervasive (Harvey 2001; Williams 1989 [1981]). The challenge therefore is to overcome the experience of particularized solidarities and make them collective.

Various forces contribute to particularized solidarities. The first is localism, bounding the space for action to those who suffer a particular aggression. An example of this is the Comité Ciudadano de Emergencia (Citizen's Emergency Committee), a citizen's committee including various neighborhood associations, cultural entities, and environmental justice activist networks that was formed to oppose the construction of a Natural Gas Plant inside the Bay of Ferrol. The plant was dangerous, did not comply with EU security regulations, and was destructive of the marine environment, thereby imperiling the livelihood of shellfish gatherers. For more than ten years, this committee has been waging a struggle on the legal front, through institutional dialogue and confrontation, and in street demonstrations. The movement, although formally united, is extremely heterogeneous, with issues ranging from fear of potentially life threatening explosions at the plant that would affect inhabitants of the area, the devaluation of adjoining property, loss of livelihood opportunities attached to destruction of marine environment, and political corruption (Narotzky 2007). This diversity in itself marks clear lines of cleavage in the movement. But the main issue is the inability of the movement to "jump scales" (Smith 1993), that is, to frame their plight in a larger framework, for example, that of general environmental justice that would link them to other national and international movements (such as Greenpeace). The argument of the leaders of the movement is that they need to combine very different interests to have a large backing locally. Opting for greater abstraction and a wider framing scale would immediately lose them local support. Because the movement toward abstraction tends to select a particular aspect of the issue to define a general logic of process, it would inevitably marginalize or even antagonize those local participants who explain the problem through a different logic.

This argument is fraught with ambivalence, however, as the main leaders of the Citizen's Committee are the heroes of the shipyard struggles of the 1960s who have found new struggles after being forced into early retirement in the 1990s. While they generally tend to frame their analysis in terms of class, in this particular struggle their strategy aims at inclusion, at keeping together a heterogeneous collective that has a unitary aim but a fragmented motivation. They also navigate the tension of their former "accomplishments" and their ultimate "defeat," as the younger participants in the movement speak of the strategy and tactics the old leaders propose both with admiration and with skepticism, but do not challenge it significantly.

A second and related form of particularization is at play in the framing of the terms of conflict. In Ferrol this is expressed by economic nationalism, the idea that the plight of workers in the autonomous region of Galicia is tied to that of firms and employers. Economic nationalism is part of an ambivalent past. Strands of economic nationalism appear at different historical moments during the nineteenth and twentieth centuries. Arguably, the autarkic project, followed by the import substitution period of the dictatorship that lasted until 1957, was a nationalist economic project, and it produced the growth of such "stable" industries as the nationalized shipyard Bazán. A different strand of economic nationalism is found in the late nineteenth century as Galician intellectuals, often following a traditional Catholic corporatist perspective, developed corporatist arguments for a national identity, seeking increased autonomy from the central Spanish government. (Afredo Brañas, one of the founders of *regionalismo* (regionalism), was inspired by equivalent traditionalist bourgeois movements in Catalonia.) During the transition, in the 1970s, a radical left version of economic nationalism was central to the development of the nationalist party (Bloque Nacional Galego, BNG) and the nationalist union (Confederación Intersindical Galega, CIG). Here economic nationalism was based on a center-periphery analysis of Galicia's position in world economic systems, also addressing the need to define a Galician-centered political economy, oriented towards an autonomous project.[15] In the present, this party (BNG) has evolved into one more accommodating to the interests of capital, while its founding leader, Xosé Manuel Beiras, has gone on to found a radical left party, Anova, in 2012.[16] Economic nationalism, therefore, has different political manifestations. Nevertheless, in everyday practice it gets mostly expressed through the endorsement of local employers' arguments for the need of rationalization. This is presented as "common sense" by the nationalist party BNG and trade union CIG, but also by leaders in other major unions.

Employees in the small local auxiliary firms often perceive competition with firms from elsewhere in Spain as the main threat to job stability. Juan, a young worker in an auxiliary company and member of the nationalist union (CIG), explains:

> What people demand is to stay for a while in the same firm; they want stability, not running around changing firms. But the main company keeps changing its contracts from one firm to the other. Now they are making contracts with companies in Madrid and the local companies don't get anything. . . . Outside firms move all the time, one day here, the other there. What I don't like is that they are destroying stable companies, with a stable labor pool, with workers who have been stable for forty years, in order to substitute them for companies where 90 percent of workers are precarious. Local employers have their capital here and they invest it locally. With the others, capital goes away. (J. C., 2006)

With a similar argument the left wing of the nationalist party Bloque Nacional Galego insists on the need to defend the Galician employers (*el empresariado gallego*) so that companies do not move to other regions.[17] Xosé Manuel Beiras described it as a recentering of Galician economy:

> We need to center the dynamics of Galician economy in itself—which does not mean isolating it; we need to strengthen its internal flows, densify its productive fabric, put an end to the extraversion of our growth potential; we need to reinvest within Galicia its economic surplus and regulate financial circuits in relation to this; we need to take public economic action to those nervous centers where the private entrepreneurial fabric is absent or frail. (XM Beiras, 2000)[18]

The idea is that the future of the worker depends on the future of local firms, so that in the face of global competitive pressures, a corporatist approach is the better solution for all. As a corollary, some of the classic corporatist themes reemerge: workers' demands have to recede in the face of the need to support the competitiveness of Galician companies; class conflict has to be superseded. Here the argument for unity and struggle is couched in the bounding of an imagined community allegedly sharing "the same" interest for the common well-being, irrespective of position in the political-economic structure.

This argument produces a lot of tension and internal contradiction within the rank and file of the unions, as workers have to negotiate struggling for better conditions with their Galician employer. Often also, they know that the local employer expands his business outside the region and makes subsidiaries of the company abroad that compete with the local firm.

A third form of militant particularism tries, paradoxically, to transcend particularity and reach for a universal level of abstraction to frame conflict. For workers, the awareness of a larger structure encompassing local developments is easier to grasp in the larger firms and generally enables shop stewards to analyze situations and engage struggles in class terms. The case of Pull & Bear's logistics department, part of the Zara-Inditex clothing empire, is a telling example. According to the local chamber of commerce president, the major Galician company, the Zara group[19] wanted to invest locally. Attracted by favorable conditions in the industrial park of Narón (in the Ferrol metropolitan area) they established the central logistic hub for their Pull & Bear brand. This was a company with no tradition of union activism, and it arrived in a region in decline with few employment expectations. But they hired young workers who were, in the words of José, the "sons of the shipyard": "they had a tradition," which they used to organize a section of the main union CCOO and eventually waged a strike for better social and working conditions that ended successfully.

The "tradition" they relate to is not only about the tactics of mobilization, but very much about the analysis of concrete issues in terms of a logic of accumulation, framed in terms of political economy. The section of Pull & Bear that engaged in mobilization is part of the Trotskyite faction of the union Comisiones Obreras (CCOO-Críticos); they have regular meetings where they study classic texts (Marx, Luxemburg, Trotsky) and analyze present-day events and conflicts. They collaborate actively in the journal *El Militante*, where they provide analyses of the economic situation and ongoing conflicts in the region. Their aim is revolutionary, and their work is to get workers to think beyond particularism, get them to "jump scales" and define the real adversary. José, however, admits that it was difficult to organize workers. This younger generation of trade unionists see themselves as distant from the institution of the union, which in the past provided the instruments for widening the scale of conflict. To them the union resembles a small business and is completely alienated from the workers. José explains:

> The institutional leadership of the union is incapable of struggle; they only know how to negotiate, make deals. The feeling is that the bureaucracy of the union is stopping us but the way to get things is through struggle. People are tired of putting up with the situation. This is a new generation of young people that does not bear the failure of the transition and does not agree on how the union manages things. There is no real authority in the union. But people are learning. (J. P., 2006)

For José, the need for struggle is present because labor conditions are deteriorating, but the union leadership has alienated itself from struggle by making deals, although it is still a useful structure to infiltrate. For this young activist, the previous generation of shipyard workers is both an example to follow and one to avoid. It is a "tradition" that enlightens as to the capacity of collective struggle and possible strategies: it situates them in a lineage as "the sons of the shipyard." But it is also the expression of the ultimate failure of the class-based unions, co-opted by the institutions that produced the practice of "agreements" and enclosed the spaces for struggle.

Collective Identities, Memories, and Struggles

What then can we conclude from these experiences in Ferrol? As in many other areas of deindustrializing Europe, struggles in twenty-first century Ferrol are very different from what they were in the past century. They have become increasingly particularized and fragmented in different ways. They trace their links to past conflicts, drawing particular lessons from both positive and negative interpretations that in turn help configure the grounds for present-day collective identity formation.

The three dimensions of feeling I have presented—defeat, suffering, and struggle—produce a dense fabric of connections and disconnections among and between ordinary subaltern people in Ferrol. Through the dimensions of time and space we can follow the production of conjunctions and disjunctions, of continuities, momentary blockages, and dead ends. We can also perceive how different levels of intimacy and distancing, of concreteness and abstraction, produce tensions that real people have to negotiate every day. It might be easy for the anthropologist observing this reality from a certain distance—which inevitably favors objectification—to define what is going on in terms of, for example, the internalization of abstract processes and logics. But this is not a possibility for those fully engaged in living their lives, making sense of it and fighting for a better future. As Raymond Williams (1989 [1977]) and Eric Hobsbawm (1984 [1971]) both point out, abstraction and organization are necessary to "jump scales" (in Neil Smith's terms) in the framing of a particular conflict in order to render it more universal and possibly more transformative of the structures. Simultaneously, however, this is a process of reification, where "relations between men are made into relations between things or relations between concepts" (Williams 1989 [1977]: 117; see also Harvey's analysis 2001). So if we want to respond to our initial question, "What kinds of collectives need to be produced to achieve a radical transformation of capitalist relations of production and a substantively democratic political space?" we need to address the central tension between the forces that produce militant particularism and those that are used to produce abstraction and expand the scale of organization and struggle. This is a tension that cannot easily be resolved for two distinct, albeit related, reasons.

The first is of an empirical nature, in that experience is always unique, and although interpersonal sharing, verbalization, and action produce commonality (Thompson 1966) there is a limit to the extension of this collective identification, of what Raymond Williams (1989 [1977]) called the "simple affirmation, affirmation with extension" of community. Further extension always requires a degree of abstraction that implies a loss of perceived realism, a "negation" of experience, while simultaneously extending the leverage of our experience and understanding. Some material realities, however, are shared in a more homogeneous way and are conducive to easier generalization, although, often, one only superficially based on an abstract understanding of the logics structuring these shared experiences. This was the case of the civil war when the conflict was simplified as the opposition of two factions—those fighting for democracy and those fighting against it—which was translated in the opposing camp as those fighting to save the Christian fatherland (the rebel armies of Franco) and those fighting to destroy it (the socialist and secular republicans). Later, during the Franco regime's violent repression of the working class and of the left, the adjective "red" often glossed over very different experiences and objectives but resulted in creating a strong sense of commonality among those opposing the regime. In both of these cases, dispossession was felt in a very direct and material way by the left all over Spain, producing solidarity and identity.

This was also the case, in a different way, for the postwar industrial and economic policies that favored the development of Fordism in key sectors of industry. These created commonality in work experience and the reconstruction of a class-based trade unionism. Class-based unionism in the context of a dictatorship was able to understand and organize labor struggle as key to the political struggle to transform society. The period of industrial restructuring and neoliberal expansion from the 1980s onward, by contrast, produced a material experience of dispossession—of employment, skills, security—that was paradoxically presented by those "representing" workers (Socialist Party, trade union leaders) as a positive program—European economic integration, increased competitiveness, growth that would bring employment, etc.—in a language of "agreements" and rational and responsible politics, where legitimate confrontation was always represented as limited to localized issues, not systemic ones. Here, a sense of alienation from those same institutions that had apparently been conquered in the struggle of the transition produced an effect of retrenchment into immediate experience, as opposed to a formalized organization that was becoming estranged and difficult to understand.

The second reason why the tensions between militant particularism and the abstraction necessary to expand the scale of organization and struggle is not easily resolved is of a theoretical nature, which can be elaborated via the insights of Henri Lefebvre (2000 [1972]). While particularism and fragmentation are facts of life, so are commonality and unity, depending on the level of abstraction and on the time and scale frames we use to make sense of reality. In both the immediate and distanced analysis of real life we confront the following issue: what appears as fragmented is part of a unit, but its imaginary fragmentation has real effects on the way the unit can be reproduced. In other words, we can understand the unitary system of capitalist accumulation as producing different forms of fragmentation at different historical moments and in different localities, which are then part and parcel of that by which the unitary system creates its conditions of possibility for social reproduction (Wolf 1982). This is, in my opinion, the deep sense of the concept of militant particularism that Raymond Williams proposes as a form of struggle that tries to capture the reality of different scales operating simultaneously. It addresses the challenge to both acknowledge the "logic" of connections within the system, both time and space connections, without losing their particular expression and the experience that drives people to think in terms of a community of interest. In Williams's words: "the concept of a practical and possible general interest, which really does include all reasonable particular interests, has to be negotiated, found, agreed, constructed" (1989 [1981]: 255). It captures the immanent contradiction that Hobsbawm (1984 [1971]) struggled with when trying to define class consciousness at the two levels of "trade union" and of "socialist" consciousness, the latter linked to the development of "organization," and formal institutions of leadership. The "lower level" consciousness of the more spontaneous trade union struggles had to be complemented by a "higher level" consciousness produced by "organization" in a purposeful manner (1984 [1971]: 27–28). The necessary mediation of organization, however, produces a "divergence, between 'class' and 'organization'" (1984 [1971]: 28), between class as experienced by people and the organization that gives it collective form and transforms it into a *subject* of history capable of enacting policy (Hobsbawm 1984 [1977]). This process of substitution and distancing through the structure of organization is both necessary to give "the people" a "reality" and often an obstacle to immediate mobilization (1984 [1977]: 293).

In Ferrol, this seems to be the case because the neocorporatist transition "agreements" became so closely bound with neoliberal policy that the expectations of workers were betrayed by those institutions representing the working class. The use of macroeconomic rationality and of pragmatic political "responsibility" on the part of the unions and the Socialist Party appeared as the ultimate "negation" of hard-won organization and community in past struggles and a blatant betrayal of immediate struggles. So, in the end, scale was in fact negated, the tension between the particular and the universal was erased, and the possibility for the unions of addressing the wrongs inflicted on the rank-and-file workers disappeared. In this conjuncture, memory has become an instrument that reintroduces time and space scales in the attempt to organize struggle.

In Ferrol people make various links between the past and the present. They see the present as an outcome of the past, as when the agreements reached by the unions during the restructuring conflict are explained as the prelude to present-day precarity. They see the present as the road to an imagined project in the future, when they define their struggles as aiming at a nationalist project of community, or at the possibility of a better life in a safer environment. These connections and disconnections are a crucial element in the local expression of systemic social reproduction. They produce both solidarity and cleavages that construct new collective identities and help redefine the conflicts that should be addressed. They generate a particular field of force that creates the conditions of possibility for engaging in transformative struggles and, in so doing, constructs the field of social reproduction.

As anthropologists we are in a particularly favorable position to explore the connection between the empirical nature of experience and the theoretical constructs developed both locally and by the distanced observer. The ways in which particular conflicts in Ferrol are being defined and struggles waged in the present are deeply embedded in the way larger forces, such as Francoist economic development, participation in the Western bloc, neoliberal imperatives of European accession, liberalization of markets, among others, became fixed in a place and inscribed in the bodies of successive generations of men and women. And that is why the ways they still find to achieve commonalities appeal to place and body and to the ties that bind them through time. The threads that situate them and commit them speak of the shipyard, the region, the lineages, and the suffering body. The realization that these elements of commonality that produce militant particularism are widely shared is central to their ability to expand and articulate collective identities. This might explain why suffering, as the immediate homology that should unite all those that share the hardship of earning a living, becomes in the last instance the metonym they appeal to as their basic commonality. However, as they try to build coalitions that will help them achieve a better life, they need to find bridges that help negotiate the cleavages set by the various experiences of space and time. Some are negotiated through lineages that bring together generations separated by disappointment; others are negotiated through a notion of region/nation that draws together different positions in the local economy and society; still others are negotiated through class pulling together those who live from a wage. All are only partial roads to inclusion through particular scale-frames that produce unity and fragmentation simultaneously, and often impair struggle. Further along the way the challenge is to define a collective identity that might achieve a significant capacity to transform the overwhelming reality of defeat, loss, and disbelief. Here, a level of abstraction that transcends particularism while expressing it has to be found, clearly defined, and transmitted.

In Europe and elsewhere the larger forces of expanding capitalism have historically become inscribed in different ways. The value of difference for capitalist expansion is *specific and place bound*, therefore, the common factor is that historically produced *specificities* are always exploited to the utmost by being reproduced as such. At the same time, the hegemony of macroeconomic thought infuses everyday experience with a transcendent reality. The focus on personal and social reproduction on the one hand, and the awareness of the simultaneous operation of different scales on the other, are in my view the best methodological inroads to understanding this process. On the ground, however, this realization is expressed as a tension between structures without soul that enable expanding the stakes of the struggle and real people who have the capacity to form solidary groups and wage immediate struggles.

Acknowledgments

The chapter is based on work done with the support of the following grants: SEJ2007–66633SOCI, Ministerio de Ciencia e Innovación; CSO2011–26843, Ministerio de Economía y Competitividad, Spain; and FP7- CT-2009–225670, European Union. I am grateful for the comments of Gavin Smith and Frances Pine to a first draft of the chapter and to Sharryn Kasmir and Gus Carbonella for further comments. I also want to acknowledge the help that discussing these issues with many friends and colleagues in Ferrol and elsewhere has provided to the formulation of my ideas.

Notes

1. Ferrol, a town of 74,799 inhabitants in 1960 (Instituto Nacional de Estadística) ranked second after Madrid in the number of ministers it provided during the Franco regime (8 out of 119) (Riquer 2010: 27).
2. Malo (2005) proposes that individual dismissal of workers was costly but easy and became an important instrument of workforce regulation in times of crisis after 1956.
3. Country Report on Spain, authors: Irene Sabaté and Claire Montgomery. Project "Models and their Effects on Development Paths: An Ethnographic and Comparative Approach to Knowledge Transmission and Livelihood Strategies" (MEDEA), FP7-CT-2009–225670, http://www.medeasteelproject.org/home.html. Accessed February 20, 2011.
4. This provided US economic and military aid in exchange for air and naval bases.
5. It is interesting to note that this also meant the ascent of economists in substitution of engineers in the ruling of the national economy (expressed in the confrontation between Suanzes — who resigned from the Instituto Nacional de Industria in 1963 — and López Rodó — who became the head of the Office of the development plan in 1962). It also meant the ascent to power of the Opus Dei, where most of these technocrats

militated. Last, it should be remembered that Laureano López Rodó, the main artifex of the modernizing development policies and the "technical" administration of the economy was very closely linked to Admiral Carrero Blanco, the right hand of Franco, like him born in Ferrol.
6. Spain asked to be admitted into the EEC in 1962 and was refused on politcal grounds, namely lack of freedom and a democratic system.
7. The Opus Dei was founded in 1928 by the Spanish priest Josemaría Escrivá de Balaguer. It was aimed at achieving sanctification through the exercise of any professional occupation by embedding Christian duties in the ordinary wake of life. After supporting the National Catholic side during the civil war, through its strength in education institutions, the congregation acquired an increasing influence in the regime, providing many members of successive governments. In 2002 the Opus Dei founder was canonized by Pope John Paul II.
8. The number of strikes jumped from 855 in 1975 to 1,568 in 1976 and 1,789 in 1979 (Navarrete and Puyal 1995: 148).
9. In general terms the Comisiones Obreras (CCOO, communist union) was less prone to sign the agreements, while Unión General de Trabajadores (UGT, socialist union) signed them all, arguing that "in a crisis situation a great sense of responsibility was necessary" (Domínguez 1990: 82). During the first ten years after Franco, CCOO signed only two (the Acuerdo Nacional de Empleo, signed in 1981 a few months after the attempted coup of February 23 by Colonel Tejero, and the Acuerdo Interconfederal of 1983) and gave tacit support to the Pactos de la Moncloa, 1977. The UGT for its part signed the Acuerdo Básico Interconfederal (1979), Acuerdo Marco Interconfederal (1980), Acuerdo Nacional de Empleo (1981), Acuerdo Interconfederal (1983), Acuerdo Económico y Social (1984).
10. However, an actor such as the socialist union leader Justo Domínguez perceived it as a new form of "trade unionism which is inserted in the state's institutions, a trade unionism of participation, that is or tries to be where decisions are made" (Domínguez 1990: 98).
11. All names of informants have been changed.
12. We have argued elsewhere, that the economic environment of scarcity, illegality, and arbitrariness was a central part of the creation of fear during the Autarky years of the Franco dictatorship (Narotzky and Smith 2006; Richards 1998).
13. This seems difficult if we think that Ferrol has the lower average income per person in all of Galicia (1,120 euro) and that more than 25 percent of salaried persons are paid under the minimum average salary of 640 euro per month. Sixty percent of households in Galicia get at least one income coming from retirement or other state subsidies (mostly unemployment), making an average of 30 percent of total household income. Twenty-three percent of households live with less than 1,000 euro per month, and 32 percent live under the 1,500 euro threshold. In 30 percent of households income from subsidies provides more than 75 percent of the total. For a nuclear family with two children the threshold of poverty was set at 1,280 euros in 2008, with 14 percent of households beneath it in Galicia. Seventy-five percent of young people (under age thirty) live with their parents, although 50 percent of them have some work (Instituto Galego de Estatística 2010).
14. *El Militante. Voz del Socialismo Marxista y de la Juventud*, July 17, 2006.
15. "Galiza, como economía periférica—só que europea, convén que reitere—non ficou á marxe dese turbulento acontecer globalizador. De xeito que se agravou unha súa patoloxía 'conxénita,' digámolo así, a saber : a carencia dun modelo de acumulación endóxena, que puidese cando menos contrarrestar a súa dinámica extravertida, como economía 'sen fronteiras,' a drenaxe do seu excedente económico monetarizado, o

seu problema de crecemento 'cara fóra,' constantemente reprodutor do seu histórico subdesenvolvemento—parafraseando agora ao recentemente finado André Gunder-Frank" (Xosé Manuel Beiras 2006, http://firgoa.usc.es/drupal/node/31657. Accessed November 2, 2010).

16. The new party ran in a coalition with two other parties in the left for the 2012 regional elections. The coalition, Alternativa Galega de Esquerda (AGE) was voted third after the Partido Popular (neoliberal right) and the Partido Socialista Galego (social democrat).
17. Some members of this left wing are now migrating to the new party Anova.
18. "Compre centrar a dinámica da economia galega nela própria–cousa ben distinta de isola-la@; potenciar os seus fluxos internos, densificar o seu entramado produtivo, acabar coa extraversión do noso potencial de crecimento, reinvertirmos dentro dela o seu excedente económico, regular en función diso os circuitos financieros, levar a acción económica pública a aqueles centros nervosos nos que o tecido empresarial privado estexa ausente ou enfraquecido" (XM Beiras, 2000).
19. Amancio Ortega, the founder and owner of a large stock of shares of the company is the seventh-richest man in the world, just following closely Lakshimi Mittal and well ahead of George Soros (forty-sixth), according to Forbes (2011), http://www.forbes.com/wealth/billionaires#p_1_s_arank_-1__-1. Accessed August 20, 2011.

References

Anderson, Charles W. 1970. *The Political Economy of Modern Spain. Policy Making in an Authoritarian System*. Madison: University of Wisconsin Press.
Beiras, Xosé Manuel. 2000. "A economía galega ante o s. XXI." *Revista Galega de Economía* 9, no. 1: 395–398.
Babiano, José. 1993. "Las peculiaridades del fordismo español." *Cuadernos de Relaciones laborales* no. 3, Universidad Complutense Madrid, 77–94.
Domínguez, Justo. 1990. "Diez años de relaciones industriales en España (1977–1987)." In *Pactos sociales, sindicatos y patronal en España*, ed. Angel Zaragoza. Madrid: Siglo XXI.
González, M. J. 1979. *La economía política del franquismo (1940–1970). Dirigismo, mercado y planificación*. Madrid: Editorial Tecnos.
Graham, Andrew. 1999. "Introduction." In *Government and Economies in the Postwar World: Economic Policies and Comparative Performance, 1945–1985*, ed. Andrew Graham and Anthony Seldon. London: Routledge.
Gutiérrez, Antonio. 1990. "Concertación social y coyuntura política en España." In *Pactos sociales, sindicatos y patronal en España*, ed. Angel Zaragoza. Madrid: Siglo XXI.
Harvey, David. 2001. "Militant Particularism and Global Ambition: The Conceptual Politics of Place, Space, and Environment in the Work of Raymond Williams." In *Spaces of Capital. Towards a Critical Geography*. Edinburgh: Edinburgh University Press.
Hobsbawm, Eric. 1984 [1971]. "Notes on Class Consciousness" In *Workers: Worlds of Labor*. New York: Pantheon Books.
———. 1984 [1981]. "The Making of the Working Class 1870–1914." In *Workers: Worlds of Labor*. New York: Pantheon Books.
———. 1984 [1977]. "Should Poor People Organize?" In *Workers: Worlds of Labor*. New York: Pantheon Books.
Instituto Galego de Estatística. 2010. "Datos Estadísticos Básicos de Galicia 2010." Santiago de Compostela, Xunta de Galicia, Conselleria de Facenda.
Lefebvre, Henri. 2000 [1972]. *"L'espace."* In *Espace et politique*. Paris: Ed. Economica.

Malo, Miguel Angel. 2005. "La evolución institucional del despido en España: una interpretación en términos de un accidente histórico." *Revista de Historia Económica* V.XXIII: 83–115.

Martínez-Alier, Joan, and Jordi Roca Jusmet. 1988. "Economía política del corporativismo en el estado español: Del franquismo al posfranquismo." *Revista Española de Investigaciones Sociológicas*, no. 41: 25–62.

Molinero, Carmen, and Pere Ysàs. 1990. "Los industriales catalanes durante el franquismo." *Revista de Historia Económica*, Año VIII, no. 1: 105–129.

———. 1993. "Productores disciplinados: control y represión laboral durante el franquismo (1939–1958)." *Cuadernos de Relaciones Laborales* no. 3, Universidad Complutense Madrid, 33–49.

Narotzky, Susana. 2010. "Gender, History and Political Activism in Spain." In *Class, Contention and a World in Motion*, ed. Winne Lem and Pauline Gardiner. Oxford: Berghahn Books.

———. 2007. "Planta de gas fora da ría: Conflictos locales, fronteras institucionales y sujetos políticos en Ferrolterra" In *Intersecçoes Ibéricas, Margens, passagens e fronteriras*, org. M.Cunha y L. Cunha. Lisboa: Graus Editora.

Narotzky, Susana, and Gavin Smith. 2006. *Immediate Struggles. People, Power and Place in Rural Spain*. Berkeley: University of California Press.

Navarrete, Montserrat, and Esther Puyal. 1995. "Conflictividad laboral: la huelgas: concepto, estadísticas y teoría." *Acciones. Investigaciones sociales* no. 3: 137–164.

Ramos-Gorostiza, José Luis, Pires Jiménez, and Luis Eduardo. 2009. "Spanish Economists Facing Indicative Planning in the 1960s." *History of Economic Thought and Policy* (1): 77–108.

Riquer, Borja de. 2010. *La dictadura de Franco*. Barcelona: Crítica.

Richards, Michael. 1998. *A Time of Silence: Civil War and the Culture of Repression in Franco's Spain 1936–1945*. Cambridge: Cambridge University Press.

Roseberry, William. 1994. "Hegemony and the Language of Contention." In *Everyday Forms of State Formation. Revolution and the Negotiation of Rule in Modern Mexico*, ed. Gilbert M. Joseph and David Nugent. Durham, NC: Duke University Press.

Sánchez Recio, Glicerio. 2002. "El sindicato vertical como instrumento político y económico del régimen franquista." *Pasado y meoria. Revista de Historia contemporánea*, no. 1: 5–37.

Smith, Neil. 1993. "Homeless/Global: Scaling Places." In *Mapping the Futures. Local Cultures, Global Change*, ed. John Bird, et al. London: Routledge.

Thompson, Edward P. 1966. *The Making of the English Working Class*. New York: Vintage Books.

———. 1978. *The Poverty of Theory and Other Essays*. London: Merlin Press.

Vilar, Margarita. 2004. "La ruptura posbélica a través del comportamiento de los salarios industriales: nueva evidencia cuantitativa (1908–1963)." *Revista de Historia Industrial* no. 25: 81–121.

Viñas, Angel. 2003. *En las garras del águila. Los pactos con Estados Unidos de Francisco Franco a Felipe González (1945–1995)*. Barcelona: Crítica.

Williams, Raymond. 1989. *Resources of Hope*. London: Verso Books.

———. 1989 [1977]. "The importance of Community" In *Resources of Hope*. London: Verso Books.

———.1989 [1981]. "The Forward March of Labour Halted?" In *Resources of Hope*. London: Verso Books.

———. 1989 [1985]. "Mining the Meaning: Key Words in the Miners' Strike." In *Resources of Hope*. London: Verso Books.

Wolf, Eric. 1982. *Europe and the People Without History*. Berkeley: University of California Press.

Zaragoza, Angel, ed. 1990. *Pactos sociales, sindicatos y patronal en España*. Madrid: Siglo XXI.

Zaragoza, Angel, and José Varela. 1990. "Pactos sociales y corporativismo en España." In *Pactos sociales, sindicatos y patronal en España*, ed. Angel Zaragoza. Madrid: Siglo XXI.

– Chapter 5 –

THE SATURN AUTOMOBILE PLANT AND THE LONG DISPOSSESSION OF US AUTOWORKERS

Sharryn Kasmir

The Saturn automobile factory in Spring Hill, Tennessee, was one of three General Motors (GM) plants put on standby during the company's bankruptcy reorganization in 2009. The decision to idle the plant—neither assuring it a short-term future, nor closing it permanently—was part of the restructuring plan orchestrated by the US government after it put up tens of billions of dollars in cash and loans and became the majority stakeholder in the company. At the time of the bankruptcy, fewer than half of the seventy-two hundred union autoworkers who had been employed just ten years earlier remained on the job. The rest had taken buyout packages, accepted early retirement, or transferred to other GM plants. As Saturn sales dropped off, Spring Hill lost bids for new products, and the plant bled jobs. GM finally made public its plan at the end of 2011. It would reopen to build a Chevrolet model and eventually employ eighteen hundred people, a fraction of its original workforce. Since many of those who moved to middle Tennessee in the 1980s–1990s to work at Saturn had already left the area, the company will likely attract new workers. Significantly, the United Automobile Workers (UAW) contract signed in the wake of the bankruptcy will permit GM to pay them roughly half of what veteran workers earn.[1] Spring Hill's lower compensation packet will now equal those offered by the nonunion Nissan, Honda, and Toyota facilities in neighboring Southern locations.

The fact that GM is currently hiring in Tennessee and elsewhere in the United States is testament to the savings it achieved from UAW concessions. In his 2012 State of the Union Address, President Obama heralded the revival of GM; indeed, the "Big Three"—GM, Ford, and Chrysler—went on a hiring spree after the government bailout helped cheapen unionized labor. Despite concessions on entry-level wages in recent contracts, the UAW held out against a permanent, widespread two-tier workforce, for the inequality among members and diminution of union power it would bring.[2] Auto companies won this giveback under threat of bankruptcy and the strong hand of the state. This situation replayed the US government bailout of Chrysler in 1979, when the UAW granted wage cuts to Chrysler and set in motion GM's own pursuit of concessions on wages, benefits, and work rules. These two moments in 1979 and 2009, when the combined power of state and capital won historic victories against labor, bookend the long dispossession of US autoworkers that marked the end of the twentieth century and the dawn of the twenty-first.

Further losses may be in the works. GM indicated that when Spring Hill reopens it will have an "innovative staffing and operating agreement." This vague statement sounded ominous to one commentator who suspected it foretold modular production, a cost-saving measure perfected by Volkswagen in Brazil, that brings nonunion employees of subcontractors into the factory to work side by side with their higher-paid, better protected, and unionized coworkers.[3] This arrangement has already been tried in Orion, Michigan, where 40 percent of the GM workforce makes entry-level wages, and lower-paid, non-GM employees work beside them in the plant.[4] A similar three-tier structure may soon follow in Spring Hill.

At first glance, Spring Hill's ignoble fate seems a dramatic reversal of fortunes. Saturn originated in the mid-1980s as a *model* plant, at a time when the US auto industry's main preoccupation was with Japanese manufacturers whose share of the small-car market was growing and whose lean, just-in-time production methods offered cost savings and flexibility that US firms could not match. Named for the rocket that launched Americans to the moon during the Cold War–era space-race with the Soviet Union, Saturn likened GM's business rivalry with Japan to the state's political and military contest with the USSR, summoning a set of symbolic markers the company would nurture through advertising and brand identity.

Saturn's advertising campaign was created by the public relations firm Hal Riney Associates, renowned for designing Ronald Reagan's 1984 reelection theme "It's Morning in America," which depicted a new dawn of American prosperity and hegemony after the recessionary years that followed the 1973 economic crisis. Like that political message, Saturn's branding cultivated an image of national revival and folksy nostalgia. The Saturn facility was pointedly built on a greenfield site in rural Tennessee on acres of farmland, some still planted in corn and encircled by a freshly painted, white wooden fence. To preserve this bucolic picture, factory buildings were set behind a man-made hill, and when approached from the highway, they were largely hidden from view. Television commercials and print ads portrayed Saturn employees as "happy workers" (Aaker 1994; Rogers 1999) and the plant as a model workplace, where the troubles of class conflict that characterized the "old world" of the Detroit-area and other long-standing industrial centers had been resolved. The brand slogan "A Different Kind of Company" advanced this idealized vision, and the company was formed as a subsidiary, rather than a division of GM, to give it autonomy as a testing ground for new labor relations.

Spring Hill's UAW Local 1853 was a partner in this process, and it set out to make the firm a laboratory for refashioning labor relations and reviving the US labor movement. Local 1853 cast aside the GM-UAW national contract for a local agreement that instituted a regime of labor-management cooperation that was the farthest reaching in the industry. Saturn boasted the most developed team concept and worker participation programs in the US, and Local 1853 collaborated with management to make Saturn workers *different from* and *more privileged than* other UAW workers. Workers transferred to Tennessee from Michigan, New York, Ohio, California, Georgia, and other states where their GM plants were in trouble or had already closed. They hoped that Saturn would be a "hundred-year company" and that union involvement in planning, managing, and sourcing would provide the security that eluded them in the places they left. Saturn, however, helped bring about the opposite: it facilitated the widespread precariousness and dispossession of autoworkers in Spring Hill and beyond. I argue in this chapter that Saturn played on and advanced the localism that had long characterized US labor unions, and it intensified competition among UAW chapters for investment, jobs, and security. Further, Saturn ruptured organizational connections with the UAW and narrowed the geography of labor precisely at a time when national and international alliances were arguably more important than ever.

I conducted fieldwork at Saturn in 1998–1999 during a period when the intense political and human stakes of the Saturn experiment had become apparent. While the team concept and employee involvement programs were in some ways a welcome change from the shop floors workers left behind, this work regime took a toll on workplace and family relationships, and it undermined collective social habits and rituals and fragmented social life; therefore, workers were left ill equipped to challenge the chronic stresses on themselves and their families that working at Saturn supposed. In return, workers hoped to secure their livelihoods, but despite Saturn's promise of shared prosperity and security through labor-management cooperation, the mutuality was decidedly circumscribed and short-lived. Rather than produce a dependable future for themselves and their families, workers were, in effect, encouraged to participate in the disorganization of their own union's power and in their own dispossession.

The case of Saturn provides an important lens for a global anthropology of labor. It shows the limitations of "militant particularism" divorced from "abstract universalism" that Raymond Williams (1989) understood to be the central problematic of working-class politics. Williams used these paired terms to capture the dialectic of working-class power—the creative relationship between the immediate, particular feelings and loyalties at the plant or community level, and the universalist sentiments and wider geography of struggle and solidarity made through organizational connections and ties (see Harvey 2001a; Narotzky 2011 and this volume). At Saturn, Local 1853's efforts to wield power at the level of the firm remained a defensive strategy in face of GM's global ambitions. The study of Saturn also affords an ethnographic vantage point from which to see how the social wage has been so determinedly undermined in the United States and elsewhere over the last decades. Capital captured for itself a greater share of the total social product not only through bald and sometimes violent attacks on labor, but also by offering privilege to select segments of national working classes.

This chapter documents the production of precariousness at Saturn. I argue that the making of insecurity was a strategy of accumulation, one that relied simultaneously on *both* expanded reproduction and dispossession. I focus on how individual workers were left to negotiate these overlapping regimes of accumulation on their own, and I show how the changing geography of production facilitated not only this individualization, but also the decline of union power. In this way, I chronicle the *long* dispossession of a privileged sector of the US working class, detailing how it was lived and experienced and pointing to the centrality of fear in this process. This account rightly troubles our old "class maps," (Denning 2004) the outmoded cultural images and understandings of class that rely on static categories of "stable working class" or "labor elite," and it points to the need for new maps that depict the more complicated social relations of production at the heart of capital accumulation.

This perspective has implications for any theoretical understanding of class formation. The dismantling of privilege among one of the most powerful sectors of the US working class was not an end unto itself, but a key aspect of the unmaking of the Fordist working class in the United States, through a process of geographical displacement, political disorganization, and individualization. This long unmaking demonstrates the extent to which the expanded reproduction of capitalism always already contains the seeds, if not the full blossoming, of what David Harvey (2003) terms "accumulation by dispossession." For Harvey, expanded reproduction and dispossession are two moments of accumulation that mark the distinct ways in which laboring people are incorporated into or pushed out of the advances of capital expansion, and they lead him to a two-fold typology of labor and popular struggles: conservative, rearguard attempts to defend the gains and privileges of expanded reproduction in the North; progressive struggles against dispossession in the global South. This typology, however, needs to be rethought (Collins 2012; Kasmir and Carbonella 2008). Responses to dispossession cannot be easily superimposed onto places or peoples; instead they are interwoven in the lives of workers and working-class communities around the world. This insight, in turn, urges us to jettison the idea of a stable working class and instead conceptualize industrial laborers as existing perpetually on the fault line of accumulation by dispossession and expanded reproduction.

Localism and the Spatial Assault on Autoworkers

The long unmaking of US autoworkers in the last decades of the twentieth century and first decade of the twenty-first necessarily centers on the extension and deepening of localism and its political consequences for working-class power. As August Carbonella shows in this volume, Fordist localism was initiated as a key aspect of monopoly capitalist control in the United States beginning in the 1920s, when corporate-led cultural campaigns, focused on citizenship, paternalism, and individualism, undermined the working-class publics of the previous decade. The imposition of localism was reinforced by the successive passage of two pieces of labor legislation: the 1935 Wagner Act, which codified a system of decentralized labor agreements into law; and the 1947 Taft-Hartley Act, which embraced anti-communism and outlawed secondary boycotts, mass picketing, wildcat strikes, and multiemployer strike actions. This cultural and legal project of capital and the state, or "Americanism and Fordism," in Gramsci's succinct phrasing, severely undermined the ability of labor unions to coordinate the actions of their members across space. The impact of localism was magnified in the 1980s, at precisely the moment when so-called "post-Fordist" work and class relationships were being introduced, particularly in the auto industry. Saturn played a key role in this development.

Capital and the state put union locals into competition with one another in the 1980s, just as they pitted towns, cities, and states against each other, all vying for investment in an age when the threat of capital flight was real, devastating, and ever present. These moves narrowed workers' worldviews and disciplined a working class that had become restive, relatively well organized, and increasingly radical in the late 1960s–early 1970s. This political consciousness was manifest in auto by the intersection of social movements for racial equality with parallel developments in the factories and union, by countercultural-inspired demands for better working conditions and more meaning on the job, and by the institutional power of the UAW. The post–World War II period is widely known as an era of "labor peace" between the UAW and the Big Three. This era was ushered in by the anti-communism of the Taft-Hartley Act and the subsequent purges of radicals from the union. It was then furthered by the 1950 contract, dubbed the "Treaty of Detroit" because it exchanged long-term contracts and union guarantees not to strike for regular cost-of-living adjustments and employer-funded health insurance and pensions. This Fordist compact surely signaled a retreat from the radical demands of 1936, when the UAW was founded as a constituent union of the industrial, class-based Congress of Industrial Organizations (CIO) against the craft exclusivity of the American Federation of Labor (AFL), and the postwar years certainly saw the consolidation of a union bureaucracy that bargained contracts at the expense of broader class concerns. Yet insurgent politics nevertheless emerged from some sectors of UAW's membership to challenge this state of affairs.

The organizations formed by African American autoworkers are indicative of this more radical development. African Americans had been relegated to the hardest, dirtiest, and lowest-paying jobs since they moved en masse to Michigan's auto factories after World War I and World War II. They were employed in the oldest and least automated plants, where harsh working conditions and inhuman speedups underpinned a system of hyper-exploitation that activists termed "niggermation" to underscore the blatant racism at its core. Despite the UAW's history as a progressive CIO union that organized workers across the industry, and contrary to its public commitment to racial equality, union locals often accepted the racial segmentation of labor. To combat the brutal working conditions and the racism in their union that allowed this inequality and super-exploitation to persist, black UAW members in Detroit formed the Dodge Revolutionary Union Movement (DRUM) in Chrysler's Dodge plant. This organization was founded in the immediate aftermath of the 1967 uprisings in Detroit and other US cities and in the context of the growing Black Power movement. DRUM challenged Dodge management and criticized the UAW leadership for its racist and imperialist policies. The Revolutionary Union Movement (RUM) quickly spread to other factories and other cities. In 1969 the League of Revolutionary Black Workers was formed to coordinate RUM activities and to build a nationwide campaign. League members ran for office in their union locals, instigated wildcat strikes, published newsletters, led marches and demonstrations, and nurtured alliances with students at nearby universities. They also brought the ideas of Black Liberation and socialism to the shop floor and union halls and, inspired by a Marxist understanding of capitalism, endorsed an internationalist politics that challenged the global lines of racial and class inequality. In its own words, the League committed itself to "help organize DRUM type organizations wherever there are black workers be it in Lynn Townsend's kitchen, the White House, White Castle, Ford Rouge, the Mississippi Delta, the plains of Wyoming, the mines of Bolivia, the rubber plantations of Indonesia, the Chrysler plant in South Africa" (quoted in Georgakas and Surkin 1998: 71). This list charted a hoped-for geography of struggle across space and across lines of difference within the US working class—from domestic to service worker to farmhand to unionized autoworker—and it extended its political map to labor conflicts then taking place beyond US borders. The League also expressed solidarity with national liberation movements in the Third World, demanded equal pay for white and black Chrysler workers in apartheid South Africa, and opposed the US war in Vietnam, standing against the UAW leadership's notorious support for the war (Georgakas and Surkin 1998; Geschwender 1977).

RUM had a counterpart in a 1973 workers' rebellion at the GM plant in Lordstown, Ohio. When Lordstown opened in 1966, it was a highly automated plant, in which the corporation had invested considerable capital. Given the strong union environment centered around the area's steel mills, GM preferentially hired young workers, who were predominantly white and Vietnam vets, counting on their lack of union experience and presumed social conservatism to keep them quiescent. In the first years, however, Lordstown workers were not quiet but waged several wildcat strikes; still, GM gave the plant the new Vega model. With a slim profit margin on the inexpensive car, the demands in the plant were intense. GM sent a special management team to reorganize production, and they loaded up jobs so the line ran one hundred cars per minute, compared with sixty to seventy per minute for the previous model. Workers were laid off and their tasks redistributed to effect the speed-up. Those who remained suffered what came to be called the "Lordstown blues" for the intense pressure and monotony of the assembly line and the extreme alienation it bred. Masked union leaders entered the factory in protest, and workers walked out in what quickly became a notorious wildcat strike (Rothschild 1973).[5]

Oral historian Studs Terkel interviewed the local union president Gary Bryner during the wildcat action. Reflecting on the mood in the plant, Bryner said that when the factory opened, unemployment in the area was low, which he thought gave workers a sense of fearlessness and power. More, younger workers had a different conception of manliness, work, and themselves than had their fathers:

> Fathers used to show their manliness by being able to work hard and have big, strong muscles and that kind of bullshitting story. The young guy now, he doesn't get a kick out of saying how hard he can work . . . Father felt patriotic about it . . . Whereas the young guy believes he has something to say about what he does . . . The almighty dollar is not the only thing in my estimation. There's more to it—how I'm treated. What I have to say about what I do, how I do it. (Quoted in Terkel 1972: 259–260)

Bryner suggests that the young white and black workers—"the guy with the Afro, the guy with the beads, the guy with the goatee" (quoted in Terkel 1972, 264)—found common cause. There was racial hostility in the plant, especially expressed by the older white workers, but the image Bryner conveys of camaraderie across racial lines, young male workers' reinterpretation of their masculine identities, their rejection of a macho work ethic, and changing working-class aspirations nevertheless signal important changes in political and cultural attitudes than ran afoul of the racial divide and social conservatism that management had banked on. The struggle at Lordstown resonated with a wider rank-and-file movement that sought the humanization of work, the reuniting of mental and manual labor to relieve the monotony of the assembly line, and a transformation of working-class subjectivity. These themes, forcefully suggested in Bryner's commentary—"The almighty dollar is not the only thing in my estimation. There's more to it—how I'm treated. What I have to say about what I do, how I do it"—sounded as well in Italy, France, and elsewhere in Europe, as workers there similarly raised questions about the meaning of their labor and struck over working conditions rather than pay (see Gorz 1964).

If the institutional capacity and staying power of the Lordstown rebellion or RUM were limited (indeed, the league split in 1971), their impact was bolstered by the UAW's response to the Lordstown blues in the form of "Operation Apache," named for its purported resemblance to the "hit-and-run tactics used by the Apaches to attack US cavalry" (Rubenstein 1992: 237). Union locals learned to pursue grievance after grievance in order to provoke a strike, and workers used this tactic to wrest some measure of collective control over the factory, the pace of work, and their time (Rubenstein 1992: 237–238). These separate but related developments together encouraged a surge of worker militancy that unsettled the labor peace.

In an attempt to flee this militancy, and to sidestep the UAW's institutional muscle at the bargaining table, GM invested in automation and devised its "Southern strategy." In the 1970s, it built new plants in rural areas in the US South where there was little industry and where deep-seated anti-union sentiment, racism, and racial violence were expected to keep workers unorganized. This spatial strategy was not new. The industry first concentrated in the Detroit area in the early twentieth century because the city's Employers' Association fought a successful open-shop campaign and maintained an anti-labor environment. But after the 1936 sit-down strike in Flint, Michigan, first established the UAW, capital repeatedly fled the spatially bounded, accumulated power of labor. GM moved factories out of Detroit to its suburbs in the 1950–1960s, and the push south followed that ground plan. (Silver 2003: 41–75).[6] The UAW initially had trouble organizing in the South, but during contract negotiations in 1976, it threatened to strike unless GM pledged neutrality in future organizing drives. After this, the UAW launched an all-out effort and successfully unionized all of the Southern plants (Rubenstein 1992: 238–241).

GM then abandoned its Southern strategy for a more decidedly global one, and it determined to implement new work rules and to win for itself the wage cuts that the UAW conceded as a condition of the US government bailout of Chrysler in 1979. In 1982, GM chairman Roger Smith demanded that the UAW reopen its contract to match the give-backs at Chrysler. When the union refused, Smith announced that it would close four plants, and within months, it shut Southgate in California. The UAW was thus pressed to concede $2.5 billion in cuts to wages and benefits.

In this way, Smith pioneered the tactic of threatening plant closings to win concessions through local-level modifications to the national contract. It thereby instigated the practice of "whipsawing" to force locals to compete against other locals, each negotiating plant-specific concessions to secure jobs for its own members. Whipsawing marked a significant blow to UAW power. It undercut the hard-won system of national contracts and pattern bargaining wherein the union negotiated what it calculated would be its most favorable national agreement with one of the Big Three and leveraged that contract to settle with the other employers. Whipsawing consequently shifted the balance of power between the UAW and GM.

This corporate tactic was immediately challenged in Van Nuys, California, where Local 645 organized a five-year campaign to keep their plant open after a wave of plant closings claimed several California auto factories (including Southgate) and thousands of jobs. Eric Mann, a worker in Van Nuys and leader of the campaign, wrote an account of the struggle in which he described how the union leaders tackled a critical issue: "[W]hy, except for the most narrow self-interest of its 5,000 workers, the plant *should* be kept open" (Mann 1987: 108). Local 645 leaders confronted in this way the meaning of industrial conflict beyond the factory gates, and they envisioned their particular struggle as a broader fight for worker and community control over economic planning and investment *and* as a challenge to the UAW leadership. The International had thus far responded to plant closures with resignation and by offering concessions and facilitating the transfer of workers from plant to plant. Local 645 activists sought a different course, one that could be followed by other chapters and that would force the UAW to take a more political stance.

The resulting campaign moved from the local to the general, developed alliances across ethnic and racial lines and geographic space, and had political aspirations beyond saving jobs. It thereby addressed the dialectic of militant particularism and abstract universalism that is a central dynamic of working-class politics (Williams 1989). The workers' histories of struggle help account for the wider progressive movement that grew out of their fight. The majority of workers were Chicano and African American, and the organization of support and multiethnic alliances that were so central to the campaign should be considered in light of the history of civil rights, anti-imperialist, anti-Vietnam War, and labor struggles within the Chicano and African American communities in Los Angeles during the 1960s–1970s. The memory of these struggles, and the trenchant analyses of imperialism and class relations that emerged from them, would have been especially vivid, both in the plant and in the wider communities (see Mann 1998; Horne 1997; Mariscal 1999).

Local 645 waged a fight on two fronts. While it battled GM, it also sent a delegation to the 1983 UAW convention to raise two related questions about labor geography and class power: "Why isn't your International union doing more to stop these plant closings?" and "Why isn't your local doing more to get other UAW locals to develop a national strategy against plant closings?" (Mann 1987: 155). Local 645 rightly identified this as a moment when the US labor movement's limited reach was not sufficient. At this juncture, the UAW might have challenged capital's spatial fix, and it might have brought the fight to preserve jobs to an international stage, where it would have necessarily confronted the globalization and financialization of capital and questions of class power. To the contrary, the UAW sounded "the constant theme [of] the battle against imports and calls for protectionist legislation. While delegates cheered wildly at every verbal assault against Japan, there was no strategy offered with which to confront the Big Three automakers on the issue of capital flight or the widespread problem of whipsawing" (Mann 1987: 156). Activists brought this agenda again to the 1986 UAW convention, where they joined the opposition union caucus New Directions Movement to fight concessions. Their protest slate did not prevail, nor ultimately did the Van Nuys campaign; activists kept the plant open for several more years, but it finally shut in 1992.

With this progressive position sidelined in the UAW, whipsawing became commonplace, and locals bid against each other for new products, investment, and jobs. Losing a bid meant that workers in one locale might face temporary layoff or see their factory permanently close; winning meant giving back on work rules. Bob Jessop (2002) used the term "competition state" to describe the maneuvering of elites and polities (national, as well as subnational) to attract mobile capital in the neoliberal era and to suggest the state's role in effecting the spatial disorganization of labor that resulted (see also Friedman 2003). I suggest that the competition state had a counterpart in the United States in the "competition union local," which bargained in direct competition with other US and international chapters. This widespread competition narrowed the political horizons of unions and their members, and it pitted insecurity in one place against employment in another. Competition union locals also had the effect of decentralizing and weakening the International UAW, turning it into "a loose federation of locals competing among themselves" (Reuther, quoted in Mann 1987: 82). Indeed, the more militant Canadian wing of the UAW so strongly opposed concessions that it left the International in 1985 over the issue (Green and Yanarella 1996: 7), thereby further restricting the union's reach at the precise time when capital was moving easily within and across nation states.

Increasingly, successful bids required locals to agree to the new, so-called cooperative work practices, including the team concept, quality circles, and other techniques associated with lean production, and this work regime became the rule of the day. In the United States, Victor Reuther, brother of longtime UAW president Walter Reuter, founded the dissident New Directions Movement to oppose this strategy (see Dandaneau 1996: 7–33). The New Directions position was developed in the left labor magazine *Labor Notes*, which considered cooperative work practices to be thinly disguised union-busting tactics. *Labor Notes* argued that the team concept robbed the union of control over job classifications and seniority rules, two sources of its power on the shop floor, and that participation and quality programs manipulated workers' pride in their work to bring a speed-up and greater stress to the shop floor (see Parker and Slaughter 1985; 1988; 1994).

If we recall that labor conflicts in auto in the 1960s–1970s were over the organization, conditions, and purpose of work, rather than simple wage disputes, we see that management "appealed to many of the workers' deepest desires—greater control over their working environment, greater respect for their input into the productive process, and greater job security through higher quality products" (Mann 1987: 87) and turned their overtures for more meaningful work into a regime that made them into petty managers of themselves and their coworkers, undermined union power, and put many out of work. GM disinherited workers of their own aspirations by distorting their collective struggle for the power to determine the purpose of work and the nature of working-class subjectivity and turning it into a managerial plan for individual "empowerment" and "self-actualization." This maneuver might be aptly characterized as a cynical inversion of their class demands.

These arrangements reached their apex at Saturn. As the standard bearer of cooperation, Saturn exerted considerable pressure on the rest of the UAW. Its impact was so great that the president of a Michigan local considered that "Saturn had become a Trojan horse in our midst. Armed with the threat of plant closing, the company is now playing local against local to see who will meet or exceed Saturn's give-backs" (quoted in Mann 1987: 82). Saturn marked an important milestone in the disorganization of working-class power that began with capital flight in the 1970s and continued in the next decade with whipsawing and labor-management cooperation. It was a short step from this narrowed field of alliance and organization to Spring Hill, where Saturn's singular labor accord, neoliberal management practices, and sophisticated cultural campaign helped to unmake the Fordist working class in the United States.

"Saturn Mania"

GM announced in 1986 that it would spend five billion dollars on a vertically integrated facility for Saturn—the largest single industrial investment in US history to that date. The budget was ultimately cut to 3.5 billion dollars, still a vast sum (Sherman 1994: 5). At a time when state and city budgets needed remedy for the punishing effects of Reaganomics and with billions of dollars in capital investment at stake, Saturn was the object of intense competition. Municipalities and states orchestrated extravagant public-relations campaigns and offered liberal incentive packages to win the company.[7] Thirty-seven states and one thousand communities vied for Saturn, and their competition garnered considerable media attention. Seven governors appeared on a popular daytime talk show to sell their states (Sherman 1994: 98), and a small record producer released a novelty song that was a tribute to the frenzy.[8] Labor studies scholar John Russo (1986) dubbed the episode "Saturn mania" for the intensity of the spectacle and to underscore its political and ideological effects.

Crushed by the decline of its steel factories, Youngstown, Ohio, bid for Saturn. Some two hundred thousand schoolchildren and residents wrote letters to GM president Roger Smith, touting the advantages of their city and imploring him to choose them. Youngstown realtors organized a hundred-car caravan to corporate headquarters to deliver the letters, and the city purchased billboard space and television time in the Detroit area to attract GM's attention. One letter, written by Russo's own school-aged son, captured the desperation of this effort:

> Dear Mr. Smith:
> I hope you will consider building the Saturn plant in the Mahoning Valley. I would like it to be here because it would make thousands of jobs and it will ease the 32.9 percent unemployment rate. Please do not rule us out because Lordstown is here. The Mahoning Valley is well suited for the Saturn plant. Some reasons are it is near transportation and resources and our people are willing to work and they work hard.
> I hope your car beats the imports and brings many Americans a job.
> Sincerely,
> Alexander Russo (age 10, quoted in Russo 1986)

This letter makes plain that the post-1973 downturn hit Youngstown hard. Alexander's plea that his city not be ruled out for its proximity to Lordstown testifies to the legacy of worker militancy: Lordstown was still on the class-conflict map, and GM was steering clear of places with traditions of labor struggle and UAW activism.

According to Russo, Saturn mania encouraged GM and other corporations to seek tax breaks at existing facilities, and it worked at a political and ideological level to deepen the anti-union environment in the United States by encouraging the public to see organized labor as the enemy of economic viability and by promoting the idea that a cooperative workplace, rather than one with a strong union, was intrinsically more "American." This contributed to the emerging common sense that rigid union rules were to blame, perhaps more so even than capitalist greed, for the decline of US industry, a bitter reversal of the actual balance of forces in an era of the globalization and financialization of capital. Russo argues that the pillorying of unions that accompanied Saturn mania encouraged many Midwest Democrats to turn against organized labor.

After a long bidding process and months of speculation, GM announced that Spring Hill, Tennessee (population 1500), was the chosen site, but it cautioned that its decision was provisional, thereby gaining yet more leverage during final negotiations. Maury County (where Saturn was located) formed an Industrial Development Board to float bonds and to hold the title to the land, thereby relieving Saturn of property tax obligations. In return, Saturn signed a forty-year in-lieu-of-tax agreement, which committed the company to pay $14.5 million over the first three years, and less still in the years to follow. GM expected the state to pay for the parkway to connect the site to the interstate and for a $30 million sewage hookup. Consumer advocate Ralph Nader criticized the deal, charging that it was millions less than the company would pay at the normal tax rate and considerably less than the county would need to meet its new fiscal burdens. A report commissioned by the State of Tennessee similarly calculated that the payments were likely to be inadequate (Borden 1986; Gilbert 1994; The Tennessee Advisory Commission on Intergovernmental Relations 1992: 37–40; Nader 1985a; 1985b; 1985 c; 1985d; Sherman 1994: 97–154).

Beyond these generous giveaways, Spring Hill was also selected for its distance from the center of UAW power in Detroit. It had been some years since the UAW posed a serious, radical threat to the auto giants—manifested by the union's failure to direct an international response to capital flight as much as by the earlier pacifying impact of the "Treaty of Detroit." The organized competition for Saturn and the pillorying of the union it encouraged was the centerpiece of a public political drama staged at a moment when the neoliberal climate encouraged GM (and other employers) to conclude that the time was ripe for a wholesale assault against organized labor. Saturn was located in a Southern, right-to-work state,[9] in close proximity to non-union, Japanese transplants, including the Nissan factory fewer than fifty miles away where UAW organizing drives twice failed. This distance from Detroit, at the same time physical, political, and symbolic, was indispensable to the unfolding of the plot, according to which labor and management would necessarily embark upon a cooperative pact to remake class relations and identities.

The Making of Difference

When I began fieldwork in 1998, Local 1853 represented the seventy-two hundred men and women who worked at Saturn. The workforce came from closed or ailing GM plants across the United States, had a higher proportion of women than did many GM facilities, and was racially and ethnically diverse—African American, Latino, and white. Most of the union leaders, whose gender and race largely mirrored that of the membership, were from the Vision Team, a caucus within 1853 that was avid in its advocacy of labor-management "partnership" and was committed to making Saturn workers different from and more privileged than other GM workers. In auto, privilege had a history of being doled out to workers along lines of race and gender, but at Saturn, work regime and cooperation were the terms of advantage. Mike Bennett, a white skilled-trades worker from Flint, who had been the longtime 1853 president and was then the union's representative to the Manufacturing Action Council, was a passionate and public champion of Saturn. From the get-go, some officials in the International UAW opposed the Saturn experiment for establishing a pattern of labor relations that would weaken the union's hand, but its devoted defenders, most notably Vice Presidents Irving Bluestone and Don Elphin, won the day. Bennett, the Vision Team, and supporters in the International believed they were pioneering a new model of labor relations that would improve the workplace and shore up jobs. My time in the plant, interviews with workers, and participant observation in training sessions and meetings, however, pointed to another reality, one that contradicted the widely circulated image of a shop floor that was better or more personally fulfilling for workers. Many workers found Saturn's work regime uniquely stressful and destructive of the relationships and identities that had made work in their old plants companionable and had engendered solidarity. The starting point for this state of affairs was Saturn's singular labor pact.

Local 1853 dispensed with the national GM-UAW contract and adopted a short, continuously bargainable local agreement that served as its only labor accord. The fact that it was only thirty-some pages, compared with the hundreds of pages of typical UAW contracts, was meant to signal a critique of "old-style" unionism as conflict-ridden, burdensome, and out of date. Saturn's memorandum of agreement granted the union rights to participate in management, which was highly unusual since US companies are not legally required to bargain over business decisions, and most contracts contain management-rights clauses that further secure managerial prerogative. Union members were paired with managers throughout the organization: they hired team members, organized workflow, became team leaders and area managers, consulted on (and sometimes modeled for) advertising campaigns, and participated in long-range planning, selection of suppliers, and manufacturing decisions as members of the Manufacturing Action Council and Strategic Action Council. A large number of UAW members therefore held what were effectively management positions, and hundreds had assignments that took them off of the shop floor. Significantly, however, the union was not involved in decisions about capital investment or new products, a fact that foretold serious limitations for its ability to retain jobs in Spring Hill and to maintain its own power within the firm (Rubinstein 1996, and Rubinstein and Kochan 2001: 19–35).

It is important to recall the global managerial climate of the 1980s–1990s. Labor-management cooperation was a popular refrain manifest in many and various forms, from such distinct corners as the Mondragón cooperative group in the Basque region of Spain, to worker-owned coops in Poland. While these expressions of cooperation were particular and historically specific, each exhibited the growing neoliberal common sense that independent workers' organizations were inefficient, unnecessary, or outmoded, and that labor and capital should be "partners." Yet ethnographic research found that cooperatives were not an effective means for workers to control the conditions of their employment, secure their livelihoods over the long term, or achieve social betterment beyond the confines of their enterprises (Kasmir 1996; Kalb this volume).

A discourse of cooperation came also from the methods of lean manufacturing that were pioneered at Toyota in Japan and that were the global benchmark of the day. Manufacturers across sectors were under competitive pressure to restore profitability after the 1973 economic crisis; their mandate was to upgrade from Taylorism's detailed task division of labor, end-of-the-line quality control, and supervisors who dispensed shop discipline. Lean production sought to use workers' own freely offered efforts, rather than the oversight of supervisors, to establish job rotation and flexibility, cut stock and waste, institute "total quality" by moving quality measures into the production process, and reduce labor time. To achieve this, workers' input and compliance was solicited through participation programs, quality circles, the team concept, and suggestions boxes. These methods received considerable attention in the United States, where proponents maintained that they relieved monotony and enriched work. Critics instead saw a cover for speed-ups, overwork, union busting, and downward pressure on wages (see, e.g., Dadeneau 1996; Graham 1995; Green and Yanarella 1996; Nissen 1997; Parker and Slaughter 1985; 1988; 1994; Rinehart, Huxley, and Robertson 1997).

Auto companies in the United States scrambled to adopt lean production in the face of significant impediments to its implementation, and the state aided capital in paving the way for managerial reform. Toyota counted on company unions to secure workers' compliance, but employer-controlled unions were banned in the United States, and the National Labor Relations Board (NLRB) traditionally ruled against employee participation programs for violating this Wagner Act prohibition. Yet shifts in state policy can be seen in the NLRB's commentary in the 1992 case of the Teamsters versus Electromation Inc. The Teamsters Union charged that Electomation's joint labor-management committee was acting as a company union. While the NLRB ruled for the Teamsters, each member of the board wrote that he would have decided in favor of the employee participation plan in different circumstances. One member suggested that as global competition mounted, the NLRB would become friendlier to "innovative employee involvement programs directed to improving efficiency and productivity" (quoted in Woolf 1994: 606). The Clinton administration, especially under the direction of Labor Secretary Robert Reich, turned the "tide of support" (Woolf 1994: 605) in favor of a cooperativist interpretation of labor law. Clinton appointed a proponent of employee participation to head the NLRB, and he established the Commission on the Future of Worker-Management Relations to "enhance work-place productivity through labor-management cooperation and employee participation" (1994: xi). The administration's plan for "reinventing government" made labor-management cooperation a foundation of neoliberal reform.

Saturn and Local 1853 contributed importantly to this cooperativist, neoliberal consensus. The memorandum of agreement eliminated job classifications and seniority rules, two provisions of the national contract that were important domains of union power. "Work unit" (Saturn's term for the team) members rotated jobs, so they could replace a fellow worker who was absent or late. Work units were "self-directed" and, like small businesses, they were responsible for their own budgets, schedules, quality, and record keeping; they held regular meetings in their team center to keep abreast of these plans. Work unit members monitored each other's attendance and confronted fellow workers who were absent or late, and they scrutinized each other's performance. They, thus, took on what had been supervisory responsibilities, and this created conflict and ill will among them. The labor accord also traded hourly wages for an incentive-based "risk and reward" formula that held a portion of compensation "at risk" and paid "reward" pegged to factory-wide training, quality, and production targets. This looked to critics like a petty form of capitalist return on investment, and it was another contractual change that made Saturn workers different from other GM workers.

Further the Saturn agreement extended job security to 80 percent of the workforce "except in situations of . . . unforeseen or catastrophic events or severe economic conditions" (Memorandum of Agreement 2000: 16). This provision substituted for the national contract's guarantee of transfer rights and assistance programs in the case of layoff—including a guaranteed income stream, subbenefits, and job banks. For the 20 percent without job security, there was no protection at all. Consequently, Saturn's memorandum left workers at risk and installed a two-tier workforce, something that codified inequality among them (Rubinstein and Kochan 2001: 16). In these many ways, Saturn's agreement set the standard for union givebacks, undermined protections for workers, and eroded union power. It was therefore central to the nexus of difference, disorganization, and insecurity that underwrote the long dispossession of US autoworkers.

A leaked 1983 memo from GM Chief of Labor Relations Alfred S. Warren indicates that Saturn's memorandum was a testing ground for GM's plans for the UAW as a whole. Warren outlined GM's goals for 1984 contract negotiations, which included much of what the corporation soon won at Saturn: a continuously bargainable agreement, rather than a formal, fixed-term contract; increased labor-management partnership and worker involvement, without surrendering management rights; increased profit sharing in exchange for wage concessions; job security for 80 percent of the workforce with diminished layoff protections and payments; and the relaxation of work rules. The lengthy wish list was meant to achieve the elimination of eighty thousand to one hundred thousand jobs by 1986. Saturn was an opening salvo in GM's plan to use labor-management cooperation to disempower the UAW and to make its labor force precarious (Russo 1984).

Saturn's Cultural and Ideological Campaign

Warren's memo also affirmed GM's commitment to a public relations campaign to sell the public and the union on its labor-relations plan, and Saturn was again a natural laboratory (Russo 1984). Along with the contractual and shop floor changes, a cultural and ideological campaign to remake class relations, much like those of the 1920s that instituted Fordism, was carried out in the factory and in the media. Saturn workers were the objects of a dense public-relations effort that extolled their difference from and superiority to other autoworkers and rehearsed the theme that labor-management cooperation was better and more American than confrontational unionism (see Kasmir 2001; 2005; 2012).

One television commercial, for example, began in an airport, where a short, stocky, casually dressed man—the narrator of the spot and the character with whom the viewer was meant to sympathize—introduced himself as "a union guy" and his taller, more formally dressed, stiff-looking partner as "management." The two were traveling to Europe and Japan to learn the best practices to bring back to their new car company. In this, they represented members of the Group of 99, the joint GM-UAW team who designed Saturn in the early 1980s. A rapid succession of edits showed them visiting factories, meeting with business executives, and waiting in airports. Once it was established that the pair traveled together a great deal, the setting changed, and they were taking a series of vacation-style snapshots together. They were posed close, donning tourist hats and standing in front of monuments, signaling that they were having fun. The manager now looked relaxed, thus softening his initial cold image, and the viewer was invited to warm up to him and to like him, as his union buddy clearly did. In the last scene, the two opened the door to a hotel room that had only one bed. They looked at eat other uncomfortably as the union narrator made reference to "being in bed with management."

"Being in bed with management" is a biting reproach in the US labor movement that charges that a union is acting in the company's interests against the welfare of its members. Here the phrase was rendered literal by the actual bed and by the prospect that the union guy and the manager might sleep together. But because these two became friends, the reference was dislodged from their adversarial locations in the labor-management hierarchy and situated in the homophobic innuendo. Being in bed with management—a compromise with serious consequence for union members—was cast as an amusing (and homophobic) joke. Commercials like this one were broadcast inside the plant on the company's closed-circuit television station. A company spokesperson explained that they were shown because workers made a good test market for the ads, but the prevalence of Saturn advertising in the factory belied this innocent reason. Workers were also being sold a version of their union and of themselves.

Saturn developed a language and set of symbols to describe its social relationships and to mark itself off from other auto factories. An early print advertisement publicized its reform of the class vocabulary of auto plants. The ad boasted, "The very first thing we did was get rid of labels like 'management.' And 'labor.'" In ad campaigns and at the factory, both labor and management were "team members," and the company was a "family." This terminology was meant to erase the language of class from everyday speech. This effort was vividly manifested in the plant by a large wall mural that depicted UAW workers in union caps on one side and white-collar employees dressed in office attire on the other. The distinct figures both went through a series of changes, and as the evolving forms moved toward the middle of the painting, the two completed their transformations and morphed into each other to become a single figure that was an amalgamation of labor and management.

Labor-management collaboration was meant to redirect workers' identities, evidenced by the many ways they were encouraged to be like managers and to embrace white-collar dispositions, and the work unit was central in this effort. One person in each work unit attended monthly meetings where profit and loss statements were distributed, as were details of work unit expenditures for wages, maintenance, and supplies. This representative then reported back to the group. An African American woman who worked in general assembly explained the purpose of these meetings:

> They are trying to get you to think about ways to save money. They try to get you involved and ask you every year, budget-wise, they ask you to come up with a figure of how much you can save, what you think you will spend. They are using numbers to direct you in certain ways. We brought scrap under control. Overtime, they are constantly squabbling about overtime, probably will continue to do so.

In this way, financial matters and cost-consciousness were made the close concern of the unit, and workers were made into managers' of their own and each other's efforts. The constant pressure to stay within a budget (for parts, labor hours, maintenance) was born by work unit members. Not surprisingly, then, teamwork was often the source of interpersonal conflict and stress, something that workers said affected them during their shifts and when they were off work, as well.

The labor-management pact also meant that workers attended work unit- and plant-wide meetings, hired coworkers, visited suppliers, and, as a requirement for reward payments, completed ninety-two hours of training per year. These obligations regularly took them off the line, and, as several people told me, made them feel as if they were "white collar." To schedule their numerous meetings, trips, and classes, every employee, assembly worker and manager alike, was provided with a Franklin Covey leather-bound planner. This was more than a calendar—it was a system for "self-actualization." In addition to entering appointments, those who used the planner properly spent time each day enumerating their personal goals, and they elaborated their long-term plans and personal mission statements on pages specially designed for those purposes. Workers could learn to use the Franklin system in a class that counted toward their training requirement. While some classes taught technical and job-related skills, many, like this one, were ideological (Yanarella 1996), meant to endorse an ethos and habits that wedded workers' own desires for self-improvement with corporate goals of efficiency and profitability. Scholars of managerial culture would consider these workplace practices and discourses—shaping an enterprise mentality, encouraging identification with management, and promoting "continuous improvement" of the product and the self—to be a project of making of neoliberal subjects who were more self-regulating than were their Fordist enculturated counterparts (see, e.g., Casey 1995; du Gay 1996; Miller and Rose 1995).

Predictably, these efforts were not wholly successful. A Mexican American worker named Jim[10] refused the Franklin planner:

> When I first got here, they were still in the mode of making you look like you were important, giving you the note planners. "This is your leather planner." And they gave everybody one. And I said I don't need one. "Well, you've got to take one." I go, "I don't want it." "Well, you've got to go to meetings, and you've got to take notes. And you're going to have agendas, and you're going to have to be able to organize like a professional." I go, "I'm not a professional. I'm a blue-collar person. I work in a factory."

Jim associated the book with an attempt to make him into "a professional" that contradicted his sense of being "a blue-collar person," an identity he brought with him when he transferred to Spring Hill from Van Nuys, where he was involved in Local 645's struggle to keep that plant open. He preferred 645's militancy to 1853's collaboration. To Jim, the leather planner did not manifest his actual advancement; rather, it was a trivial symbol of individual status that signified the defeat of community control and collective betterment that he had fought for in California.

Many people I talked to joined Jim in resisting efforts to "Saturnize" them, as they put it. Others, however, welcomed the opportunity to reflect upon their life goals and to plot the steps they could take to achieve them, and they felt personally "empowered" by some of the life skills they learned at Saturn. Saturn's workplace symbols, discourse, and practices were attractive to those who wanted to reconsider the purpose of work and to reshape their own subjectivity, desires much in evidence just twenty to thirty years earlier when auto workers protested the monotony of the assembly line and the strict division between mental and manual labor it imposed. Saturn, however, turned those past collective aspirations for working-class *power* into a plan for managing one's self and one's coworkers and for individual feelings of *empowerment*. The implications of this reversal for disorganizing labor were all the more significant since they rested upon a growing rift between Local 1853 and the International union.

A Different Kind of Union

The Vision Team prided itself on the distinctiveness of Saturn's labor-management agreement, and it echoed the brand slogan "A Different Kind of Company" with its own motto, "a different kind of union." In proclaiming this difference, it accumulated a track record of acting out of self-interest rather than solidarity. This fact was on display during a 1992 strike at Lordstown. The Lordstown plant was the only supplier of some Saturn parts, and in short order the Spring Hill plant was unable to build cars. Mike Bennett, then 1853 president, complained to the press that the International should allow those Lordstown workers who made parts for Saturn to cross the picket line and return to work (Parker and Slaughter 1997). In effect, he suggested that rather than expecting 1853 to show common cause with striking workers, as other chapters had done, Lordstown should respect Spring Hill's distinctiveness and support its maverick experiment. Bennett did not support the strike; on the contrary, he insisted that the role of a local union should be to help the company find ways to compete. Bennett's dismissal of solidarity is evident, as is his conviction that 1853 was different from other locals, but it also reflected his staunch position on the proper scale of working-class alliance and struggle.

On this occasion and others, Bennett argued that "if unions have a future . . . it's 'at the local level' where they can help companies 'explore opportunities to compete.'"[11] These comments showed particular insensitivity since the walkout was "widely viewed as a test of GM's toughness" after the corporation announced a plan to shut twenty-one plants and eliminate seventy-four thousand jobs over three years, and since the walkout began on the very day that Van Nuys was finally closed.[12] Bennett's words were therefore a declaration that the Vision Team put the success of Saturn and the achievements of its local—the local "wage bargain," in Williams's (1989) terms—before the interests of fellow autoworkers and before the national strategy of the UAW. This was a stunning expression of the profound limitations of militant particularism.

Because of this record of acting out of self interest, in conjunction with the company's reputation for having nontraditional labor relations, Saturn was often mistaken for a nonunion factory, even by UAW members. Friends and former coworkers back home were sometimes under the impression that those who left for Saturn were no longer union members. A worker from Linden, New Jersey, told me that when he went to visit his old plant, "I brought the union card because people told me Saturn didn't have a union." Another worker was warned off Saturn: "Our local union at Willow Run [Michigan] told us to stay away from Saturn, told it was a union-busting plant, and to stay away from it. That's what our local union told us." While Saturn was always controversial within the International, these developments further eroded UAW support. Uneasiness with Local 1853 was widespread. The head of Central Tennessee's Service and Employees International Union considered that Saturn's local was estranged from the regional labor movement. He thought that Saturn might be "good internally for their people, but not good externally for the rest of us." But, there was strong evidence that Saturn was not "good internally" either. The part Saturn played in the development of a public anti-union discourse, the reframing of class relations and identities, and the intensification of localism, all facilitated the dispossession of US autoworkers, and these conjoined processes, in turn, played out in ways that had important personal and social consequences for workers in Tennessee.

Fragmentation and Insecurity in Tennessee

When I first visited the Spring Hill area in 1996, I saw a housing boom in full swing, in good measure because of the influx of GM autoworkers, but also because the growth of Nashville, thirty-five miles to the north ignited suburban development. Residential neighborhoods were under construction, where tract homes and townhouses were for sale and recently built roads lead to new strip malls. Saturn's massive manufacturing complex was encircled by farmland, creating a buffer zone around the factory that deferred to local concerns that the plant not be ringed with bars, fast-food restaurants, or payday loan operations, precisely the sorts establishments often found outside factory gates. Without a dense municipal center nearby, and with no ready after-work meeting places, workers typically left the plant and drove home in various directions to neighboring towns, suburbs, and cities. Many had thirty- to forty-five-minute commutes, while some drove an hour or more to distant, rural communities. This residential dispersal shaped social life and hindered the emergence of a public, working-class culture.

I interviewed Howie, a white general assembly worker from a New Jersey facility, and his wife, Joanne (who worked for a firm that had a contract with Saturn), at their home and horse farm in a rural area thirty miles southwest of the plant. When I asked how Saturn workers spent their time outside of work, Joanne listed a wide range of a residential patterns and pastimes. "Some live in Nashville. They are into the city thing, it is their hobby, they play racquetball. People in the country have cattle, horses, some sheep or goats. People in the subdivisions, gardening or golf." While this list offered a choice of lifestyles, it did not include shared rituals or common places, nor did it enumerate collective habits of daily life that social historians associate with working-class publics, solidarity, and power.

There were no places where workers regularly gathered, and Howie commented that one of his coworkers sorely felt the lack. "Yes, Ralph lived in a town with a corner bar. Every day after work he went there. He ate there. His wife and kids would meet him there, and they ate there. He was there for two, three hours every day. I don't have anything against it, but he just couldn't adjust." Howie and Joanne were not nostalgic for a working-class culture that took place in bars, a pattern of socializing they associated with excessive drinking and male exclusivity. Until 1991, Spring Hill banned liquor sold by the glass, and, unlike other UAW union halls, Local 1853's did not have a bar, out of respect for the town ordinance and because, as Joanne put it, their union hall was "family oriented" and "more focused on the community." Despite their praise for this kind of social life,

Howie was not active in the union, and he and Joanne did not go to the family- and community-oriented activities that they commended.

I attended 1853's fall festival, an event Howie and Joanne singled out as exemplifying the family-minded union culture, one that "they wouldn't have had in Michigan." The union hall was filled with hand-crafted goods displayed for sale, children's rides and games, food, a dominoes competition, and a booth with health information. When I arrived, a Gospel choir was performing. The singers paused between songs to thank the audience: "We are happy to be here at the Saturn company picnic." Of course, this was not a company picnic but a union event. This inadvertent slip, which no one from the union corrected, revealed a good deal. In towns with histories of unionization and labor struggles, the line between labor and management has cultural and social consequence, both in the workplace and the broader community. This mistake, and equally the fact that the union did not put it right, betrayed a lack of labor consciousness that characterized the area. A comment Joanne made further explained the slip. When I asked her why the union made the changes it did in its social activities, she offered, "It branched off from Saturn philosophy. We are going to do all this community stuff." Here she identified a porous boundary between company and union, one that encouraged forms of socializing that included women and children and did not depend upon alcohol, but also did not foster an independent working-class culture.

For many workers this absence of a public culture along with residential dispersal meant that their social connections in Tennessee were diminished and they lived more isolated lives. One African American man who lived in the Detroit suburbs before transferring to Saturn told me he had closer social connections back home. "At my old plant, when my shift was over, I would go do something, go play ball." In Tennessee, he went directly home. When he had several days off, he left the area altogether: "I try to spend time with my family or get somewhere out of here, Atlanta, Memphis, Birmingham. Just for a couple of days, at least." Others, like John, a white general assembly worker, sought social ties in their subdivisions but not with fellow workers. John and his wife spent free time with their neighbors, who, like them, owned single-family homes in Franklin, an upscale suburb midway between Spring Hill and Nashville. John was not close to his coworkers, even though some of them lived nearby.

An African American worker named Bill lived with his wife and children in a modest subdivision nearly an hour northeast of the plant. His long commute meant that he spent little time in Spring Hill. He transferred to Saturn, in part, because he liked the idea of moving to Tennessee; he imagined a slower-paced life for his family and a reversal of the migration that took his parents from the rural South to Michigan after World War II (see Stack 1996). He also wanted to get away from the dense social networks of Saginaw, where he grew up and where his father was also a GM worker. Everyone in Saginaw knew him, and while his family had a good reputation, he and his wife wanted to "start fresh" and gain some "freedom." Bill's choice of residence in Tennessee reflected his desire to start anew, but it also was shaped by race. Spring Hill had a small black population, which was largely impoverished, and there was a dearth of black leadership. For this reason, African American workers were not inclined to stay close to the plant. I heard stories of the racism experienced by some who came to the area when Saturn first opened. They had been stopped by the police for speeding or other infractions in a pattern of enforcement they recognized as racially biased. More commonly, the lack of black institutions or a substantial black middle class sent them to look elsewhere for a place to live. But despite their move away from the plant, they did not select common destinations; they, too, spread out, choosing suburbs closer to Nashville or cities or towns with larger African American populations.

Bill's and his family's social life did not involve his coworkers nor did it include union activities. They were Jehovah's Witnesses and spent a lot of time in the Kingdom Hall near their home. Bill thought that many workers (white, black, and Latino) who had not been church-going back home went to church in Tennessee. In some measure, this was because they had moved to the Bible belt, where churches were important community institutions. It was also a reflection of the fact that since worked-based identities and friendships were less central than they had previously been, other social bonds became more salient. Saturn workers remade their lives in myriad, individual ways, dispersed over a wide area and varied social landscape. This may have permitted many to realize individual dreams—owning a farm, getting a fresh start, buying a nice home—but it did not make for ready conditions for the creation of a common social life or a working-class public.

The spatial fragmentation and individual patterns that characterized their social lives were partly predicated upon the different circumstances under which workers transferred to Saturn. The men and women who moved to Tennessee came from many different US cities, and they arrived in distinct waves. Those hired early came mostly from plants that were still operating. They chose Spring Hill because they were persuaded by the Saturn experiment and saw a better future for themselves, or because they saw signs of insecurity at their plant and decided to get out before an impending layoff. Those who came later did so after long layoffs and after the International pressured Saturn to preferentially hire out-of-work GM employees. For many, this was not their first transfer, but the latest of three or four. These workers called themselves "GM gypsies," since they were so often on the move. The US auto industry is perpetually sensitive to market downturns, and autoworkers have always been vulnerable to layoff, but since the 1980s, the pace, duration, and impact of layoffs have greatly intensified. As a result, workers expended considerable individual effort to strategize their transfers, searching for plants that would provide more years of steady work, and trying to clock the thirty years of employment that would qualify them for full GM retirement benefits.

These differences in workers' motivations for coming to Saturn were exacerbated by geography and housing prices. Some left strong real estate markets and were able to sell their homes for a lot of money. Those from Flint or Detroit sold homes for little, since prices there were severely depressed by factory shutdowns and urban decay, and houses remained abandoned as unemployed workers fled in search of work.[13] Hard times followed these people to Tennessee. One woman recalled the difficult circumstances that those from Michigan faced when they first arrived: "They didn't have a whole lot. One guy lost his job in Michigan. He slept in his station wagon when he came here. He did not get a motel or apartment or have a trailer. He slept in his car. People were desperate. That group who came down was hard off. They had nothing." Residential dispersal was partially a reflection of what people could afford and the degree of enthusiasm and amount of energy for building a new life that they could muster.

When workers first moved to Tennessee, many came without their families, preferring to make the initial transition by themselves. Some were anxious that the job would not last and that the transfer would only be followed by another; others wanted to get settled before their families joined them; others had children with only one or two years left until high school graduation, and the family stayed to avoid disrupting their educations; some were divorced, and when they moved they left their children with the custodial parent. These choices meant long drives on days off to visit spouses and children, and it put a strain on marriages that some were unable to survive. Even families who remained together after the months or years of separation felt the time had taken a toll on them.

Rotating shifts caused further strain. Saturn had a unique work schedule, another point of difference from the national UAW. Each crew (three in all) worked four ten-hour days and then had two days off. Days off did not necessarily fall on weekends, as the plant operated on Saturdays (but not Sundays). (Neither the ten-hour shift nor the Saturday earned overtime, as they would have under the national contract, since workers still had a forty-hour schedule. This was another way that Saturn achieved flexibility and cost-savings that other union locals would not concede.) Following the two-day break, there was a shift change, and those who had been on days worked nights. After four days on nights, the crew got five days off. Workers often used this stretch to work overtime, and in this way, they boosted their pay considerably, but it also meant that they spent a lot of time at work. Others preferred to use the five days to visit family and friends back home, and this meant that they forewent local relationships in favor of distant ones.

Shifts were hard on families and marriages. A general assembly worker told me that he and his wife went on different crews so that they could care for their kids, albeit separately. Their twenty-year marriage could not withstand the strain; his wife met someone else on her new crew, and they were divorcing. Andy, a representative from the International, was vehement in his condemnation of rotating shifts:

> [They] very insidiously isolated people from the larger social fabric. The family comes in and the boy wants to play in little league, Boy Scouts, but the father can't do any of those things with him. Same for what the girl wants to do. Parents can't belong to a bowling league together. Can't belong to any type of social thing together. There were 8 x 11 placards on people's refrigerators. All 365 days of year blocked out in color-coded blocks for the crews. The rotation for each spouse is different. They are not even off together.

Predictably, there was a high divorce rate in the plant. Workers thought there were many reasons for this: the shifts; the stress of moving a family or of leaving them behind; the fact that spouses (wives and husbands alike) had trouble finding employment in the area and might be unhappy; long hours in the plant and the intense work culture left people susceptible to feeling distant from their spouses and to having affairs. Workers spoke about divorce so often and considered its causes so carefully that I fully understood that marital difficulty loomed large in their assessment of the emotional and social toll of working at Saturn.

Prosperity and Insecurity

In return for their social isolation and the strain on the marriages and family relations, Saturn workers earned good money. Assembly workers earned a base rate that was approximately $4,000 below other GM workers; this reflected the portion of their pay "at risk." When the plant achieved production, training, and quality targets, they recuperated that shortfall and more. "Reward" bonuses reached $10,000, making workers total earnings almost $50,000. As many supplemented this with considerable overtime, it was not uncommon for them to earn $60,000 a year. Skilled trades workers earned even more. This prosperity differentiated them from local working people, as Saturn workers were notably better off than others in the Spring Hill area.

Since laid-off GM workers had priority for Saturn jobs, local residents were for the most part unable to secure employment in the plant. Therefore, the arrival of Saturn did little to increase local wages. When Spring Hill was selected for the plant, politicians and economic development experts assured residents that they would have the opportunity for high-wage employment at the many parts suppliers that would undoubtedly relocate to the area, yet those businesses never came. The demand at Saturn was not enough to pull them to Spring Hill, and they saw the unionized factory and kept away. This employment pattern meant that there were effectively two labor markets in the area, one of highly paid GM transplants, the other of low-paid local residents. A 1994 survey of area manufacturers showed that Saturn had not affected their wage rates because they drew from a different labor pool. Saturn created geographically contiguous but distinct working-class communities in the area, just as it created divisions within the UAW.

For local working people, Saturn did not mean jobs or affluence, but a higher cost of living, as rents, property taxes, and utilities all went up. Farmers faced higher property taxes and were pushed into neighboring counties where prices were lower (Gilbert 1994). Locals believed "people that work at Saturn think they are all that, all rich," as one longtime resident maintained, and they frequently spoke of "Saturn people" and their "Saturn kids," as those who had big houses, swimming pools, and boats and who played golf. Reportedly, the area's swimming pool and recreational vehicle dealerships were, for a time, the most successful in the country.

For many, this prosperity was predicated upon mortgages, car and boat loans, and credit card debt that was manageable only with reward pay and overtime. This caused competition among workers for overtime and led to jealousy and ill will. One Mexican-American worker from Van Nuys told me that there was,

> A lot of jealousy. And it breeds hate here, a lot of jealousy. How can Mary buy a new car, a new van? How can . . . ? They resent people that live up here in Williamson County [a wealthy county]. There's a lot of that. A lot of who has the bigger house. Fighting over the overtime, in debt. We've got one guy that he'll work every day. He'll go anywhere in the plant and beg, borrow, and steal overtime.

On a visit I made to interview Greg, this affluence and its "others"—low-paid local workers, unemployed autoworkers in other cities, coworkers begging overtime—was plain. Greg, a white worker in his late forties, transferred to Saturn in 1988. He was divorced, and his daughter stayed in Missouri, with his ex-wife. He bought a small tract home in Spring Hill, where he lived alone, and that he decorated nicely with new furniture, carpeting, and window treatments. As a skilled tradesman, he was making over $70,000 with reward pay and extra shifts. He had a new GM truck and a Saturn in his two-car garage, and he showed me pictures of his recently purchased bass boat that was docked in the lake where he went fishing with his girlfriend. Greg's girlfriend grew up in the area and was not a Saturn transplant. Greg told me that she thought he was "rich." He laughed nervously when he said this. He seemed proud that she saw him this way, but he also seemed anxious. His lifestyle depended upon paychecks padded with overtime and reward, and both had recently been cut as a result of a decline in the small-car market and poor sales at Saturn. This loss of income dealt a blow to household budgets. According to Greg, some workers were already filing for bankruptcy, and he was concerned that he too would fall behind in his truck and boat payments and that harder times were to come.

Even as they led comfortable lives, Saturn workers were insecure. Flint, Michigan lost thirty thousand jobs from 1978 to 1992; GM downsized in Linden, New Jersey, and shut plants in Southgate, Fremont, and Van Nuys, California (Dandeneau 1996: xxi; Mann

1987: 68; Milkman 1997). Saturn workers came from these places and others like them; they lived through layoffs, saw their home cities decline, and moved from plant to plant to get thirty years in GM. Workers had seen that those plants were "disposable," and they had devoted considerable energy to reading the cycles of production to predict the future. One woman transferred to Tennessee when she suspected that her plant might be in jeopardy: "GM made it almost seem like [we] were a disposable plant. They kept bringing in product, and eliminating product, and bringing in new product, and that worried me." A middle-aged white worker from upstate New York was ever vigilant, constantly looking over his shoulder for the warning signs of dispossession.

> People had come up to our plant in '90, recruiting people to come down to Saturn. I went to listen. I was interested. At that time, my plant was doing good. We were working overtime, but I started seeing things change at our plant. I noticed the way management was acting. The biggest thing was we purchased new machinery that was four to five years old. Management locked out ten machines. We were told, "Don't take parts off those machines." In my mind they put "sold" signs on those machines. I would take out the Saturn application and fill it out a bit at a time, take it out from time to time when things looked bad, but then they would look better again, and I would put it away.

This man considered himself fortunate; the relative health of this plant and his careful assessment of its future shielded him from layoff. Others were not so lucky. "Most of the people here moved three, four times. I am one of the lucky ones. I hadn't moved before," he reflected. That individual workers were left to make these estimations and negotiate these situations on their own suggests an infinite fractioning of the workforce, whereby each person strategized his or her own next best move.

Andy from the International vividly described the fear that drove this process and brought workers to Spring Hill. "Saturn, 'The 100 Year Car Company,' was stimulus enough for them and their families to uproot and go to Spring Hill for the promise of 'no layoffs.' Keep in mind, in those times the word 'layoff' was extremely traumatic, if not life threatening, for the workers in GM." Saturn workers were ever aware of insecurity. They had recently left economically devastated places; they depended on overtime and reward pay, two unsure sources of income, to cover their bills; and they lived in an area with a divided labor market, with a low-wage bottom tier. Life in

Tennessee thus bore the imprint of the long dispossession that began in the 1980s with whipsawing and concessions and continued with GM's "regime shopping" (Collins 2003: 12) for a setting far from the sites of labor militancy. This dispossession was written into Saturn's work rules and into the ways the labor-management accord weakened the national agreement; it was felt in the stresses on family life and the lack of working-class rituals and places in Tennessee; and it was manifest in the constant dread that layoff or plant closure was imminent.

Small-car sales slumped nationally in the late 1990s, and with no guarantee of a new product, workers feared that Saturn was not the hundred-year-company they had been assured it would be. Saturn's labor accord provided job security for 80 percent of the workforce, except in case of an "unforeseen or catastrophic event" or "severe economic conditions," and workers now worried over precisely how this language would be interpreted (Slaughter 1998). Amidst growing insecurity, shop-floor activists began to challenge Saturn's supposed difference. They organized to reform Local 1853 and to shift the geography of class identity, alliance, and power.

Activism and Expanding the Scale of Struggle

Saturn began car production in 1990, and sales were strong by the middle of the decade. After good years in 1995 and 1996—when reward payments reached $10,000—sales fell 10 percent in 1997, and reward pay plummeted to $2,000; Saturn workers then earned less than their counterparts in GM. Sales fell another 20 percent by March 1998, and by the end of that year, Saturn had lost $25 million and rewards remained low.[14] The plant was seriously under its five-hundred-thousand-unit capacity, as annual sales of Saturn's single subcompact model, which was by then eight years old and widely considered stale, never reached more than 278,000. These disappointing numbers were all the more distressing given GM's plans to centralize its global production by standardizing sourcing and adopting a common manufacturing platform. These moves would make GM plants worldwide more interchangeable, and they would diminish Saturn's autonomy. Meanwhile, the International pressured GM to give Spring Hill's much-needed and long-awaited new product, a midsize sedan, to Wilmington, Delaware. This boded ill for Spring Hill. It signaled the UAW's ever-dwindling support for Saturn's labor model and GM's similarly waning commitment to the experiment. Though the Wilmington plant remained under the national agreement, it offered concessions on the team concept and employee involvement to win the bid, evincing Saturn's continuing impact on whipsawing. This was the first Saturn model to be produced outside of Spring Hill. Workers there had seen the brand as theirs, and they felt worried and betrayed.

In this atmosphere of mounting insecurity and fear, a small group of dissident Local 1853 members calling themselves Concerned Brothers and Sisters met in the winter of 1998 to discuss their dissatisfaction with the Saturn labor agreement, the corporation, and their union officers. Bruce, a middle-aged white worker from Michigan who was a leader of the group, explained their plan:

> If the workers can look into the future and see the door, the thirty-year door when they can get out and retire, they're okay. But when they start to get insecure, that's when you organize. You organize when your enemy is the weakest. Our enemy was the Vision Team, the partnership . . .
>
> And the role of a union activist is to throw matches . . . We created the kindling by educating the workers what they were being cheated out of, how they were being taken advantage of, what was wrong with this agreement, and there was a solution: it's the national agreement. And, then, once we got the fire going, we fanned the fire.

The campaign was directed at recouping the layoff protections and supplemental pay, seniority and transfer rights, and hourly wages provided in the national contract but that the Saturn accord had given up. Notably, dissidents made the union Vision Team, not management, their target. Some of the leaders of Concerned Brothers and Sisters were affiliated with the national New Directions Caucus, and they had developed a trenchant critique of labor-management cooperation and of Local 1853's leadership. The Vision Team held union office since the plant opened, and many officers had been involved even earlier as members of the original Group of 99. They were seen as forming a clique, being too close to management, and wielding too much power over fellow workers on the shop floor. Dissatisfaction with the union leadership had led to unsuccessful challenges by rival caucuses in the past.

Over the next weeks, Concerned Brothers and Sisters gained support, and they organized a meeting of several hundred workers in the Spring Hill High School gym, which they rented after union officers refused them use of the union hall. At the meeting, they determined that

Local 1853 should hold a referendum on returning to the national contract to regain the protections they had given up. A move to amend the Saturn agreement and bring Spring Hill closer to the national pattern had been put forward once before in 1993, but it was handily rejected. This time the proposal was ratified by a vote of 87 percent.

Concerned Brothers and Sisters enlisted workers to send letters and e-mails to the International, detailing their criticisms of the Saturn agreement and of Local 1853. They asked the International for support: "Please, brothers and sisters of the International," one worker pled, "Don't forget us down in 1853 for our local leadership has lost the way" (Dalton n.d.). The International helped orchestrate the effort from its offices in Michigan. The campaign centered on layoff protections, pay, and GM transfer rights, but it also expressed the conviction that to return to the national contract was an act of solidarity with the rest of the UAW, one that would begin to undo Local 1853's years of difference. In a letter to the International, one activist suggested that he and his coworkers were cognizant of the damage Saturn and their local had done to the union, "This membership is tired of being the *Experiment that is Tearing down the Foundation Our Great Union was Built Upon*" (Benavides, February 6, 1998, emphasis in original). Concerned Brothers and Sisters also was able to garner considerable press attention and put public spotlight on the conflict. The referendum to adopt the national contract was defeated by a vote of 2:1. Despite this loss, organizers were emboldened by their stronger ties to the International and by their success in orchestrating dissent. For its part, The Vision Team interpreted the vote as a mandate for its partnership-style unionism.

Concerned Brothers and Sisters rallied again in July 1998, during a seven-week strike that began at GM's Flint Metal Center parts plant over the outsourcing of work to nonunion plants. There was general concern that GM intended to spin off the Delphi parts division and leave some fifty-three thousand workers outside of the GM system (a fear that was realized later that summer). A second Flint parts facility struck in short order, and the labor action spread quickly throughout GM. Some plants walked out over local issues, others closed for lack of parts, and their combined action had the distinct appearance of a solidarity strike in support of Delphi workers. Twenty-seven of twenty-nine North American assembly plants and scores of parts facilities shut down and 186,000 workers were out in the biggest work stoppage at GM since the 1970s. It was an exciting time when the constraints of localism were briefly overcome and the

UAW demonstrated international, coordinated resistance (see Collins 1999). Saturn workers, however, remained on the job.

This situation was a disturbing reminder of Local 1853's response to the 1992 Lordstown strike, when Mike Bennett publically insisted that Saturn's success was so important that workers should cross the picket line to ensure its supply of parts. It looked as if 1853 would once again eschew solidarity and demonstrate its difference. Indeed, Vision Team officers actively sought alternative sources for the Delphi parts in order to keep Saturn operating. "In the name of preserving the nation's best-known experiment in cooperation between labor and management," reported *The New York Times*, "they have set aside union solidarity by assembling cars using parts from Japan and at least one nonunion American company, instead of parts from Flint" (July 22, 1998, A1, D2). One white worker from Michigan described how distressing this was for men and women who came from auto families and communities in which such acts of UAW solidarity were fundamental to a collective sense of right and wrong and were a matter of habit and convention. The betrayal of that ethos suggested that there was something terribly wrong with their local union, and it threatened their closest social ties:

> [During] the strike, a lot of the people went on their five [days off] up to Michigan. And they had relatives, and they were being harassed. A lot of them told me, "I have a brother-in-law just gave me a hard time. I couldn't even drink a beer with him because he says, 'How can you justify my being on strike and you guys are out there working, it's not right. What kind of a union are you guys?' And a lot of them, . . . when they went home . . . their dads, brother-in-laws, asking them, 'What kind of a union do you guys belong to?'

Saturn workers were deeply troubled that they were still working and that their union leaders helped the company source nonunion and non-US suppliers. Concerned Brothers and Sisters began to organize. Bruce recounted,

> We were the only GM facility working. Bowling Green was still working, but for the only reason that they had parts, and they were at a slower production than most. So we were still working with the local union, with management to outsource the parts. And we were getting parts from Nip and Denso and Japanese suppliers for the spark plug, and we were also getting parts from "Red China," to keep the Saturn lines going . . .
>   So it made the workers just feel like shit. Here we were building cars with convicts' and child labor. And that really made the people think, even the pro-partnership people. That really made them think, what in the hell is going on with our union that they would agree to this with management. And that really opened a lot of the eyes. So we called ourselves "scabs." That's what we were.

The outsourcing of parts gave the lie to Saturn's brand image of the revival of American industry and a better deal for US workers. It also exposed the extreme particularism of 1853 leaders, who worked with managers to find non-US and nonunion suppliers to protect *their* local and *their* plant, the very strategy Mike Bennett had publicly endorsed during the Lordstown strike. Bruce's telling suggests that the shop floor response to this realization was complicated, and that workers rehearsed the anti-Japanese, now anti-Chinese, framing of labor politics that the UAW encouraged in the 1980s when it squandered the opportunity to develop an international strategy and instead pursued a doomed politics of jingoism. Although their analysis did not encompass an international perspective on their class interests and alliances, they nonetheless saw that their localism had gone too far.

In uttering "scab," dissidents used a powerful term of class betrayal. It was a word taken from the language of the US labor movement that drew fixed lines of class identity and solidarity quite distinct from Saturn's class-erasing vocabulary of "cooperation," "partnership," and "family." "Scab" was meant to shame Local 1853 members and push them toward solidarity and a broader geography of struggle and alliance. Concerned Brothers and Sisters set out to force 1853's leadership to support the strike. "We started a write-a-letter campaign," Bruce continued, " . . . the UAW, Solidarity House, AFL/CIO, the UAW Website. And we encouraged the workers to write letters in opposition to what was going on in Saturn, the outsourcing of the parts." Organizers urged workers to communicate and seek alliances beyond their plant, and in this way, they began to challenge the extreme localism that characterized 1853. This shop-floor militancy, combined with pressure from the International, compelled Spring Hill to hold a strike authorization vote.

It was the first time Saturn workers took such a vote, and it was an exciting time. John, the assembly worker who was not close to his coworkers and who preferred to socialize with neighbors in his subdivision, recalled with great enthusiasm and emotion how the vote brought workers together:

> That was the greatest thing that ever happened to this place. There were tears in my eyes. I mean the roads were jammed. People coming on a Sunday, an off day, to vote. I couldn't believe that people came together. It was really amazing. I've never seen anything like that. I wish you had interviewed me when it happened, I was jumping I was so excited.
>
> The successful strike vote got the International behind us again. I think that it showed the International that we were union and that we would help the International. I think it helped our relationship with the International.

John's assertion that the vote "showed the International we were union," points to the issues of class identity and alliance that were at stake. Saturn workers knew that others wondered whether or not they were truly union, and the vote affirmed their class commitments and brought them closer to the rest of the UAW.

The strikes were a month and half old when the vote was taken, nevertheless, 1853's decision to join was momentous. Dozens of national and international newspapers covered the story, featuring headlines such as one carried by Britain's *The Independent*: "Elite car workers ready to strike" (July 21, 1998, 13). Saturn's union leadership agreed to talk to management for thirty days before they staged a walk out, and the Vision Team used the threat of a job action to get Spring Hill the promise of a sorely needed new product, a Sports Utility Vehicle (SUV). The strikes were settled before Saturn ever walked out, but the vote strengthened solidarity with the UAW, unleashed workers' dissatisfaction with the Saturn difference, and won them a pledge from GM for investment in a new model.

Feeling confident after getting a pledge for the SUV, the Vision Team called union elections early, for February 1999. Concerned Brothers and Sisters organized again, this time to support candidates from the opposition Members for a Democratic Union (MDU) Caucus, who ran on a platform of reform and of bringing Spring Hill closer to the national contract. Fliers, newsletters, and palm cards flooded the shop floor, and representatives from rival caucuses crowded factory doors, handing out campaign literature to workers who came in and out for their shifts. On a visit I made to the plant just before the election, I passed a team center where a handmade sign put all on notice: "This is a Vision free team center." Posted on another team center was a sign displaying a crossed-out bed labeled "management's bed." As when activists spoke the word "scab," this sign used the combative language and symbols of the US labor movement, an expression of working-class identity and protest that had been rare in the plant. The sign harkened also to the television ad in which the manager and union guy became so friendly that they almost shared a hotel room bed, but in this rendition, the two would not be so cozy.

The Vision Team fought back with a palm card that featured a red SUV and the slogan, "The Vision Team is Leading the Way to 500K." On the front grille of the vehicle were the words "Vision Team." The back of the card listed the Vision candidates running for office. The card proclaimed that under Vision Team leadership, Spring Hill would finally get a new product and finally bring production to the five-hundred-thousand-unit capacity.

Someone close to MDU learned that the red SUV was not a picture of a future Saturn (as many had assumed) but a photo of a Hyundai downloaded from the internet. This discovery ignited the plant in controversy and fueled leaflets, e-mails, and team-center debates. Despite the fact that the Vision Team did not intend to suggest that the red SUV was the new Saturn model—it meant only to provide a generic image of a similar vehicle—workers felt deceived. When the membership learned that the photo was actually a Hyundai, it spoke to the inability of the Vision Team to guarantee the new model and secure their jobs, and it suggested that their isolation from the UAW, which had been so painfully and publicly displayed during the Flint strike, had won them little. The palm card helped turn the election. In an overwhelming defeat, all thirteen Vision Team officers, including Mike Bennett and others who had been in power since the plant opened, were unseated.

Some months later, the new MDU officers negotiated to bring the Saturn risk and reward formula closer to GM wages. In the next years, there was continued discussion of returning to the national contract, and in 2004, Local 1853 members voted by more than 3:1 to scrap their labor agreement. This momentous decision marked Spring Hill workers' unity with the International and suggested an expanded scale of identity and struggle. However, it did little to forestall their insecurity. Saturn workers got the SUV after they agreed to a speed-up, only to find that their jobs were permanently under threat. GM continued to give new Saturn models to other plants in the United States and Mexico, and while Spring Hill won bids for some products, its workforce steadily dwindled. Although the seniority, transfer, recall rights, and layoff benefits guaranteed by the national contract proved crucial for individual workers who were trying to secure their livelihoods and retirement, the UAW could not keep jobs in Spring Hill or anywhere else.

Conclusion: The Long Dispossession of US Autoworkers

GM announced a massive corporate restructuring in 2005: It would shut twelve plants and layoff thirty-five thousand North American workers over three years. GM did not identify the factories it would close, rather it instigated another round of whipsawing to determine which plants would be spared. Spring Hill lost one production line, and downsized workers transferred, retired, and took buyouts. In 2007, Spring Hill manufactured the last of its Saturn subcompacts and the last of its much-fought-for SUVs. Of the forty-seven hundred workers employed at the time, twenty-four hundred went on layoff while the plant was retooled to build a Chevrolet model.[15] To stay afloat, workers relied on layoff protections and transfer rights, regained when they returned to the national contract. Fewer than three thousand were on the job in 2009, when GM declared bankruptcy and idled the facility. There was an 18 percent unemployment rate in the area when GM announced two years later that it would reopen Spring Hill with an "innovative staffing and operating agreement" and eighteen hundred employees, many of whom would earn entry-level wages.

The press carried numerous stories of Saturn's tragic failure to be enduring model for new labor relations or a hundred-year-company. However, another postmortem is in order. This chapter has chronicled Saturn's role in the more than three-decades-long project of capital and the state to unmake a powerful sector of the US working class. This process of geographic displacement, disorganization, and individualization began before the development of Saturn, when GM fled to the US South in the 1970s in a spatial assault on organized labor in Detroit, Lordstown, and the other places where there was growing worker militancy. It continued after Chrysler's bailout by the US government, when GM also sought to cheapen labor and so turned local unions into competitors for investment and jobs. In the first instance, Saturn was heir to these losses, as it was to the UAW's inability or unwillingness to mount a hard-hitting and internationalist response to whipsawing and capital flight. In the second instance, Saturn facilitated this disorganization and defeat.

Saturn advanced this long dispossession by extending and deepening the localism that historically afflicted the US labor movement. Competition locals, like competition states, marketed themselves to mobile capital by offering givebacks and concessions that eroded union power and the social wage, and whipsawing turned an international union that had won pattern bargaining into a "federation of locals," feverishly bidding against each other for their own futures. Local 1853's leaders believed in this extreme localism, in securing privilege for their own members at the expense of others, and in cooperating with management to do so. They rehearsed this ideology and politics before their members and the press, and they practiced it when they refused solidarity with other plants, even during critical strikes when UAW strategy called for a united stance. Local 1853's effort to win job security and better working conditions in Spring Hill, while at the same time straining alliances within the larger labor movement, was doomed to fail against GM's global plans. Narrowing their demands in this way did not win Saturn workers privilege, but it guaranteed their insecurity.

The case of Saturn thus shows how destructive militant particularism can be when disconnected from more universalist sentiments and struggles to create solidarity. From the onset, Saturn contributed to the very precariousness Local 1853 imagined it would overcome. Marxist geographers have pointed out that unevenness, as much as homogeneity, is the lifeblood of accumulation, and that as capitalism creates uniformity, it also makes and exploits difference across space and laboring populations (e.g., Harvey 2001b; Smith 1984). But workers and their unions make difference in ways that capital alone cannot. Local 1853 collaborated with GM to draw a line between Saturn workers and the rest of the UAW, and it used the promise of difference and superiority in the service of this division. As GM set out to create a "Different Kind of Company," 1853 energized and animated this divide by attempting "a different kind of union" with a singular labor accord, a commitment to labor-management cooperation, and a localist ideology and politics.

When Spring Hill reopens and offers entry-level wages to its newly hired workers, these men and women will not be rich by local standards, as the veteran workers were seen to be, and the dual labor market in the area will flatten. This one form of unevenness will be ameliorated not by lifting all boats, as the economic planners predicted when GM selected Tennessee, but by lowering them. June Nash reminds us that job loss and disempowerment in one locale is not matched by advances elsewhere, but "capital gains at the expense of labor loss is ultimately a zero sum game with no winners and all losers" (2012: 29) The ethnography of the long dispossession of US autoworkers presented in this chapter offers a close view of the ways in which social wage was determinedly undermined, labor was disorganized and defeated, and working people were impoverished in the United States and elsewhere over the last decades. To be sure capitalists secured a greater portion of the social product for themselves and created generalized precariousness through present-day versions of "conquest, enslavement, robbery [and] murder" (Marx 1977: 874), as some chapters in this volume vividly show. But capitalists also achieved these ends by offering privilege (always temporary) for particular segments of working classes. Different working-class fractions, divided and divided again in innumerable ways, lived through specific histories of advances and losses over long periods of time.

The dismantling of privilege of US autoworkers was a protracted and uneven process. This understanding has important implications for a global anthropology of labor, for it suggests the bifurcation of politics that Harvey (2003) uses to map the globe does not adequately capture the experiences of working people. We recall that for Harvey, accumulation by dispossession in the global South spurs progressive actions and movements, while conservative politics characterizes workers' and their unions in the North, as they attempt to prolong their relative advantage within the regime of expanded reproduction. It is not that this latter doomed effort is not apparent in the history of Spring Hill, but too fast a demarcation misses important complexities in the lived experiences and political responses of workers (see Collins 2012). Harvey's categorization leads us to imagine that dispossession is a relatively bounded process or the outcome of a given event, but there was no single point when Spring Hill workers were first or finally dispossessed, rather there were many such moments over decades, and resistance, limited as it was, came after the long accrual of insult and also of defeat. The case of Saturn suggests that dispossession is often a slow, deliberate project of capital, aided at critical junctures by the state, with all of the complications for resistance that this set of political facts necessarily implies.

The easy mapping of global labor does not adequately capture the mutability of class and social relations. Even as Saturn supposedly reinstated a "labor elite," this moment of expanded reproduction was riddled with dispossession. Workers came to Tennessee from devastated, disposed-of places, from which capital had fled; the UAW had already been weakened by whipsawing and localism by the time Saturn opened. The making of widespread insecurity counted on *both* expanded reproduction and dispossession. These two moments of capital accumulation do not correspond to disparate epochs, places, or peoples, thereby giving rise to distinct politics of struggle or categories of labor. In the lives of workers and working-class communities, they are closely intertwined. It is important to keep this in mind as we chart an anthropology of labor that takes into account the overlapping histories and geographies and seeks to understand the connections between the many, diverse laborers in different parts of the world.

Acknowledgments

My research was funded by the Robert Penn Warren Center for the Humanities at Vanderbilt University, the National Endowment for the Humanities, Knox College, and Hofstra University. At the Robert Penn Warren Center, I was fortunate for the support, assistance, and intellectual companionship of Mona Frederick, Sherry Willis, and my wonderful colleagues in the Center's "Meanings of Work" seminar. Ananth Aiyer, Jennifer Alvey, Lawrence Bretiborde, Jane Collins, Kirk Dombrowski, Benjamin Dulchin, Paul Durrenberger, Lesley Gill, Elena Glasberg, Karen Judd, Don Kalb, Christopher Matthews, June Nash, Joy Nolan, Sabina Sawhney, Gerald Sider, Gavin Smith, Judy Whitehead, and Ara Wilson all contributed to development of this chapter. I owe a great debt to August Carbonella, who has been an indispensable intellectual colleague for many years. My most sincere thanks to the many people in Spring Hill who very generously spent time with me and shared their experiences and insights.

Notes

1. *The Tennessean*, December 29, 2011; http://www.tennessean.com/article/20111229/BUSINESS03/312290032. Accessed January 3, 2012.
2. There were earlier instances of two- and even three-tier concessions in individual plants, and the 2003 and 2007 national contracts contained some concessions along these lines. However, the post-bailout agreement more firmly entrenched this practice and facilitated the wider use of entry-level wages throughout the industry, such that experts predict that a bifurcated workforce will become commonplace.
3. Colias, Mike. 2011. "Despite UAW Vows, GM Labor 'Innovations' Spread to Former Saturn Plant." *Automotive News on the Go.*" September 30. http://www.autonews.com/article/20110930/BLOG06/110939989/-1/mobile04&template=art4. Accessed January 26, 2012.
4. *The New York Times*. July 12, 2011. http://www.nytimes.com/2011/07/13/business/with-chevrolet-sonic-gm-and-uaw-reinvent-automaking.html. Accessed February 1, 2012.
5. See also *Akron Beacon Journal*. 1996. "Lordstown, Ohio, Has History of Wildcat Strikes." April 8. http://archives.econ.utah.edu/archives/aut-op-sy/1996-04-20.015/msg00060.html. Accessed February 12, 2014.
6. This recalled GM founder Billy Durant's first such power play in 1891, when he threatened Flint officials that he would relocate to Saginaw if the city was not forthcoming with capital (Mann 1987: 18–19).
7. The Reagan administration jump-started the competition state in auto some years earlier, when it pressured Japan to limit imports and to locate assembly plants within the United States. For their part, states sought to attract these transplants with public monies and commitments, therein setting the stage for the intermunicipal and interstate rivalry that characterized the Saturn spectacle. While the Canadian government similarly limited imports and encouraged competition for the new plants, its federal government controlled the process, and only Ontario and Quebec were major competitors. Their rivalry was heightened by ethnic and linguistic divides (Green and Yanarella 1996: 6).
8. *Columbia Daily Herald*. July 12, 1985, 7; July 28, 1985, 1, 2; July 29, 1985, 1.
9. The Taft-Hartley Act enabled states to enact right-to-work laws that allowed open shops, in which workers who are represented by a union and work under a union-negotiated contract can choose *not* to be union members or pay an agency fee in lieu of

union dues. Nearly all Southern states, and increasingly some Northern states, have passed right-to-work legislation.
10. Except in cases where the person is a public figure, I have changed the names of my informants to protect their anonymity.
11. Bennett quoted in *The Wall Street Journal* September 4, 1992, A8.
12. *Los Angeles Times.* August 28, 1992. http://articles.latimes.com/1992-08-28/news/mn-6025_1_uaw-strike. Accessed February 12, 2014.
13. Filmmaker Michael Moore's *Roger and Me* documents the devastation of auto cities that followed in the wake of this unmaking, and Detroit's declaration of bankruptcy in 2013 serves to underscore its long-term impact.
14. *Newsday*, August 23, 1998, F08; see also Rubinstein and Kochan 2001: 42.
15. *Detroit Free Press.* December 12, 2006, March 30, 2007. http://www.freep.com/article/20070330/BUSINESS/01/703300301/1014. *The Tennessean.* December 31, 2008. http://www.tennessean.com/article/20080131/BUSINESS/8013103.

References

Primary Sources

Newspapers

Akron Beacon Journal
Automotive News on the Go
Columbia Daily Herald
Detroit Free Press
Newsday
The Independent
The New York Times
The Wall Street Journal

Letters and Leaflets

Benavides, Richard. February 6, 1998. Letter to Richard Shoemaker. UAW. V.P.-GM Dept., xerox.
Dalton, Kevin. n.d. "Get a Real Job Roland." Flier.

Corporation, Union and Government Documents

Memorandum of Agreement. 2000. Saturn and the U.A.W.
Commission on the Future of Worker-Management Relations. 1994. "Fact Finding Report." US Department of Labor, US Department of Commerce, May.
The Tennessee Advisory Commission on Intergovernmental Relations. 1992. "Growth and Change in Maury County."

Secondary Sources

Aaker, David. 1994. "Building a Brand: The Saturn Story." *California Management Review* 36, no. 2: 114–133.

Borden, Anthony. 1986. "GM Comes to Spring Hill." *The Nation* June 21: 852–854.
Casey, Katherine. 1995. *Work, Self, and Society After Industrialism*. London: Routledge.
Collins, Jane. 1999. "Industrial Innovation and Control of the Working Day: The 1998 General Motors Strike." *Social Politics* 6, no. 1: 76–84.
———. 2003. *Threads. Gender, Labor and Power in the Global Apparel Industry*. Chicago: The University of Chicago Press.
———. 2012. "Theorizing Wisconsin's 2011 Protests: Community-Based Unionism Confronts Accumulation by Dispossession." *American Ethnologist* 39, no. 1: 6–20.
Dandaneau, Steven P. 1996. *A Town Abandoned: Flint, Michigan Confronts Deindustrialization*. Albany: State University of New York Press.
Denning, Michael. 2004. *Culture in the Age of Three Worlds*. New York: Verso Books.
Du Gay, Paul. 1996. *Consumption and Identity at Work*. London: Sage Publications.
Friedman, Jonathan, ed. 2003. *Globalization, the State, and Violence*. Walnut Creek, CA: AltaMira Press.
Georgakas, Dan, and Marvin Surkin. 1998. *Detroit: I Do Mind Dying. A Study in Urban Revolution*. Cambridge, MA: South End Press.
Geschwender, James A. 1977. *Class, Race and Worker Insurgency: The League of Revolutionary Black Workers*. London: Cambridge University Press.
Gilbert, Stuart C. 1994. "Observations on the Saturn Project: Site Selection, Financial Incentives, and Impact." *Economic Development Review* 12, no. 4 (fall): 35–44.
Gorz, Andre. 1964. *Strategy for Labor: A Radical Proposal*. Boston: Beacon Press.
Green, William, and Erenest Yanarella, Jr., eds. 1996. *North American Auto Unions in Crisis: Lean Production as Contested Terrain*. Albany: State University of New York Press.
Graham, Laurie. 1995. *On the Line at Subaru-Isuzu: The Japanese Model and the American Worker*. Ithaca: ILR Press.
Harvey, David. 2001a. "Militant Particularism and Global Ambition: The Conceptual Politics of Place, Space and Environment in the Work of Raymond Willliams." In *Spaces of Capital: Towards a Critical Geography*. New York: Routledge.
———. 2001b. "Capitalism: The Factory of Fragmentation." In *Spaces of Capital: Towards a Critical Geography*. New York: Routledge.
———. 2003. *The New Imperialism*. Oxford: Oxford University Press.
Horne, Gerald. 1997. *Fire this Time: The Watts Uprising and the 1960s*. New York: Da Capo Press.
Jessop, Bob. 2002. *The Future of the Capitalist State*. Cambridge: Polity Press.
Kasmir, Sharryn. 1996. *The Myth of Mondragon: Cooperatives, Politics and Working Class Life in a Basque Town*. Albany: State University of New York Press.
———. 2001. "Corporation, Self, and Enterprise at the Saturn Automobile Plant." *Anthropology of Work Review* 22, no. 4: 8–12.
———. 2005. "Activism and Class Identity at the Saturn Automobile Factory." In *Social Movements: A Reader*, ed. June Nash. Malden. Oxford: Blackwell Publishers.
———. 2012. "Difference and Dispossession: Considerations on the Making and Un-Making of a Labor Elite at Saturn." In *The Anthropological Study of Class and Consciousness*, ed. Paul Durrenberger. Boulder: University Press of Colorado.
Kasmir, Sharryn, and August Carbonella. 2008. "Dispossession and the Anthropology of Labor." *Critique of Anthropology* 28, no.1: 5–25.
Mann, Eric. 1987. *Taking on General Motors: A Case Study of the UAW Campaign to Keep GM Van Nuys Open*. Los Angeles: Center for Labor Research and Education, Institute of Industrial Relations, University of California.
———. 1998. "Class, Community, and Empire: Toward an Anti-Imperialist Strategy for Labor." In *Rising From the Ashes? Labor in the Age of 'Global' Capitalism*, ed. Ellen Meiksins Wood, Peter Meiksins, and Michael Yates. New York: Monthly Review Press.

Mariscal, George. 1999. *Aztlan and Viet Nam: Chicano and Chicana Experiences of the War.* Berkeley: University of California Press.
Miller, Peter, and Nikolas Rose. 1995. "Production, Identity and Democracy." *Theory and Society* 24, no. 3: 427–467.
Milkman, Ruth. 1997. *Farewell to the Factory. Autoworkers in the Late Twentieth Century.* Berkeley: University of California Press.
Nader, Ralph. 1985a. "GM Saturn Plant." March 4. http://www.nader.org/index.php?/archives/709-GM-Saturn-Plant.html. Accessed February 12, 2014.
———. 1985b. "Production Seems More Important than GM's Product." August 2. http://www.nader.org/index.php?/archives/752-Production-Seems-More-Important-than-GMs-Product.html. Accessed February 12, 2012.
———. 1985c. "Saturn Plant in Tennessee." December 10. http://www.nader.org/index.php?/archives/764-Saturn-Plant-in-TN.html. Accessed February 12, 2014.
———. 1985d. "New GM Plant Brings Higher Costs to a Community." December 13. http://www.nader.org/index.php?/archives/763-New-GM-Auto-Plant-Brings-High-Costs-to-a-Community.html. Accessed February 12, 2014.
Marx, Karl. 1977. *Capital. A Critique of Political Economy.* Volume One. New York: Vintage Books.
Nash, June. 2012. "Capital Gains and Labor Losses: Corporate Strategies in the War Against American Workers." Unpublished paper.
Narotzky, Susana. 2011. "Structures without Soul and Immediate Struggles: Rethinking Militant Particularism in Contemporary Spain." *Identities: Global Studies in Culture and Power* 18, no. 2: 92–116.
Nissen, Bruce, ed. 1997. *Unions and Workplace Reorganization.* Detroit: Wayne State University Press.
Parker, Mike, and Jane Slaughter. 1985. *Inside the Circle: A Union Guide to QWL.* Detroit: Labor Notes.
———. 1988. *Choosing Sides: Unions and the Team Concept.* Detroit: Labor Notes.
———. 1994. *Working Smart: A Union Guide to Participation Programs and Reengineering.* Detroit: Labor Notes.
———. 1997. "Advancing Unionism on the New Terrain." In *Unions and Workplace Reorganization,* ed. Bruce Nissen. Detroit: Wayne State University Press.
Rinehart, James, Christopher Huxley, and David Robertson. 1997. *Just Another Car Factory? Lean Production and Its Discontents.* Ithaca: ILR Press.
Rogers, Brishen. 1999. "The New Myth of the Happy Worker." *The Baffler* 12: 41–50.
Rothschild, Emma. 1973. *Paradise Lost: The Decline of the Auto-Industrial Age.* New York: Vintage Books.
Rubenstein, James M. 1992. *The Changing Auto Industry. A Geographical Analysis.* London: Routledge.
Rubinstein, Saul. 1996. "Saturn, the GM/UAW Partnership: The Impact of Co-Management and Joint Governance on Firm and Local Union Performance." Ph.D. dissertation, Massachusetts Institute of Technology.
Rubinstein, Saul and Thomas A. Kochan. 2001. *Learning from Saturn: Possibilities for Corporate Governance and Employee Relations.* Ithaca: ILR Press.
Russo, John .1984. "'Killing Jobs with Cooperation': The GM Memo." *Labor Research Review* 1, no. 5 (article 10).
———. 1986. "Saturn's Rings: What GM's Saturn Project is Really About." *Labor Research Review* 9: 67–77.
Sherman, Joe. 1994. *In the Rings of Saturn.* New York: Oxford University Press.
Silver, Beverly. 2003. *Forces of Labor: Workers' Movements and Globalization since 1870.* Cambridge: Cambridge University Press.

Slaughter, Jane. 1998. "Union Votes to Keep Separate Contract: As Sales Slip, Saturn Workers Worry About Job Security Under 'Cooperation' Regime." *Labor Notes*, no. 229 (April): 16.
Smith, Neil. 1984. *Uneven Development: Nature, Capital and the Production of Space*. New York: Basil Blackwell.
Stack, Carol. 1996. *Call to Home: African-Americans Reclaim the Rural South*. New York: Basic Books.
Terkel, Studs. 1972. *Working. People Talk About What They Do All Day and How They Feel About What They Do*. New York: Ballantine Books.
Williams, Raymond. 1989. *Resources of Hope*. New York: Verso Books.
Wolf, Eric. 2001. *Pathways of Power: Building an Anthropology of the Modern World*. Berkeley: University of California Press.
Woolf, David J. 1994. "The Legality of Employee Participation in Unionized Firms: The Saturn Experience and Beyond." *Columbia Journal of Law and Social Problems* 27, no. 4: 557–609.
Yanarella, Ernest J. 1996. "Worker Training at Toyota and Saturn: Hegemony Begins in the Training Center Classroom." In *North American Auto Unions in Crisis: Lean Production as Contested Terrain*, ed. Ernest J. Yanarella and William C. Green. Albany: State University of New York Press.

– Chapter 6 –

"WORTHLESS POLES" AND OTHER DISPOSSESSIONS
Toward an Anthropology of Labor in Post-Communist Central and Eastern Europe

Don Kalb

Many of the parameters of globalization that have been around for some three decades are shifting and turning dramatically since the collapse of the Western financial sector. This renders recent core concepts such as "neoliberalism" and the "Washington Consensus" less stable and illuminating than they once were, for policy as well as analysis. Nevertheless, few analysts would disagree that worker-citizens in contemporary transnationalizing states will inevitably continue to feel the competitive heat of the one billion new workers that have been added to the capitalist system since 1989, as well as the two billion that might be added in the next two decades. This will remain one of the basic determinants of the current epoch, *n'importe* the exact paradigms under which it gets signified. The consequences of the tripling of the global proletariat, now more fragmented than ever before and spread over a wider array of regional blocs and national states, will persist for a while, pace Immanuel Wallerstein's often repeated prognosis that the end of "capitalism as we know it" is in sight.

Within anthropology, Jonathan Friedman (2003) suggested that the conjoined decentralization and globalization of capital will inevitably lead to major challenges to the legitimacy of states and state-elites in the regions of capital flight. This has been a relative truism for global systems throughout history, as the Friedmans show with examples from antiquity, as for the contemporary West (Friedman and Friedman 2008a; 2008b). Bob Jessop adds that neoliberal states have become locked in a global regime that inescapably works to set them up as "competition states" (Jessop 2002), designed to compete with each other for mobile capital by offering their populations and territories up as profitably exploitable factors. While this may not necessarily lead to outright social dumping across states, over time it does shift the balance of forces within states and across states from labor and citizens toward capital, exerting downward pressure on the social wage on behest of the capitalist wage. This is in fact the underlying cause of the recent financial collapse in the West. As the pool of capital liquidity in search of speculative investment grows and the relative social wage shrinks, credit driven consumption and speculation-based life planning take the place of social reproduction based on incomes and savings, after which asset prices first bubble and then deflate, while debts cannot be repaid and must be downgraded or reinflated with more debt (See Dumenil and Levy 2004; 2011; Harvey 2010).

This was the conjuncture within which the transition to "post-politics" (Crouch 2004; Mouffe 2005) and the unstoppable rule of experts in the last thirty years must be explained. States and societies in general, but in Europe perhaps in particular, have seen a steady narrowing of the domain of the political. Democratic decision-making was rendered increasingly meaningless as the technical competencies of law and accountancy displaced social deliberation in public and political spheres. The whole edifice of the EU itself is a case in point and a major cause as well as effect of the spiral of post-politics in Europe. It lifted huge chunks of core policy-making from democratic national forums and placed them into transnational, technocratic, and officially secret Coreper committees. It also imposed elite consensus, both as desired outcome and as mandatory procedure as the only form of legitimate politics (Anderson 2009). Neoliberalism was a crucial part of the ideological background to this dwindling of the political.

Anthropologists were certainly aware and critical of the process but could not entirely escape its pull. Narotzky and Smith (2006) have rightly pointed out that the anthropology of Europe in the preceding period focused rarely in a straightforward way on the problems of social and individual reproduction under "corporate capitalism's" regained hegemony. Anthropologists tended to focus instead on issues of governance, migrants, religion, and ethnicity, even though many researchers certainly sensed, to speak with Zizek, that capitalism might well be "the real that lurks in the background" (quoted in Smith 2006: 621). The financial collapse in the Western banking sector now perhaps helps expand the space for anthropologists to face up to that "real." And indeed what we are seeing lately is an interesting resurgence of economic anthropology (Carrier 2006; Gudeman 2008; Hann 2006; Hann and Hart 2009; Wilk and Cligget 2007) and a cross-disciplinary interest in Polanyi and commodification. But rereading Polanyi does not necessarily lead immediately to a renewed interest in labor, capital and class (see Carrier and Kalb forthcoming; Robotham 2009).

The classic populist view says that the decline of politics is a conspiracy against the people and they would blame incumbent politicians. But the cause was much more systematic and robust than that. It was driven by an identifiable and large-scale material process: the globalization and financialization of capital (Arrighi 1996; Friedman 2003; Friedman and Friedman 2008; Harvey 2003, 2005; Kalb 2005; Kalb et al. 2000; Sassen 2007) and the consequent collective transformation, with few exceptions, of national welfarist, socialist, and developmentalist states into Jessop's "competition states" starting in the late 1970s as a response to, among other social factors, labor activism and popular insurgencies in the West (Silver 2003), industrial overproduction in the core (Brenner 2003), and stagnation and indebtedness in the global South and global East. Again, this general process did not hit every polity in Europe and elsewhere with identical force and consequences: different locations, different stages of development, different histories of citizenship and the histories of the modern *res publica*, facilitated different outcomes and different emphases within what was nevertheless quite a universal process.

As a combined consequence of the rule of post-politics and the reinvigorated capitalism that has been visibly lurking in its background, Europe (like other places) has been undergoing the spread, generation, and regeneration of new hybrid and volatile populisms (see classically Betz 1994; Canovan 1999; Di Tella 1997; Westlind 1996; for the recent wave see Berezin 2009; Kalb and Halmai 2011; Mudde 2007). Significantly, the launching date seems somewhere around 1989. Such populist sensibilities and discourses reject some of the foundations of liberal rule and are composed of ethno-national or ethno-religious, symbolic sources eclectically combined with some of the socioeconomic demands of the classical Left. As Piccone wrote in 1993, reflecting on the first wave of the *Front National* in France:

"The French New Right seems to be onto something when it counterposes a universalizing New Class seeking to impose an abstract liberal agenda on everyone, and populists wanting to live their lives in their communities, with their particular cultures, institutions, religions etc" (1993: 21).

These European populisms are not just interruptions of the daily business of post-politics, as described by political scientists, but also, and ultimately more importantly, the vehicles by which disenfranchised populations try to make sense of their discontents with globalizing modernisms. Even people who do not speak out loudly for the radical Right these days often blame incumbent political classes sotto voce for their complicity with the perceived conspiracies against "the people." Like the public ideologists of the new Right they articulate their bricolages of critique from combined bits of direct experience and mass-mediated right-wing protests. Unlocking these dialectics between popular anger and resentment and the organized radical Right seems an urgent project that anthropological methods might well help forward. We need to uncover the hidden histories of labor, dispossession, disenfranchisement, and imposed subalternity that feed the particular alienations of the resenting classes in their volatile dialectic with the histories of neoliberal transnationalization by which they are shaped (Kalb and Halmai 2011).

My focus in this chapter is on hidden histories of labor and dispossession within post-socialism, in particular in Poland. Eastern Europe seems to cry out for such an exercise. I have worked in the region since 1997 and in my experience it has been hard to talk about issues of class at all until around 2003. References to systematic social process beyond individual choice or cultural preference, or beyond race and gender, certainly if phrased in languages that seemingly harked back to Marxist traditions, still often hit at a traumatic spot. The new neoliberal regimes and elites in the region have advertised themselves as the bringers of democracy and economic growth; and on the surface this is indeed what they did. After the "transitional recession" and the consolidation of parliamentary democracy in the first post-1989 decade, from around 2000 onward they could point to high economic growth and faster average wage growth than Western Europe. In 2004 the great majority of these countries were accepted into the EU, ending half a century of violently enforced exclusion from the imagined liberal cornucopia. In that celebratory context, histories of dispossession and disenfranchisement could not be easily narrated and revealed and were often blamed on the victims. What is rarely highlighted is that not just Roma in Eastern Hungary or former kolchoz workers in Northeastern Poland, both with high levels of alcoholism and the predictable objects of public alarm, have fared badly, but so too have skilled industrial workers and technical personnel above forty years old, even in boom regions such as Wroclaw, close to the Polish/German border, or Gyor in West Hungary close to Vienna (see Kalb and Halmai 2011). I am interested in laying bare the hidden histories of dispossession and disenfranchisement that have helped to shape the particular forms of political and cultural resentment of this latter group. My aim is to probe the agonistic lived inside of processes of class formation that are usually framed by the media as nothing less than a "successful" democratic transition.

Anthropologies of Neoliberal Globalization, Fear, and the Populist Nation

In recent anthropology, Andre Gingrich and Marcus Banks (2005) and Arjun Appadurai (2006) highlight the importance of social insecurity, fear, and anger in generating the popular receptiveness for ideologies of ethnic or religious neonationalism. They also invoke the association of such receptiveness with the general conditions generated by neoliberal globalizations. Their work resonates with Friedman's (2003) general notion of "double polarizations" associated with globalization: polarizations that pair widening social divides with spreading idioms of deep cultural difference in an era in which ruling elites and their allies are structurally invited to transform themselves into cosmopolitan classes and forsake the project of the nation as a community of fate. In the process, the erstwhile "Fordist" working classes are unmade, in representation as well as fact, into a new "ethnic folk," and the lower tiers are turned, in representation and fact, into racialized *classes dangereuses*. These very different works combine, then, in suggesting that any explanation of the surge of neonationalism in Europe must be placed against the combined background of what I would call the "dual crisis" of popular sovereignty, on the one hand, and of labor, on the other hand. They also suggest that spirals of nationalist paranoia, although structurally derived from the dual crisis, receive their precise historical dynamics, meanings, and symbolisms from demonstrable configurations—confrontations, alliances, and divisions—of class, within specific local histories.

Actual local outcomes, then, are intermediated by what I call various "critical junctions" that link global process via particular national arenas and local histories, often hidden, to emergent and situated local events and narratives, and back again (Kalb 1997; 2000; 2002; 2005; Kalb and Tak 2005). Critical junctions are multilevel mechanisms that link the global levels of what Eric Wolf (1990) called structural power with the respective institutional fields of tactical power on the scale of the national state and with the agential power of "common people" in situated everyday circumstances. Such critical junctions, moreover, have a path dependency, a historical weight and a direction of their own that cannot always easily be turned around. They keep pushing in particular directions and remain captured by particular fields of signification, until some major event happens, often spanning local, regional, and global spaces at the same time. Critical junctions are thus densely structured, albeit punctuated, and suffused with systematic relationships of inequality, power and dependence. Now my claim is that it is precisely in these dynamic interlinkages that the politics of fear and anger gets incubated.

The politics of fear is not the direct consequence of cultural implosions and global cascades, such as in Appadurai's account of ethnic riots in India (Appadurai 1996). Rather, while turbulence does happen, fear gets generally nurtured step by step within the grinding mechanisms that link livelihoods and neighborhoods with mass mediated national level political articulations and mobilizations. Specifically, I would suggest, it is the contradictions and disjunctures between everyday agential power fields, tactical state-based political environments (including political and media opportunity structures), and global structural power relationships—that move the popular anxiety and paranoia. Such anxieties, in their turn, energize the nationalist populisms that are taking the place of the liberal modernisms gone awry. In a more narrowly political sense, populism, in the current conjuncture, is the rejection of liberal elites and ideologies that fail to use the resources of the democratic national state to harness global process to local needs and desires, that celebrate an elite cosmopolitanism, or that use state power and cosmopolitan ideologies for outright local dispossession. The narrowly political outcome is the generation of media-genetic and charismatic ideologues that create havoc among established political classes and institutions. But more broadly conceived, working-class populism refers to the moods and sensibilities of the disenfranchised as they face the disjunctures between everyday lives that seem to become increasingly chaotic and uncontrollable and the wider public power projects that are out of their reach and suspected of serving their ongoing disenfranchisement. In Tilly's (2003) definition of democracy, this implies dedemocratization and a consequent return to particularized trust networks crucial for working-class reproduction. Examining how the politics of fear gets incubated and nurtured within the relevant critical junctions therefore requires an obsession with local historical discovery and a critical reading of large-scale global and national process from the vantage point of the particular and situated livelihoods of laboring classes.

Approaching Post-socialist Hidden Histories of Labor: The Specter of 1989

In the particular case of post-socialist Eastern Europe the repression is even more intractable. For one, class language after socialism has been even more ostensibly delegitimized than in the West, with a broad popular rejection of Soviet imposed ideology and a broad popular appeal of notions of rights, democracy, and reform, at least until recently. Indeed, "joining the West," democracy and reform have been such powerful public symbols of redemption in Eastern Europe that analyzing the systemic contradictions of world capitalist development and post-socialist social change was all but tabooed among intellectuals (but see Szalai 2008). Such public narratives have simply not been available (though they spread rapidly after the financial crisis). What was available was a growing rightist undercurrent, sometimes rising dramatically to the surface, that sensed the injustices against the people and sought to unmask the enemy within and without. To analyze this process, we need an anthropology of labor that takes the actual processes of popular disenfranchisement and dispossession that have been silenced under the "oppressive signs" of neoliberalized democracy seriously.

This anthropology of class and labor should start with a reappraisal of the causes and significations of the velvet revolutions of "1989." We need this for three reasons: first, as said, the symbol of the democratic revolutions of 1989, with their language of civil society, anti-authoritarianism, and freedom still weighs as a specter on our current dominant public perceptions, both in the East and the West, as well as in the South. Secondly, labor having actively lived through the tumultuous moment of 1989 has been grappling with its shifting meaning over time. There is a need to understand the connections of and within laboring lives, their evolving "structures of feeling" over time, as people lived, worked, and acted toward 1989, through it, and after it. And most importantly, as we will see, labor played a crucial role in producing the revolutions in Central Europe in 1989, but in more paradoxical ways than one would think. This anthropology of labor and 1989 is what I will try to sketch out first.

By the summer of 1989, opposition forces, underground youth, peace, and environmentalist groups, empowered by a diffusion of news and civil society networks connecting East and West Europe, were emboldened to come out and press claims for free elections and the end of socialist party rule. Even where such dissent had not openly existed before, such as in the GDR or Romania, this swiftly led to mass movements claiming the end of socialist party rule. These movements were different from country to country but reinforced each other, and produced nothing less than the fall of the Berlin Wall on November 9, 1989. It was the end of state-socialism.

As in the classical revolutions (England, the United States, France, Russia, China), intellectuals of diverse sorts (dissidents, pastors, actors, writers) were substantially involved in 1989. But instead of claiming the victory of a rising class and articulating new ideas for social and political order for which the center of the state had to be captured, if necessary by armed insurrection—"Jacobinism"—they walked peacefully under the banners of "civil society" and a "return to Europe." Their ideas were framed in universal notions of human rights as revitalized by the "Helsinki process" (1975), notions that pictured the state not so much as the guardian or guarantor of such rights, but as the first offender. These were merged with recent and older local traditions of anti-politics and what the writer Milan Kundera has once called "the republic of the mind," traditions that rejected centralized power over peoples' lives in general. The desirability and possibility of an anarcho-liberal utopia was pictured, a position that offered basically no thoughts about capitalism and inequality, and even about social reproduction, at all. Indeed, notions of class and labor were for the first time in modern history decidedly absent from a major wave of European revolutions.

However, except in Poland and Hungary, such intellectuals had in the 1980s been thoroughly marginalized by security apparatuses. In countries such as Czechoslovakia, the GDR and Romania, even a few weeks before the factual revolutions, dissident groups appeared hardly relevant. Stephen Kotkin and Jan Gross have therefore argued that the idea that 1989 was produced by strong civic movements is ludicrous (Kotkin and Gross 2009). "This was not an explosion," the Polish philosopher Leszek Kolakowski later wrote about the revolutions, "it was like the breaking of an egg from inside the shell" (Kolakowski 1999). There is an emergent consensus that the unexpected cycle of regionwide peaceful revolutions can only be explained in a complex multiscalar narrative, a critical junctions perspective indeed, that proceeds on several temporal planes simultaneously, going beyond the usual modernist focus on separate nation states and intrastate social movements. In that perspective, the protest wave was in fact the crystallization of a set of diffuse structural processes within the socialist bloc that were only weakly perceived in their full dimensions by contemporary participants and commentators. The contradictions of labor and accumulation in "workers' states" were crucial.

Stalinism was designed to turn backward agricultural societies into urban industrial societies within a uniquely compressed period of time enabled by forceful illiberal methods. East Central Europe in 1948 was overwhelmingly rural with anywhere between 50 percent and 80 percent of the population living off the land. By 1980 these agricultural populations had been largely transformed into modern literate urban working classes and white-collar workers. After the initial high-speed social transformation a seemingly stable "socialist mode of production and consumption" had developed. Against its self-image, however, that mode of production was not well planned and had its own irrationalities, among others a heavy bias toward capital and military goods controlled by the party-state, and a massively underperforming agricultural sector. After 1970 it also became ever more dependent on Western loans. While it did produce the basics for a modern way of life, it did not live up to Khrushchev's famous promise of 1961: it never surpassed the West. By the 1980s the "capitalist" other, that had been stuck in deep crisis in the 1930s and had been broadly associated with Nazism and war, was thoroughly transformed into a wealthy space of social democracy and individual freedom. Life in socialism seemed bleak in comparison. Socialism had produced modern subjects with modern desires, but characteristically left the desires suspended and therefore politicized, both in production and in consumption. This was one aspect of what was growing inside Kolakowski's eggshell.

More immediately politically momentous, "really existing socialism" left a large measure of control over production to its lower level managers and workers. This was one of the basic insights of Katherine

Verdery's (1996) seminal theory of socialism—one of the more robust attempts at theorization in an anthropological field that often lacks the will to do so. Socialism penetrated much less forcefully into the sphere of production than capitalism did. The center controlled the sphere of public discussion but not quite the sphere of work. Workers' control had been a recurrent inspiring idea in the anti-Soviet revolts in Poznan 1953, Budapest 1956, Prague 1968, and of course in Poland under Solidarnosc and, in more complex ways, in 1989 as I will show. It was a core aspect of the claim for "socialism with a human face." In reality however quite a bit of control from below on the workshop floor already existed. This was part of the bargain to get sodalities of workers who could not be fired nor incentivized by high wages to commit themselves to the Plan (See Burawoy 1985; Verdery 1996). As a consequence, the more complex the socialist economy became, the less the party-state seemed capable of securing the central appropriation of surplus from workers and firms.

Workers were also aware that they were ruled in their own name, and they had learned to use this to their own advantage. Although independent labor unions were outlawed, workers did not go easy on the party state if it raised food prices. In Poland in 1971, 1976, 1979, 1980, and 1988 massive worker unrest, increasingly coordinated, emerged precisely around this issue, with cumulative political consequences. Paradoxically, socialism unraveled as a consequence of informally empowered workers demanding formal rights of the "workers' state." Poland was the prime example, but elsewhere similar logics were unfolding under the surface too.

One response to stagnation, pioneered in Hungary since 1968, was "reform." It was an effort to decentralize control and responsibility to lower levels of execution in the firms and the bureaucracy. It empowered the technocrats vis-à-vis the central planners and the party leadership. Such experts would then subsequently claim further "reform." In the daily running of socialist societies after 1970 therefore, technocrats, increasingly with university credentials, pushed back party ideologists and became a force both within and without the parties, further hollowing out party rule.

Verdery has rightly emphasized that this shift in leadership downward and outward from the party center was further exacerbated as socialist countries from the mid-1970s were given access to Western loans as part of the "Helsinki" deal with the West ("human rights for loans"). In the 1980s, indebted socialist countries desperately tried to export their way out of their newly acquired capitalist servitude.

Their products however were hardly competitive in the West and the export strategy failed (in contrast to a similar strategy at a later point in time by China). By 1989 CEE had run up some $90 billion in debt to the West. Instead of partially defaulting, as Mexico did, the state socialist economies, desperately tried to integrate further into the Western markets. Hungary became the first Comecon (Council for Mutual Economic Assistance; the international economic coordination agency of the Warsaw Pact) nation to become a member of the IMF in 1982. The Soviet Union rejected an invasion into Poland in 1981 because the politburo feared a Western economic blockade. In an effort to fend off this possibility, socialist parties therefore became increasingly bent on exacting higher productivity and a larger surplus from workers. Ceaucescu's Romania imposed a new homebred Stalinism, including permanent nightly curfews and a severe rationing of energy, and in fact paid off its debts by 1989. More "liberal" socialist states were squeezed in between the demands of an ever less paternalist Kremlin, hardnosed Western finance, and workers with little liking for the party.

Poland, for various reasons, only one of them being its strong Catholic church, had always enjoyed a more open political scene than other Warsaw-pact countries. It was therefore the most vulnerable to the growing squeeze. From the mid-1970s, young left-wing intellectuals, in particular Jacek Kuron, began seeking alliances with an increasingly restless working class, resulting in 1976 in the making of the KOR (the "Workers' Defense Committee"; see for example Ekiert 1996; Ekiert and Kubik 1999; Kubik 1994). The KOR was of signal importance in helping to turn a new bout of isolated worker protests in the shipyards of the Baltic Coast in 1980 into the making and then the legalization of an independent nation-wide labor union, Solidarnosc, with the electrician Lech Walesa at is head. This took place after the new Polish pope, Karol Woytjla, had brought the nation together in massive public religious rituals in 1979, the collective spirit of which was now increasingly turned into defiance against the party state. This powerful alliance between intellectuals, workers and the Catholic Church at once fractured and delegitimized the party. With a membership of 8 million by late 1980, it openly demanded worker self-management and a pluralist civic sphere. This claim prefigured the end of state-socialism as we knew it. Solidarnosc was not just a blue-collar union: the new middle classes of technocrats were substantially part of it, including a good million communist party members who were delighted to use the space offered for dissent and discussion and push for a more democratic socialism. On December 13, 1981, General Jaruzelski's martial law destroyed the union in a few weeks and incarcerated thousands of its activists. But it did not defeat for good the spirit of defiance and the sodalities in the factories, nor could militarization be a durable solution to the mounting problems of socialism in Poland. In 1985 an amnesty was announced. In April 1988, in response to price hikes of meat, several mines in the South and various factories along the Baltic Coast were once again occupied by workers, now led by a new generation of young and more openly rebellious leaders. In a large national consultation/referendum in 1987 people rejected further "economic reforms" in defiance of the party's expectations. DADA-like street performances by students, mocking the regime and socialist morality, were spreading again in the cities (Kenney 2003).

The coming of Gorbachev as general secretary of the Communist Party of the Soviet Union in 1985 signaled the start of a rejuvenation of the aging Kremlin leadership. Glasnost (openness) and Perestroika (restructuring) were the symbols under which the new Politburo set about tackling the social and economic stagnation. In talks with the Polish generals following the renewed strikes and occupations in Poland in the spring of 1988, the Kremlin accepted that the Polish generals would negotiate with individuals in the opposition and offer political concessions in exchange for economic reform and the reduction of price subsidies. The idea of the Round Table was born, a method for reconciliating a state elite that was losing its capacity to rule with an entrenched popular opposition. Gorbachev and even the Polish party leadership did not fully sense that the legitimacy of the party in Poland was beyond repair, and elsewhere soon too. Poland started its Round Table in January 1989, ushering in partly free elections in June that the regime was confident it would win. They did not, and against everyone's expectations Solidarnosc elites formed a government in September.

While this was broadly seen in Poland as the final victory of labor over the party, the victory was in fact immensely contradictory. It gained pluralism, "civil society," parliamentary democracy, national sovereignty vis-à-vis the Soviet Union (and later Russia), and further integration with the West, in time even accession to the European Union. But it lost "socialist paternalism," the "workers' state" and the socialist organization of the economy that had made it so strong in the first place. Workers who had actually fought for "sovereignty" and "autonomy" would be forced to face the realities of dispossession and disenfranchisement in a liberal democratic and globalized context, even amidst fast economic growth. After twenty years, the "silent" contradictions of 1989 and the contradictory experiences of labor in Central and Eastern Europe are still unfolding.

In what follows, I delve into the stories of a group of workers in the Polish city of Wroclaw to dig up the narrated realities that pushed skilled and semiskilled industrial workers, arguably the largest population segment in post-socialist Europe, to articulate an increasingly biting populist rejection of their liberalizing elites after 1989. This is meant to be a microarchaeology of workers' resentment in response to misrecognized and misrecognizing processes of dispossession initiated at state and global levels, liberal disenfranchisements that are not merely related to their work but to their whole habitat, as we shall see.

Between 1997 and 2007, I followed a group of workers organized around Solidarnosc unions in Polar, a white-goods factory (refrigerators and washing machines), and other local factories in Wroclaw, southwest Poland.[1] These workers had built the local Solidarnosc units against communist repression and state accumulation in the late 1970s–early 1980s. They subsequently sustained their underground self-organization throughout the period of military rule and into the creeping transition processes from 1985 onward. They laid strong de facto as well as de jure claims to "their" factories, and actively tried to secure these claims, their factories and communities throughout the crises of shock therapy (see Kalb 2009a). I argue that these crises served, paradoxically, to facilitate outright the dispossession into state hands of what were in fact seen as people's assets—a process of dispossession legitimized by and misrecognized as regained sovereignty, parliamentary democratization and "Europe." My aim is to probe the lived inside of processes largely understood and fetishized from the outside as a "successful democratic transition."

"History Repeats Itself," Conversations with a Polish Populist

The best lead into working-class experience and its contentious signification that I can give is to share conversations my colleagues and I had with Krysztof Zadrozny, a vocational teacher born in Wroclaw in 1953, a worker activist who, in the end, never exchanged his job on the assembly lines of the local Polar factory for a paid career in unionism, politics, or a foreman position. He had been the leader of the anti–martial law strike and factory occupation in December 1981, was interned by General Jaruzelski in 1982, edited and published an underground factory journal from 1983 to 1988 called *Our Home*, was jailed again and then dismissed from further industrial work in Wroclaw for resurrecting Solidarnosc in 1988, temporarily became a high-altitude chimney sweeper, and later became a youth basketball coach and an organizer of "home-church" holiday camps with other lay Catholics. He is the older brother of a Solidarnosc forewoman of both local and national importance. Above all, he is a persistent fighter for "living in truth" and for demanding "normality" in Poland.[2] He is the father of three children, the oldest born while he was interned, who are all studying pedagogy-related subjects. Like many workers we interviewed, he now still lives in the small apartment that was allocated to him in the late 1970s not far from the factory complex. In the Polar factory environment, in which more than 50 percent of employees had no more than a primary education, he stood out for the trust he had gained among hundreds, even thousands, of workers and inhabitants. As a vocational teacher and production-line worker, he mediated between working-class sensibilities and politics, on the one hand, and the more highly educated actors in the institutional fields, including his sister, on the other hand.[3]

When we first met him in the small and sober union office in the Polar administration building in 1998, some of the Polar shares were just about to be sold by the state to a French industrial group. The European Union, which had insisted on the full liberalization of imports into Poland while still maintaining specific tariffs against Polish exports until the early 2000s, loomed large in his internal conversations and exchanges with friends at the time. Fifteen hundred redundancies (in a labor force of forty-five hundred in 1997) had recently been announced. An investigation by McKinsey and Company consultants, commissioned by the State Treasury, had, predictably, shown that Polar employed more workers than comparable white-goods firms in the West. "The EU is a huge Soviet Union," Zadrozny stated with self-conscious cynicism. "There has been so much talk about self-governments, locality, etc., and what they finally do is create a huge monopoly."

Monopoly, in the language of the anti-communist resistance, stood for social and material waste, lack of accountability, misinformation, and corruption. Self-government, in contrast, meant "normality" and "living in truth." These were the ultimate symbols for which Polish workers had sustained their fight with the party-state, arguably more important than the idea of "civil society" or even "pluralism," which remained rather tactical and intellectual concepts. Normality and living in truth were the complex popular (and Christian) symbols that had ultimately energized the people's mobilization (see, e.g., Kubik 1994; Ost 1990). They remained magnets of signification and desire all through the 1990s and into the 2000s and were increasingly targeted against the liberal state and its transnational allies.

We met Zadrozny again in the same small office ten years later in April 2007. He was still working on the conveyor belt of what is now Polar-Whirlpool. "History repeats itself," he exclaimed.

> Our naïveté and kindheartedness have been exploited. In all these years after 1989 we were told that we are nothing; that the West has come to take it all over; that the Poles happen to have their national vices. And in this way the ground was prepared for people to accept the status quo. But in my opinion, what was missing in 1989 was a spirit of resistance against abnormality. Also in Solidarnosc and the church. See, for example, this recent issue of women working in supermarkets not being allowed to go to the toilet and therefore wearing Pampers! Where was Solidarnosc? Where was the church? They should have reacted sharply. Then other things could not have taken place either. And here, I think, quite intentionally, the enterprises and Polar too, were broken into pieces. They were left to fight for themselves. And in that way solidarity was broken. We were told that this is how it has to be, that there is this transition going on, and that we should just be happy that we have work at all. Well, labor is a great value but our dignity and our incomes are important too. I think we should at least revisit the process of privatization, even in Polar, whether it was real privatization or, as people say, mere theft. My sister, when the privatization was pending in 1998, had to travel to a dinner with Prime Minister Buzek, talk at night, lots of alcohol, to convince him to get the social package done. Absurd! He was meant to be our own Solidarnosc prime minister! But in the ministry he let an undersecretary deal with our case, and this guy was of the Proszkow mafia [secret services]. Such things must be investigated, show the truth! It would be odd that those who bought the enterprises for almost nothing would be doing it for the people? We cannot undo what was done. Still it would be psychologically important to find out whether this company was sold for less than its real value. Then it could become easier to enforce something now, like better wages. It is a question of honor. I myself never believed that this was how it had to be, that Poles are such that they cannot do this or that . . . it was a big mistake to say that Poles were worthless.

Some words are immediately in order to help contextualize and disentangle this superficially straightforward but in fact thickly layered narrative. Privatization, counterintuitively, was something that workers in Poland had fiercely believed in, from the moment that the term was first circulated in public in 1989–1992 (see also Kalb 2009a, b; Ost 2005). In their view, though, it had a totally different connotation than it did in the West or when used by the Polish liberal elite. It was not about selling a public asset to a private investor but, rather, the other way around. For Polish workers in the late 1980s, it initially signified a transfer of firms—which, under communism, were the anchor of total community life, including health care, holidays, housing, kindergartens, loans, and so on—out off the hands of the communist state, which was seen as an external force encroaching on the nation, scheming to appropriate its properties, and into those of the workers, seen as the factual national public. More particularly, privatization meant ideally turning state property into workers' owned cooperatives, including all the social functions such enterprises had under socialism. In fact people talked about "self-government" rather than self-management (same word in Polish).[4]

The period of the late 1980s and early 1990s in Poland, indeed, probably everywhere in central and eastern Europe, was one in which the early-twentieth-century idea of workers' self-management, indeed, workers' self-government, was very much in the air; more precisely, it was materially real and very close to being a daily lived experience, in Raymond Williams's sense of a structure of feeling, in many sites and locations, including Wroclaw. Few analysts of postsocialism have focused on this lived reality sufficiently, so it requires a further excursion. It is the starting point for understanding local popular experience.

Remarkably enough, under martial law, one of the first civil acts of the military regime was to implement a crucial demand made by Solidarnosc in its General Assembly in September 1981—workers' self-management (Poznanski 1996). It is often assumed that this demand had figured as one of the radicalizations of the Polish rebellion that convinced Moscow and the Polish generals of the increasing inevitability of armed intervention to defend the position of the nomenklatura. But with Solidarnosc outlawed and dismantled, the military regime felt that new institutions for self-government at the factory level would help to pacify the population, sever the links between local workers and national intelligentsia, and create some legitimacy for the regime. On top of that, self-management could help to solve, at one stroke, some systemic problems of socialist accumulation.

First, by making them responsible for their own finances, the regime hoped that firms would be forced to become more financially responsible and entrepreneurial. Second, lawmakers hoped to prevent, or at least deflect to plant and local level, eventual new waves of collective wage claims by workers. In this way, they hoped to take away one of the structural impediments to socialist accumulation: the inability of the state to control wages, profits, and investment and, indeed, the inability to forestall state-focused working-class collective action. Workers would now preside over their own wage funds as part of limited budgets with "hard constraints," in Janos Kornai's (1980) sense. And because workers had considerable control over the overall budget, they would have to weigh their own wages in relation to productive investments and the extensive social funds. They were expected to become responsible caretakers of and investors in their own social reproduction (see Kasmir, this volume, for a discussion of similar strategies of "worker responsibilization" among capitalist employers in the United States). This was meant to be the end of the socialist paternalist state and its uncontainable contradictions (see Ekiert and Kubik 1999; Poznanski 1996). And, in retrospect, this is indeed what happened, although not in the form anticipated by Jaruzelski or Moscow. It became the end not of paternalism but of the socialist state tout court: The state would ultimately lose its control over "people's property" and crumble—after which, the new neoliberal state would emerge to take it all back under the contradictory sign of democratic market reform.

Communist technocrats in Poland had launched new regime-friendly unions (confederated in the Ogolnopolskie Porozumienie Zwiazkow Zawodowych [All-Poland Alliance of Trade Unions], or OPZZ) in 1982, which were expected to take control of the self-management institutions now that Solidarnosc had been outlawed. But at those sites where Solidarnosc had been strong and had gone underground, as, for example, at Polar and several other factories in Wroclaw, OPZZ proved only capable of organizing some sections of the white-collar workers. The new worker councils got very rapidly colonized by cohesive and democratic worker collectives that now used formally legal ways to wrestle de facto control over productive property from the state. Zadrozny and his colleagues had been deeply involved in this fight for working-class and national repossession vis-à-vis the Moscow-backed military communists; in fact, Zadrozny had been the key actor and, in the process, had gained the trust of hundreds, even thousands, of workers at Polar. In the course of the late 1980s, workers had succeeded in pushing back the power of the nomenklatura over the Polar factory and its social assets; they had subsequently prevented nomenklatura privatization and asset stripping; and, by 1989, they were starting to actually choose and nominate their own directors. In other core factories in Wroclaw, such as the computer maker Elwro and the train-maker Pafawag, the same was happening. Tens of thousands of workers in this city alone felt substantially in control of factory and community assets. The personnel director of Polar in 1998, in explaining the moral and practical difficulty of firing hundreds of workers, stressed repeatedly to us that there was still an overwhelming sense of factory ownership among workers at Polar.

The juridical notion of "privatization," in contrast to its popular connotation, of course, came from a totally different corner. It was introduced in public speech by liberal economists from Gdansk, in particular, Leszek Balcerowicz, in 1988–1989. They had been invited into the core team of political liberals organized around Bronislaw Geremek and Adam Michnik to help educate them in economic matters to which they had given less than serious thought, even though they had already begun to reject ideas of workers' self-management around 1985 (Ost 1990). But in the context of an economy that was de facto managed, legally co-owned, and morally claimed by victorious worker collectives while the other formal co-owner, the illegitimate and Soviet-backed communist state, was finally collapsing, the idea of privatization was perceived by workers to signify something like the endgame of their struggles over people's property. Privatization was, first and foremost, popularly understood as the final realization of the original 1981 Solidarnosc demands that had triggered military rule. It was something like the crowning ritual of the workers' rebellion.

Let me emphasize that worker self-management/self-government was not only a blue-collar affair and not exclusively a blue-collar connotation of the idea of privatization. Self-management was endorsed by many university-educated people as well, particularly in more high-end factories. In the first two parliaments after 1989, a faction sprang from local self-management institutions that defended the idea of the worker cooperative as one of the desirable paths of privatizing the economy. From the self-managed factories, a nationwide movement of well-trained cadres had already emerged in 1988 that pushed for an outcome of the Round Table talks between the communist government and the opposition, and for subsequent financial and economic regulations, that were conducive to worker-managed democratic cooperatives.[5] But these "organic" actors quickly discovered that the liberal intellectuals at the Round Table, who by now had very weak ties with constituencies on the ground, as correctly anticipated by the generals, and had very little patience with the idea of letting workers consolidate power (Ost 1990). Meanwhile, the crucial economic and fiscal aspects of liberal state making were delegated to "experts" who were working in silence on their shock-therapy program (see also Wedel 2001). One of our informants from Wroclaw, Andrzej Piszel, a computer scientist, was a member of the self-management group in parliament after 1989. He is now a successful entrepreneur with few political illusions and recalls vividly how the core group of dissident parliamentarians would regularly silence him with whistling and other less-than-polite methods when he made the case for policies that would help consolidate the worker-managed sector of the economy. He is still convinced that a great and feasible socioeconomic option was thus intentionally killed off for political reasons that he does not like to think about.

At the same time, shock therapy, with its full liberalization of the market at one stroke and its mythic focus on consolidating the state budget amidst economic collapse, was punishing all productive enterprises and affiliated social institutions so heavily that their sheer survival became a more crucial concern for activists than the skewed discussion about the legal form. While the new regime gently silenced the public debate about the particular legal paths of privatization by leaving it to groups of sheltered experts and by slowing down the actual decision-making processes (even by the late 1990s, a majority of Polish enterprises were not yet formally privatized, in contrast to the country's post-socialist neighbors), it engineered a rough beating of the national economy that, by 1991, had left most firms begging for loans and help from the state and the state-run banking sector. In this way, through bankrupting the popularly controlled sector of the economy, the new liberal state gradually wrestled de facto ownership claims away from worker collectives. Property titles were channeled into state banks and the State Treasury, while this move was publicly advertised as the definitive blow against the communists. In the same process, by forcing factory-based sodalities to fight for their own survival, it destroyed worker solidarity and fragmented the movements for self-management and cooperatives. By 1993, with Poland again witnessing massive worker protests against shock therapy and poverty (Ekiert and Kubik 1999), the cooperative option had all but vanished from the political debates, and privatization came more and more to connote bringing a firm under the wing of the State Treasury and onto the Warsaw stock exchange to find desperately needed new sources of capital abroad.

If 1985–1989 had thus seen the repossession of productive assets by worker-citizens from the militarized party-state, 1989–1995 saw the dispossession of worker collectives by a liberal state through financial engineering, thus shrewdly recentralizing the nation's assets under a now-independent treasury in globalizing mode. One of the crucial legal details was that a firm whose ownership had been transferred to the Treasury was immediately lifted out of the self-management legal regime and lost the right to a workers' council and its nomination of the director. State appropriation had thus become legally secured against still-prevailing popular structures of feeling that workers were actual owner-occupiers of their factories. By the time we started our interviews, in 1997, workers in Polar and elsewhere had begun to see their legal defeat, as their property claims had been annulled while they were shocked into sheer survival mode, as Klein (2007) analyzed so well and more generally.[6]

"Real privatization," in Zadrozny's words, signifies, in its purest form, a worker cooperative and, in a diluted and compromised form, at least a privatization that is beneficial for the plant and its workers, in which a measure of control from below is exchanged for growth, investment, and better wages.[7] The opposite he calls "theft." Theft, of course, is a motif in populist narratives par excellence. But it does rather realistically connote the dispossession of assets from worker constituencies and their subsequent transfer into the hands of the state and the global market by purely legal and financial procedures beyond the control of the assets' moral proprietors. It also describes the consequent deprivation of communities of workers—not just communities but actual sodalities with known fighting histories in a national rebellion—as the proceeds of privatization disappeared into the hands of state bureaucrats and international bidders.

Recall that in the interview excerpt above, Zadrozny moves from the issue of "theft" into a little tirade about Poles being told that they had their vices and, hence, should not want to trust their own sources of agency. Here he immediately connects material dispossession to the wider public culture of neoliberalism in Poland after 1989. He is referring to the nasty public rhetoric spawned by the liberal elite and its following of media and academic pundits after the discovery of the yawning state debt. None of the liberals had the guts to even discuss canceling the debt as "odious" (as Klein 2007 importantly points out).[8] But with shock therapy shaking the nation and the specter of economic failure becoming a realistic possibility, intellectuals and media people began desperately picturing themselves as "middle class" while increasingly depicting workers and peasants as gross liabilities for a Poland now openly exposed to world capitalist competition. Workers and peasants were systematically associated in the media with alcoholism and laziness, and labor unions were openly decried as dysfunctional for the new civil Poland. In fact, the whole concept of "civil society" was regularly turned against them. Even such an honorable person as Michnik, at a 1999 commemoration of the events of 1989, which was held in the Kaiserliche Hofburg in Vienna and which I attended,[9] openly devalued Polish industry by talking about "ex-socialist workers who were merely producing busts of Lenin." In the same elite ceremonial event, Balcerowicz showed himself still almost religiously satisfied at having finally unleashed "healthy" market forces and creative destruction, punishing Polish workers for "the crowding out of conscience" that he saw as their self-chosen fate under the state-led economy (Kalb 2002; for further examples, see Buchowski 2006). The supposed inevitability of it all was mentioned regularly, but speakers were keen to turn such perceived necessity into (their own) virtue. While they celebrated their peaceful victory over the Evil Empire of Communism in lusty Vienna, there was no audible dissent to the silencing of the workers' fight and plight among the ex-dissident new Polish elite at this particular banquet.[10]

This was the context that Michal Buchowski has recently described with the notion of "internal orientalization" (also Kideckel 2002; 2007), which "blames workers and peasants for their own degraded circumstances and for society's difficulties" (2006: 467). It refers to a public climate in which workers "have proven to be "civilizationally incompetent" (Sztompka 1993), show a "general lack of discipline and diligence" (Sztompka 1996: 119) and obstruct the efforts of those who are accomplished and the progress of whole societies in the region" (Buchowski 2006: 469) By regularly invoking the *Homo Sovieticus* syndrome, liberal intellectuals displaced workers out of the bounds of Europe and into a timeless Asia. At the same moment, they passionately claimed a place for themselves in the new European pantheon, invoking their conscientious and peaceful advocacy of liberal civil society against the communist Goliath and their successful liberalization and privatization of "the economy." More than that, they prided themselves on their successful imposition of Western-type civil society and individualism on backward, populist eastern nations.

Zadrozny is basically speechless in response to this inflicted symbolic violence. As a tenacious fighter for justice, he keeps uttering that he has always refused to believe that "Poles were worthless." But he clearly recognizes how important this public attack, the withdrawal of recognition, has been in breaking resistance and disqualifying collective action in working-class communities. Internal orientalization served as one of the style figures of a process of cultural dispossession that accompanied, deepened, and smoothed the material dispossession simultaneously taking place. It was one of the cultural mechanisms that helped produce a Polish ethnic folk figure against a cosmopolitanizing elite, as Friedman and Friedman (2008a, b) would have anticipated.

Zadrozny makes another important observation that merits further decoding: "Enterprises were broken into pieces and left to fight for themselves," and he blames, among others, Solidarnosc and the church for this. He also mentions, in the same breath, "Poles having their vices" and the related "absence of a spirit of resistance." In fact, he addresses the whole liberal complex of dispossession at once. Again, when he talks of "enterprises," he, in fact, is talking about whole living communities with all the necessary supportive social services. In a more narrow sense, he refers to the self-government movement and its failure to protect the firms against the attacks by the neoliberal state. He correctly registers the fragmentation of working-class power around 1990 and its failures in the face of the emerging liberal state-making project under Western capitalist vassalage.

But for all his experientially based insights into the liberal complex of dispossession in Poland, he all but ignores the way in which this outcome was to some extent intentionally inscribed by the communist generals when they introduced worker self-management and cut the links between local worker sodalities and national dissidents. The growing control by worker constituencies over factories was clearly not anticipated by the regime, which underestimated the cohesiveness of working-class communities and overestimated its own legitimacy. But the displacement of the point of struggle from the national center down to the single local firm, and the erasure of the dangerous liaisons between them, was shrewdly intended and subsequently guaranteed by military rule and repression. Thus, the conditions that allowed worker groups to repossess assets from the communist state were the same conditions that subsequently prevented them from fighting in concerted ways against dispossession by the liberal state (see the chapters by Carbonella and Kasmir in this book for related arguments about local bargaining and the disempowerment in relation to larger conditions in the

US context). Remember that it had been precisely the worker–dissident alliance that had made the 1980 national rebellion possible in the first place (see Kubik 1994; Ost 1990; among others). Cut off from its civil base in working-class communities, the intelligentsia, now nurtured by the generals and their technocrats and selectively put in control of the state by a dying regime in 1988–1989, did exactly what the communist generals had scripted for it: it turned against the local working-class owner-occupiers, destroyed their cohesion, power, and emergent alliances, attacked their "public credit" and reputation, and secured their assets for the state, of which they themselves were now increasingly the "owner-occupiers." Zadrozny will understandably not picture this longer-run logic of almost scripted fragmentation. It would be a devastating insight for him; the cynical flip side of the victorious ascent of local self-management. That is why he must sense conspiracy or at least perverse complicity of the "liberal intellectuals" with the generals. Before picking up Zadrozny's narrative, I discuss one last aspect of how resistance had been undermined by the institutionalization of self-management itself, an aspect that helps elucidate his disappointments.

As self-management got consolidated, a predictable shift occurred in leading personalities. And this shift contributed significantly to the lack of mobilization and popular energy after 1989. Zadrozny, the vocational teacher, was recognized as an honorable fighter for living in truth and had the trust of his coworkers, but the technicalities of self-managing a mid-tech firm with around ten thousand workers (in the mid-1980s) inevitably brought people to the fore with a different habitus. In that shift, Zadrozny rightly felt that some other people were better qualified to lead than he was. His sister, Malgorzata Calinska, a strong woman and a bookkeeper in the accounting department, was brought in and successfully used the symbol of kinship to ask for a transfer of workers' trust from her brother to her, which she received and retained until at least 2008. She is still a democratically chosen paid union representative in Polar (and a national political backbench figure in the right-wing coalition). Zbigniew Kostecki, working at the department of quality control and with an MA in economics in hand, was asked to lead the workers' council; later he became the chairman of Polar's supervisory board and a director of a large local firm. The Wroclaw-wide club of the leaders of self-management, which had emerged in the later 1980s to answer the need for more coordination among self-management activists, was chaired by Andrzej Piszel. He had a managerial position in the computer firm Elwro and a university degree in computer science and later became a member of the national parliament and a successful entrepreneur. But these were not the people who would mobilize working-class communities to fight a regime still seen as their own democratic achievement and hailed by the wider world as an example of successful peaceful political transition. Certainly, Kostecki and Piszel tended to retrospectively view worker self-management as an intermediate technical solution to the problems of a centrally led economy on its way to full marketization rather than as a popular claim for justice, as it was for Zadrozny and his coworkers.

I continue with Zadrozny's narrative at the precise point at which it broke off above:

> Now it is all coming out, that it was prepared by the Secret Services. But this knowledge should have been there before. I was saying this but nobody listened. When people raised critical voices they were set apart as lunatics. I still work in production and I was always chided, first for [Lech] Walesa's betrayal, then for the corruption of AWS [the political party coalition Akcja Wyborcza Solidarnosc (Solidarity Electoral Action)]. And it was me who had to excuse their failures while those high up did not have to excuse themselves at all. They were uninterested. I am surprised that all these smart people find lustration unimportant.

He explains that, because crucial things were never investigated, including the choice of who would be at the Round Table and all that came after, accusations can always be lodged. The press, in turn, will immediately turn them into a spectacle, which destroys reputations and politics but never leads to more insight into how and why things actually happened. In this vision, widely shared among my informants, the secret services become the actual agencies behind the scene, profiting in corrupt ways from privatization and controlling all sorts of knowledge about persons. When groups organize politically and become an obstacle for inside networks, Zadrozny argues, the secret services can always break them apart by releasing bits of information about their members or concocting falsehoods. "And then finally all the scandals are supposed to discredit lustration itself because, as you can see, everyone has done it" (see also Los and Zybertowicz 2000).

Many people were compromised under communism because they were concerned about their career, Zadrozny explains. "But you do not necessarily need to have a career. Just live in truth!" And he continues with a story about his own illegal company journal, *Our Home*, in the 1980s:

We actually cleared things up. We investigated. But now there are a lot of lies. And the press has been given away while we are passive onlookers. This is just outrageous, giving away the press and the banks [90 percent of which are foreign owned]. There is a good chance that the banks started steering privatization for their own ends when they at once shortened the payback periods of loans in the early '90s. For us at Polar it became at once impossible to pay. I was not against Solidarnosc entering politics. But Solidarnosc entered politics without doing politics. I have always thought that politics should be everywhere. Different people, not just liberals, should have been at the Round Table, people less eager to strike a deal.

Thus, the Round Table, so cherished in the liberal press worldwide as peaceful transition, comes to signify nothing less than popular betrayal by actors handpicked by the socialist generals for their willingness to make "deals"; in other words, the opposite of "living in truth." Since 1998, Zadrozny has identified with the far-right party of the League of Polish Families, which he sees as not yet morally compromised, and he became a big supporter of former President Lech Kaczynski and his brother Jaroslaw. He was utterly disappointed by the weakness of Solidarnosc and its right-wing parliamentary branch, the AWS party, in 1997–1998. He was, first of all, disappointed about the actual paths and outcomes of privatization. Neither Solidarnosc nor AWS was willing to do politics and take privatization out of its neoliberal orbit. Polar was first "X-rayed" against Western standards by McKinsey. Then, after 30 percent of its jobs were axed, it was pushed into the hands of a French investor who was reluctant to commit investments or even sign a "social package." It was the refusal to do the latter, in particular, that hurt the old unionists at Polar. It at once made clear to them that they had lost all institutional clout and were at the full mercy of market forces. The French owner went bankrupt in the early 2000s, and Polar could be cherry-picked, without much negotiation, by Whirlpool.

But, ultimately, Zadrozny's disappointment was about far more than Polar's acquisition by foreign corporations, just as factories and self-management used to be about far more than mere production for the market. It was about self-government, community, *Our Home*, and about human value at large. Zadrozny narrates a long story of decline of neighborhoods, of safety, of sports, of youth, and of the rise of criminality. He strongly believes that the ex-communist security forces benefited from street crime, hooliganism, and fear and happily let them thrive. In his neighborhood homeowners' associations are asked to pay extra contributions to the police if they want to have better security. And they all pay. Fear makes people weak and makes them long for the beautiful past of communism, he claims, a popular nostalgia that he as previous anti-communist fighter is contemptuous of. He sometimes serves as a court juror and remarks that the courts are heavily underfunded, not able to deal with the pressures on society at all. Zadrozny, the vocational teacher and basketball trainer, deplores the demoralization of working-class youth, and he slips finally into a glorification of Jozef Pilsudski, the interwar Polish populist dictator with socialist leanings, and compares him favorably against the current regime. He then jumps to excess: "If we were to put the middle-ranking communists in prison (as supposedly Pilsudski would have done), then the margin of error would have been negligible. The vast majority was corrupted. They are simply unfit for patriots."

Fighting Amnesia with the Kaczynskis

Zadrozny therefore cheered up during the creation of the Kaczinskis' right-wing populist government in 2005. The Kaczsyinski brothers, dubbed by the *Economist* magazine Europe's "Terrible Twins," brought a resurgent Right to power with precisely the election themes that were close to Zadrozny's heart. In fact, the Kaczynskis finally lifted the anger and concerns of Zadrozny's class and generation out of the local communities and onto the level of the nation-state. They combined nationalist and protective economic policies, conservative family and gender policies, and zero-tolerance and anticrime positions with vitriolic anti–European Union reflexes and authoritarian fantasies of "lustration." Their policy visions culminated in an assertive anti-German stance within the European Union, mobilizations against the emergent European Constitutional Treaty, which supposedly would corrupt Polish sovereignty, and anti-liberal diatribes. Most spectacularly, their law-and-order vision was not conveniently restricted to the petty street crime of neighborhood youth but extended to exposing the middle and top-level corruption that people like Zadrozny had been singling out for years.

Populists are fighting official and imposed amnesia, by definition. That is because the historical and cultural narratives of the new liberal regimes inevitably obscure the actual cultural and material dispossession that has been going on. The Kaczynski government adopted this stance, and it therefore invited the contempt of liberals in Poland and elsewhere. The Kaczynskis engineered two excellent occasions for fighting amnesia. The first was based in the attack on the secret services and their collaborators and was aimed at the imposed historical amnesia of the "thick line"; the second concerned the amnesia about poverty and social rights and was instantiated in struggles around the Equality Parade in Warsaw. Both had strong working-class connotations and resonance.

The Kaczynski regime was, above all, meant to be the end of the "thick line" that leading ex-dissident liberals like Michnik and Geremek had defended all through the1990s. The thick line, in Polish parlance, refers to the no-blame, no-punishment policy in relation to past behavior, agreed to in the Round Table pact between the "chosen" democrats and the socialist generals. None of my working-class informants in Wroclaw ever said a good word about the policy of the thick line.[11] Without exception, they favored "lustration" and punishment. The Kaczynski government channeled these popular and populist feelings into the creation of a very well-endowed anticorruption watchdog that, among other tasks, compiled a register of some seven hundred thousand Polish individuals suspected of collaboration with the communist secret services. Very tellingly, the most prominent potential traitor in the eyes of the Kaczynski government was Geremek, by now a widely respected former minister of foreign affairs, a professor of history, a member of the European Parliament, and an active participant in liberal–conservative European think tanks. Geremek was among hundreds of thousands of academics, judges, administrators, engineers, and businesspeople who were summoned to submit declarations that they were not guilty of collaboration, an intentional inversion of the liberal procedures for establishing innocence and guilt: suspicion was sufficient for an accusation, and proof had to be shown to refute a suspicion. The full Western press joined *Gazeta Wyborcza*, Michnik's liberal daily, in a sustained public outcry against the demeaning picture of Geremek, for some, the icon of dissident incorruptibility, pushed into submission by a populist government in Warsaw and desperately pleading his innocence before a hardly friendly committee of populists, judging him under the eyes of a less than civil media public.

But, of course, as Buchowski (2006) would appreciate, it was both the material history as well as the public culture of working-class dispossession that worked to place Geremek in the top position on the corruption list. This was all posed as the Polish ethnic nation taking revenge on those of its own who had sold it out, socialists as well as liberals. There was an ominous underlying, if not explicit, message to the Polish liberal elite in this: that it might not have been you who were "the people" in 1989, but we. Zadrozny agreed wholeheartedly.

Consider in this context the symbolism of the Equality Parade, previously called the "Gay Parade." This international parade was intentionally scheduled to take place in post-socialist Warsaw to challenge then mayor Lech Kaczynski's "anti-multiculturalism." Mayor Kaczynski had forbidden the parade in 2004 and 2005, his refusal spiced up with politically incorrect anti-liberal and anti-gay rhetoric. A youth organization associated with the League of Polish Families (a conservative Catholic organization), had beaten up local parade participants in the years before. West European political classes from the multicultural Left had intervened and had officially warned Warsaw about spreading "intolerance." That pressure helped secure the event for 2006 and 2007, which now included the participation of high-level Western politicians, mostly from the German Greens, under the banner of promoting human rights in Poland. The League of Polish Families, however, was allowed to schedule a counterdemonstration at the same time. Zadrozny participated in it. He was annoyed by the multicultural and human rights imagery sponsored by the European Union. "Why is the EU making so much fuss about that parade," he asked? "Nobody in Brussels says a word if Polish workers starve on low wages, have to work like dogs, and get exploited." In contrast, the "Equality Parade" was seen among his imputed politically correct liberals as a measure of Poland's belonging in Europe.

For him, apparently, the Equality Parade was a travesty that served another important amnesia. He recalled that the *equality* in the title of this parade once meant a concern with broad social rights, which included multicultural and gay rights among a wider palette of social justice struggles. And he therefore hinted at Western Europe's forgetfulness of its own history of social struggle. Many of my informants in Wroclaw would have concurred. Of course, a clash of class often surrounds multicultural events such as gay parades. From the point of view of post-socialist industrial workers, who had lost control over their factories and communities, had barely saved their skins in the collapse of their industries, and had been confined to a life of hard work and material stagnation in a hostile public environment that openly fetishized consumption, they appeared as rituals extolling the pleasure of licentious, free-choice consumerism. They were part of a festival of never-ending free circulation, as it were. Not just a circulation of objects, however, but of objectified intimate relations. Workers' lives taught different lessons, Zadrozny seemed to imply. One of those lessons was the importance of solidarity within families and among trusted friends rather than of free circulation. Free circulation had turned out to be precisely a threat to solidarity, trust, and intimacy. Another lesson was that the liberal promise of mass consumption had simply been false and that the opportunities of a world of endless circulation and unlimited pleasure had been very unfairly distributed. The Equality Parade seemed not just an indecent public act, as it was for the Polish Catholic church. It was, rather, an indecent public myth that served to silence the Polish popular reality of scarcity, of toil, and of confinement for many; a reality that received much less attention and respect from the European Union and the Polish elite, they felt, than that frivolous parade. Hence, it was again a case of public amnesia. A festival used as a signifier to obscure an uncomfortable reality. And the Polish ethnic nation was again positioned against the promiscuous cosmopolitans who were pictured as literally willing to sell themselves out to everybody.[12]

History Still Repeating Itself

Throughout our conversations, Zadrozny pointed out several times that "history repeats itself." Polish people have lost their sovereignty and dignity repeatedly throughout history, and he firmly doubts whether an end to national victimization will be found in this era of liberal capitalist globalization. "The power is still the same," he argues. "There is big disillusionment. Also I am disillusioned. We thought that if some Western companies come in, there will be good order and justice and that all these things so typical of socialism would be over; like petty fighting for pay-raises, all that petty bargaining. We thought it would be wisely and humanely ordered."

In 2005, Polar was taken over by Whirlpool. Wroclaw will become the main European production and development location of this US oligopolist in the white-goods sector. Substantial investments are finally being made in new production lines, machinery, and buildings. Nevertheless, Zadrozny is often addressed by fellow workers about the stepped-up productivity norms and the petty despotism on the shop floor. "It is just abnormal," he says, invoking the symbolic heritage of the workers' fight for "normality."

> Certain things from communism, such as the singular focus on productivity, on work, and not on the human being, are persisting. This is an American firm but it is a beggars' firm. The West should imply quality. They all complain

about socialism, but these masters nowadays seem just hell-bent to churn out these five hundred items—everything has become so tense and tight. Compared with socialism, our current piecework norms are much tougher. And the style of being a master derives directly from socialism. The worst aspects of communism are retained and are combined with the worst things from the West.

Real wages on the shop floor have hardly risen since 1997, when we started research. They are still just over 300 euros (roughly $400) per month. Our interviews with workers, personnel directors and local researchers indicate that production-line wages had completely stagnated at least until early 2007. In fact, Zadrozny's generation has experienced generalized and lifelong stagnation in earnings. Against that, there had been a 700 percent rise in productivity per worker in the Polar-Whirlpool factory as a whole in the three years since Whirlpool took over. New investments certainly played a role in this, but so too did a notable hierarchization of the shop floor. The number of overseers, who impose work discipline, had roughly doubled. Such bosses now earned wages that were often twice as high as those of line workers, something unheard of in the past. Workers cannot remember that labor had ever been so stressful before. Union people note that young workers find the pace of work very hard to bear and often leave the factory after a few weeks. Zadrozny, the teacher and sports trainer, often helps them to control their bodies, energy, and concentration, but even the best of them need three full weeks to learn to cope with the pressure, and they need months to get used to it.

He is genuinely concerned:

> Young people have been cheated. They studied hard but still can't get decent jobs here. It is a rat race. Young people and their potentials have been exploited. I think there is gross disappointment. On the one hand there were great promises, but in fact very little has been delivered. There is this shallowness of life and the old role models are falling apart. There is less patriotism. It is easy for people just to leave, to migrate. They are not held back by anything. They even make kids abroad, but not here. And they do not appreciate the unions that we've built. But we could have gone so much further! If only we didn't have to bother about certain things [the Soviet Union, in 1988–1989], we could have turned it all upside down, formed a government of our own, a parliament earlier. All these antilabor regulations would not have been so advanced and the employers that were coming in would have been coming on different terms. And that, ultimately, is the great loss. People were willing. There was zest. We could have been building a new society. And I think that this is what the Poles expected to happen. It was just like after the war. There was this re-building atmosphere and people had

the will to switch to another system and to other habits too. But I guess it didn't work out too well. Wild capitalism emerged. It was all great on the surface but on the inside it was not the human relations that we craved.

Conclusion

In this chapter I have focused on one particular Polish path to right-wing working-class resentment. I have shown how analyzing critical junctions among Wolf's levels of structural, tactical, and agential power through time and space can help to build an anthropology of labor that can unlock the hidden and entangled histories of disenfranchisement, dispossession, and resistance that feed the current anger articulated in Central European right-wing populisms. This helps one to recognize that dominant celebratory discourses of successful democratization, economic growth, transition, and EU accession in Central and Eastern Europe obscure local histories of dispossession and de-democratization that force themselves onstage via biting populisms that are increasingly shaking the post-political liberal-cosmopolitan scene in uncanny ways. In its general properties this is far from a typical Polish story. Similar though always necessarily different critical junctions of disenfranchisement create similar, though always different, bouts of political havoc elsewhere in the post-socialist region (Kalb and Halmai 2011). Petrovici has shown how the city of Cluj in Romania drifted into twelve long years of vigorously nationalist rule (1992–2004) as ethnic political brokers displaced working-class anxiety over the collapse of socialist industry and the consequent spread of unemployment, poverty and informalization onto claims to their "eternal" right to modern urban citizenship (Petrovici 2011). Vetta (2011) told us how the Serbian city of Kikinda in 2004, the very same year in which it won the OSCE award for multicultural tolerance, shifted en masse to voting for the radical nationalist party of Seselj for whom even Milosevic was a moderate: It was the only party that openly dared denounce the "theft" and destruction of local factories by European capital. Socialist factories were assets on which local modernity had depended for a generation and for which no substitute was offered beyond an abstract story of European humanist values. Hungary as a whole, meanwhile, was increasingly embracing nationalist populism of both the radical (the Jobbik party and affiliated uniformed vigilantes) and the slightly more genteel variants (Fidesz) as narratives of social decline, theft, crime, and corruption all but overwhelmed the elite liberal consensus of 1989–2009. Such narratives were grounded, as Halmai (2011) and

Bartha (2011) have shown, in creeping processes of material and cultural dispossession.

Such eventful stories are not at all limited to the post-socialist world (see Kalb and Halmai 2011): in northern and western Europe comparable processes have been playing out in the Netherlands, in Denmark, in France, Italy, Norway, and Finland. The recent "True Finns" movement is a fascinating example: the collapsing paper mill economy in Southeastern Finland led ex–trade unionists to become interested in a religiously inspired neo-nationalism that extols healthy Finnishness against alien influences and against the supposed slackers of Southern Europe in the EU; this is a situation where neither immigrants nor ethnic minorities were even at hand to project anger upon. It reminds us of the basic insight that it is not the presence of political scapegoats that help explain the process, it is the anthropology of labor and dispossession that allows us to see where the motivations come from, how they emerge over time, how they are embedded in real life trajectories, and how they get articulated, displaced and distorted by right-wing political brokers after left wing alternatives have been ruled out, have bankrupted themselves, or have just lost traction.

I conclude with a note on recent developments in the anthropology of post-socialism. In this field, contrary to earlier trends (see Kalb 2002), there is a recent sprinkling of cultural essentialism and old style substantivism going on; perhaps, one suspects, in response to the rise of populist non-liberal subjectivities studied in this chapter. A recent publication from an author who has done excellent work on relatively poor older people in East German towns (Thelen 2007) rejects an earlier focus on analytic questions of property, shortage economies, regional development paths etcetera, and advocates a search for "genuine anthropological theory" to assess how socialist subjectivities were radically different as compared to subjectivities in capitalism (Thelen 2011). She takes her cue from Marilyn Strathern's work on the "non-Western" subjectivities of Melanesians, who seem to be much more relationally oriented than the typical modern Western ego-centered subject. (Post)-socialist persons, the argument goes, were genuinely and humanly attached to their colleagues in the collaborative work groups on which socialist labor processes relied. Hence her subjects do not feel at home in the new, anonymous, and alienating relationships of the East German towns that were swallowed by West German capitalism.

I easily concur with this last purely empirical observation. But on a theoretical level we should resolutely reject the return to "culture and personality" studies placed against an imagined background of cohesive ethnographic culture areas. In fact, in empirical terms I would rather go well beyond Thelen's claim: socialist urban subjects were often not just attached to the people they worked with, they were even in a rather sober way simply enchanted by the idea of "people's property," as I showed in this chapter, even though they were disillusioned about its actual practice. They were also positively inclined toward the idea of worker self-government. In Poland people sometimes even put their lives on the line for trying to realize it. And people remember this and not just in an agonistic way; such recollections often continue to inform their present politics, albeit in hardly predictable ways. In short, post-socialist subjects indeed entertain visions of the good life and the just society that are not smoothly consonant with capitalist ideologies. But so what? Should this mean that post-socialist subjects are therefore essentially different from something like the "modal western personality"? Where is class and labor in this vision? Who has ever suggested that working classes in the West are essentially enthralled by endless accumulation and limitless circulation and not somehow personally attached to their colleagues or living spaces or actual work contexts? This is an old-style Cold War perspective on cultural difference: an orientalism depending on an occidentalism. What is absent here is a purchase on the anthropology of labor, class, and the contradictory lived experiences and politics to which labor, in any mode of production and accumulation, must give rise. Vulnerable people everywhere tend to feel real attachments to what they have, to whom they know, and to whom and what they can trust. And they do not like to let that habitual context go just on behalf of the supposed pleasures and virtues of circulation without end. We do not need a Central or East European essentialist exceptionalism to be aware of such basic starting points. What this chapter has also shown is that an anthropology of labor and class that fails to work through the dynamic critical junctions of nested power fields, and instead bases itself on conventional place-based synchronous ethnography of "communities," "local knowledges," and "ontologies," will predictably fall in the politically perverse trap of "essential otherness."[13]

Acknowledgments

This article is based on intermittent periods of local research and interviewing over a period of ten years, sponsored by the Netherlands Science Organization (1997–2001) and Central European University's Research Board (2007). I am deeply grateful for the research support offered by Herman Tak, Ewa Tak-Ignaczak, and Kacper Poblocki. I have enormously benefited from comments from, and discussions with, Istvan Adorjan, Eszter Bartha, Johanna Bockman, Glenn Bowman, Gus Carbonella, Jan Drahokoupil, Doug Holmes, Marc Edelman, Sharryn Kasmir, Tamas Kraus, Lesley Gill, Mathijs Pelkmans, David Ost, Kacper Poblocki, Tony Robben, Oscar Salemink, Gavin Smith, Luisa Steur, Sid Tarrow, Katherine Verdery, and Nico Wilterdink. I thank the editors of this volume for their editorial acumen and for the chance to participate in the undertaking.

Notes

1. From 1997 to 2000, I worked with small teams of interviewers, following a snowball method set in train by two key informants involved in Solidarnosc labor unions. We interviewed some sixty local workers at length, often two or more times, sometimes at their homes, sometimes at the factory premises or in Solidarnosc office. We also interviewed labor union leaders at the *Polar* factory, personnel managers, specialists on the local economy, and leaders of self-management. In 2007, Kacper Poblocki and I did extensive follow-up interviews with twenty-five of our informants and with some of their children. Other sources we consulted were private archives of activists (see below) and (unsystematically) the local and national press.
2. Rather, then, than giving a "definition" of these notions, I will try to show their "meaning" in situated and class structured practice in the course of this chapter.
3. Zadrozny received an important medal of honor from President Kaczynski in 2009.
4. I am grateful to Johanna Bockman and Dora Vetta for pointing out to me that similar meanings of the symbol of privatization were current among Yugoslav workers at the time; see also Uvalic (1997). Professor Tamas Krausz (personal communication, June 2008) confirms that, in Hungary, workers' management was, for a short while around 1988–1989, popularly felt to be an option. Bill Lomax (1980), Paul Lendvai (2008), and others have shown that the Hungarian revolution in 1956 was not just about sovereignty and democracy but also very much about worker councils opposing the Stalinist command economy.
5. This history is based on interviews with Andrzej Piszel and Zbigniew Kostecki, two key actors, as well as on Kostecki's private archive of newspaper clippings and other writings on worker self-management from the early 1980s to early 1990s. I am very grateful to Kostecki for allowing us to see these materials.
6. How seriously worker collectives identified with their role of owners can be sensed from the fact that workers in *Polar* made significant savings on their wage fund to modernize its production lines and launch a new dishwasher plant, the kind of behavior well-known from studies of worker cooperatives such as Mondragón in Spain. The first thing Whirlpool did after its takeover in 2005 was relocating precisely that dishwasher's line to Slovakia: the symbolic politics of transnational capital and its contested ownership claims.
7. My oral research generated extensive insight into the politics of privatization of *Polar* workers, who basically tried to keep a branch investor from taking over the firm after transnational corporations such as Siemens had killed off the large local Pafawag firm and after Elwro, the computer maker, had been destroyed too. They also tried to secure as many shares in Polar as possible for themselves as a group (not individual-

ized shares), which ultimately left them with 15 percent. The state got the rest after it floated Polar on the Warsaw stock exchange and sold 35 percent to Brandt, the French investor that went bankrupt in the early 2000s. I have no space here to go into this. But the intensity of workers' sustained mobilization and consultation about the particular choices in the privatization of "their" plant must be emphasized.

8. The debt, in the end, got substantially reduced in two waves in the early and mid-1990s. Western creditors had kept up the pressure on the debt from 1989 to 1992 and had waited to alter its terms until the new regime had fully implemented the emerging Washington Consensus agenda of trade liberalization and fiscal stabilization and crucial choices in the direction of wholesale privatization had been made. When the communists were voted back into power in 1993, the West panicked and decided it had to cut the debt to keep Poland, and, with it, perhaps the whole of Eastern Europe, in the Western camp and to prevent it from slipping out of control. Poland was the first nation to be so kindly served by the "international community." Significantly, Yugoslavia was denied similar treatment, which contributed in multiple ways to its violent implosion (see Woodward 1994). After 2000, as a consequence of the successful Jubilee Debt Campaign, some African nations received "debt forgiveness," followed up under strict guidance by the World Bank. Left-wing economists agree that the failure of rapid all-over-the-board privatization in Poland, a consequence of strong popular opposition combined with the reduction of the debt, explains a good part of Polish economic success after 2000.

9. I served as director of the Soco program at the Institute for Human Sciences in Vienna and, as such, was part of the "Ten Years After" celebration. Soco was a support program for social policy research in East Central Europe and was funded by the Ford Foundation and the Austrian Federal Chancellery. Soco was one of the Western responses to the surprise election of the postcommunists in 1993 in Poland. To some extent it was a product of Western panic.

10. The exception was the Catholic ex–prime minister of Poland, Tadeusz Mazowiecki, whose duty it was to announce the shock-therapy program in the parliament in September 1989 and who still suffered visibly from the recollection. See also Klein (2007: 180–181).

11. John Borneman (1997) argued correctly that post-socialist regimes would suffer from legitimacy problems generated by the impunity conferred by the "thick line." He also partly foresaw that such problems would be deflected onto "cultural others," including other nations and minorities. However, he did not foresee that "liberals" would be turned into "cultural aliens" and "traitors" by populist nationalists. See also Narotzky and Smith (2006) on working-class dissatisfaction with impunity and how, combined with neoliberal restructuring, it creates problems for regime legitimacy in post-fascist Spain.

12. It should be superfluous to add that I do not necessarily agree with my informants here. There is no necessary contradiction between social rights, multicultural rights and gay rights, of course.

13. For a more or less similar argument against postcolonial studies see Chibber (2013).

References

Anderson, Perry. 2009. *The New Old Europe*. London: Verso Books.
Appadurai, Arjun. 1996. *Modernity at Large*. Minneapolis: University of Minnesota Press.
———. 2006. *Fear of Small Numbers: An Essay on the Geography of Anger*. Durham, NC: Duke University Press.
Arrighi, Giovanni. 1996. *The Long Twentieth Century: Money, Power and the Origins of our Time*. London: Verso Books.

Bartha, Eszter. 2011. "'It Can't Make Me Happy that Audi is Prospering': Working-Class Nationalism in Hungary after 1989." In *Headlines of Nation, Subtexts of Class: Working Class Populism and the Return of the Repressed in Neoliberal Europe*, ed. Don Kalb and Gabor Halmai. Oxford: Berghahn Books.

Berezin, Mabel. 2009. *Illiberal Politics in Neoliberal Times: Culture, Security and Populism in the New Europe*. Cambridge: Cambridge University Press.

Betz, Hans-Georg. 1994. *Radical Right-Wing Populism in Western Europe*. New York: Palgrave Macmillan.

Borneman, John. 1997. *Settling Accounts: Violence, Justice, and Accountability in Postsocialist Europe*. Princeton: Princeton University Press.

Brenner, Robert. 2003. *The Boom and the Bubble: The US in the World Economy*. London: Verso Books.

Buchowski, Michal. 2006. "The Specter of Orientalism in Europe: From Exotic Other to Stigmatized Brother." *Anthropological Quarterly* 79, no 3: 463–482.

Buroway, Michael. 1985. *Politics of Production*. London, Verso.

Canovan, Margaret. 1999. "Trust the People! Populism and the Two Faces of Democracy." *Political Studies* 47: 2–16.

Carrier, James G., ed. 2006. *A Handbook of Economic Anthropology*. Cheltenham: Edward Elgar Publishing.

Carrier, James, and Don Kalb, eds. Forthcoming. *Anthropologies of Class*. Cambridge: Cambridge University Press.

Chibber, Vivek. 2013. *Postcolonial Theory and the Specter of Capital*. London: Verso Books.

Crouch, Colin. 2004. *Postdemocracy*. London: Polity Press.

Di Tella, Torcuato. 1997. "Populism into the Twenty-first Century." *Government and Opposition* 32: 187–200.

Dumenil, Gerard, and Dominique Levy. 2004. *Capital Resurgent: Roots of the Neoliberal Revolution*. Cambridge, MA: Harvard University Press.

Dumenil, Gerard, and Dominique Levy. 2011. *The Crisis of Neoliberalism*. Cambridge, MA: Harvard University Press.

Ekiert, Grzegorz. 1996. *The State Against Society: Political Crises and Their Aftermath in East Central Europe*. Princeton: Princeton University Press.

Ekiert, Grzegorz, and Jan Kubik. 1999. *Rebellious Civil Society. Popular Protest and Democratic Consolidation in Poland 1989–1993*. Ann Arbor: University of Michigan Press.

Friedman, Jonathan, ed. 2003. *Globalization, the State and Violence*. Walnut Creek, CA: Altamira Press.

Friedman, Kajsa Ekholm, and J. Friedman. 2008a. *Modernities, Class, and the Contradictions of Globalization. The Anthropology of Global Systems*. Lanham, MD: Altamira Press.

———. 2008b. *Historical Transformations. The Anthropology of Global Systems*. Lanham, MD: Altamira Press.

Gingrich, Andre, and Marcus Banks, eds. 2005. *Neo-Nationalism in Europe and Beyond: Perspectives from Social Anthropology*. New York: Berghahn Books.

Gudeman, Stephen. 2008. *Economy's Tension: The Dialectics of Community and Market*. New York: Berghahn Books.

Halmai, Gabor. 2011. "(Dis)possessed by the Spectre of Socialism: Nationalist Mobilization in 'Transitional' Hungary." In *Headlines of Nation, Subtexts of Class: Working Class Populism and the Return of the Repressed in Neoliberal Europe*, ed. Don Kalb and Gabor Halmai. Oxford: Berghahn Books.

Hann, Chris. 2006. *Not the Horse We Wanted: Post-socialism, Neo-Liberalism, and Eurasia*. Münster: LitVerlag.

Hann, Chris and Keith Hart, eds. 2009. *Market and Society: The Great Transformation Today*. Cambridge: Cambridge University Press.

Harvey, David. 2003. *The New Imperialism*. Oxford: Oxford University Press.

———. 2005. *A Brief History of Neoliberalism*. Oxford: Oxford University Press.

———. 2010. *The Enigma of Capital and the Crisis of Capitalism*. London: Profile Books.
Jessop, Bob. 2002. *The Future of the Capitalist State*. Cambridge: Polity Press.
Kalb, Don. 1997. *Expanding Class: Power and Everyday Politics in Industrial Communities, The Netherlands 1850–1950*. Durham, NC: Duke University Press.
———. 2000. "Localizing Flows: Power, Paths, Institutions, and Networks." In *The Ends of Globalization*, ed. Don Kalb, et al. Boulder and London: Rowman and Littlefield.
———. 2002. "Afterword: Globalism and Postsocialist Prospects." In *Postsocialism: Ideals, Ideologies and Practices in Eurasia*, ed. Chris Hann. London: Routledge.
———. 2005. "From Flows to Violence: Politics and Knowledge in the Debates on Globalization and Empire." *Anthropological Theory* 5, no. 2: 176–204.
———. 2009a. "Conversations with a Polish Populist: Tracing Hidden Histories of Globalization, Class, and Dispossession in Post-Socialism (and Beyond)." *American Ethnologist* 36, no. 2: 207–223.
———. 2009b. "Headlines of Nationalism, Subtexts of Class: Poland and Popular Paranoia, 1989–2009." *Antropologica* 51, no. 2: 289–301.
Kalb, Don, et al., eds. 2000. *The Ends of Globalization: Bringing Society Back In*. Boulder, CO: Rowman and Littlefield.
Kalb, Don, and Herman Tak, eds. 2005. *Critical Junctions: Anthropology and History beyond the Cultural Turn*. New York: Berghahn Books.
Kalb, Don, and Gabor Halmai, eds. 2011. *Headlines of Nation, Subtexts of Class: Working Class Populism and the Return of the Repressed in Neoliberal Europe*. Oxford: Berghahn Books.
Kenney, Padraic. 2003. *A Carnival of Revolution: Central Europe 1989*. Princeton: Princeton University Press.
Kideckel, David. 2002. "The Unmaking of an East-Central European Working Class." In *Postsocialism: Ideals, Ideologies and Practices in Eurasia*, ed. Chris Hann. London: Routledge.
———. 2007. *Getting by in Postsocialist Romania: Labor, the Body, and Working Class Culture*. Bloomington: Indiana University Press.
Klein, Naomi. 2007. *The Shock Doctrine: The Rise of Disaster Capitalism*. London: Penguin Books.
Kolakowski, Leszek. 1999. "Amidst Moving Ruins." In *The Revolutions of 1989*, ed. Vladimir Tismaneanu. London: Routledge.
Kornai, Janos. 1980. *The Economics of Shortage*. Amsterdam: North Holland Publishing.
Kotkin, Stephen, and Jan Gross. 2009. *Uncivil Society: 1989 and the Implosion of the Communist Establishment*. New York: Random House.
Kubik, Jan. 1994. *The Power of Symbols against the Symbols of Power: The Rise of Solidarity and the Fall of State Socialism in Poland*. University Park: The Pennsylvania State University Press.
Lendvai, Paul. 2008. *One Day that Shook the Communist World: The 1956 Hungarian Uprising and Its Legacy*. Princeton: Princeton University Press.
Lomax, Bill. 1980. *Eye-Witness in Hungary: The Soviet Invasion of 1956*. Nottingham: Spokesman Books.
Los, Maria and Andreiz Zybertowicz. 2001. *Privatizing the Police State: The Case of Poland*. Basingstoke: Palgrave Macmillan.
Mouffe, Chantal. 2005. *The Return of the Political*. London: Verso Books.
Mudde, Cas. 2007. *Populist Radical Right Parties in Europe*. Cambridge: Cambridge University Press.
Narotzky, Susana, and Gavin Smith. 2006. *Immediate Struggles: People, Power, and Place in Rural Spain*. Berkeley: University of California Press.
Ost, David. 1990. *Solidarity and the Politics of Anti-Politics: Opposition and Reform in Poland since 1968*. Philadelphia: Temple University Press.

———. 2005. *The Defeat of Solidarity: Anger and Politics in Postcommunist Europe*. Ithaca: Cornell University Press.
Petrovici, Norbert. 2011. "Articulating the Right to the City: Working Class Neo-Nationalism in Postsocialist Cluj, Romania." In *Headlines of Nation, Subtexts of Class: Working Class Populism and the Return of the Repressed in Neoliberal Europe*, ed. Don Kalb and Gabor Halmai. Oxford: Berghahn Books.
Piccone, Paul. 1993. "Confronting the French New Right: Old Prejudices or a New Political Paradigm?" *Telos* 98/99: 3–23.
Poznanski, Kazimierz. 1996. *Poland's Protracted Transition: Institutional Change and Economic Growth, 1970–1994*. Cambridge: Cambridge University Press.
Robotham, Donald. 2009. "Afterword: Learning from Polanyi 2." In *Market and Society: The Great Transformation Today*, ed. Chris Hann and Keith Hart. Cambridge: Cambridge University Press.
Sassen, Saskia. 2007. *A Sociology of Globalization*. New York: Norton.
Silver, Beverly. 2003. *Forces of Labor: Workers' Movements and Globalization since 1870*. Cambridge: Cambridge University Press.
Smith, Gavin. 2006. "When the Logic of Capital is the Real that Lurks in the Background." *Current Anthropology* 47, no. 4: 621–639.
Szalai, E. 2008. *New Capitalism, and What Can Replace It*. Budapest: Pallas.
Sztompka, Piotr. 1993. "Civilizational Incompetence: The Trap of Post-Communist Societies." *Zeitschrift für Soziologie* 22, no. 2: 85–95.
———. 1996. "Looking Back: The Year 1989 as a Cultural and Civilizational Break." *Communist and Post-Communist Studies* 29, no. 2: 115–129.
Thelen, Tatjana. 2007. "'Veteran Care': Shifting Provision, Needs, and Meanings of Enterprise-centered Pensioner Care in Eastern Germany." *Focaal—European Journal of Anthropology*, no. 50: 35–50.
———. 2011. "Shortage, Fuzzy Property and Other Dead Ends in the Anthropology of (Post)socialism." *Critique of Anthropology* 31, no. 1: 43–61.
Tilly, Charles. 2003. *Contention and Democracy in Europe, 1650–2000*. Cambridge: Cambridge University Press.
Uvalic, Milica. 1997. "Privatization in the Yugoslav Successor States: Converting Self-management into Property Rights." In *Privatization Surprises in Central and Eastern Europe*, ed. Milica Uvalic and Daniel Whitehead-Voughan. Cheltenham: Edward Elgar Publishing.
Verdery, Katherine. 1996. *What Was Socialism and What Comes Next?* Princeton: Princeton University Press.
Vetta, Theodora. 2011. "'Nationalism is Back!' Radikali and Privatization in Serbia." In *Headlines of Nation, Subtexts of Class: Working Class Populism and the Return of the Repressed in Neoliberal Europe*, ed. Don Kalb and Gabor Halmai. Oxford: Berghahn Books.
Wedel, Jeanine. 2001. *Collision and Collusion: The Strange Case of Western Aid to Eastern Europe*. London: Palgrave Macmillan.
Westlind, Dennis. 1996. *The Politics of Popular Identity: Understanding Recent Populist Movements in Sweden and the United States*. Lund: Lund University Press.
Wilk, Richard, and Lisa Cligget. 2007. *Economies and Cultures: Foundations of Economic Anthropology*. Boulder, CO: Westview Press.
Woodward, Susan. 1994. *Balkan Tragedy: Chaos and Dissolution after the Cold War*. Washington, DC: Brookings Institution.
Wolf, Eric. 1990. "1990. Facing Power: Old Insights, New Questions." *American Anthropologist* 92: 586–596.

Contributors

August Carbonella is associate professor of anthropology at Memorial University of Newfoundland. He has published widely on the historical memory of the Viet Nam War, 19th century transatlantic social movements, the historical anthropology of labor, and working class life, politics and organization in the United States.

Lesley Gill is professor of anthropology at Vanderbilt University. She is the author of several books, including *Teetering on the Rim: Global Restructuring, Daily Life, and the Armed Retreat of the Bolivian State* (Colombia 2000) and *The School of the Americas: Military Training and Political Violence in the Americas* (Duke 2004).

Don Kalb is university professor of sociology and social anthropology at Central European University, Budapest, and senior researcher at Utrecht University, the Netherlands. He is the author of *Expanding Class: Power and Everyday Politics in Industrial Communities, The Netherlands, 1850–1950* (Duke 1997) and the editor of several volumes, including *The Ends of Globalization: Bringing Society Back In* (Rowman and Littlefield 2000), *Globalization and Development: Key Issues and Debates* (Kluwer 2004), *Critical Junctions: Anthropology and History beyond the Cultural Turn* (Berghahn 2005), *Headlines of Nation, Subtexts of Class: Working Class Populism and the Return of the Repressed in Neoliberal Europe* (Oxford and New Berghahn Books/EASA Series 2011). He is founding editor of *Focaal: Journal of Global and Historical Anthropology*.

Sharryn Kasmir is professor of anthropology at Hofstra University. She is the author of *The "Myth" of Mondragón: Cooperatives, Politics, and Working Class Life in a Basque Town* (State University of New York Press 1996). She has written about working-class life and politics in the Basque region of Spain and in the southern United States, and she has published several works on the anthropology of labor.

Susana Narotzky is professor of social anthropology at the University of Barcelona, Spain. She has recently published the edited collection *Economías Cotidianas, Economías Sociales, Economías Sostenibles* (Icaria 2013) and various articles, including "Alternatives to Expanded Accumulation and the Anthropological Imagination: Turning Necessity into a Challenge to Capitalism?"; "Europe in Crisis: Grassroots Economies and the Anthropological Turn"; and "Memories of Conflict and Present Day Struggles in Europe: New Tensions between Corporatism, Class, and Social Movements." Her new project "Grassroots Economics: Meaning, Project and Practice in the Pursuit of Livelihood," has been funded by a European Research Council Advanced Grant.

Judy Whitehead is professor of anthropology at the University of Lethbridge. She is the author of *Development and Dispossession in the Narmada Valley* (New Pearson 2010) and coeditor of *Of Property and Propriety: Gender and Class in Colonialism and Nationalism* (University of Toronto 2011). She has published widely on space, power, inequality, and activism in India, including "John Locke and Dispossession in India" (*Journal of Contemporary Asia* 2011), "Inside/Outside Global Accumulation: An Examination of Micro-enterprises in a Mumbai Slum" (*Critique of Anthropology* 2011), and "Is Mumbai a Global, Revanchist City? The Political Economy of Ground Rent in Contemporary Mumbai" (*Anthropologica* 2008).

Index

American Federationist, 97
American Federation of Labor (AFL), 12, 85, 89, 97, 101, 208
American Plan, 80–81, 89
anger, 41, 116n1, 253–255, 275
anti-imperialism, 36, 37, 38
Appadurai, Arjun, 254, 255
AUC (Autodefensas Unidas de Colombia), 50–52, 57, 66
auto industry, US competition with Japan, 204
automation, 82, 105

Balandier, Georges, 8
Balcerowicz, Leszek, 267
Banks, Marcus, 254
Barranca Commune, 39
Barrancabermeja
    demographics, 36, 41–42
    employment decline, 41–42
    foreign oil enclave, 35–37
    massacre (May 16, 1998), 51–52
    massacre (taxi drivers' union, 2000), 60
    residential segregation, 37, 42
    refugee flight, 51
    working-class culture, 36–37
Basque nationalist party, 180
Bazán, 168, 191
BCB (Bloque Central Bolívar), 51–53, 55, 57, 65
Beiras, Xosé Manuel, 191
Benjamin, Walter, 110–111
Bennett, Mike, 218, 225–226, 239, 241
Berquist, Charles, 69–70

Betancur, Belesario, 48
Bharatiya Janata Party, 146
Bhowmik, Sharit, 149
Black Eagles (Colombia), 65
Black Liberation movement, 209
blacklist, 175. *See under* International Paper Company
Bloque Nacional Galego (BNG), 191–192
Bluestone, Irving, 218
Board for Industrial and Financial Reconstruction, 152
Bogan, Louise, 84
Bombay. *See* Mumbai
Bombay Environmental Action Group, 150, 153
Breman, Jan, 23
Brihamumbai Municipal Corporation (BMC), 124, 125, 154, 159
Brodkin, Karen, 19
Bryner, Gary, 210–211
Buchowski, Michal, 270, 276
Buck-Morss, Susan, 2

Cano, María, 34, 38
capital flight, 15, 90, 208
Carey, James, 92–93
Catalan nationalist party, 180
Catholic Church, 43, 95, 140, 142, 149, 260, 278
Catholicism, 37, 176, 179, 191, 263. *See also* liberation theology; National Catholicism
Castaño, Carlos, 51, 52
Castaño, Vicente, 51

Central Labor Unions (CLU), 79, 81–82, 86–87, 95–96
Chacón, Manuel, 34, 47
Chatterjee, Partha, 24
Chile, 1973 coup, 15, 33, 112
Chrysler bailout, 204
civic strikes, 41, 42
civil society, 24, 45, 64, 256–257, 261, 270
class
    cross-class alliances, 38–39, 129
    debates on, 172–174
    memories of, 4–5, 207
    racialized, 254
    spatial arrangements, 78
clientalism, 32, 40, 47, 60, 67, 187
    authoritarian, 60, 63
Clinton administration, 220
Collins, Jane, 9–10
Colombian Communist Party (CP), 49
Comisiones Obreras (CCOO), 178, 193, 200n9
Comisiones Obreras, Críticos (CCOO-Críticos), 187, 193
Comité Ciudadano de Emergencia (Citizen's Emergency Committee), 190–191
Communist International (Comintern), 130–131
Communist Party of India (CPI), 129–131, 132–134, 146, 149
    trade unions, 132–33, 135, 146 (*see also* Girni Kamgar Union)
Communist Party of India (Marxist), 157
Communist Party, Spain, 180, 185
competition states, 214, 242, 245n7, 251–252
Confederación Intersindical Galega (CIG), 187, 191
Congress of Industrial Organizations (CIO), 100, 101–102, 118n49, 208–209
Congress Party, 127, 130–132, 154
    support for mill owners, 136
    trade unions, 136 (*see also* Rashtraya Mill Mazdoor Sangh union)

Congress Socialist Party, 130
Conservative Party, 39, 41
Cooper, Fred, 21
cooperation, labor-management, 1, 78, 109, 206, 219, 221, 223–225. *See also under* neoliberalism
Coordinadora Popular de Barrancabermeja, 43, 45, 47, 48

Davis, James, 97
Davis, Mike, 83
death squads. *See* dirty war; paramilitary; violence: paramilitary
Debs, Eugene, 81
debt, 251, 260, 269
democratic transition, Spain, 174–175, 179–180, 181, 183
Denning, Michael, 3–4, 9
Desai, Krishna, 133–134
Detroit, 209, 211, 246n13
dirty war, 47–56
disposable people, 22–25, 158
dispossession, 21, 32, 88, 125, 137, 144, 167
    and difference, 8–15
    and disenfranchisement, 253–254, 256, 261–262
    effect on families, 98, 144–145, 164n8, 206, 230–232
    politics of, 15–18
District 50, United Mine Workers, 100–102, 118n52
Dodge Revolutionary Union Movement (DRUM), 209
Dos Passos, 116n1
Du Bois, William Edward Burghardt, 7, 12–13
Durrenberger, Paul, 19

economic restructuring, Spain, 179, 181, 196
ECOPETROL (Empresa Colombiana de Petróleos), 31, 40–41, 55, 59–60
Ejército Popular de Liberación (EPL), 45

ELN (National Liberation Army, Colombia), 44–45
Elphin, Don, 218
Empresa Nacional Bazán. *See* Bazán
Erem, Suzan, 19
European Economic Community (EEC), 176, 179, 200n6
European Union (EU), 251, 253
experts, rule of, 176, 177, 183, 251, 259, 266, 268, 272

FARC (Revolutionary Armed Forces of Colombia), 44–45, 48–49, 53–54
fear, 15, 61, 186, 188, 254, 255, 275
and destruction of working-class sociality, 55–56, 61
Federici, Sylvia, 10
Ferrol
shipyards, 178–181
strike (1972), 179
financial crisis, 1, 251, 252, 256
New York City, 15
financial industry, 123, 124, 150
financialization, 252
Flint sit-down strike, 211
Flynn, Elizabeth Gurley, 81
Fordism, 3, 89, 117n30, 123, 125–126, 177, 195–196, 207, 208
Franco, Francisco, 168
Franco regime, 15, 168, 175, 195
economic policies, 175–179, 184, 198
relations with trade unions, 176, 178–179, 180
French Canadian immigrants, 81, 83–84, 93, 94, 97
Friedman, Jonathan, 250, 254, 271

Gaitán, Jorge Eliécer, 39–40
Gandhi, Mohandas, 130
Gazeta Wyborcza, 276
gender
division of labor, 18, 37, 106–107, 141–145, 176
feminization of survival, 141
idealized masculinity, 146–148, 210–211

General Motors (GM)
global strategy, 206
plant, Lordstown (*see* Lordstown, GM plant)
Southern strategy, 211
See also Saturn
Geremek, Bronislaw, 267, 276
Gingrich, Andre, 254
Girni Kamgar Union (GKU, Textile Workers' Union), 128, 129, 131, 133
globalism, 250–251, 252, 254
labor struggles, 6
North vs. South, 6
Gluckman, Max, 8
González, Felipe, 179
Gorbachev, Mikhail, 261
Gramsci, Antonio, 89, 131, 174, 208
Grandin, Greg, 32–33
Great Recession, 9. *See also* financial crisis
guerrilla insurgency
alienation of Barrancabermeja residents, 53–54, 68
criminality, 46
influence in Barrancabermeja, 45
labor support, 44
national political participation, 48–49
relations with popular movements, 46

Harvey, David, 6, 33, 243
accumulation by dispossession, 2, 5, 207
Haywood, William Dudley, "Big Bill," 81
Hillquit, Morris, 81
Hitler-Stalin pact, 131
Hobsbawm, Eric, 18, 172–173, 195, 197
human rights, 33, 59, 64, 257, 259, 277

Iglesias, Pablo, 168
import substitution, 127, 155, 175, 176, 184, 191
incarceration, 10

Industrial Workers of the World
    (IWW), 81–82, 85
industrial unionism, 81–82, 89
    attacks against, 79–80
informal economy, 23–24, 56, 123, 144
International Bank for Reconstruction
    and Development (IBRD), 176,
    177
International Brotherhood of
    Papermakers (IBPM). *See* Paper
    Makers
International Brotherhood of Pulp,
    Sulfite, and Paper Mill Workers
    (IBPSPMW). *See* Pulp Sulfite
International Dockworkers Council
    (IDC), 20
International Longshoremen and
    Warehousemen Union, 100,
    118n49
International Longshoremen's
    Association, Local 1422, 19–20
International Paper Company (IP),
    77, 79
    blacklist, 94, 98
    control of timber resources, 108
    ethnic segmentation, 81, 83, 93, 94
    paternalism, 96
International Transport Workers
    Federation, 20
International Woodworkers of
    America, 100
invisible labors, 22–23
Irish/Anglo immigrant workers, 83,
    94–95, 97, 116n7
Italian immigrant workers, 83–84, 93

Jacobinism, 257
Jaruzelski, Wojciech, 261
Jay/Livermore Falls, Maine, 78, 82, 99,
    103, 104
Jessop, Bob, 214, 251, 252
Jiménez, Carlos Mario (Macaco), 51,
    64–65

Kaczynski, Jaroslav, 274, 275–277
Kaczynski, Lech, 274, 275–277
Kellman, Peter, 110, 111

Keynsianism, 4, 5
Klein, Naomi, 269
Kolakoski, Leszek, 258
KOR (Workers' Defense Committee),
    260
Kornai, Janos, 266
Kotkin, Stephen, 257–258
Kramer, Paul, 35
Krushchev, Nikita, 258
Ku Klux Klan, 89, 97
Kundera, Milan, 257
Kuron, Jacek, 260

Labor Notes, 214
Lavoie, Casey, 109
League of Polish Families, 274, 277
League of Revolutionary Black
    Workers, 209–210
lean manufacturing, 219–220
Lefebvre, Henri, 20–21, 196
Legere, Benjamin, 81
LePage, Paul, 77, 115
Liberal Party, 39, 41
liberation theology, 43–44, 149
localism, 21, 89–91, 114, 207–208, 226
London docks, 11
Lordstown, GM plant, 210–211, 216,
    225
    "Operation Apache," 211
    wildcat strikes, 210
Luxemburg, Rosa, 5, 9, 193

M-19, 45
Magubane, Bernard, 13
Mahécha, Raúl Eduardo, 34, 38
Mancuso, Salvatore, 65–66
Marx, Karl, 5, 8–9, 24, 44, 82, 111, 124,
    193
Marxism, 38
Marxism-Leninism, 18
Mbembe, Achille, 23
McKinsey & Company, 124, 157, 263,
    274
memories, 19, 56, 68, 70, 72n25, 96–97,
    110, 115, 155, 167–168, 182, 275.
    See also under class
Merserve, Bill, 112

Mexico, 9, 241, 260
  oil industry expropriation, 40–41
  oil workers, 35
  Revolution, 79, 81
Michnik, Adam, 267, 270, 276
militant particularism, 102–108, 109, 114, 174, 190–193, 213. *See also under* Williams, Raymond
El Militante, 188, 193
Mintz, Sidney, 8
MNS (Maharashtra Navnirman Sena), 148–149, 162, 164n10
Mondragón cooperative, 219, 283n6
Monnet, Jean, 176
Moore, Michael, 246n13
Mumbai
  housing stock, 128
  Janata Colony, 139, 140–142, 145, 149, 156–158, 160
  labor recruitment, 128
  spatial and economic history, 126–128
  working-class culture, 128
Mumbai Girni Kamgar Union (MGKU, Mumbai Textile Workers' Union), 136, 138–139, 145–146, 148–149, 155
  housing activism, 150, 157

Nash, June, 18–19
National Catholicism, 176, 200n7
National Food and Beverage Workers Union (SINALTRAINAL), 65
National Front government, 41
National Labor Relations Board (NLRB), 99, 220
National Liberation Army. *See* ELN
National Textile Corporation, 127, 136, 154, 155
National Union of Domestic Workers, 142
nationalism, 124, 254
  economic, 176 (*see also* import substitution)
  ethnic identity, 95
  Third World, 40
  working-class, 37, 38

Narotzky, Susana, 251
nativism, 79, 89, 97, 239
Nehru, Jawaharlal, 130
neoliberalism, 2, 6, 15, 31–32, 111–113, 115, 124, 141–142, 196–197, 198, 251
  labor-management cooperation, 1
  management, 215
  paramilitary preparation for, 56–58
New Deal, 99–100
New York Call, 86
Nicaragua, 37, 45
Nugent, Daniel, 90

Obama, Barack, 204
Occupy movement, 4, 77
oil workers
  cross-class alliances, 38–39
  relative prosperity, 42
Ogolnopolskie Porozumienie Zwiazkow Zawodowych (All-Poland Alliance of Trade Unions), 266
open shop. *See* American Plan
Opus Dei, 178, 199–200n5, 200n7
Osborne, William, 78
Our Home, 263, 273, 274
overproduction, 82

Pacto de la Moncloa, 180, 200n9
Palmer, A. Mitchell, 80
Palmer Raids, 89
Paper Makers (IBPM), 82, 91, 93, 96, 101, 104
  craft exclusion, 84
  early history, 84
  nativism, 84–85
paper worker strikes, 78
  1908, 85
  1910, 85–86, 89
  1921–1926, 81, 89–98, 100, 110–111
  1987–1988, 77, 109–114
paramilitary, 89
  credit racketeering, 61–62
  drug trafficking, 55
  fusion with state, 54–55

military cooperation with, 47, 50, 52–53
peasant dispossession, 50
repressive moral order, 62
takeover of Barrancabermeja, 51, 56–57
targeting labor, 57–58, 60
transformation to NGOs, 64–65
US support, 50
See also AUC; BCB; Black Eagles; Semillas de Paz

Patriotic Union (UP), 48–49
Petrovici, Norbert, 280
Phoenix Mills, 152–153
Piccone, Paul, 252–253
Pinochet, Augusto, 33, 112
Polanyi, Karl, 9, 252
Polish immigrant workers, 83–84, 93
populism, 252–253
  definition, 255
  nationalist, 255
  working-class, 255

Prabhu, C., 154
Pragati Kendra (Progress Center), 142, 149, 162
precarious work, 10, 111–112, 181, 183, 189, 192, 205–206, 221
primitive accumulation, 5, 8–11, 124
privatization, 264–265, 267–269
proletarianization, 5, 23, 250
Pulp Sulfite (IBPSPPMW), 82, 85, 91, 93, 97, 101
  Local 14, 104

Quit India movement, 131

race
  colonial context, 13, 14
  labor solidarity, 12–13
race riots, East St. Louis (1917), 12–13
racial segmentation, 209
racism, 12, 19, 209
Rangel, Rafael, 39
Rangel, Ramón, 42, 44

Rashtraya Mill Mazdoor Sangh union (RMMS), 131–132, 135
Reagan, Ronald, 112, 204
Red Scare (1919–1920), 80, 89
Reich, Robert, 220
rent gap, 150–151, 154
residential segregation
  Barrancabermeja, 37, 42
  Jay/Livermore Falls, 83–84, 95
  See also individual areas, cities
Reuther, Victor, 214
Reuther, Walter, 214
Revolutionary Armed Forces of Colombia. *See* FARC
Revolutionary Union Movement (RUM), 209–211
Richani, Nazih, 57
right to work laws, 80, 217, 245–246n9
Roseberry, William, 174
Round Table, 261, 267–268, 273–274, 276
Roy, Arundhati, 24
Russia, 113, 261
  Revolution, 79, 81, 257
  See also Soviet Union
Russo, Alexander, 216
Russo, John, 215–216

Sacco, Nicola, 80
Samant, Datta, 135–136, 139, 146, 149
Samyukta Maharasthra, 132–133, 146
Saturn
  advertising campaign, 204–205, 221–223
  compensation, 220–221, 232
  competition for facility location, 215–217
  insecurity of work, 233–235
  two-tier workforce, 221
Sassen, Saskia, 160
Semillas de Paz, 65
Shiv Sena, 132–134, 141, 145–149
  criminality, 147–148
  masculine subjectivity, 147–148
  nativism, 133, 135, 143, 146–148
  real estate, 148
  trade unions, 132–133, 134–135

shock therapy, 268–270
Sindicato de Trabajadores Disponibles y Temporales (SINTRADIT), 60
Slum Rehabilitation Scheme, 156–158
Smith, Gavin, 251
Smith, Neil, 151, 195
Smith, Roger, 212, 216
socialism, really existing, 258–259
Socialist Labor Party (US), 81
Socialist Party (Partido Socialista Obrero Español), 168, 196
Sociedad Unión Sindical, 38. *See also* Unión Sindical Obrera
Solidarnosc, 259, 260–261, 263–267, 273–274
South Africa, 13, 209
Soviet Union, 131
Spring Hill, Tennessee, 216–217, 227–233
Stalinism, 258, 260
Steel Strike of 1919 (US), 80
Steward, Julian, 8
Strathern, Marilyn, 281
street theater, 129, 157, 261
Striffler, Steve, 15
strikebreaking, 91, 92, 93, 98, 110, 112, 129, 137, 225, 239
strikes. *See* civic strikes; *also individual companies, industries, unions*
structural adjustment, 4, 79, 186
structural power, 22, 255
structures of feeling, 18, 186, 189, 190, 269. *See also* Williams, Raymond
subcontracted labor, 31, 58–61, 125–126, 139, 153, 187, 204. *See also* informal economy
surplus populations, 24. *See also* disposable people
surveillance, 85–86, 273

Taft-Hartley Act, 80, 104–5, 112, 208
Taylor, Frederick, 116n9, 117n30
Taylorism, 219
Terkel, Studs, 210
terror, 12–13. *See also* paramilitary
textile industry

Bombay Textile Strike (1982–1984), 134–139, 149–150
colonial history, 126–128
deindustrialization, 135–139
nationalization, 134
real estate investment, 150
Thackeray, Bal, 133, 147–148
Thackeray, Raj, 148
Thackeray, Uddhav, 148
Thatcher, Margaret, 112
Thelen, Tatjana, 281–282
Thompson, Edward Palmer, 5, 7, 18, 110, 172, 173
Tilly, Charles, 256
Torres, Camilo, 34–35
Toyota, 219
Trade Union Joint Action Committee (TUJAC), 136, 157
Tronti, Mario, 89
Tropical Oil Company (TROCO), 35–40
Trotsky, Leon, 193
Trotskyism, 187

Unión General de Trabajadores, 200n9
Unión Sindical Obrera (USO), 31, 48, 59
  anti-imperialism, 59
  class solidarity, 42
  nationalism, 59
  See also Sociedad Unión Sindical
United Automobile Workers (UAW)
  Canada, 214
  concessions, 203–204
  GM-Delphi strike, 237–240
  imports, opposition to, 213
  leadership opposition to Saturn, 218, 235–237
  Local 645 (Van Nuys, California), 212–213
  New Directions Movement caucus, 213–214, 236
  Southern organizing, 211–212
  "Treaty of Detroit," 208
United Automobile Workers, Local 1853 (Spring Hill), 206, 217–221

Concerned Brothers and Sisters caucus, 236–240
Members for a Democratic Union Caucus (MDU), 240–241
national GM-UAW contract, 218–219
Vision Team caucus, 218, 225–226, 236, 240–241
United Fruit Company, 35, 37
United Mine Workers, District 50. *See* District 50, United Mine Workers
United Paperworkers International Union (UPIU), 112
Local 14, 109, 111–114
universalism, 2, 169, 175, 181, 193, 252, 253. *See also* militant particularism

Vanzetti, Bartolomeo, 80
velvet revolutions, 256–257
Verdery, Katherine, 258–259
Vetta, Theodora, 280
violence, 31, 97
paramilitary, 47
police, 46, 137–138, 158
strike, 91, 117n34
against trade unionists, 31–32, 33, 133–134, 137–138
See also dirty war; dispossession; paramilitary
La Violencia, 40

wage
family, 97–98, 168
monetarization, 10–11
wagelessness, 9, 23
Wagner Act, 99–100, 101, 102, 104–105, 208, 220
Walesa, Lech, 260
Warren, Alfred S., 221
Weinstein, Liza, 155
welfare state, 5
whipsawing, 103, 105, 118n54, 212–213, 215, 235–236
whiteness, 12, 14, 94
Williams, Raymond, 195, 226, 265

experience vs. abstraction, 169–172, 193, 195
militant particularism, 19, 40, 102, 105, 171, 196–197, 206
Wilson, Godfrey, 8
Wilson, Monica Hunter, 8
Wolf, Eric, 7–8, 22, 255
worker self-management, 40, 259, 260, 265–268, 271–273
dismantling, 268–269
worker-owned cooperatives, 219
working class
abandonment of struggle, 182–183
cross-ethnic/racial solidarity, 85, 86–87, 210–211
democratic struggle, 183
ethnic and status divisions, 83–84, 93
generational transmission of knowledge, 184–185
immigrant, 93–94
linguistic divisions, 132–133
precarity, 10, 79, 82, 97, 114, 183–184, 186, 207, 243
radicalism, 35, 81, 85, 86, 99
regional public sphere, 86–88, 90
shared identity, 5
See also class
Wojtyla, Karol (Pope John Paul II), 260

Zadrozny, Krysztof, 264, 266, 269, 271–275, 277–279, 283n3

DISLOCATIONS

General Editors: August Carbonella, *Memorial University of Newfoundland*, Don Kalb, *University of Utrecht & Central European University*, Linda Green, *University of Arizona*

Volume 1
Where Have All the Homeless Gone? The Making and Unmaking of a Crisis
Anthony Marcus

Volume 2
Blood and Oranges: European Markets and Immigrant Labor in Rural Greece
Christopher M. Lawrence

Volume 3
Struggles for Home: Violence, Hope and the Movement of People
Edited by Stef Jansen and Staffan Löfving

Volume 4
Slipping Away: Banana Politics and Fair Trade in the Eastern Caribbean
Mark Moberg

Volume 5
Made in Sheffield: An Ethnography of Industrial Work and Politics
Massimiliano Mollona

Volume 6
Biopolitics, Militarism, and Development: Eritrea in the Twenty-First Century
Edited by David O'Kane and Tricia Redeker Hepner

Volume 7
When Women Held the Dragon's Tongue and Other Essays in Historical Anthropology
Hermann Rebel

Volume 8
Class, Contention, and a World in Motion
Edited by Winnie Lem and Pauline Gardiner Barber

Volume 9
Crude Domination: An Anthropology of Oil
Edited by Andrea Behrends, Stephen P. Reyna, and Günther Schlee

Volume 10
Communities of Complicity: Everyday Ethics in Rural China
Hans Steinmüller

Volume 11
Elusive Promises: Planning in the Contemporary World
Edited by Simone Abram and Gisa Weszkalnys

Volume 12
Intellectuals and (Counter-) Politics: Essays in Historical Realism
Gavin Smith

Volume 13
In Blood and Fire: Toward a Global Anthropology of Labor
Edited by Sharryn Kasmir and August Carbonella

Volume 14
The Neoliberal Landscape and the Rise of Islamist Capital in Turkey
Edited by Neşecan Balkan, Erol Balkan, and Ahmet Öncü

Volume 15
Yearnings in the Meantime: 'Normal Lives' and the State in a Sarajevo Apartment Complex
Stef Jansen

Volume 16
Where Are All Our Sheep? Kyrgyzstan, a Global Political Arena
Boris Petric, Translated by Cynthia Schoch

Volume 17
Enduring Uncertainty: Deportation, Punishment and Everyday Life
Ines Hasselberg

Volume 18
The Anthropology of Corporate Social Responsibility
Edited by Catherine Dolan and Dinah Rajak

Volume 19
Breaking Rocks: Music, Ideology and Economic Collapse, from Paris to Kinshasa
Joe Trapido

Volume 20
Indigenist Mobilization: Confronting Electoral Communism and Precarious Livelihoods in Post-Reform Kerala
Luisa Steur

Volume 21
The Partial Revolution: Labor, Social Movements and the Invisible Hand of Mao in Western Nepal
Michael Hoffmann

www.ingramcontent.com/pod-product-compliance
Lightning Source LLC
Chambersburg PA
CBHW070911030426
42336CB00014BA/2368